INTRODUCTION TO MONTAGUE SEMANTICS

SYNTHESE LANGUAGE LIBRARY

TEXTS AND STUDIES IN
LINGUISTICS AND PHILOSOPHY

VOLUME 11

INTRODUCTION TO MONTAGUE SEMANTICS

by

DAVID R. DOWTY

Dept. of Linguistics, Ohio State University, Columbus

ROBERT E. WALL

Dept. of Linguistics, University of Texas at Austin

and

STANLEY PETERS

CSLI, Stanford University

D. REIDEL PUBLISHING COMPANY

A MEMBER OF THE KLUWER ACADEMIC PUBLISHERS GROUP

DORDRECHT / BOSTON / LANCASTER

Library of Congress Cataloging in Publication Data

Dowty, David R.
Introduction to Montague semantics.

(Synthese language library; v. 11)
Bibliography: p.
Includes index.
1. Montague grammar. 2. Semantics (Philosophy).
3. Generative grammar. 4. Formal languages–Semantics.
I. Wall, Robert Eugene, joint author. II. Peters, Stanley, 1941–
joint author. III. Title. IV. Series.
P158.5D6 415 80-20267
ISBN 90-277-1141-0
ISBN 90-277-1142-9 (pbk.)

Published by D. Reidel Publishing Company,
P.O. Box 17, 3300 AA Dordrecht, Holland.

Sold and distributed in the U.S.A. and Canada
by Kluwer Academic Publishers,
190 Old Derby Street, Hingham, MA 02043, U.S.A.

In all other countries, sold and distributed
by Kluwer Academic Publishers Group,
P.O. Box 322, 3300 AH Dordrecht, Holland.

3-0185-500 ts

First published 1981
Reprinted 1983, 1985

Printed in The Netherlands

TABLE OF CONTENTS

PREFACE ix

1. INTRODUCTION 1

2. THE SYNTAX AND SEMANTICS OF TWO SIMPLE LANGUAGES 14
   - I. The Language L_0 14
     - 1. Syntax of L_0 14
     - 2. Semantics of L_0 16
   - II. The Language L_{0E} 23
     - 1. Syntax of L_{0E} 23
     - 2. Semantics of L_{0E} 25
     - 3. Alternative Formulations of L_{0E} and L_0 35
   - III. A Synopsis of Truth-Conditional Semantics 41
   - IV. The Notion of Truth Relative to a Model 44
   - V. Validity and Entailment Defined in Terms of Possible Models 47
   - VI. Model Theory and Deductive Systems 50
   - Exercises 53
   - Note 54

3. FIRST-ORDER PREDICATE LOGIC 56
   - I. The Language L_1 56
     - 1. Syntax of L_1 56
     - 2. Semantics of L_1 59
   - II. The Language L_{1E} 66
     - 1. Syntax of L_{1E} 69
     - 2. Semantics of L_{1E} 72
   - Exercises 81
   - Notes 82

4. A HIGHER-ORDER TYPE-THEORETIC LANGUAGE 83
I. A Notational Variant of L_1 83
II. The Language L_{type} 88
1. Syntax of L_{type} 91
2. Semantics of L_{type} 92
III. Lambda Abstraction and the Language L_λ 98
Exercises 110
Notes 111

5. TENSE AND MODAL OPERATORS 112
I. Tense Operators and Their Interpretation 112
II. The Other Varieties of Modal Logic; the Operators □ and ◇ 121
III. Languages Containing Both Tense and Modal Operators: Coordinate Semantics 131
Exercises 139
Notes 139

6. MONTAGUE'S INTENSIONAL LOGIC 141
I. Compositionality and the Intension–Extension Distinction 141
II. The Intensional Logic of PTQ 154
1. Syntax of *IL* 155
2. Semantics of *IL* 157
III. Examples of 'Oblique Contexts' as Represented in *IL* 162
IV. Some Unresolved Issues with Possible Worlds Semantics and Propositional Attitudes 170
Notes 175

7. THE GRAMMAR OF PTQ 179
I. The Overall Organization of the PTQ Grammar 179
1. The Syntactic Categories of English in the PTQ Grammar 181
2. The Correspondence Between Categories of English and Types of *IL* 184
II. Subject-Predicate and Determiner-Noun Rules 190
III. Conjoined Sentences, Verb Phrases, and Term Phrases 198
IV. Anaphoric Pronouns as Bound Variables; Scope Ambiguities and Relative Clauses 203
V. **Be**, Transitive Verbs, Meaning Postulates, and Non-Specific Readings 215
VI. Adverbs and Infinitive Complement Verbs 232
VII. *De dicto* Pronouns and Some Pronoun Problems 237

VIII. Prepositions, Tenses, and Negation 243
Exercises 245
Notes 248

8. MONTAGUE'S GENERAL SEMIOTIC PROGRAM 252

9. AN ANNOTATED BIBLIOGRAPHY OF FURTHER WORK IN MONTAGUE SEMANTICS 269

APPENDIX I: Index of Symbols 277

APPENDIX II: Variable Type Conventions for Chapter 7 278

APPENDIX III: *The Temperature Is Ninety and Rising* 279
Notes 286

REFERENCES 287

ANSWERS TO SELECTED PROBLEMS AND EXERCISES 294

INDEX 307

PREFACE

In this book we hope to acquaint the reader with the fundamentals of truth-conditional model-theoretic semantics, and in particular with a version of this developed by Richard Montague in a series of papers published during the 1960's and early 1970's. In many ways the paper 'The Proper Treatment of Quantification in Ordinary English' (commonly abbreviated PTQ) represents the culmination of Montague's efforts to apply the techniques developed within mathematical logic to the semantics of natural languages, and indeed it is the system outlined there that people generally have in mind when they refer to "Montague Grammar". (We prefer the term "Montague Semantics" inasmuch as a grammar, as conceived of in current linguistics, would contain at least a phonological component, a morphological component, and other subsystems which are either lacking entirely or present only in a very rudimentary state in the PTQ system.) Montague's work has attracted increasing attention in recent years among linguists and philosophers since it offers the hope that semantics can be characterized with the same formal rigor and explicitness that transformational approaches have brought to syntax. Whether this hope can be fully realized remains to be seen, but it is clear nonetheless that Montague semantics has already established itself as a productive paradigm, leading to new areas of inquiry and suggesting new ways of conceiving of theories of natural language.

Unfortunately, Montague's papers are tersely written and very difficult to follow unless one has a considerable background in logical semantics. Previous introductions to Montague's framework, e.g., Partee (1975a) and Thomason (1974a), have served very well to bring Montague's ideas to the attention of linguists and philosophers generally, but within the relatively brief space they occupy they could not provide the detailed account that seems to be required for a thoroughgoing understanding of these ideas. The increasing interest in Montague Semantics thus seemed to call for a textbook that would start from a minimal basis of set theory and logic and proceed stepwise toward the goal of the PTQ system and a view of Montague's overall program. This book is an attempt to provide what is necessary for understanding Montague's work itself as well as the recent literature based on this approach.

The plan of the book is as follows. In Chapter 1 we sketch some of the basic assumptions underlying the truth-conditional, model-theoretic, and "possible worlds" approaches to semantics and attempt to justify these assumptions in very general terms. In Chapter 2 we illustrate the truth-conditional and model-theoretic methods using a formal language which is essentially the propositional calculus and a small fragment of an analogous language bearing some resemblance to English. In the next three chapters the complexity of the languages is gradually increased – first by the addition of variables and quantifiers, and then by the addition of tense-, modal-, and λ-operators – and the model-theoretic semantics is correspondingly augmented to take account of the new constructions. A number of notational alterations along the way prepare the reader gradually for the rather intricate and sometimes confusing system used by Montague.

In Chapter 6 the language under consideration is the Intensional Logic which Montague employs in PTQ as an intermediate translation language connecting English to its model-theoretic interpretation. The PTQ system itself is the subject of Chapter 7. Chapter 8 contains a discussion of Montague's general semiotic program as set forth in his paper 'Universal Grammar' (Montague 1970b), and Chapter 9 consists of an annotated bibliography of publications in which Montague's framework has been extended and applied to other problems in the domain of natural language.

From a certain point of view, it would have been desirable to include a detailed discussion of many of the extensions of Montague's system in this textbook. For while the syntax of the original PTQ fragment is relatively rudimentary, these extensions show that Montague's original program is compatible with a syntax that achieves the degree of sophistication found in current transformational theory, and that it allows a precise examination of the interconnection of syntax and semantics in a way that is rarely achieved in other semantic frameworks. Thus it is really these extensions rather than the PTQ grammar itself which justify Montague Grammar as an interesting and productive paradigm for linguistic research. Unfortunately, a detailed discussion of this work would have lengthened this book to ungainly proportions; and in any event, such a discussion should not be absolutely essential since this book will equip the reader to attack the original articles quite easily. We simply issue the warning here that the reader should examine this literature before drawing any final conclusions about the usefulness of Montague's program for linguistics.

As background for this textbook, we presuppose acquaintance with such rudiments of logic and set theory as might be found, for example, in the first five chapters of Wall (1972) and perhaps some familiarity with the basic principles and goals of generative transformational grammar (see, for example, Baker, 1978; Akmajian and Heny, 1975). For those readers who have no previous knowledge of formal semantics, there is no denying the fact that it will require diligent application to get through it all. Montague Semantics is manifestly of an intensely formal nature. Yet the ideas involved are not in themselves really difficult, and the systems considered here are built up progressively and in an orderly way. Furthermore, there are numerous problems and exercises sprinkled throughout, which the reader is encouraged to work through as a check on how well the preceding material has been understood. Answers for many of these are provided at the end of the book. By the end of Chapter 7 the reader should be prepared to read the current literature in the field.

This book is an outgrowth of a manuscript prepared by Dowty as an introduction to his book on word meaning (Dowty, 1979). But the length of that book made it impractical to include the introduction there, and this introduction was instead distributed temporarily by the Indiana University Linguistics Club under the title *A Guide to Montague's PTQ*. Wall and Peters had independently undertaken to write an introduction to Montague Semantics, and they then invited Dowty to join them as collaborator on this project, in which Dowty's *Guide* could be incorporated. This *Guide* forms the basis of chapters two through seven of the present textbook. It was revised and expanded by Wall, who added discussions of the languages L_{0E} and L_{1E} as well as other material, and was further emended by the other two authors. Dowty wrote 5-IV and Appendix III, Wall and Peters the Preface and Chapter 1, and Peters Chapter 8. Chapter 9 was assembled by Peters with the aid of students. Barbara Partee generously offered us the exercises she had constructed for Dowty's *Guide*; these make up the bulk of the problems and exercises in the book. We are grateful to her for this contribution and for her comments. Those who have made helpful suggestions and/or assisted with the preparation of the manuscript are too numerous to mention individually here, but we would like to single out in particular Jon Barwise, David Cohen, Edit Doran, Will Dowling, Douglas Fuller, Simon Gray, Charles Kirkpatrick, Doug Moran, Marlene Deetz Payha, Joseph Queen, Robert Starr, Gregory Stump, and Hans Uszkoreit.

D.R.D., R.E.W., and S.P.

CHAPTER 1

INTRODUCTION

Linguists who work within the tradition of transformational generative grammar tend to regard semantics as an intractable, perhaps ultimately unfathomable, part of language. In diagrams of the overall organization of the theory of grammar the semantic component is that box ritually drawn next to the one labelled "Syntactic Component" and connected to it by arrows of uncertain significance. The semantic box itself is generally empty – which is fitting for a component of grammar about which, it is believed, next to nothing is known.

Philosophers and logicians, on the other hand, find semantics perfectly tractable but are made uncomfortable by the idea that approaches to semantics which work very well for systems of formal logic could be usefully applied in the domain of natural languages. In constrast to the tidy, well-behaved languages of the predicate calculus and of various tense and modal logics, a natural language such as English seems hopelessly messy – full of ambiguities and unruly exceptions. Richard Montague challenged this assumption: in Montague (1970a) he wrote, "I reject the contention that an important theoretical difference exists between formal and natural languages," and in his work he built up a framework which has already shown great promise for the development of an explicit, substantive theory of semantics for natural language. It is that framework, of course, which is the subject of this book.

There is no doubt that semantics has a somewhat more abstract character than does syntax or phonology. Semantics, after all, deals with such notoriously slippery entities as "meanings," and this fact sometimes leads people to assume that it must be approached in ways that are quite unlike those used in the study of other components of grammar. We would content, however, that there is no reason in principle to regard the problems of theory construction and testing in semantics as significantly different from the corresponding enterprises in other domains of linguistics. This book will itself comprise an extended justification of this contention, but a few words of a general nature in its defence might be in order here.

When we construct the syntactic component of a grammar for a particular language, we do so with the intention of accounting for certain facts that are intuitively regarded as syntactic in nature. For example, we would certainly expect the syntactic component of a grammar of English to predict, in accord with native speakers' intuitions, that "John hit the ball" is a grammatical sentence, while "*Ball John the hit" is not. Some facts are, of course, much harder to account for than others. The fact about English just mentioned generally poses no overwhelming problem for anyone's theory of grammar. Facts that are more difficult to account for, on the other hand, become puzzles, and these play a crucial role in the construction and testing of new hypotheses. For example, it was something of a triumph for the early theory of transformational grammar that it was able to "solve" the puzzle of why "John is easy to please" and "To please John is easy" are both grammatical, while in the apparently parallel cases, "John is eager to please" is grammatical but "*To please John is eager" is not.

In constructing the semantic component of a grammar, we are attempting to account not for speakers' judgements of grammaticality, grammatical relations, etc. but for their judgements of synonymy, entailment, contradiction, and so on. Although giving a completely formal and explicit account of *any* linguistic fact is seldom a wholly trivial task, it is nonetheless true in semantics, just as in syntax, that some facts are harder to account for than others. As we will see later, it is relatively easy to account for the fact that if "John stayed and Mary left" is true, then "John stayed" must be true (i.e., the former entails the latter). It is somewhat more difficult, on the other hand, to account for the fact that "Every man loves a woman" is ambiguous, while sentences such as "Every man loves Mary" and "John loves Mary" are not (or at least not in the same way as the first). Or consider the following rather notorious semantic puzzle. Suppose that my neighbor is the Mayor. Then the sentence "The Mayor keeps a pet alligator" and the sentence "My neighbor keeps a pet alligator" must be either both true or both false. The truth values of these sentences seem to depend only on the facts of the situation and not on the particular way in which the individual who is both my neighbor and the Mayor is referred to. In contrast, the sentence "John believes that the Mayor keeps a pet alligator" might well be true, while the sentence "John believes that my neighbor keeps a pet alligator" is false. This could happen, for example, if John did not know that the Mayor is in fact my neighbor. The puzzle here is why substitution of a different description for the same individual should preserve truth value in the one case but not necessarily in the other.

To mention just one other sort of case which poses problems for any semantic theory, consider the following argument. "Every teacher is better than any student. John is better than every teacher. Therefore, John is better than any student." This argument seems valid, in that the conclusion follows logically from the premises. Why then is the following argument, which is apparently parallel, not valid: "Nothing is better than a long and prosperous life. A ham sandwich is better than nothing. Therefore, a ham sandwich is better than a long and prosperous life."?

Puzzles such as these will be the test of any adequate semantic theory of English, and it is to the credit of Montague's approach that it fares rather well in accounting for them and for a number of others as well. Furthermore, in semantics, just as in syntax, we require our theory to provide *principled* explanations for the facts, i.e., explanations that emerge from a tightly interconnected system of general statements and which lead to further predictions about as yet undiscovered facts. The theory must also be capable of being joined in a plausible way with theories of related domains. In these respects also, Montague semantics has shown a good deal of promise, and it is for these reasons that many linguists and philosophers have found it an attractive paradigm within which to work. There are, to be sure, many remaining difficulties – as indeed there are with any developing theory. For a number of semantic puzzles, Montague semantics offers no satisfying solution, and we will point out certain of these as they arise later in the book. Another considerable difficulty for Montague semantics which should be mentioned at the outset is the problem of connecting it with an adequate theory of syntax. As we will see, Montague assumed as the basis for his semantics a view of syntax which, by current linguistic standards, could hardly be considered satisfactory. A good deal of current research has been directed toward this problem, i.e., making Montague's formal approach to semantics compatible with the syntactic insights gained over the past twenty years or so by transformational generative grammar. What success these efforts will have remains to be seen, but enough has already been accomplished in this area to suggest that the difficulties may not be insuperable. The reader will find in Chapter 9 a number of references to such work.

SOME BASIC ASSUMPTIONS OF MONTAGUE SEMANTICS

Much of this book will be concerned with an exposition of Montague semantics, but we should prepare the way by mentioning here a few of the fundamental ideas on which the program rests. Specifically, we will discuss briefly each of the following characteristics of Montague's approach: (1) it is truth conditional; (2) it is model theoretic; and (3) it makes use of the notion of *possible worlds.*

1. *Truth-Conditional Semantics*

A truth-conditional theory of semantics is one which adheres to the following dictum: To know the meaning of a (declarative) sentence is to know what the world would have to be like for the sentence to be true. Put another way, to give the meaning of a sentence is to specify its truth conditions, i.e., to give necessary and sufficient conditions for the truth of that sentence. (Note, by the way, that we are using "true" to indicate something like "corresponding to the way the world is." We are thus implicity adopting a *correspondence theory* of truth.)

Plausible as this may sound, we should note that it is not logically necessary that it be so; other approaches to the explication of the notion of meaning are at least conceivable. To mention just two that have had their adherents at various times, one might propose that the meaning of a sentence is a mental image or idea formed by someone who understands it, or alternatively, that the meaning is the totality of all situations in which the sentence can be appropriately used. Such theories of meaning run immediately into serious difficulties, but there are also various moves that can be made in an attempt to salvage them. We will not pursue the subject here, but the reader might wish to consult the relevant articles in *The Encyclopedia of Philosophy* (Alston, 1967) for more information about these and other theories of meaning. Our point is simply that the truth-conditional analysis of meaning that we will henceforth take for granted is one which does have imaginable alternatives.

It is clear that one of the central notions of the truth-conditional approach is the relationship which sometimes holds between a sentence and the world. ("The world" is here simply intended to refer to the vast complex of things and situations that sentences can be "about.") Many philosophers of language – and many linguists also, for that matter – would contend that it is an essential requirement of any semantic theory that it specify the nature of this relationship. In support of this, they cite the fact that a fundamental characteristic of natural language is that it can be used by human beings to communicate about things in the world. Any theory which ignores this essential property, it is argued, cannot be an adequate theory of natural language. Examples would be theories which, in effect, give the meaning of a sentence by translating it into another language, such as a system of semantic markers or some sort of formal logic, where this language is not further interpreted by specifying its connection to the world. The approach of Katz and his co-workers seems to be of this sort (Katz and Fodor, 1963;

Katz and Postal, 1964), as is that of Jackendoff (1972) and of the framework known as Generative Semantics (Lakoff 1972; McCawley, 1973; Postal, 1970). The point is controversial, and we will not enter into a discussion of the issues and alternatives here. We merely wish to emphasize that truth-conditional semantics, in contrast to the other approaches mentioned, is based squarely on the assumption that the proper business of semantics is to specify how language connects with the world – in other words, to explicate the inherent "aboutness" of language.

Let us inject a little concreteness into this rather abstract discussion by taking a particular example. Consider the sentence: "The Washington Monument is west of the Capitol Building." What would a truth-conditional account of the meaning of this sentence be like? We have said that we will consider ourselves successful in producing such a meaning once we have specified what the world would have to be like in order for the sentence to be true. What condition of the world, what state-of-affairs would this be? Clearly, on the basis of our knowledge of English, and in particular of our knowledge of what English sentences mean, we can say that this sentence would be true just in case a certain physical object (entity) named by the words "the Washington Monument" and another entity named by the words "the Capitol Building" stand in a certain spatial and temporal relation named by the words "is west of." We might go on to specifiy these entities and the relations between them in greater detail, but doing so would not be relevant to the basic point here, which is simply this: in truth-conditional semantics we answer a question of the form "What is the meaning of sentence *S*?" by providing some sort of description of how things would have to be arranged in some relevant corner of the world in order for *S* to be true.

One commonly has the feeling at this point that the wool has been pulled over one's eyes. What has been put forth as the meaning of a particular English sentence looks like just a longer and more complex, but perhaps synonymous, English sentence, *viz.*, "A certain physical object, etc., etc." Isn't this then just another case of translating a sentence of the language under study (English) into a sentence of a language (again, English) whose connection to the world is yet to be specified? The whole enterprise seems hopelessly circular.

What we have done is in fact not circular, but in order to demonstrate this we must disentangle some possible sources of confusion. First, we observe that sentences (linguistic entities) and states-of-affairs (configurations of objects in the world) are altogether different sorts of things. There is nothing, in principle, wrong with attempting to explicate a certain property of the former, *viz.*, their meanings, in terms of the notion "state-of-affairs." How then does the air of paradox arise? It comes from the fact that we used *a sentence of English* to describe the state-of-affairs. We relied on the fact that you, the reader, understand English in order to indicate to you just which state-of-affairs we intended. This suggests that at least a part of the air of paradox would be dissipated if we had chosen an example from French or Swahili. If one did not know, say, French, and were told (in English) that a certain French sentence would be true just in case the world were such-and-such, this would be informative – indeed, one would have thereby learned the meaning of the French sentence. In such a case, French would be the ***object language,*** the language under analysis, while our statements about the object language would be couched in English, the so-called ***meta-language.*** In our initial example, of course, English was both the object language and the meta-language.

But this is not the whole story. We have not answered the objection that the meta-language has not yet been connected up with the world in the required way, and thus whatever object language we choose will likewise remain unanchored. Consider, in this regard, other means that we might have employed in specifying a state-of-affairs. Suppose that the required information could be conveyed to another person by drawing a picture, or by an elaborate system of gestures, or by telepathy. Then we might show how the world would have to be arranged in order for "The Washington Monument is west of the Capitol Building" to be true by producing, say, a picture representing the relevant state-of-affairs. Disregarding various practical difficulties that might arise (e.g., we would have to get across to our audience not only that the picture *is* a picture of a certain state-of-affairs but also that it is *intended as* a representation of the truth conditions of a particular sentence), if it succeeded in its objective, then our picture would accomplish what is necessary for a truth-conditional account of the meaning of the sentence at hand. The point is that we must have *some* system within which to construct theories, whether they be theories of atoms, or rocks, or meanings, but there is nothing in principle which limits this system to natural languages. A meta-language of pictures, gestures, or whatever, would do as well, provided that it had the resources to specify states-of-affairs and pair them with object-language sentences. But in a book such as this the most convenient mode of communication with the reader is a natural language, and that is, of course, what we will use throughout in specifying truth conditions.

It should now be apparent that there was in fact no vicious circularity in giving the truth conditions for our example sentence as we did. Understanding this point at the outset is very important since the situation will be encountered repeatedly in the following chapters: English (really, fragments of English) will often be the object language, and the meta-language will be English also. The latter is a practical necessity since it is the language we, the authors, are most familiar with, but the use of English as an object language will also have certain advantages. For example, since the reader knows English, he or she will be in a position to evaluate the accuracy of the claims made by our theories about the meanings of object-language sentences. If this two-level use of English becomes too confusing at any point, the reader might try imagining that the English meta-language has been replaced by some favorite system of non-linguistic communication.

The principal business of the next six chapters will be to explain in some detail just how the program of truth-conditional semantics is carried out in the specific cases of certain logical languages and fragments of English. It may be helpful here, however, to give a general indication of some of the procedures and strategies we will follow.

We note first that since there are infinitely many nonsynonymous well-formed sentences of any natural language (and of any interesting logical language), our semantics must be prepared to specify an infinite number of truth conditions. A simple list will therefore not do; just as in syntax, recursive devices will be required. But what are the pieces that enter into a recursive specification of states-of-affairs? This is not an easy question to answer since it asks, in effect, What is there in the world? But we need not meet the ontological question head-on; as a first approximation let us simply assume that the world contains various sorts of objects – call them "entities" – and that in a particular state-of-affairs these entities have certain properties and stand in certain relations to each other. In a different state-of-affairs there will be some change in the inventory of entities and/or some difference in the distribution of properties and relations.

It is still not clear how we could construct a system for recursively specifying an infinite class of states-of-affairs; and there is also the serious problem of ensuring that the truth-conditions – however generated – are matched up in the right way with the well-formed sentences of the object language. A particular strategy for attacking both these problems at once is to let the rules for specifying truth conditions work, as it were, in tandem with the syntactic rules. The idea is that the syntactic generation of each sentence will be mirrored or "recapitulated" semantically, and in this way we will generate an infinite class of truth conditions *while* putting them in correspondence with object-language sentences. Adherence to this strategy has in fact become one of the cornerstones of truth-conditional semantics, and it is known as Frege's Principle or the Principle of Compositionality.

Here, in a little more detail, is how such a system would work. A sentence is composed ultimately of some finite number of words or morphemes – call them "basic expressions" – which are combined according to the syntactic rules of the grammar into successively larger expressions. Each syntactic rule can be regarded as a statement that certain input expressions combine in a certain way to produce an output expression. If we suppose now that each basic expression of the syntax is associated with something in the world – an entity, a property, a relation, or whatever – then we will have formed a basis for the recursions that are to operate on both the syntactic and semantic sides. What should be the "semantic values" associated with the basic expressions? In many cases it will be reasonably clear what the answer ought to be; for example, we would naturally be inclined to associate with a proper name, e.g., "David Kaplan," the person whom we commonly refer to by this name, i.e., David Kaplan. In other cases it will not be so clear what to do, but let us suppose for the moment that suitable correspondences have somehow been established. Now whenever there is a syntactic rule R taking inputs $\alpha, \beta, \ldots, \eta$ and from them giving ξ as output, our strategy calls for a corresponding semantic rule R' which takes as input the semantic values of $\alpha, \beta, \ldots, \eta$, respectively, and yields as output something which is the semantic value of ξ.

It should be clear that if the semantics and syntax match up point-for-point in this way, each sentence (and indeed each well-formed constituent of a sentence) will be provided with a semantic value. It remains to be seen, of course, whether we can contrive to make such a system yield the correct results in particular cases and whether the overall framework can be made sufficiently general to apply to all the languages we might want to treat in this way.

Notice that we have said nothing so far to indicate that any expression other than declarative sentences have meanings. Indeed, since truth is not a property of nouns, verb phrases, etc., the dictum of meanings as truth conditions would not be applicable here – at least not directly. It is tempting, however, to regard the semantic value given to an expression which is not a sentence as "the meaning" of that expression, and if we allow ourselves to do so as a first approximation, we can state Frege's Principle in the form in which it is most often quoted: The meaning of the whole is a function of the meaning of the parts and their mode of combination. Put in this way, it appears to be a truism, but in fact when it is taken seriously within the framework of truth-conditional semantics, it places some fairly severe constraints on the systems of syntactic and semantic rules we can construct. Note, for example, that "the parts" referred to in the statement of Frege's Principle must be the syntactic constituents of the expression in question. Moreover, the meanings of those constituents must enter into the meaning of the whole expression *in a fixed way,* determined once and for all by the semantic rule corresponding to the syntactic rule by which those constituents were joined. We will have more to say on this subject later, but for the moment it should not be too hard to imagine that many conceivable systems of syntactic and semantic rules would be in violation of this principle.

It is sometimes suggested (e.g., by Chomsky 1975) that to import this principle from logic into the study of natural language semantics is mere dogma – false dogma at that. We do not believe this suggestion to be correct. Rather, the Principle of Compositionality seems to us to be supported by considerations much like those which reveal the existence of phrase structure in syntax. Syntactically, one assigns strings like *most dentists, the dogcatcher*, and *John's teacher* to a common grammatical category, in this case noun phrase, because of the fact that where one of these strings occurs in a grammatical sentence, e.g. (1-1), it can be replaced by the others to yield other grammatical sentences, (1-2) and (1-3).

(1-1) Most dentists won't make house calls.

(1-2) The dogcatcher won't make house calls.

(1-3) John's teacher won't make house calls.

Nonconstituents like *make house* do not have this property. Although grammatical sentences are obtained when this string is replaced in any of (1-1) through (1-3) by *accept collect,* for instance, the same substitution in *A real estate agent can make house hunting easy* produces an ungrammatical string of words. Semantically, it appears that the meanings of (1-1) through (1-3) depend in a regular way on which of these noun phrases the sentences contain. If we attribute the differences in meaning among the sentences to the different contributions made by *most dentists, the dogcatcher,* and *John's teacher,* then these same noun phrases make the same contributions to the meanings of (1-4) through (1-6).

(1-4) I dislike most dentists.

(1-5) I dislike the dogcatcher.

(1-6) I dislike John's teacher.

What each noun phrase contributes can be regarded as its meaning. The meaning of any sentence or other category of expression containing one of these noun phrases seems to be a function of which of them it contains, as the Principle of Compositionality asserts. So a reasonable strategy is to assign meanings to syntactically complex expressions as a function of the meanings of their parts. The consequence that these noun phrases each have a meaning but *make house* does not is certainly in agreement with pretheoretic intuition. Thus the Compositionality Principle is rather a plausible one.

2. *Model-Theoretic Semantics*

The second characteristic of Montague's semantic theory we mentioned above is that it is model theoretic. This means, roughly, that it involves the construction of abstract mathematical models of those things in the world making up the semantic values of expressions in the object language. Model theory is a method – the most successful one developed to date – for carrying out the program of truth-conditional semantics. We will spend a good deal of time in subsequent chapters showing how it is done, but we can perhaps here convey something of the general idea involved.

The leading idea of model theory is that one can learn about the meaning of expressions and the correlations between expressions and meanings by investigating in detail how the meaning of complex expressions is related to the meaning of the simpler expressions they are constructed from. Given that the meanings in question are objects or configurations in the world, a sensible strategy is to study the relationships among those objects and configurations in order to gain insight into the relationships between meanings that get associated with expressions by the compositional process. In practice, this often means using the apparatus of set theory to represent semantically relevant aspects of the relationships between objects and configurations, and employing appropriate set-theoretic constructs as the objects in a model that are assigned as semantic values of expressions. Numerous examples of this procedure will be seen in the following chapters.

In studying the connection between expressions and their meanings it is common practice to take advantage also of the fact that many expressions might have meant something different than what they actually do, without the language therefore having been significantly different than it is. It happens, for example, that in English we use the proper name "David Kaplan" to denote a particular individual in the world; but any other name, logically speaking, would have served as well, and by the same token we might well have used the name "David Kaplan" to denote any other individual. This fact allows us to systematically vary the meaning assigned to such expressions, and observe the effect on the meaning of related expressions. By such means we may learn various things about the appropriate assignment of meaning to make to expressions of the language. To cite just one example, note that the meaning and even the truth value of "David Kaplan is a philosopher" may change as we vary the semantic value of "David Kaplan" (or of "philosopher"), since we can assign the President of the U.S. (i.e., Jimmy Carter) as the semantic value of the name (or assign the property of being a bricklayer as the semantic value of the common noun). Note, though, that however we might change these semantic values, the truth value of "If David Kaplan is a philosopher, then there is at least one philosopher" stays the same; that is, this sentence remains true. This observation gives useful information about the appropriate semantic values to assign to "if," "is," "a," "there," "at least," and "one."

To go into slightly greater detail, we might say, taking into account all the possible correspondences between expressions and semantic values, that each pairing represents a possible *interpretation* of the language in question. A *model* begins by specifying what sorts of thing there are in the world, and then, with respect to this assumed ontology, specifies an interpretation of the object language. Given this notion of a model, we can investigate certain interesting things which remain invariant under changes in interpretation. For example, it is generally assumed that certain basic expressions of English such as *and, or, not, every,* etc. have a fixed interpretation, i.e., they remain invariant from model to model. We can then characterize a certain class of sentences of English containing these words as *logically true* and another as *logically false*; specifically, these will be sentences which are true or false, respectively, in every model (i.e., under every assumed ontology and under every possible interpretation).

To take just one more illustration of the usefulness of the notion of a model, consider the sentence "Every man loves a woman." It is ambiguous, but the ambiguity arises from the interpretations of the words *every* and *a* and the particular syntactic configuration in which they occur, not from the interpretations of the words *man, woman,* and *loves.* We want our theory to say, therefore, that the ambiguity persists in every model – or to put it another way, we want it to give the *same* account of the ambiguity of the sentence "Every noise annoys an oyster."

3. *Possible Worlds Semantics*

We have already observed that in giving the truth conditions for a sentence we make reference to "how the world would have to be" in order for the sentence to be true. Thus, the meaning of a sentence depends not just on the world as it in fact is, but on the world as it might be, or might have been, etc. – i.e., other *possible worlds.* One quite naturally understands *I wish that I were richer,* for example, as expressing a certain relation between a speaker of the sentence and possible worlds differing from the actual one by an increase in the speaker's wealth.

We will be at some pains to justify the introduction of this notion into the framework of truth-conditional semantics in Chapter 5. For the moment, we should note that the intuitive significance of a possible world is that of a *complete* specification of how things are, or might be, down to the finest semantically relevant detail. A particular world – one of all the possible ones – is to contain everything that could affect the truth value of some sentence, i.e. everything that a sentence can be *about.* We have also spoken of states-of-affairs as providing the truth conditions of sentences. As we are using the terms, a "state-of-affairs" is a less comprehensive or detailed notion than a "possible world," since a state-of-affairs may concern only some aspects of a world. A particular sentence, after all, is *about* only a small part of the world. Thus, a state-of-affairs which makes a sentence true amounts to what is common to all those worlds in which the sentence is true.

Before we set about our task of constructing truth-conditional semantic systems for particular languages, we should issue a word of warning about what will *not* be found in this approach. For one thing, there is little to be said about lexical semantics, i.e., word meanings and relations among word meanings. This is often disappointing to those who are just becoming acquainted with the theory, expecially to those who are already familiar with previous linguistic work in semantics, but the synonymy of *bachelor* and *never-married adult human male* and a myriad of other such cases will not be of much concern to us. The truth-conditional approach, and in particular Montague's version of it, is able to *accommodate* such facts, but it is not taken as one of the principal tasks of the theory to account for them. Indeed, if our semantics adheres rigorously to the Principle of Compositionality, we can understand why matters of lexical semantics lie somewhat outside the domain of the theory. Since the semantic value of any expression is to be a function of the semantic values of its syntactic constituents, expressions which are syntactically unanalyzable, i.e., basic expressions, will be treated as semantically unanalyzable as well. Various extensions of the truth-conditional approach can be envisioned which will encompass at least a part of lexical semantics; for an extensive discussion of this matter, the reader is referred to Dowty (1979).

Neither will one find in this book, or in truth-conditional approaches generally, much discussion of the semantics of non-declarative sentences. In part, the reason for the exclusive attention to declaratives is the historic source of truth-conditional semantics within mathematical logic, an area where illocutionary acts other than statements play no role. This difference between logical and natural languages is one of considerable magnitude, and that is why it is a rather radical position to maintain that there is "no important theoretical difference" between them. Other features of natural language which are also absent from the usual formal languages – indexicals, subjunctive mood, etc. – will readily come to mind. For references to recent attempts to extend the methods of truth-conditional semantics to questions, imperatives, etc., the reader is referred to Chapter 9.

Finally, we should observe that we will have nothing to say here about the very important issue of the "psychological reality" of our proposed semantic theories. There is a sense, of course, in which any semantic theory of a natural language has psychological implications in that its predictions about matters of synonymy, entailment, and so on, must square with the intuitions of native speakers on these matters. And as in the case of syntactic theories, one can raise questions of the connection, if any, between the constructs postulated in the theory of semantics and the intrinsic competence of the native speakers that we seek to characterize. This exceedingly vexed question is just as difficult with respect to the semantic domain as it is with the syntactic. For some discussion of these matters, the reader should see Dowty (1979, ch. 9) and also Partee (1979c).

CHAPTER 2

THE SYNTAX AND SEMANTICS OF TWO SIMPLE LANGUAGES

I. THE LANGUAGE L_0

We begin by considering a very simple language, which anyone familiar with symbolic logic will recognize as essentially the propositional calculus with propositions analyzed into predicates and arguments. Truth-conditional semantics was first developed in connection with logical languages, and it is instructive to look at such cases to understand the motivations for certain features that may appear peculiar in the context of natural languages.

In the logical tradition it is customary to specify the syntax of a language not by a phrase-structure grammar but by a recursive definition of the *well-formed expressions* of the language. This is done by giving first a list of *basic expressions* divided into various categories. (These will correspond to the terminal symbols and lexical categories of a phase-structure grammar.) Then a set of *formation rules* states how expressions of various categories are combined into other more complex expressions. These rules apply recursively, and each is of the following form: given expressions $\alpha, \beta, \ldots, \eta$ of categories $C_\alpha, C_\beta, \ldots, C_\eta$, respectively, these expressions can be combined in a specific way (stated by the rule) to yield an expression of category C_ω. One notices certain similarities here to the phrase-structure rules of a phrase-structure grammar but certain differences as well. We will have more to say on this point later, but let us first consider as a specific instance the syntax of our language L_0.

1. *Syntax of L_0*

A. The *basic expressions* of L_0 are of three syntactic-categories:

(2-1)

Category	*Basic Expressions*
Names	d, n, j, m
One-place predicates	M, B
Two-place predicates	K, L

B. The *formation rules* are of two kinds. First, there are rules for combining predicates with an appropriate number of names to produce *atomic sentences*

(sentences having no other sentences as parts). These are rules 1. and 2. below. Second, there are rules (3.–7. below) which form a sentence out of one or more other sentences.

(2-2)
1. If δ is a one-place predicate and α is a name, then $\delta(\alpha)$ is a sentence.
2. If γ is a two-place predicate and α and β are names, then $\gamma(\alpha, \beta)$ is a sentence.
3. If ϕ is a sentence, then $\neg\phi$ is a sentence.
4. If ϕ and ψ are sentences, then $[\phi \wedge \psi]$ is a sentence.
5. If ϕ and ψ are sentences, then $[\phi \vee \psi]$ is a sentence.
6. If ϕ and ψ are sentences, then $[\phi \rightarrow \psi]$ is a sentence.
7. If ϕ and ψ are sentences, then $[\phi \leftrightarrow \psi]$ is a sentence.

Note that in the statements of the foregoing rules we used the Greek letters "α," "β," etc. to refer to expressions of L_0. These symbols function in effect as variables taking expressions of L_0 as values, and it is important not to confuse such symbols with symbol of the language itself. Here L_0 is the *object language*, the language under study. The rules in (2-2) are statements *about* certain expressions of L_0 and are couched in English (albeit of a somewhat stilted, technical variety). Thus, English is the *meta-language*, the language used in talking about the object language and "α," "β," etc. are *meta-language variables*, or simply *meta-variables*. To help forestall possible confusion between meta-variables and object language symbols, we will adopt henceforth the following notational convention:

(2-3) Notational Convention 1: Lower-case letters of the Greek alphabet are used only as meta-language variables, never as symbols of an object language.

The rules in (2-2) constitute a recursive definition of the infinite set of expressions of the category "sentence" in L_0. Rules 1. and 2., together with (2-1), comprise the base of the recursive definition, and rules 3.–7. together make up the recursion. It is assumed in all such statements of formation rules that nothing else is a member of any syntactic category except what qualifies by virtue of the rules; i.e., the exclusion clause is assumed whether explicitly stated or not.

By rule 1. we can form, for example, the atomic sentence $M(d)$ from the one-place predicate M and the name d. Similarly, rule 2. allows the formation of the atomic sentence $K(d, j)$ from the two-place predicate K and the names d and j. Now given that $M(d)$ and $K(d, j)$ are sentences, we can form by rule 3. the (non-atomic) sentences $\neg M(d)$ and $\neg K(d, j)$. The reader can verify on the basis of the formation rules given that each of the following is a well-formed sentence of L_0:

(2-4) 1. $[K(d, j) \wedge M(d)]$
2. $\neg[M(d) \vee B(m)]$
3. $[L(n, j) \rightarrow [B(d) \vee \neg K(m, m)]]$
4. $[\neg\neg\neg B(n) \leftrightarrow \neg M(n)]$

One should note carefully that the parentheses, comma, and square brackets are symbols of L_0 just as K, d, etc. are. They are not basic expressions, however, and are not assigned membership in any syntactic category. Such symbols are called *syncategorematic* because they are introduced into expressions by the formation rules along with the regular, or *categorematic*, symbols. Besides the symbols that might be regarded as punctuation, other syncategorematic symbols of L_0 are the *connectives* "$\wedge$," "$\vee$," "$\neg$," "$\rightarrow$," and "$\leftrightarrow$."

2. *Semantics of* L_0

Our strategy for determining the semantic values of the sentences and other constituents of L_0, for connecting each well-formed expression of L_0 with some "object in the world," will follow the Principle of Compositionality mentioned in Chapter 1. We first assume that a semantic value has been given to each basic expression (somehow or other – the way in which this is done does not concern us at the moment). We then state *semantic rules*, whose job it is to determine the semantic value of each larger constituent in terms of the semantic values of its components. In other words, semantic values are assigned to successively more inclusive constituents of the sentence until finally the semantic value of the entire sentence has been determined.

With respect to sentence (2-4) 2., for example, we would assume the semantic values for the basic expressions "M," "d," "B," and "m" to be antecedently given. Then by means of the semantic rules, we would determine the semantic values of the constituents "$M(d)$," "$B(m)$," "$M(d) \vee B(m)$," and finally of the whole sentence. Since the semantic rules will be designed in such a way that they retrace or "track" the syntactic structure, every well-formed sentence of L_0 as well as every well-formed constituent of such a sentence will be assigned a semantic value by this procedure.

What sorts of things are the semantic values to be? First, it is a basic assumption of the truth-conditional approach that semantic values come in various varieties or types, and that *in general* (but not always, as we shall see later), members of different syntactic categories take on semantic values of different types. Different theories of truth-conditional semantics will, however, make different assumptions about the exact range of possible semantic values and about the pairing of syntactic categories with types of values.

For the moment, we will assume a rather elementary version of the theory. In this system, names take as their semantic values just what our common sense would probably tell us they ought to take, namely, individuals. We are not obliged to say at this point just what counts as an individual; we would certainly want to include human beings, animals, and other countable physical objects, but we need not take a stand on such philosophically controversial problems as whether events, propositions, actions, etc. are to count. For illustrative purposes, let us assume that the universe consists of just four individuals, namely, Richard Nixon, Noam Chomsky, John Mitchell and Muhammad Ali. To each name in L_0 we might then assign one of these individuals as its semantic value, as in the following table:

(2-5)	*Name*	*Semantic Value*
	d	Richard Nixon
	n	Noam Chomsky
	j	John Mitchell
	m	Muhammad Ali

Other pairings would have served as well, but let us adopt this one now for purposes of illustration. We will in general insist that each basic expression be assigned a single semantic value, so that cases of lexical ambiguity will be treated as separate lexical items that happen to have the same pronunciation. We will not require, however, that every individual in the domain of discourse be assigned to a name as its semantic value. Thus, there could be individuals for whom our language had no names. It is also allowed for one and the same individual to have two or more names (just as "Samuel Clemens" and "Mark Twain" are names of the same person). In short, what we want is a *function*, in the mathematical sense, from the names of the language into the set of individuals in the domain of discourse; more specifically, it must be a *total function*, since no names are to be left unpaired. The table in (2-5) is intended to represent one such total function.

PROBLEM (2-1). Given a language with *n* distinct names and a universe of discourse consisting of *m* distinct individuals, how many different assignments of semantics values to names are possible?

It is important to recognize that there are two very different sorts of entities involved in (2-5). In the left-hand column there are *linguistic entities* – lexical items of a particular syntactic category in a particular language. In the right-hand column we find not linguistic entities but "*real-world*" *entities*, in this case, real people. There would be little chance of confusion on this matter were it not for the fact we are communicating with the reader by means of the printed page, and so we could not put in (2-5) the people themselves but rather have let them be represented by their conventional names in English. The reader is encouraged to mentally transcend this limitation and to imagine that in (2-5) we have persuaded Messrs. Nixon, Mitchell, Chomsky and Ali to participate in a *tableau vivant* in which they wear their respective names from L_0 as, say, signs hanging around their necks. In this way, the reader will not be tempted to think that the semantic value of *d* is "Richard Nixon" (i.e., Mr. Nixon's name); rather, it is Richard Nixon himself, the ex-President of the United States of America, the man who said "I am not a crook," etc. The point is worth belaboring since it is central to the program of truth conditional semantics, as we said in the preceding chapter, that a connection is made between language and extra-linguistic reality, i.e. "the world." (The sanitizing quotes here are prompted by the fact that we will eventually want to consider not only the world in which we live as it actually is but also the world as it was, as it will be, as it might have been, etc. i.e., other "possible worlds").

What sort of semantic value should the one-place predicates *B* and *M* have? What "objects in the world" could we connect these predicates with? For purposes of L_0, we will let this semantic value be a set of individuals – intuitively, the set of individuals of which the predicate is true. Our semantics is said to be *extensional* because our semantic treatment of a predicate here involves *only* its "extension." Thus, we will let the semantic value of *B* be the set of all individuals that are bald and the semantic value of *M* be the set of all individuals who have moustaches. We might digress at this point to admit that from the point of view of a speaker's understanding of the meanings of predicates, it is not very natural to identify our understanding of, say, "is bald" with the set of bald persons; there are, after all, bald individuals we have never met. Instead, what seems more relevant is our grasp of a certain attribute or characteristic that all these individuals share that distinguishes them from others. (For this reason we have avoided use of the term "meaning" here and have employed the more neutral term "semantic value.") But one implicit effect of the use of "is bald" by all speakers of English is potentially to single out this set of persons, however this is done mentally by individual speakers, and this set will serve our present purposes quite well. Our treatment of the semantic values of predicates in later languages will be more complex and will more closely approximate our intuitive understanding of their "meaning."

We can now see how the truth value of a sentence formed from a name and a one-place predicate is to be determined. A sentence like $M(j)$ should be true if and only if the individual denoted by the name j (John Mitchell in this case) is a member of the set of individuals denoted by the predicate M (the set of individuals that have moustaches). Since we will need to use the phrase "the semantic value of α" often, we will introduce a special notation for it:

(2-6)	Notational Convention 2: For any expression α, we use $[\![\alpha]\!]$ to indicate the semantic value of α.

Thus our semantic rule for sentences formed from a one-place predicate and a name will say that if δ is a one-place predicate and α is a name, then $\delta(\alpha)$ is true iff (if and only if) $[\![\alpha]\!] \in [\![\delta]\!]$.

For two-place predicates, we will adopt an approach that parallels that used for one-place predicates: we let the semantic value of a two-place predicate be a set of pairs of individuals; intuitively, these are the pairs of which the predicate is true when the first argument names the first individual and the second argument names the second individual. In particular, we will let $[\![K]\!]$ be the set of pairs in which the first knows the second, and $[\![L]\!]$ will be the set of pairs in which the first loves the second. For example, $\langle$Richard Nixon, John Mitchell$\rangle$ is a member of $[\![K]\!]$, but to the extent of our knowledge, $\langle$Muhammad Ali, Noam Chomsky$\rangle$ is not a member of $[\![K]\!]$. Our semantic rule for sentences formed from a two-place predicate and two names will then state that if γ is a two-place predicate and α and β are names, then $\gamma(\alpha, \beta)$ is true iff $\langle [\![\alpha]\!], [\![\beta]\!] \rangle \in [\![\gamma]\!]$ (that is, if the ordered pair consisting of the denotations of the two names, in that order, is a member of the set of pairs denoted by the predicate). By this rule, for example, $K(d, j)$ is true, because $\langle [\![d]\!], [\![j]\!] \rangle \in [\![K]\!]$, in other words, because $\langle$Richard Nixon, John Mitchell$\rangle \in \{\langle x, y\rangle \mid x \text{ knows } y\}$. Note that we want the semantic values of two-place predicates to be sets of *ordered* pairs (and not merely sets of two-meber sets) in order to allow for the possibility that $\gamma(\alpha, \beta)$ can be true while

$\gamma(\beta, \alpha)$ is false (or vice versa), for some two-place predicate γ and names α and β.

Before going on to a formal statement of the semantic rule or rules involved, we must pause to consider our obligations to the Principle of Compositionality. We want our semantic rules to be such that the semantic value of a syntactically complex expression is always a function of the semantic values of its syntactic components and of their "mode of combination," i.e., the way the parts are combined to form the expression in question. As we said in Chapter 1, in order to ensure that the semantic component adheres to the Principle of Compositionality, it is common practice to construct the semantic rules so that they are in one-to-one correspondence with the syntactic rules. For example, $\neg[M(j) \wedge K(j, d)]$ is generated by the grammar of L_0 through the application of the four syntactic rules B1, B2, B4 and B3. Therefore, four of the semantic rules we formulate will correspond to these syntactic rules. The semantic rules will, in effect, "compute" the semantic values of successively larger parts of this sentence, starting with the semantic values of the basic expressions.

The semantic rules for L_0 that remain to be formulated are therefore those that will correspond to the syntactic rules producing $\neg\phi$, $[\phi \wedge \psi]$, $[\phi \vee \psi]$, $[\phi \rightarrow \psi]$, and $[\phi \leftrightarrow \psi]$ from sentences ϕ and ψ. These will be designed to have the effect of the familiar truth tables for these connectives and thus require little comment. Though here formulated in our English metalanguage in a way that requires our understanding of English "and," "or," "not," etc., we will see shortly that these semantic rules could, if desired, be given a mechanical formulation that avoids these metalanguage words. We now state the complete semantic system for L_0: the assignment of semantic values to basic expressions, and the rules that recursively determine the semantic value for any sentence of L_0 in terms of the basic expressions and syntactic rules from which it is formed.

(2-7) A. Basic Expressions:

$[\![d]\!]$ = Richard Nixon $[\![j]\!]$ = John Mitchell
$[\![n]\!]$ = Noam Chomsky $[\![m]\!]$ = Muhammad Ali
$[\![M]\!]$ = the set of all living people with moustaches
$[\![B]\!]$ = the set of all living people who are bald
$[\![K]\!]$ = the set of all pairs of living people such that the first knows the second.
$[\![L]\!]$ = the set of all pairs of living people such that the first loves the second.

(2-8) B. Semantic Rules:

1. If δ is a one-place predicate and α is a name, then $\delta(\alpha)$ is true iff $[\![\alpha]\!] \in [\![\delta]\!]$.
2. If γ is a two-place predicate and α and β are names, then $\gamma(\alpha, \beta)$ is true iff $\langle [\![\alpha]\!], [\![\beta]\!] \rangle \in [\![\gamma]\!]$.
3. If ϕ is a sentence, then $\neg\phi$ is true iff ϕ is not true.
4. If ϕ and ψ are sentences, then $[\phi \wedge \psi]$ is true iff both ϕ and ψ are true.
5. If ϕ and ψ are sentences, then $[\phi \vee \psi]$ is true iff either ϕ or ψ is true.
6. If ϕ and ψ are sentences, then $[\phi \rightarrow \psi]$ is true iff either ϕ is false or ψ is true.
7. If ϕ and ψ are sentences, then $[\phi \leftrightarrow \psi]$ is true iff either ϕ and ψ are both true or else ϕ and ψ are both false.

Given these semantic rules and the assignments of semantic values to basic expressions, one can, in principle, determine the truth values of all sentences of L_0. We say "in principle" because values are assigned to the predicates M, B, K, and L in terms of what is in fact the case in the world at present. Anyone's knowledge of this factual situation may be limited, but the functions which are the semantic values are well-defined nonetheless (if we ignore for the sake of the example any problems connected with the assumed preciseness of the predicates; i.e., we assume that we can determine for any living individuals whether they are bald or not, have moustaches or not, etc.). Thus, at the time of writing, $B(n)$ is false, since Noam Chomsky is not bald, but $B(j)$ is true, since John Mitchell is bald. Given this, it follows that $\neg B(j)$ is false (since $B(j)$ is true), and $\neg B(n)$ is true (since $B(n)$ is false). $K(d, j)$ is true, since Richard Nixon knows John Mitchell, and thus $[B(j) \wedge K(d, j)]$ is true, both conjuncts being true. $K(n, m)$, we suspect, is false, since we doubt that Noam Chomsky knows Muhammad Ali.

PROBLEM (2-2). Determine the truth values, insofar as your knowledge allows you to do so, of each of the sentences of L_0 given in (2-4).

This system of syntactic and semantic rules thus specifies an infinite set of sentences of L_0 and assigns to each a semantic value, either *true* or *false* (and, as it happens, the assignments are unique since L_0 contains no "syntactically ambiguous" sentences). But in the preceding chapter we promised a system that would supply for each sentence of a language its *truth conditions* – necessary and sufficient conditions for the truth of that sentence – and it appears that we have delivered only a *truth value*. Where is the rest? The answer is that the foregoing semantic rules do in fact give the truth conditions for sentences of L_0, and they do so, as it were, *while* determining truth values. Consider an atomic sentence of L_0, for example, $M(n)$. Let us ask under what circumstances it would be true. This information is contained in semantic rule B.1, where we learn that for any sentence of the form $\delta(\alpha)$, it will be true just in case $[\![\alpha]\!] \in [\![\delta]\!]$. That is, for the case of sentence $M(n)$, it will be true just in case $[\![n]\!] \in [\![M]\!]$, which, given the assumed semantic values for M and n, amounts to saying that Noam Chomsky is a member of the set of all living people with moustaches. In summary, $M(n)$ is true iff Noam Chomsky has a moustache.

If we examine any sentence of L_0 of the form $[\phi \wedge \psi]$ and ask for its truth conditions, we find that they are given by rule B.4. $[M(n) \wedge B(d)]$ is true, for example, just in case both $M(n)$ is true and $B(d)$ is true. But we know under what conditions each of these is true by virtue of rule B.1, so we therefore know the truth conditions of $M(n) \wedge B(d)$. Similar reasoning applied to any sentence of L_0, and so we have in fact delivered what we promised.

A further, related point may perhaps make this clearer yet. As we will explain in section IV, a quite different status is possessed by the assignment of semantic values to basic expressions in (2-7) and that of the semantic rules in (2-8). Precisely what semantic values are assigned in (2-7) depends crucially on certain facts about the world, e.g., on just who is bald, who in fact knows whom, etc. If these facts were different than they actually are, different semantic values would have to be assigned to "*B*", "*K*", etc. But regardless of how these facts might change, the semantic rules in (2-8) would stay the same. These rules are an integral part of the language L_0, as opposed to the world this language might be used to talk about. They state relationships between the semantic value of one expression and the semantic values associated with other, syntactically related expressions – relationships which must hold just by virtue of what language L_0 is, irrespective of precisely what objects in the world turn out to be connected with L_0's expressions. The game plan of model theory is to describe the semantics of a language by characterizing these necessary relationships between associated objects, capitalizing on the fact that the relationships do not change depending on contingent facts about the condition of things in the world.

We have given the syntactic and semantic rules for L_0 in the general form usually adopted for formal languages by logicians. But in fact many of the features of our statements of these rules were essentially abritrary, as we could have defined a language with the same expressive capability as L_0 in somewhat different ways while still adhering to the Principle of Compositionality and the goal of a truth-conditional semantics. For example, while we used recursive definitions to specify the syntax of L_0, we could instead have used a phrase-structure grammar of the sort linguists are accustomed to, and instead of introducing the connectives $\wedge$, $\vee$, $\rightarrow$, etc., syncategorematically, we could have treated them as basic expressions in a category of sentence conjunctions. Similarly, several aspects of our semantics could have received alternative but equivalent formulations. In order to better illustrate which features of L_0 are crucial to our program and which are matters of convenience and, at the same time, to show how this program can be applied to a language that resembles English to a much greater degree than L_0, we now turn to an English-like but semantically similar language which we will call L_{0E}.

II. THE LANGUAGE L_{0E}

1. *Syntax of* L_{0E}

The syntax of L_{0E} is given by the following context-free phrase-structure grammar:[1]

(2-9)

$$S \rightarrow \left\{ \begin{matrix} S\ Conj\ S \\ Neg\ S \\ N\ VP \end{matrix} \right\} \qquad VP \rightarrow \left\{ \begin{matrix} V_i \\ V_t\,N \end{matrix} \right\}$$

Conj → *and, or*
N → *Sadie, Liz, Hank*
V_i → *snores, sleeps, is-boring*
V_t → *loves, hates, is-taller-than*
Neg → *it-is-not-the-case-that*

By trying a few derivations with this grammar the reader will see that it generates a small fragment of quasi-English. For example, the following are grammatical according to (2-9):

(2-10)
1. *Sadie snores.*
2. *Liz sleeps.*
3. *It-is-not-the-case-that Hank snores.*
4. *Sadie sleeps or Liz is-boring and Hank snores.*
5. *It-is-not-the-case-that it-is-not-the-case-that Sadie sleeps.*

One should note that the hyphenated items *is-boring*, *is-taller-than*, and *it-is-not-the-case-that* are understood as unanalyzable terminal symbols of L_{0E} just as *Liz* and *snores* are. This is merely a device to allow us to introduce a bit of variety into this rather limited language without having to deal with certain syntactic complexities prematurely. We do not wish to suggest that the corresponding expressions "is boring," etc. should be treated this way in a more complete and accurate grammar of English, and there is nothing essential to our semantic approach involved here.

L_{0E} contains five *lexical categories* (those which are immediately rewritten as terminal symbols), namely N, V_i, V_t, *Neg*, and *Conj*. For convenience, let us call these by their traditional linguistic designations: proper nouns (or names), intransitive verbs, transitive verbs, negation, and (co-ordinating) conjunctions, respectively. The two remaining non-lexical categories are *VP* (for verb phrase) and *S* (for sentence). We assume that the derivation of any sentence of L_{0E} can be represented by a tree structure in the usual way (described in Note 1), and given such a tree we will use the commonly accepted terminology, saying, for example, that any string of terminal symbols which is exhaustively dominated by a category stands in the "is a" relation to that category. The sentence *Hank snores and Liz is-taller-than Sadie* would thus be associated with the following tree structure according to the grammar of (2-9):

(2-11)

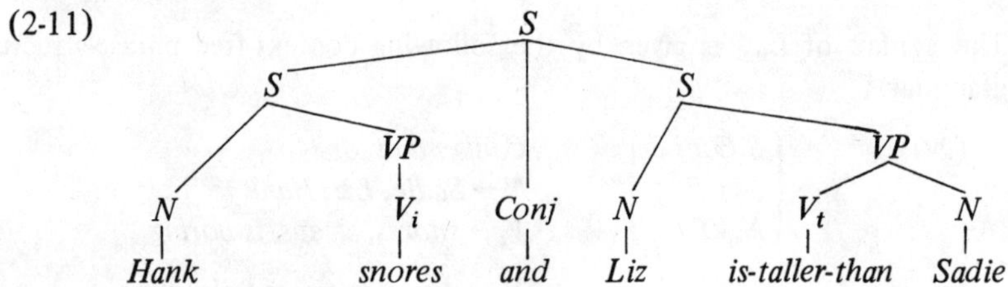

With respect to this tree, we can say that *Hank* stands in the "is a" relation to *N*, or briefly, that *Hank* is an *N*. Similarly, *is-taller-than Sadie* is a *VP*, the entire terminal string is an *S*, "snores and" is not a constituent at all, etc.

Although the grammar in (2-9) generates only a fragment of English (or near-English), it is worth noting that it generates an infinite language – by means of the recursive rules $S \rightarrow S\ Conj\ S$ and $S \rightarrow Neg\ S$. Further, there are sentences, in fact an infinite number of them, which have more than one syntactic derivation. Sentence (2-10) 4. is one such.

PROBLEM (2-3). Construct all phrase-structure trees associated with the sentences in (2-10). The fourth sentence should have two trees. Set your results aside for use in Problem (2-11).

PROBLEM (2-4). Are there any syntactically ambiguous sentences (those having distinct tree structures) in L_{0E} which do not involve an application of the phrase-structure rule $S \rightarrow S$ Conj S?

2. *Semantics of* L_{0E}

Even though we have used a phrase-structure grammar to formulate the syntax of L_{0E} we will still adopt the Principle of Compositionality in our interpretation of L_{0E} in much the same way as with L_0. We will assign a semantic value to each lexical item as we did to each basic expression in L_0, and for each syntactic constituent there will be a rule for determining its semantic value from the semantic value(s) of its sub-constituents. Though we may think of the phrase-structure rules as defining a tree "from top to bottom," our semantic rules will be formulated as proceeding from the bottom of the tree (its terminal nodes) to the top. Nevertheless, there will be a semantic rule corresponding to each phrase structure rule in the semantics of L_{0E}, just as there was a one-to-one correspondence between syntactic and semantic rules in L_0. More formally, for each phrase structure rule $\alpha \rightarrow \beta_1\ \beta_2 \ldots \beta_n$, there will be a semantic rule for determining the semantic value of the constituent labelled α in a tree in terms of the semantic values of the constituents $\beta_1, \beta_2, \ldots \beta_n$ which the node α dominates.

Purely for convenience, we will make a slight change in the way the semantic values for sentences are stated. Instead of simply classifying sentences into the (meta-language) categories "true" and "false" as we did for L_0, we will select two objects to represent truth and falsity, respectively, and assign one of these to each sentence as its semantic value. Following common practice among mathematical logicians (including Montague), we will select the number 1 to indicate truth and 0 to indicate falsity. The intuitive significance of these semantic values is the same as before: sentences assigned 1 are to be thought of as those that correspond to some (real or hypothetical) state-of-affairs, while sentences assigned 0 are those that don't. Thus our choice of these two objects has no particular ontological significance; we could just as well have selected the Empire State Building for the value assigned to true sentences and the planet Venus for false ones.

Turning now to the lexical categories of L_{0E}, we will first assign values to the names. As with L_0, we will want names to denote individuals, so we may assign the names *Sadie*, *Liz* and *Hank* values as in (2-12):

(2-12) $[\![Sadie]\!]$ = Anwar Sadat
$[\![Liz]\!]$ = Queen Elizabeth II
$[\![Hank]\!]$ = Henry Kissinger

We wish to give the semantic values of intransitive verbs, V_i, the effect of singling out a set of individuals, just as we did with the one-place predicates of L_0. We will achieve this effect in a different way here, however.

Sets of individuals are in a one-to-one correspondence with functions that map individuals to 0 or 1, as will emerge momentarily. It is very convenient to follow Montague in the common mathematical practise of not distinguishing between the two isomorphic sorts of object in cases like this, and to consider an object sometimes as a set, sometimes as a certain kind of function. For this reason we digress briefly to define the association which justifies this identification.

If A is the set of individuals and S is any subset of A, we define a function f_S on the set A by letting

$$f_S(a) = \begin{cases} 1 \text{ if } a \in S \\ 0 \text{ if } a \notin S \end{cases}$$

for each a in A. This function is called the *characteristic function* of S (with respect to A) and belongs to $\{0, 1\}^A$, where X^Y is in general the set of all functions from Y into X. The characteristic function divides the domain A in two parts, the subset mapped into 1 (namely S) and the complementary subset, which is mapped into 0.

Two fundamental properties of sets guarantee that sets of individuals and their characteristic functions are in a one-to-one correspondence. First, membership in a set S is a strictly yes-or-no matter, i.e., each particular individual either does or else does not belong to S. Thus every set included in A is characterized by some way of saying "true" or "false" to each individual. Secondly, two sets are distinct if they differ in membership. Therefore, different ways of saying "true" or "false" to individuals correspond to different sets.

The semantic values of V_i's in L_{0E} will all be characteristic functions of sets of individuals. Assuming for the sake of simplicity that the three individuals mentioned in (2-12) are the only individuals in the world, we might for example stipulate that the V_i *snores* has as its semantic value the following function:

(2-13)
$$[\![snores]\!] = \begin{bmatrix} \text{Anwar Sadat} \to 1 \\ \text{Queen Elizabeth II} \to 1 \\ \text{Henry Kissinger} \to 0 \end{bmatrix}$$

(Recall that a function is technically a set of ordered pairs: thus (2-13) is simply a convenient graphic representation of the set {⟨Anwar Sadat, 1⟩, ⟨Queen Elizabeth II, 1⟩, ⟨Henry Kissinger, 0⟩}). Note that this semantic value is a set-theoretic construct made from individuals (NB: here, real people!) and truth values. (In the extensional semantic theory we will be constructing in this and the following two chapters, *every* kind of semantic value will in fact be made out of these same basic ingredients – individuals and truth values – by means of the combinatory apparatus of set theory.)

For the sake of completeness, let us assume that semantic values of the remaining V_i's are as follows:

(2-14)
$$[\![\textit{sleeps}]\!] = \begin{bmatrix} \text{Anwar Sadat} \rightarrow 1 \\ \text{Queen Elizabeth II} \rightarrow 0 \\ \text{Henry Kissinger} \rightarrow 0 \end{bmatrix}$$

(2-15)
$$[\![\textit{is-boring}]\!] = \begin{bmatrix} \text{Anwar Sadat} \rightarrow 1 \\ \text{Queen Elizabeth II} \rightarrow 1 \\ \text{Henry Kissinger} \rightarrow 1 \\ 0 \end{bmatrix}$$

PROBLEM (2-5). Assuming that the world contains *n* individuals, how many different semantic values for V_i's are possible?

Given now the semantic value for both the names and the intransitive verbs of L_{0E}, what kind of semantic rule will be required to "compute" the semantic value of a sentence of the form $N + V_i$? It is clear that the simplest rule will be: apply the function which is the semantic value of the V_i to the argument which is the semantic value of the *N*. The result will be the semantic value (i.e. 1 or 0) of the sentence. For example, given that $[\![\textit{Sadie}]\!] =$ Anwar Sadat and that $[\![\textit{snores}]\!]$ is the function in (2-13), the truth value of the sentence *Sadie snores* will be the value of the function at the argument Anwar Sadat, i.e., 1 (true). In the usual notation for functions in which the argument is written to the right of the name of the function and enclosed in parentheses, the foregoing could be expressed as:

(2-16) $[\![\textit{snores}]\!]([\![\textit{Sadie}]\!]) = 1$

In the same way we could determine that given our assumed semantic values, $[\![\textit{Hank sleeps}]\!] = 0$ and $[\![\textit{Liz is-boring}]\!] = 1$.

In L_0 we let one-place predicates denote sets and specified that a sentence formed from such a predicate plus a name was to count as true just in case the individual denoted by the name belonged to the set denoted by the predicate. The function given in (2-13) as the semantic value of *snores* is the characteristic function of the set {Anwar Sadat, Queen Elizabeth II}, and applying such a function to an individual, as we did in (2-16), results in the value 1 (truth) just in case that individual belongs to the set characterized by this function, false just in case that individual does not belong to that set. Thus, our semantic treatment of one-place predicates in L_0 turns out to be equivalent to that of sentences with V_i's in L_{0E}. In many approaches to truth conditional semantics, sets rather than characteristic functions are assigned as semantic values of certain syntactic categories. As we see, nothing crucial is involved in this choice, since sets and characteristic functions are essentially two ways of looking at what amounts to the same thing. It may be more elegant to formalize semantic values as characteristic functions rather than sets in that the semantic rules which produce a truth value as output are assimilated to other rules which work by applying a function to an argument. Montague preferred the elegance and uniformity of stating semantic rules as *rules of functional application* wherever possible, and thus we will adhere to his practice of using characteristic functions rather than sets in the formal definitions. But, again following Montague's practice, we will often talk in terms of sets rather than functions when it is intuitively more congenial to do so. The reader should be prepared to make the necessary conversion without being explicitly directed to do so in each case.

As a further preliminary to stating the semantic rules for L_{0E}, we note again that sentences like *Sadie sleeps or Liz is-boring and Hank snores* are derivable in nonequivalent ways. It is intuitively clear that the semantic value such a sentence has may depend on how it is derived, in particular on the phrase-structure tree associated with its derivation, so that it will be semantically as well as syntactically ambiguous. For this reason, we shall not assign semantic values directly to sentences in an ambiguous language like L_{0E}, but in the first instance to phrase-structure trees. Otherwise we could not continue assigning a unique semantic value to each part of the language we interpret. Sentences and other phrases naturally inherit the semantic values assigned to their one or more tree structures.

Turning now to the semantic rules of L_{0E}, we will provide a semantic rule for each syntactic rule used in producing sentences. In order to interpret the structure (2-17) of the sentence *Sadie snores*, which will ultimately involve applying the function $[\![snores]\!]$ to $[\![Sadie]\!]$, we need semantic rules for the phrase-structure rules that introduce the intervening nodes N, V_i and VP.

(2-17)

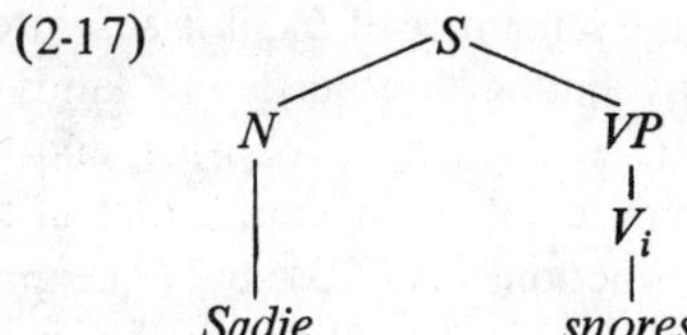

Clearly the semantic value of the nodes labelled with the lexical categories N and V_i should just be the semantic values of the respective lexical items which they immediately dominate. Thus, the semantic rule corresponding to the syntactic rule $N \rightarrow$ *Sadie* should be something like the following:

(2-18) If α is $\overset{N}{\underset{\beta}{|}}$ and β is *Sadie*, then $[\![\alpha]\!] = [\![\beta]\!]$.

The semantic rule corresponding to $V_i \rightarrow$ *snores* would be similar, and in fact we could abbreviate all such semantic rules by means of the following rule schema:

(2-19) If α is any $\overset{\gamma}{\underset{\beta}{|}}$, where γ is lexical category and β is any lexical item, and $\gamma \rightarrow \beta$ is a syntactic rule, then $[\![\alpha]\!] = [\![\beta]\!]$.

For the grammar of L_{0E}, this schema is instantiated by twelve semantic rules, each one corresponding to a lexical rule of the grammar.

Corresponding to the nonlexical syntactic rule $VP \rightarrow V_i$, we will want a semantic rule which attaches the semantic value of the V_i node to the VP node. Here and below, we use triangles (in a way familiar to linguists) as meta-variables over trees; e.g., $\overset{V_i}{\triangle}$ stands for any tree rooted in the node V_i.

(2-20) If α is $\overset{VP}{\underset{\beta}{|}}$ and β is $\overset{V_i}{\triangle}$, then $[\![\alpha]\!] = [\![\beta]\!]$.

Finally, we come to the more interesting semantic rule which corresponds to the branching syntactic rule $S \rightarrow N\ VP$:

(2-21) If α is $\overset{N}{\triangle}$ and β is $\overset{VP}{\triangle}$, and if γ is $\overset{S}{\alpha \frown \beta}$, then $[\![\gamma]\!] = [\![\beta]\!]([\![\alpha]\!])$.

PROBLEM (2-6). Determine by means of the semantic rules just given the semantic values of the phrase-structure trees of *Hank sleeps* and *Liz is-boring*.

As we emphasized in our discussion of the semantics of L_0, it is absolutely essential to keep in mind the distinctions among three different kinds of things: (1) expressions in the object language (e.g. *Sadie, is-boring*, and the tree in (2-17)), (2) entities serving as semantic values of expressions in the object language (e.g. Anwar Sadat and the functions in (2-13), and (3) expressions in the meta-language which are used in talking about the entities in (1) and (2) (e.g. α and the other expressions in (2-21)). In light of this discussion, the reader should now consider the following question: according to the semantic values given for L_{0E} so far and the semantic rules given for L_{0E}, what is the truth value of *Henry Kissinger sleeps*? Anyone who answers "0" or "false" has fallen into a trap. *Henry Kissinger sleeps* is not a sentence of L_{0E} since *Henry Kissinger* is not in its terminal vocabulary. Thus, not being a sentence of the object language, it is not assigned any semantic value by what has been given so far. Of course "Henry Kissinger sleeps" is a sentence of *English*, and in a semantics of that language we would want to be sure that some truth value is assigned to it.

Let us now ask what sort of values the V_t's should have. Semantically they seem to express relations between individuals. According to the grammar, a V_t followed by an *N* forms a *VP*. Is this consistent with the need for a *VP* to have as its semantic value a function from individuals to truth values (so that semantic rule (2-21) will function correctly)? The answer is "Yes" because we can take advantage of the isomorphism between relations and functions of a certain type. We need the semantic value of a V_t to be something that maps the semantic value of an *N* (i.e., an individual) into the semantic value of a *VP* (i.e., a function from individuals to truth values). Thus, we take the value of a V_t to be a function which yields other functions as its "outputs". Its domain will be the set of individuals, and its co-domain (i.e., set within which its "outputs" must lie) will be the set of all functions from individuals to truth values. For example, the V_t "loves" might have the following semantic value:

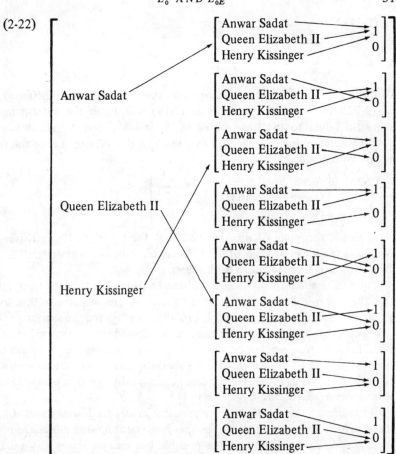

(2-22)

Anwar Sadat →	[Anwar Sadat → 1, Queen Elizabeth II → 1, Henry Kissinger → 1]
	[Anwar Sadat → 0, Queen Elizabeth II → 1, Henry Kissinger → 1]
Henry Kissinger →	[Anwar Sadat → 1, Queen Elizabeth II → 0, Henry Kissinger → 1]
	[Anwar Sadat → 1, Queen Elizabeth II → 1, Henry Kissinger → 0]
	[Anwar Sadat → 0, Queen Elizabeth II → 0, Henry Kissinger → 1]
Queen Elizabeth II →	[Anwar Sadat → 0, Queen Elizabeth II → 1, Henry Kissinger → 0]
	[Anwar Sadat → 1, Queen Elizabeth II → 0, Henry Kissinger → 0]
	[Anwar Sadat → 0, Queen Elizabeth II → 0, Henry Kissinger → 0]

(In this diagram we have listed every characteristic function in the co-domain, including those that do not lie in the range of function (2-22).)

We now state the semantic rule corresponding to the syntactic rule $VP \rightarrow V_t N$:

(2-23) If α is $\underset{\triangle}{V_t}$ and β is $\underset{\triangle}{N}$, and if γ is $[_{VP}\ \alpha\ \beta]$, then $[\![\gamma]\!]$ is $[\![\alpha]\!]([\![\beta]\!])$.

To illustrate, the grammar associates with the *VP* "loves Hank" the following tree structure:

(2-24)

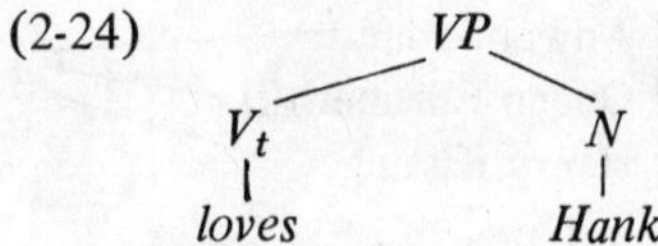

Given that ⟦*Hank*⟧ = Henry Kissinger and that ⟦*loves*⟧ is the function given in (2-22), the semantic rule schema (2-19) will assign the corresponding semantic values to the trees rooted by V_t and N. Then, by semantic rule (2-23) we determine that the semantic value of the *VP* tree, i.e. of the verb phrase *loves Hank,* is:

(2-25)

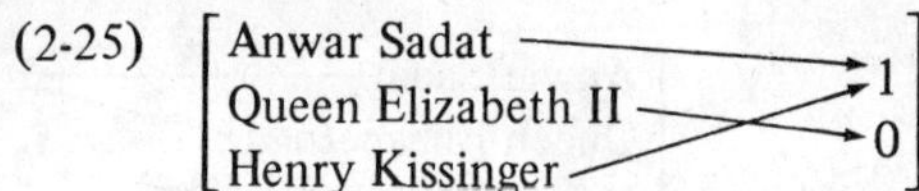

since this is the value of function (2-22) at the argument Henry Kissinger. Note that the semantic value of the *VP loves Hank* is, as it was designed to be, a function from individuals to truth values.

The reader should now be in a position to determine that the truth value that the sentence *Liz loves Hank* inherits from its tree structure is 0, according to our assumptions about ⟦*Liz*⟧, ⟦*Hank*⟧, ⟦*loves*⟧, and the semantic rules.

(Recall that in L_0, two-place predicates denoted sets of ordered pairs of individuals. In fact, we will be able to show that by assigning V_t's a denotation like that in (2-22) we are giving a semantic treatment that is essentially equivalent to that in L_0; we will explain precisely why this is so on pp. 38–39, when we compare L_0 and L_{0E} in detail.)

Returning to the specification of semantic values for lexical items of L_{0E}, let us assume that *hates* and *is-taller-than* have the following values. (In order to save space, we will not list the possible but unused values as we did in (2-22).)

(2-26)

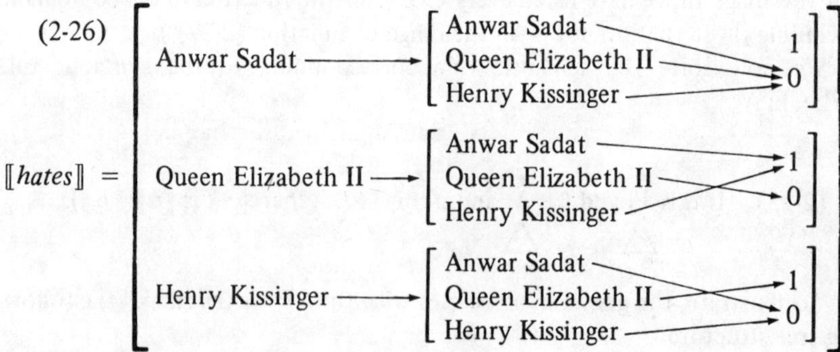

(2-27)

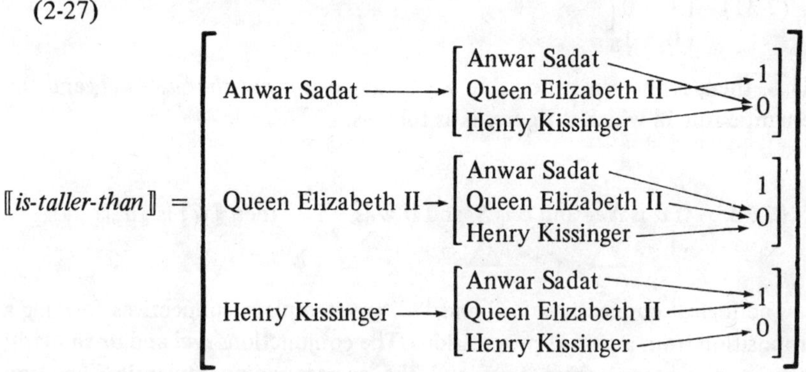

PROBLEM (2-7). Given our assumed universe consisting of three individuals, how many distinct semantic values are possible for a V_t? How many are possible given a universe of *n* individuals?

The remaining lexical items are the negation operator *it-is-not-the-case-that* and the two co-ordinating conjunctions *and* and *or*. We will assume that these have semantic values corresponding to the logical connectives "¬," "∧," and "∨" as defined by the customary truth tables:

(2-28)

p	$\neg p$
1	0
0	1

(2-29)

p	q	$p \wedge q$
1	1	1
1	0	0
0	1	0
0	0	0

(2-30)

p	q	$p \vee q$
1	1	1
1	0	1
0	1	1
0	0	0

Syntactically, *it-is-not-the-case-that* combines with a sentence to form another sentence. Therefore, given our "functional" approach to the semantics of L_{0E} we may treat it as a function mapping a truth value into a truth value, and this is in fact just what the truth table in (2-28) represents. Written in our diagrammatic notation it would appear as in (2-31):

(2-31) $\begin{bmatrix} 1 \to 0 \\ 0 \to 1 \end{bmatrix}$

This, then, is the semantic value we assign to *it-is-not-the-case-that*, and the semantic rule in which it figures is as follows:

(2-32) If α is $\underset{\triangle}{Neg}$ and ϕ is $\underset{\triangle}{S}$, and if ψ is $[_S\ \alpha\ \phi]$, then $[\![\psi]\!]$ is $[\![\alpha]\!]([\![\phi]\!])$.

The logical connectives "∧" and "∨" are two-place connectives forming a proposition from a pair of propositions. The conjunctions *and* and *or* similarly form one sentence from two, and the corresponding semantic operation ought therefore to take a pair of truth values and give a single truth value as a result. Accordingly, the semantic values assigned to *and* and *or* are the following functions:

(2-33)

$$[\![and]\!] = \begin{bmatrix} \langle 1, 1\rangle \to 1 \\ \langle 1, 0\rangle \to 0 \\ \langle 0, 1\rangle \to 0 \\ \langle 0, 0\rangle \to 0 \end{bmatrix}$$

(2-34)

$$[\![or]\!] = \begin{bmatrix} \langle 1, 1\rangle \to 1 \\ \langle 1, 0\rangle \to 1 \\ \langle 0, 1\rangle \to 1 \\ \langle 0, 0\rangle \to 0 \end{bmatrix}$$

Only one semantic rule is required, of course, corresponding to the syntactic rule $S \to S$ Conj S.

(2-35) If α is $\underset{\triangle}{Conj}$, ϕ is $\underset{\triangle}{S}$, and ψ is $\underset{\triangle}{S}$, and if ω is $[_S\ \phi\ \alpha\ \psi]$, then $[\![\omega]\!]$ is $[\![\alpha]\!](\langle [\![\phi]\!], [\![\psi]\!]\rangle)$.

This completes the inventory of assumed semantic values for the terminal symbols of L_{0E} and of the semantic rules. Given these, the reader should now be able to determine the semantic value of any well-formed syntactic constituent of L_{0E}, and, in particular, of any sentence of L_{0E}.

PROBLEM (2-8). Determine the truth value assigned to each of the phrase-structure trees constructed in Problem (2-3), under the assumed assignments of semantic values to terminal symbols of L_{0E}. The fourth sentence in (2-10) would have posed a problem if we had attempted to assign semantic values to terminal strings rather than trees or labelled bracketings. Why? Why could we assign semantic values directly to terminal strings if we were dealing with a syntactically unambiguous language?

PROBLEM (2-9). Suppose new Conj's *if-and-only-if* and *only-if* were added to L_{0E} with semantic values appropriate to the logical connectives "$\leftrightarrow$" (the biconditional) and "$\rightarrow$" (the material conditional), respectively. Express their semantic values as functions of the sort given in (2-33) and (2-34). What semantic rules need to be added to accommodate these new Conj's?

3. *Alternative Formulations of L_{0E} and L_0*

The syntax and semantics of the two languages we have just described are similar in the overall effect of their semantic interpretations but differ in a number of details. In this section we digress to consider several "intermediate" languages borrowing various syntactic and semantic features of one or the other language. Our purposes here are to help us see what is essential to the truth conditional method and what is a matter of convenience or choice. We show, for example, that it is unimportant to our semantic method that L_{0E} is "English-like" and is defined syntactically by a phrase-structure grammar, while L_0 has neither of these properties, and we likewise show that it does not matter that two-place predicates were assigned relations as semantic values in L_0 while transitive verbs were assigned "function-valued" functions in L_{0E}. (Readers who already perceive these differences as inconsequential and do not desire additional practice in formulating languages of this sort may wish to skip directly to section III, p. 41.) The differences between the two languages may be summarized as follows:

1. While the basic expressions of L_0 look like those of the formal languages found in logic textbooks, as does the ordering of these in formulas, the lexical items of L_{0E} are deliberately designed to resemble English, and the word order in L_{0E} is much like that of English sentences.
2. We used recursive definitions to specify the syntax of L_0, but we used a context-free phrase structure grammar to specify that of L_{0E}.

3. Our semantic rules for L_0 classified sentences as "true" or "false" in the meta-language, while those of L_{0E} simply assigned 1 or 0 as the semantic value of a sentence.

4. The semantic values of one-place predicates were sets in L_0, but the semantic values of V_i's were characteristic functions of sets in L_{0E}.

5. The semantic values of two-place predicates were sets of pairs in L_0, but the semantic values of V_t's in L_{0E} were functions from individuals to the kind of semantic values assigned to V_i's.

6. The logical symbols $\neg$, $\wedge$, $\vee$, $\rightarrow$, and $\leftrightarrow$ were treated syncategorematically in L_0 but the corresponding lexical items *it-is-not-the-case-that*, *and*, etc., in L_{0E} were introduced as members of the category *Neg* or *Conj*, and their semantic values were therefore defined as functions on truth values (or pairs of them), independently of the semantic rules corresponding to $S \rightarrow Neg\ S$ and $S \rightarrow S\ Conj\ S$.

However, these six characteristics are not in any essential way tied to the differences between natural languages and the formal languages of logicians, but rather are independent and somewhat arbitrary choices which we made for convenience (and for expository purposes). We could in fact alter the syntax or semantics of L_0 or L_{0E} with respect to almost any one of these characteristics while keeping the other five the same, as the reader can now assist us in demonstrating.

PROBLEM (2-10). Reformulate the syntax of L_{0E} as a set of recursive definitions. In this formulation the rules will produce only *sentences* of English (i.e. strings of words), not labelled bracketings or trees.

PROBLEM (2-11). Can the syntax of L_{0E} also be formulated as recursive definitions in such a way as to produce labelled bracketings for sentences (e.g. "$[_S [_N Sadie_N] [_{VP} [_{V_i} snores_{V_i}]_{VP}]_S]$" instead of *Sadie snores*)? If so, write a couple of rules of L_{0E} to illustrate how this is done.

The choice of sets versus characteristic functions for the semantic values of V_i's is likewise rather arbitrary, but does relate to the semantic rule (2-21). If we had assigned as the values of *snores*, *sleeps*, and *is-boring* the respective sets of which (2-13), (2-14) and (2-15) are the characteristic functions, then semantic rule (2-21) would have to be stated as follows:

(2-36) If α is N and β is VP, and if γ is $[_S\ \alpha\ \beta]$ then $[\![\gamma]\!] = 1$ iff $[\![\alpha]\!] \in [\![\beta]\!]$, and is 0 otherwise.

Note that the functions given in (2-22), (2-26), and (2-27) as the semantic values of the V_t's are *not* characteristic functions inasmuch as their co-domains are not the set $\{1, 0\}$ (or any other set of two elements, one of which is specified as a "marked" or "distinguished" element). Rather, the *values* of these functions are themselves characteristic functions. If these values were reformulated as sets, in keeping with the modification (2-36) above, (2-22), for example, should be rewritten as:

(2-37)

Anwar Sadat ⟶ {Anwar Sadat, Queen Elizabeth II, Henry Kissinger}
Queen Elizabeth II ⟶ {Queen Elizabeth II}
Henry Kissinger ⟶ {Anwar Sadat, Henry Kissinger}

In this representation it is perhaps somewhat easier to grasp the import of the semantic value assigned to *loves*. Recall that the argument of (2-37) is the individual named by the N which is the direct object of *loves*. That is, if the N is *Hank*, then since $[\![$*Hank*$]\!]$ = Henry Kissinger, we take the value of (2-37) at the argument "Henry Kissinger" and find that it is the set {Anwar Sadat, Henry Kissinger}. This, then, is the set of individuals who "love Hank." (Compare this set with the characteristic function in (2-25)). Similarly, it is easy to see from (2-37) that the set of those who "love Sadie" is the entire domain of discourse and that the set of those who "love Liz" is just {Queen Elizabeth II}. Given this modification, only one more step is needed in order to think of a sentence $N + V_t + N$ in L_{0E} as expressing the proposition that two individuals named by the subject and object nouns stand in the binary relation named by the verb, just as we explicitly did with sentences like $L(j, m)$ in L_0. Given the universe we assumed for the semantics of L_{0E}, the semantic value given to the V_t *loves* would correspond to this set of ordered pairs:

(2-38)

{⟨Anwar Sadat, Anwar Sadat⟩, ⟨Queen Elizabeth II, Anwar Sadat⟩,
⟨Henry Kissinger, Anwar Sadat⟩, ⟨Queen Elizabeth II, Queen Elizabeth II⟩,
⟨Anwar Sadat, Henry Kissinger⟩, ⟨Henry Kissinger, Henry Kissinger⟩}

While (2-38) represents exactly the same information as (2-22), notice that the function is 'backward'with respect to the ordered pairs. That is, an argument in (2-22) appears as a *second* coordinate of an ordered pair while individuals appearing in the values of the function turn up as *first* coordinates. Note, for example, that in (2-22) Anwar Sadat is mapped into a function which in turn maps Queen Elizabeth II into 1; thus, the ordered pair ⟨Queen Elizabeth II, Anwar Sadat⟩ appears in (2-38).

Representing the semantic values of a V_t like *loves* as a set of ordered pairs suggests that we might formulate the associated semantic rule in the following way:

(2-39) If α is V_t, β is N, and γ is N, and if δ is [$_S$ β α γ], then $[\![\delta]\!]$ is 1 iff $\langle [\![\beta]\!], [\![\gamma]\!] \rangle \in [\![\alpha]\!]$, and is 0 otherwise.

While this would give the correct semantic values for sentences of the form $N + V_t + N$, it runs afoul of the condition that the semantic rules should be in one-to-one correspondence with the syntactic rules. Since the syntax does not contain a rule of the form $S \rightarrow N\, V_t\, N$, there will be no semantic rule of the form given in (2-39). It is nonetheless possible to adhere to our stipulation of one semantic rule for one syntactic rule and still represent the semantic value of a V_t as a set of ordered pairs. We simply restate the semantic rule corresponding to the syntactic rule $VP \rightarrow V_t + N$ as follows:

(2-40) If α is V_t and β is N, and if γ is [$_{VP}$ α β] then $[\![\gamma]\!]$ is the set of all x such that $\langle x, [\![\beta]\!] \rangle \in [\![\alpha]\!]$.

PROBLEM (2-12). Verify that (2-40) yields the same semantic value for *loves Hank* (where $[\![$*loves*$]\!]$ is as in (2-38)) as does (2-23) (where $[\![$*loves*$]\!]$ is as in (2-22)).

It may be useful to many readers to consider in a bit more mathematical detail the identification we have made between relations and function-valued functions. Any binary relation R between members of sets A and B can be regarded in a standard way as a subset of $A \times B$, the set of ordered pairs $\langle a, b \rangle$ such that a is in A and b is in B. Being a set, R can thus be identified with a function in $\{0, 1\}^{A \times B}$ – recall our earlier discussion. From this characteristic function, f_R, of R we can define functions $g_{R,b}$, for every b in B, and the function h_R which we will identify with R. Let

$$g_{R,b}(a) = f_R(\langle a, b\rangle) \text{ for every } a \text{ in } A \text{ and each } b \text{ in } B,$$

$$h_R(b) = g_{R,b} \text{ for every } b \text{ in } B.$$

Each $g_{R,b}$ is a characteristic function of a subset of A, and thus the range of h_R is included in $\{0, 1\}^A$. Hence h_R, which maps each b in B to the set of members of A which stand in relation R to b, is a member of $(\{0, 1\}^A)^B$.

Note that $h_R(b)(a)$ means a stands in R to b – i.e., $h_R(b)(a) = f^R(\langle a, b\rangle)$, where the notation reverses the order of a and b. We have chosen to identify R with a function on B because English syntax treats a transitive verb + direct object as a constituent of a sentence, rather than subject + transitive verb. One must take care not to confuse $h_R(b)(a)$ with $f_R(\langle b, a\rangle)$, which is defined if $b \in A$ and $a \in B$ – as, for example, with the relation expressed by *loves*, where $A = B$.

PROBLEM (2-13). Let A consist of the colors red, white, and blue, and B consist of the countries of the world; and let R be $\{\langle a, b\rangle | a$ appears in the flag of $b\}$.

What is h_R(Switzerland)? h_R(Great-Britain)?

PROBLEM (2-14). Let $A = B$ = {Anwar Sadat, Queen Elizabeth II, Henry Kissinger} and let R be the relation {⟨Anwar Sadat, Queen Elizabeth II⟩, ⟨Queen Elizabeth II, Henry Kissinger⟩, ⟨Henry Kissinger, Anwar Sadat⟩}. Diagram the corresponding function h_R in the form exemplified in (2-22).

PROBLEM (2-15). Of what set is (2-31) the characteristic function? If this set were assigned as the value of *it-is-not-the-case-that*, how would (2-32) be stated?

PROBLEM (2-16). Suppose *and* and *or* were assigned as semantic values the sets corresponding to the respective characteristic functions given in (2-33) and (2-34). How would semantic rule (2-35) then be stated?

PROBLEM (2-17). Find the two-place relation R on individuals such that $\langle x, y\rangle \in R$ iff α *hates* β is true, where $[\![\alpha]\!] = x$, $[\![\beta]\!] = y$, and $[\![hates]\!]$ is as given in (2-26).

PROBLEM (2-18). Express (2-33) and (2-34) as functions with domain $\{1, 0\}$ and having as values functions from $\{1, 0\}$ to $\{1, 0\}$. Write the semantic rule corresponding to (2-35) under this new formulation of $[\![and]\!]$ and $[\![or]\!]$.

As we remarked, we could reformulate the syntax and semantics of L_0 in such a way that the logical symbols are treated as basic expressions and assigned semantic values directly. One way to do this would be as follows:

Add to the basic expressions of L_0:

Category	*Basic Expressions*
Sentence operators	$\neg$
Sentence connectives	$\wedge, \vee, \rightarrow, \leftrightarrow$

Replace formation rule 3. in (2-2) by:

3. If ϕ is a sentence and α is a sentence operator, then $\alpha\phi$ is a sentence.

and replace formation rules 4. through 7. by the single rule:

4. If ϕ and ψ are sentences, and α is a sentence connective, then $[\phi\alpha\psi]$ is a sentence.

The reader can easily determine that this modified syntax specifies exactly the same set of well-formed sentences as did (2-2) (although of course not the same set of well-formed expressions of all categories, since we have added new categories).

To the semantics we add the specifications of the semantic values of the sentence operator and the sentence connectives corresponding to their truth tables. "$\neg$," for example, will receive the semantic value given in (2-31), and "$\wedge$" will be assigned the same semantic value given to *and* in (2-33).

The semantic rules will then be amended in the following way. Replace semantic rule 3. in (2-8) by:

3. If ϕ is a sentence and α is a sentence operator, then $[\![\alpha\phi]\!] = [\![\alpha]\!]([\![\phi]\!])$.

and replace semantic rules 4. through 7. by the single rule:

4. If ϕ and ψ are sentences, and α is a sentence connective, then $[\![[\phi\alpha\psi]]\!] = [\![\alpha]\!](\langle[\![\phi]\!], [\![\psi]\!]\rangle)$.

The reader should have little difficulty in ascertaining that the same semantic values will be assigned to the sentences of L_0 as before.

PROBLEM (2-19). Revise the syntax and semantics of L_{0E} so that *and*, *or*, and *it-is-not-the-case-that* are introduced syncategorematically.

PROBLEM (2-20). Revise the syntax and semantics of L_0 so that the parentheses and square brackets as well as the logical connectives are treated as basic expressions.

PROBLEM (2-21). Give a syntax and semantics for L_0 in which each sentence connective (i.e., "$\wedge$," "$\vee$," "$\rightarrow$," and "$\leftrightarrow$") combines syntactically with a single sentence to yield an expression of the category "sentence operator." For example, $\wedge$ and $M(b)$ wil form the sentence operator $M(b) \wedge$, which will, in turn, combine with another sentence, say $B(j)$, to give $[M(b) \wedge B(j)]$. Write the semantic rules in such a way that each non-basic sentence operator will be assigned an appropriate semantic value.

III. A SYNOPSIS OF TRUTH-CONDITIONAL SEMANTICS

We now summarize the essential points that are common to the applications of truth-conditional semantics we have presented so far.

First, we must emphasize that any truth-conditional semantics is always tightly interconnected with the syntax of the language in question. This is why the first step in the consideration of our example languages L_{0E} and L_0 was to specify the syntax. One should not infer from this, however, that in order to do truth-conditional semantics on, e.g., English, that all syntactic questions must first be settled. Quite the contrary. The close interconnections between syntax and semantics mean that certain decisions made with respect to the syntax will have consequences for the semantics, and the converse is also true, but nothing prevents research in both areas of a language from proceeding in parallel. L_{0E} and L_0, of course, were deliberately chosen to be very simple languages with relatively few problems in the syntax so that we could illustrate the truth-conditional semantic method.

What is the minimum that a truth-conditional semantics requires of the syntax in order to operate? There must be at least a set of *syntactic categories*, one of which is the category "sentence" or something of the sort – the category associated with truth or falsity. There must in addition be some initial assignment of expressions of the language to these categories, and then, since in every interesting case we will be dealing with an infinite language, there must be rules which effect the assignment of the remaining well-formed expressions to their respective categories. We have seen how all this can be accomplished by a system of context-free phrase-structure rules in the case of L_{0E} or by a system of initial assignments of basic expressions to categories and recursive formation rules in the case of L_0. We will return in a moment to consider some important ways in which these systems of syntactic specification differ, but for now it suffices to note that either one accomplishes syntactically what is necessary for the semantics.

What, then, are the essential ingredients of a truth conditional semantics, given the aforementioned syntactic information? They are as follows:

1. A set of things which can be assigned as semantic values. In the system assumed thus far these are (1) a set of individuals, (2) a set of truth values, and (3) various functions constructed out of these by means of set theory.

2. A specification for each syntactic category of the type of semantic value that is to be assigned to expressions of that category (e.g., names are to have individuals assigned, etc.) Sentences are to be assigned truth values.

3. A set of semantic rules specifying how the semantic value of any complex expression is determined in terms of the semantic values of its components.

4. A specific assignment of a semantic value of the appropriate type to each of the basic expressions.

It might be helpful for the reader at this point to return to the relevant sections of this chapter and check that it was in fact just this information that was specified in giving the semantics of both L_{0E} and L_0.

Item 3 above contains an implicit assumption that our semantics is to adhere to the *Principle of Compositionality*, which we referred to earlier. As we saw, adherence to this principle leads us to construct our syntax and semantics so that they work in tandem.

Consider, for example, a syntactic formation rule of the form "if α is an A, and β is a $B, \ldots,$ and μ is an M, then $f(\alpha, \beta, \ldots, \mu)$ is an N" (where $A, B, \ldots, M, N$ are syntactic categories). The function f specifies how the inputs are to be mapped into the output, i.e., it specifies the mode of combination of the arguments. Corresponding to this syntactic rule there will be a semantic rule of the form "if α is an A, and β is a $B, \ldots,$ and μ is an M, then $[\![f(\alpha, \beta, \ldots, \mu)]\!]$ is $g([\![\alpha]\!], [\![\beta]\!], \ldots, [\![\mu]\!])$". Here, g is a function which, so to speak, specifies the "semantic mode of combination" of the semantic values which are its arguments. The situation can be represented by a diagram such as the following:

(2-41) *Syntactic formation rule* *Semantic rule*

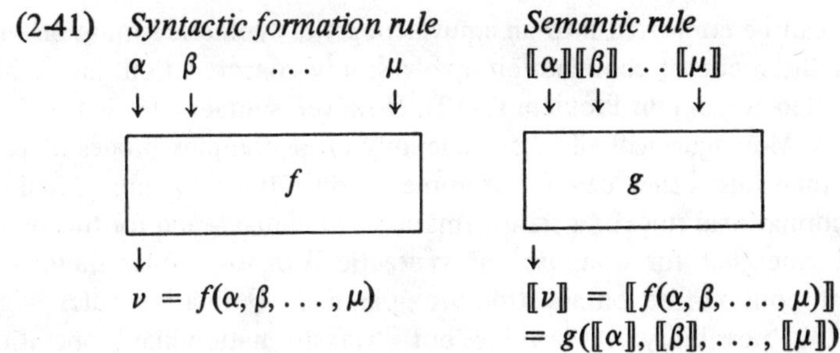

To use a precise mathematical term for this situation, we may say that there is a *homomorphism* from syntax to semantics. Since the mapping is not an isomorphism but only a homomorphism, different syntactic structures can receive the same semantic value.

As an example, consider the first syntactic formation rule for L_0 in (2-2). This rule takes as inputs a one-place predicate and a name and yields an expression of the category "sentence." The function f which expresses the syntactic mode of combination can be stated as follows: write the one-place predicate followed by a left parenthesis followed by the name followed by a right parenthesis. The corresponding semantic rule, rule 1. of (2-8), says that if δ is a one-place predicate and α is a name, then the semantic value of $\delta(\alpha)$, i.e., of $f(\delta,\alpha)$, is a function of the semantic values of δ and α; specifically, this function is one which assigns to $\delta(\alpha)$ the semantic value *true* just in case $[\![\alpha]\!]$ is a member of $[\![\delta]\!]$, and assigns it *false* otherwise. Examination of the remaining syntactic and semantic rules of L_0 in (2-2) and (2-8) reveals that the homomorphism dictated by the Principle of Compositionality is indeed present. It was in fact the ease of constructing the desired homomorphism between syntax and semantics that led logicians to give their syntactic rules the form that they did. To the linguist, who is accustomed to phrase-structure rules as devices for expressing immediate constituent structure, the logician's syntactic formation rules may at first appear rather strange, but then, after some reflection, the two systems may appear to be, in effect, notational variants. It is easy to see that a phrase-structure rule of the form $A \to B\ C \ldots M$ (where $A, B, C, \ldots, M$ are all non-terminal symbols) expresses roughly the same sort of syntactic information as does a formation rule of the form "If β is a member of category B, . . . , and μ is a member of category M, then $\beta \ldots \mu$ is a member of category A." Note that the function which specifies the mode of syntactic combination in this rule merely concatenates the arguments in a particular order, and in fact any context-free phrase-structure grammar can be converted into an equivalent set of syntactic formation rules in which the mode of combination involves only concatenation, just as was demonstrated for L_{0E} in Problem (2-12). However, syntactic formation rules as used by Montague will allow considerably more complex modes of combination than this – they can, for example, be operations that are carried out by transformational rules of a transformational grammar – and for this reason it is not true that for every set of syntactic formation rules there is an equivalent context-free phrase-structure grammar. Formation rules which exploit this possibility of carrying out "transformation-like" operations figure prominently in Montague's system for English in PTQ.

IV. THE NOTION OF TRUTH RELATIVE TO A MODEL

Let us return now to the list of four essential components of a truth conditional semantics we gave earlier. If we look at them more carefully, we see that the items in the list fall into two broad classes corresponding to the kinds of factors which go into determining the semantic values of a sentence. We could say, roughly, that a particular sentence gets the semantic value that it does – is either true or false – because of certain formal structural properties that it has on the one hand, and on the other hand because of certain facts about the world. To take an example from L_{0E}, the sentence *Liz snores* gets the semantic value 1 (true) because all the following considerations interact to yield this result:

1. *Liz* has as its semantic value Queen Elizabeth II.
2. *snores* has as its semantic value a function from individuals to truth values which maps Queen Elizabeth II into 1.
3. *Liz* is a name, and *snores* is an intransitive verb, and the truth value of any sentence composed of a name plus an intransitive verb is determined by applying the function which is the semantic value of the intransitive verb to the argument which is the semantic value of the name.

Of these, the last is a theory-internal condition which is specified as a part of our semantic theory for L_{0E} in particular. The first two, however, are conditions which have to do with assumed facts about the connections between the language and the world and facts about the way the world is. That is, *Liz snores* might receive a different semantic value if *Liz* referred to (had as its value) someone other than Queen Elizabeth II or if *snores* referred to some other set of individuals (i.e., if different people snored than those who are assumed to snore). The truth value of *Liz snores* might also be different if we computed the semantic value of $N + V_i$ sentences in some way other than that given, but if so, that would be an essential modification of the semantic system of L_{0E}, and that is a different sort of variation than is involved in imagining, say, a different set of snorers.

All this discussion is by way of introducing the notion of a *model*. Formally, a model is an ordered pair $\langle A, F \rangle$, where A is a set, the set of individuals, and F is a function which assigns semantic values of the appropriate sort to the basic expressions. All the rest (for which there seems to be no standard name in the literature) is taken as the fixed part of the semantics for a particular language, and we may then examine the effect on the semantic values of expressions in the language as we allow the model to vary. The various choices of a model, then, are intended to represent the various ways we might effect the fundamental mapping from basic expressions to things in the world, while the fixed remainder represents the contribution to semantic values (and in particular, to truth values of sentences) made by the semantic theory itself. Having made this distinction, it is no longer sufficient to say that S is true *simpliciter*; rather, we must say that S is *true with respect to (a particular) model M*. As a notation for this, we use the notation for semantic values together with a superscript for the model.

(2-42) Notational Convention 3: For any expression α, we use $[\![\alpha]\!]^M$ to denote the semantic value of α with respect to model M.

The model we chose to illustrate the semantics of L_{0E} is $\langle A_{0E}, F_{0E} \rangle$, where A_{0E} is the set {Anwar Sadat, Queen Elizabeth II, Henry Kissinger}, and F_{0E} is the function which is the union of the sets given in (2-12) (represented as a function), (2-13), (2-14), (2-15), (2-22), (2-26), and (2-27). Why do we not include in this list the functions assigning values to *and*, *or*, and *it-is-not-the-case-that*, i.e., (2-31), (2-33), and (2-34)? The reason is that, although these are indeed a part of the assignment of semantic values to basic expressions, these particular basic expressions are distinguished from all the others in being a part of the "logical" vocabulary of the language; hence, their values are taken to be fixed once and for all and are not considered as part of the variable model. That is, after all, what we would expect of the constants of a particular logic: we can easily imagine different situations in which the set of snorers varies, but it is difficult to imagine a situation in which *and* means something other than what it does in our world. Thus, we amend our characterization of a model given above to say that the function F assigns semantic values to all the basic, *non-logical* expressions of the language.

Since the notion of *truth with respect to a model* plays a central role in most versions of truth-conditional semantics (and all versions discussed in this book), the term *model-theoretic semantics* is often used as a broad term for the kinds of approaches to semantics we are concerned with: we will henceforth adopt this term ourselves.

In the model we chose for L_0 the set A was the set of all living persons and the function F was given in (2-7). It may be helpful to consider some other possible models for L_0 in order for the reader to grasp firmly the point that a sentence may be true with respect to one model and false with respect to another.

The model M_1 $(= \langle A_1, F_1 \rangle)$

A_1 is the set of states of the United States. F_1 is defined as follows: $F_1(m) =$ Michigan, $F_1(j) =$ California, $F_1(d) =$ Alaska, $F_1(n) =$ Rhode Island, $F_1(M) = \{$Maine, New Hampshire, Vermont, Massachusetts, Connecticut, Rhode Island$\}$, $F_1(B) =$ the set of states that have Pacific coasts, $F_1(K) =$ the set of pairs of states such that some part of the first lies west of some part of the second (e.g., both ⟨Washington, Oregon⟩ and ⟨Oregon, Washington⟩ are in this set), $F_1(L) =$ the set of pairs of states such that the first is larger than the second. (Note that we have expressed the semantic values of K and L as ordered pairs. The reader should make the mental translation to functions from states to characteristic functions of sets of states.)

The model M_2 $(= \langle A_2, F_2 \rangle)$

A_2 is the set of all integers (positive and negative whole numbers and 0). $F_2(j) = 0$, $F_2(m) = 2$, $F_2(d) = 9$, $F_2(n) = -1$, $F_2(M) =$ the set of all odd integers, $F_2(B) =$ the set of all perfect squares, $F_2(K) =$ the set of all pairs of integers such that the first is greater than the second, i.e., $F_2(K) = \{\langle x, y \rangle | x > y\}$, and $F_2(L) =$ the set of all pairs of integers such that the first is the square of the second, i.e., $F_2(L) = \{\langle x, y \rangle | x = y^2\}$.

The model M_3 $(= \langle A_3, F_3 \rangle)$

A_3 is the set of all chemical elements. F_3 is defined as follows: $F_3(m) =$ magnesium, $F_3(j) =$ iodine, $F_3(d) =$ krypton, $F_3(n) =$ sodium, $F_3(M) =$ the set of "rare-earth" elements, $F_3(B) =$ the set of halogen elements, $F_3(K) =$ the set of all pairs of elements such that the first has a greater atomic number than the second, $F_3(L) =$ the set of all pairs of elements such that the two form a chemical compound containing no other elements.

The sentence $M(d)$ is false with respect to M_1 (because Alaska is not in $F_1(M)$, i.e., not a New England state), true with respect to M_2 (because 9 is odd), and false in M_3 (because krypton is not a rare-earth element). The sentence $B(j)$, on the other hand, happens to be true in all three models (because California has a Pacific coast, 0 is a perfect square, and iodine is a halogen). The sentence $K(j, n)$ is true in M_1 (California is west of Rhode Island), true in M_2 (0 is greater than -1), and true in M_3 (iodine has a greater atomic number than sodium). Finally, $L(n, m)$ is false in all three models (Rhode Island is not larger than Michigan, nor is -1 the square of 2, nor does sodium form a compound with magnesium).

PROBLEM (2-22). Construct a model for L_0 in which $M(d)$, $B(j)$, $K(j, n)$, and $L(n, m)$ are all true.

V. VALIDITY AND ENTAILMENT DEFINED IN TERMS OF POSSIBLE MODELS

There are various advantages that the notion of truth relative to a model has over the notion of truth *simpliciter*. The logician (or linguist, for that matter) may not actually be very interested in, say, the set of all bald persons and the question of just which persons belong to the set and which do not, or in similar questions about the denotations of other basic expressions, the answers to which would involve a great deal of empirical knowledge but would not be particularly enlightening for the overall theory of semantics. But it is nevertheless of interest to formulate one's semantics explicitly enough that *if* these basic denotations were ever specified in some way or other, then the precise definitions of truth for the sentences of the whole language would follow automatically. Or the logician might be interested in describing the syntax and basic semantic procedure for an "all-purpose" formal language that might profitably be put to use in talking about various domains of discourse.

But there is an even more important reason for being interested in the notion of truth relative to a model: Consider the difference between the sentences $[B(j) \wedge K(d,j)]$ and $[B(j) \rightarrow [K(d,j) \rightarrow B(j)]]$ of L_0 in the model given earlier in (2-7). Both of these sentences are true in this interpretation, but there is more to be said about the truth of the second sentence than just this. Its truth does not really depend in any way on the semantic values assigned to the basic expressions in it, but rather can be traced to general properties of its syntactic form and to the way we have given truth conditions for the conditional connective (viz., the semantic rule 6. in (2-8)). In fact, any sentence of the form $[\phi \rightarrow [\psi \rightarrow \phi]]$ will turn out to be true in L_0, given any possible model whatsoever. (A sentence with this form will no doubt be recognizable to the reader as one of the *valid sentences*, or *tautologies*, of the propositional calculus, of which our language is a rather simple extension.) The former sentence, on the other hand, will be true in some models and false in others, depending on the denotations assigned to B, K, d and j by the model. It turns out that by distinguishing those sentences of L_0 that are true with respect to *all* models from those that are true only with respect to *some* of the possible models, we can give a definition of *valid sentence* of L_0 (or *logically true sentence* of L_0) that satisfies the usual expectations as to which sentences of this language ought to count as logically valid:

(1) A sentence of L_0 is *valid* iff it is true with respect to every possible model for L_0.

Other familiar logical properties of sentences and relations between sentences can also be defined by using the notion of truth with respect to a model, quantifying over the class of possible models:

(2) A sentence of L_0 is *contradictory* iff it is false with respect to every possible model for L_0.

(3) Two sentences of L_0 are *logically equivalent* iff the first is true in exactly the same models in which the second is true and in no others.

(4) A sentence ϕ of L_0 is a *logical consequence* of a set of sentences Γ (or equivalently, Γ *logically entails* ϕ) iff every model in which all the sentences of Γ are true is a model in which ϕ is true also.

Now the possibility of giving definitions of these notions will be of as much interest to the linguist as to the logician since it is widely held among linguists that an account of these properties of English sentences and relations among English sentences is an important goal (some would say *the* goal) of semantics.

For the relation *logically equivalent* we would like to be able to substitute *synonymous* but cannot because most philosophers of language and linguists hold synonymy to be a much narrower relation among sentences, their synonymy taking into account various subtleties such as focus, conventional and conversational implicature, perhaps stylistic connotations of particular words, all of which we are ill-equipped to deal with formally at present. But fortunately the relation of logical equivalence seems to be a more workable and useful relation in the initial stages of developing a semantic theory for natural language.

Although we have defined logical entailment as a relation between a *set* of sentences Γ and a sentence ϕ, we can obviously consider entailment between a pair of sentences as the special case of this definition in which the set Γ contains only one sentence. Logical equivalence is of course simply mutual logical entailment between a pair of sentences.

PROBLEM (2-23). For the model of L_{0E} given in the text find an example of each of the following: (1) a valid sentence, (2) a sentence which is true but not valid, (3) a contradictory sentence, (4) a sentence which is false but not contradictory, (5) two sentences which are logically equivalent, (6) a non-empty set of sentences Γ and a sentence ϕ (not in Γ) such that ϕ is a logical consequence of Γ but not of any proper subset of Γ.

There are, to be sure, other properties of sentences or parts of sentences and relations among them that linguists have traditionally treated under the rubrics of synonymy (or logical equivalence) and entailment. For example, the validity of the sentence *If John is a bachelor, then he is an unmarried man* is attributed to the 'synonymy' of the phrases *bachelor* and *unmarried man*. Yet it is not at all obvious how the notion of truth with respect to a model can be extended to account for this example, since the unvarying truth of this last example cannot be traced to the syntactic form of the sentence but rather depends *only* on the particular basic expressions *bachelor, unmarried* and *man.* (If we were to follow Quine's terminology, we would refer to this latter kind of example as an *analytic sentence* and the former example, in which the syntactic form is responsible for validity, as a *logically true sentence.*) More will be said about such cases later.

VI. MODEL THEORY AND DEDUCTIVE SYSTEMS

The reader is probably aware that there is an older, more traditional way of characterizing validity and entailment for formal languages in terms of the notions of a *deduction* and *rules of inference.* This may be accomplished either through an *axiom system* or, in most contemporary logic texts, a system of *natural deduction* (cf., e.g. Blumberg, 1967). By the axiomatic method, a list of *axioms* (or *axiom schemata*) and a *rule* (or *rules*) *of inference* are given for a formal language, and then a *proof* is defined as any sequence of sentences of the language such that each sentence is either an axiom (or instance of an axiom schema) or follows from one or more of the preceding sentences of the sequence by the rule(s) of inference. A *theorem* (which is to correspond to our intuitive notion of a logically true sentence) of the language is any sentence ϕ of the language for which there is a proof ending in ϕ. To illustrate, the following is a possible axiomatization for a propositional language which resembles L_0, except that it treats $\wedge$, $\vee$, and $\leftrightarrow$ as defined in terms of $\neg$ and $\rightarrow$. We have here axiom schemata rather than axioms proper because they are stated in terms of meta-language variables rather than actual sentences of L_0; hence each line is a schema for an infinite number of sentences of L_0 with similar syntactic forms, each of which is an axiom.

(A1) $[\phi \rightarrow [\psi \rightarrow \phi]]$

(A2) $[[\phi \rightarrow [\psi \rightarrow \chi]] \rightarrow [[\phi \rightarrow \psi] \rightarrow [\phi \rightarrow \chi]]]$

(A3) $[[\neg\psi \rightarrow \neg\phi] \rightarrow [[\neg\psi \rightarrow \phi] \rightarrow \psi]]$

With these axiom schemata, one rule of inference would suffice to complete the axiomization of L_0, the rule of *modus ponens* (also known as the *rule of detachment.*) This is the rule that permits one, when given ϕ and $[\phi \rightarrow \psi]$, to infer ψ.

With such a deductive apparatus, definitions of properties of sentences and relations among sentences can be given which can be proved to correspond exactly to the semantic definitions given earlier in terms of possible models. This correspondence is illustrated by the table below:

Definitions in terms of possible models:	*Corresponding deductive definition*:
1. A sentence of L_0 is *valid* iff it is true with respect to every possible model for L_0.	1. A sentence of L_0 is a *theorem* of L_0 iff there is a proof of it from the above axiom schemata alone.
2. A sentence of L_0 is a *contradiction* iff it is false with respect to every possible model for L_0.	2. A sentence of L_0 is a *contradiction* iff its negation is a theorem of L_0.
3. A sentence ϕ of L_0 is *logically entailed* by a set of sentences Γ iff every model in which all the sentences of Γ are true is a model in which ϕ is true.	3. A sentence ϕ of L_0 is *deducible* (or *provable*) from a set of sentences Γ iff there is a sequence of sentences of L_0 such that each is either an axiom or belongs to Γ or else follows from some of the preceding sentences in the sequence by the rule(s) of inference, and ϕ is the last sentence of the sequence.
4. Two sentences of L_0 are *logically equivalent* iff they are true in exactly the same models (or equivalently, if each logically entails the other.)	4. Two sentences of L_0 are *logically equivalent* iff each is deducible from the other.

The possibility of giving corresponding deductive and semantic definitions for logical systems is of fundamental significance in modern logic, and indeed much research in logic is devoted to producing the semantics and corresponding axiomatizations for various logics and proving mathematically that the semantic definitions of validity and logical consequence are in fact exactly equivalent to the definitions of theoremhood and deducibility that result from the axiomatization. (See Blumberg 1967 and Henkin 1967 for additional discussion.)

The method of axiomatization is relevant to our present discussion because it has suggested to some linguists that an axiomatization (or perhaps natural deductive system) might be given for an appropriately formalized language of semantic representations (or as Lakoff (1972) has called it, a *natural logic*), thus enabling us to account for all the relations of entailment, logical equivalence, etc., that exist among English sentences, without appeal to model-theoretic semantics. This would be particularly appealing to the linguist in view of the ideal of the "autonomous semantic representation" that has no defined relation to non-linguistic (or non-mental) objects. 'Linguistics and Natural Logic' (Lakoff 1972) seems to suggest that a deductive system of some sort is to be the means of achieving Lakoff's goal of "a logic which is capable of accounting for all correct inferences made in natural language and which rules out incorrect ones." (p. 589).

But two points need to be made in response to this suggestion. First, to take the construction of an axiomatic system (but not a formally interpreted language) as the goal of the semantic analysis of natural language is, in an important sense, to miss the point of what semantics is all about. It is true that the advantage of symbolic logic, in its early form, was that it allowed one to completely ignore the meaning of the propositions involved in an argument and concentrate on the form of the argument entirely. Deductive systems are purposefully formulated in just such a way as to make interpretation of the primitive symbols irrelevant for carrying out proofs. Nevertheless, the ultimate interest in formal deductive systems for philosophers of language has always lain in the way they mimic certain properties of natural languages and how people use them, and languages in turn have the essential feature of referring to objects and situations beyond themselves. Without their reference to things in the world, human languages would be impossible to imagine. Notions such as "synonymy" and "entailment" thus always have lurking behind them the connection of languages with the world, and it is these connections which ultimately give the logical properties of sentences their interest for us, whether we temporarily ignore the connections with the world or not. The definition of truth with respect to a model has the advantage that it allows us to capture the definitions of logical truth, logical entailment, and related notions *and* at the same time to capture our intuitions of the essential "aboutness" of natural language; deductive systems satisfy only the first of these two objectives.

A second reason for preferring the semantic method to the deductive is that certain logics *cannot* be given axiomatic definitions of validity and entailment, though model-theoretic definitions of these notions are perfectly feasible for them. It can be proved mathematically that the set of valid sentences of second-order logic (logics involving quantification over predicates) cannot be finitely axiomatized (cf. Henkin 1950), whereas a semantic definition of validity and entailment can be given.

One might wonder whether there is an axiomatization of the fragment of English which Montague described in PTQ. We conjecture that such an axiomatization exists. A partial positive answer is given in Gallin (1975, p. 40), but the general question seems still to be unsettled. Natural language certainly contains devices (grammatical constructions and lexical items), however, whose semantic analysis precludes any complete axiomatization (Barwise, personal communication). For example, the semantic analysis of a sentence like (2-43)

(2-43) There is no way for all boys to take different girls to the party.

will necessarily involve quantifying over arbitrary functions from individuals to individuals (representing ways of pairing a boy with a girl whom he takes to the party).

Thus from this point on, we will concentrate exclusively on model theoretic definitions of semantic entailment, validity and related notions, rather than deductive systems. This is not to say that the study of deductive systems has *no* interest for semantics and pragmatics of natural language. It might, for example, have particular applications in the psycholinguistic study of how people draw inferences from sets of sentences, or in artificial intelligence studies. Rather, this means that we can safely ignore formal deductive systems in what follows, since our model-theoretic method renders them superfluous for our purposes.

EXERCISES

1. Suppose the phrase-structure grammar in (2-9) were expanded to allow an adverb to modify the *VP* by adding the rules

$$VP \rightarrow VP\ Adv$$

and

$$Adv \rightarrow \textit{restlessly, harmlessly}$$

Decide on an appropriate type of semantic value to assign to items belonging to the lexical category "*Adv*" and add the required semantic rule or rules. Though the same set of sentences would be generated if $VP \rightarrow VP\ Adv$ were replaced by $S \rightarrow S\ Adv$, this syntactic analysis would have untenable semantic consequences. What are they? (Hint: think about the semantic rule you would associate with $S \rightarrow S\ Adv$, and the difference between the type of semantic value associated with sentences versus verb phrases.)

2. The sentence *John sleeps restlessly* intuitively implies *John sleeps*. Amplify the semantic analysis you gave in Exercise 1 so as to guarantee formally that this implication holds. (Hint: Place a set-theoretic restriction on a function used in Exercise 1.) Note that the treatment we have given to "logical vocabulary" (e.g., *and, or*) is just the limiting case of what you must do for *restlessly, harmlessly*, etc. The restrictions on the logical vocabulary are so strong as to uniquely determine what semantic values may be assigned. The model-theoretic method of studying relationships between the semantic values of expressions makes it possible to capture necessary relationships of lexical meaning, like

those between *bachelor* and *man* or *unmarried* noted on p. 50, by mandating that certain relationships hold between the semantic values assigned to the items in question.

3. Write a set of formation rules for a language like L_0 but written in "Polish" notation. In this notation the connectives precede the formulas they connect, and parentheses are unnecessary. The letters *N*, *K*, *A*, *C*, *E* are generally used as symbols for the Polish connectives corresponding to "¬," "∧," "∨," "→," and "↔" respectively. Thus, $[p \wedge [q \vee r]]$ in standard notation becomes *KpAqr* in Polish notation, and *ECpqAqNr* corresponds to $[[p \rightarrow q] \leftrightarrow [q \vee \neg r]]$ in standard notation. What changes must be made in the semantic rules for L_0 to accommodate the "Polish" syntax? What changes are necessary if the connectives are not treated syncategorematically but are assigned semantic values directly?

4. Give a syntax and a semantics for a language which is like L_0 except that it contains only one logical connective, "|," defined by the following truth table:

p	q	$[p \mid q]$
1	1	0
1	0	1
0	1	1
0	0	1

5. Give a syntax and a semantics for the propositional calculus (the language like L_0 except that propositions are not analyzed into predicates and names).

6. Suppose the following rules were added to the grammar in (2-9):

$$VP \rightarrow V_s\ S$$

$$V_s \rightarrow \textit{believes-that, hopes-that}$$

What type of semantic value would be appropriate for verbs belonging to the lexical category V_s? What difficulty arises in attempting to formulate the semantic rule for $V_s + S$ constructions?

7. Consider a syntactic system in which each formation rule is of the form (2-41) where $\nu = \alpha\beta \ldots \mu$ (the concatenation of $\alpha, \beta, \ldots, \mu$). Prove that there is an equivalent context-free phrase structure grammar, i.e., one with the same categories and generating the same expressions of each category.

NOTE

[1] The notation is to be understood as follows. An expression of the form $A \rightarrow \begin{Bmatrix} \omega_1 \\ \omega_2 \\ \vdots \\ \omega_n \end{Bmatrix}$ or $A \rightarrow \omega_1, \omega_2, \ldots, \omega_n$ abbreviates the n rules: $A \rightarrow \omega_1, A \rightarrow \omega_2, \ldots, A \rightarrow \omega_n$. The grammar may be used to derive sentences by first writing the symbol S (or, to derive phrases of any category A, by writing A) and then carrying out a series of steps using the rules to rewrite strings until no further rewriting is permitted. If at a given stage the last string produced is $\alpha_1 \alpha_2 \ldots \alpha_m$, and for some i there is a rule $\alpha_i \rightarrow \omega$, then it is permitted

to rewrite the string further and produce $\alpha_1 \ldots \alpha_{i-1} \omega \alpha_{i+1} \ldots \alpha_n$. For example, S may be rewritten as *S Conj S* or as *Neg S* or as *N VP*. If one rewrites it as *N VP*, the derivation may continue either by rewriting the latter string as *Sadie VP* or as $N\ V_i$ (or as any of three other possibilities). It is irrelevant which of the symbols *N* or *VP* one replaces first; since the grammar is context-free any string of words that can be derived one way can also be derived the other way.

One can construct a structural description as the derivation proceeds which omits the irrelevant information about order of rewriting but records the very relevant facts about what string replaced each nonterminal symbol. The information can be represented as either a tree structure or a labelled bracketing. To construct, say, a tree, while carrying out a derivation, begin by simply writing the same symbol that initiated the derivation. As each step of the derivation replaces a nonterminal symbol by a string, augment the tree by adding the replacing string of symbols beneath the nonterminal symbol corresponding to the one replaced and connecting these new symbols to that one. If one starts from *S*, for instance, the tree begins simply as *S* too. If *S* is replaced by *NVP* the tree grows to

```
  S
 / \
N   P
```

. If the string is then rewritten as *Sadie VP*, the tree becomes

```
    S
   / \
  N   P
  |
Sadie
```

.

On the other hand, if one had rewritten *NVP* as $N\ V_i$, the second tree above would have grown instead to

```
  S
 / \
N   VP
    |
    Vi
```

.

If after replacing one of the symbols *N* and *VP*, one then makes the other replacement in the resulting string, he gets the string *Sadie* V_i in either case. The two different derivations of this string both correspond to the tree

```
    S
   / \
  N   VP
  |   |
Sadie Vi
```

, and are thus seen to be equivalent.

CHAPTER 3

FIRST-ORDER PREDICATE LOGIC

I. THE LANGUAGE L_1

We turn now to the construction of a formal language L_1, which adds individual variables and quantifiers over these variables to the syntactic apparatus of the language L_0. In fact, this language L_1 *contains* L_0, in the sense that all the sentences of L_0 will also be sentences of L_1 (but not conversely), and these sentences of L_0 will have to be interpreted just as before. As these new individual variables (for which we will use the symbols $v_1, v_2, v_3, \ldots$) behave syntactically just like individual constants, we will introduce the new syntactic category of *individual terms* (or simply *terms*) to include both variables and constants.

1. *Syntax of* L_1

A. The *basic expressions* of L_1 are of four categories:

1. the *names d, n, j,* and *m*
2. a denumerably infinite supply of *individual variables* $v_1, v_2, v_3, \ldots$ (To avoid having too many subscripts in our formulas we will sometimes use x to stand for v_1, y to stand for v_2, and z to stand for v_3.) Together, the names and individual variables of L_1 comprise the *terms* of L_1.
3. the *one-place predicates M* and *B*.
4. the *two-place predicates K* and *L*.

B. The formation rules of L_1 consist of the following:

1. If δ is a one-place predicate and α is a term, then $\delta(\alpha)$ is a formula.
2. If γ is a two-place predicate and α and β are terms, then $\gamma(\alpha, \beta)$ is a formula.

3.– 7. If ϕ and ψ are formulas, then so are:

3. $\neg\phi$
4. $[\phi \wedge \psi]$
5. $[\phi \vee \psi]$
6. $[\phi \rightarrow \psi]$
7. $[\phi \leftrightarrow \psi]$

8. If ϕ is a formula, and u is a variable, then $\forall u\phi$ is a formula.
9. If ϕ is a formula, and u is a variable, then $\exists u\phi$ is a formula.

(Note that in clauses (8) and (9) u is used as a meta-language variable ranging over the variables of L_1; this is the only case of a non-Greek letter being used as a meta-language variable.)

In these rules we have used the term 'formula' where the term 'sentence' was used earlier. This follows the traditional practice of reserving the term *sentence* for a formula containing no free occurrences of variables, whereas formulas may or may not contain free occurrences of variables. The distinction between *free* and *bound* occurrences of variables is no doubt already familiar to the reader: an occurrence of a variable u in a formula ϕ can be defined as *bound in* ϕ if it occurs in ϕ within a sub-formula of the form $\forall u\psi$ or $\exists u\psi$; otherwise, that occurrence is *free* in ϕ. The syntactic rules do nothing to avoid so-called *vacuous quantification,* quantification over a formula with respect to a variable that does not occur in it; e.g. we can form $\forall xK(j, m)$ from $K(j, m)$, or $\exists yB(x)$ from $B(x)$. It would complicate the syntax greatly to prohibit such formulas, and moreover, the semantic rules will turn out to treat such vacuously quantified formulas as if the vacuous quantifier simply weren't there: $\forall xK(j, m)$ will be interpreted exactly like $K(j, m)$, and $\exists yB(x)$ will be interpreted like $B(x)$. Hence the vacuous quantifiers are harmless if we are willing to ignore them.

The novelty in the interpretation of L_1 over L_0 lies primarily in the notion *satisfaction of a formula by an assignment of objects to variables* (which is Tarski's term) or, to use the completely equivalent notion found in PTQ, the *truth of a formula with respect to an assignment of values to variables.*

The need for such a notion within a compositional semantics can perhaps be best grasped intuitively in the following way. In introductory treatments of elementary logic it is usually said that formulas with free variables cannot be either true or false as they stand because the variables themselves do not denote any particular individuals, hence the formulas make no real assertion until the variables have been quantified (or perhaps replaced with names in the course of a deduction). Thus we have Russell's term *propositional function* for such formulas; they are regarded not as propositions but as functions which give propositions when supplied with individuals as arguments. Quantified expressions are then treated in the following way: a sentence $\forall xB(x)$ is true just in case $B(x)$ is always true when x is regarded as denoting any member of the domain of discourse whatsoever; similarly, $\exists xB(x)$ is true if there is at least one individual in the domain such that

$B(x)$ is true when x is regarded as denoting that individual. (Alternatively, $\forall xB(x)$ may be said to be true when the result of substituting for x in $B(x)$ a name of any individual in the domain of discourse always gives a true sentence. This approach leads to the *substitutional theory of quantification*, but we will not be concerned with that theory here.) The treatment of multiple quantifiers and quantifiers binding arbitrarily complex sentences is then left pretty much to intuition, except for pointing out that it is necessary to distinguish scope relations carefully. For example, it might be said that to find out whether $\forall x\exists yL(x, y)$ is true we must "try out" all values for x, and for each one of these values of x we must try to find some value for y that makes $L(x, y)$ true. On the other hand, for $\exists y\forall xL(x, y)$ we must find a single value for y according to which $L(x, y)$ will remain true as the value of x is allowed to range over every member of the domain in turn. Such procedures are usually not rigorously specified, though of course explicit procedures may be given for carrying out *deductions* involving multiple quantifiers and arbitrarily complex formulas.

A little thought should convince the reader that something new will be needed if we are to give explicit truth conditions for quantified sentences by the compositional principle followed for L_0. Since the rules introducing quantifiers (B.8 and B.9) make a sentence $\forall u\phi$ from any sentence ϕ and any variable u, we must be able to give a completely general semantic rule for the truth conditions for $\forall u\phi$ in terms of the truth or falsity of ϕ, no matter what ϕ is. Now consider what will happen when we try to determine the truth conditions for $\forall x\exists yL(x, y)$ by this method. This formula is syntactically formed by first constructing the atomic sentence $L(x, y)$, then adding a quantifier by B.9 to give $\exists yL(x, y)$, then finally adding a second quantifier to B.8 to give $\forall x\exists yL(x, y)$. The semantic rules will retrace these stages. Thus the truth definitions corresponding to syntactic rule B.9 will have to give the truth condition for $\exists yL(x, y)$ in terms of $L(x, y)$ (and later, the rule corresponding to B.8 will have to give the conditions for $\forall x\exists yL(x, y)$ in terms of $\exists yL(x, y)$). But at the stage where y is quantified, the formula $L(x, y)$ has, in addition to the variable y being quantified at this step, the variable x which is still free as far as B.9 is concerned. Note also that in some syntactic derivations involving $\exists yL(x, y)$ the variable x will later be bound by a universal quantifier, and in other derivations by an existential quantifier. Of course this is the minimally simple case of multiple quantifiers; other cases will require that the semantic corresponding to B.8 be able to give truth conditions for $\forall u\phi$ where ϕ has besides u any number of other free variables which will be bound at later stages. Obviously, free variables have to be dealt with *as such* by the semantic rules if a compositional semantics is to be given. As Tarski put it, "compound sentences are constructed from simpler sentential functions [i.e., formulas that may have free variables], but not always from simpler sentences" (Tarski 1944, p. 353).

It seems that what we need for these cases is some systematic means of "pretending" that each free variable denotes some individual or other, and then later systematically revising our assumption about which individual is denoted by these variables as we reach the appropriate quantifier at the "outer" or "higher" stages of the syntactic formation of the formula. Tarski's notion of *satisfaction* (or *truth relative to an assignment to variables*) is designed to do just that. Accordingly, we will add to the semantic machinery already described for L_0 the notion of a function assigning to each variable of L_1 some value from the domain A. Such a function is called an *assignment of values to variables*, or simply a *value assignment*. We will use the symbol g to denote such a function. (Since we have given L_1 an infinite supply of variables, the domain of g will be infinite, but functions with infinite domains present no particular problems.) The function g need not be one-to-one of course; in fact, it is important that we allow some value assignments to assign the same individual to more than one variable. For that matter, there is nothing wrong with a value assignment that assigns the same individual from A to every variable.

The definition of truth relative to a model will now be given in two stages. First, we will give a recursive definition of *true formula of* L_1 *with respect to a model* M *and value assignment* g. Then, on the basis of this intermediate definition, we can very simply state the final definition of *true sentence of* L_1 *with respect to a model* M. (Note that the value assignment g is not to be considered part of the model M – it has nothing to do with how we interpret the *constant* basic expressions of the language.)

The reader may ask at this point how we decide which value assignment to pick. The answer is, it doesn't matter at all, so long as we pick a particular one. The ultimate definition of truth with respect to a model will turn out not to depend at all on which assignment g was initially picked to "compute", as it were, the intermediate truth definition, since the semantic rules systematically make reference to *other* value assignments differing from the original g in specified ways. The formal definitions are as follows:

2. *Semantics of* L_1

A *model for* L_1 is an ordered pair $\langle A, F\rangle$ such that A is a non-empty set and F is a function assigning a semantic value to each non-logical constant of L_1

(i.e., names, one-place predicates, and two-place predicates). The set of possible semantic values for names is A; the set of possible semantic values for one-place predicates is $\{1, 0\}^A$; the set of possible semantic values for two-place predicates is $(\{1,0\}^A)^A$, (Here we again use the standard set-theoretic notation "X^Y" to stand for the set of all functions from Y to X.) A *value assignment* g is any function assigning a member of A to each variable of L_1. We abbreviate "the semantic value of α with respect to M and g" as $[\![\alpha]\!]^{M,g}$.

A. Semantic values of basic expressions:
1. If u is an individual variable of L_1, then $[\![u]\!]^{M,g} = g(u)$.
2. If α is a non-logical constant of L_1, then $[\![\alpha]\!]^{M,g} = F(\alpha)$.

B. Truth conditions for formulas of L_1 relative to M and g:
1. If δ is a one-place predicate and α is a term, then $[\![\delta(\alpha)]\!]^{M,g} = [\![\delta]\!]^{M,g}([\![\alpha]\!]^{M,g})$.
2. If γ is a two-place predicate and α and β are terms, then $[\![\gamma(\alpha,\beta)]\!]^{M,g} = [[\![\gamma]\!]^{M,g}([\![\beta]\!]^{M,g})]([\![\alpha]\!]^{M,g})$.

3.-7. If ϕ is a formula, then $[\![\neg\phi]\!]^{M,g} = 1$ iff $[\![\phi]\!]^{M,g} = 0$; otherwise, $[\![\neg\phi]\!]^{M,g} = 0$. Similarly for $[\phi \wedge \psi]$, $[\phi \vee \psi]$, $[\phi \rightarrow \psi]$, and $[\phi \leftrightarrow \psi]$.

8. If ϕ is a formula and u is a variable, then $[\![\forall u\phi]\!]^{M,g} = 1$ iff for every value assignment g' such that g' is exactly like g except possibly for the individual assigned to u by g', $[\![\phi]\!]^{M,g'} = 1$.
9. If ϕ is a formula and u is a variable, then $[\![\exists u\phi]\!]^{M,g} = 1$ iff for some value assignment g' such that g' is exactly like g except possibly for the individual assigned to u by g', $[\![\phi]\!]^{M,g'} = 1$.

As should be clear, the semantic value $[\![\alpha]\!]^{M,g}$ of any expression α can depend on the particular assignment g only with regard to what values g assigns to variables that are free in α. That is, if $g(u) = g'(u)$ for all variables u that are free in α, then $[\![\alpha]\!]^{M,g} = [\![\alpha]\!]^{M,g'}$. If α is a basic expression, this follows directly from A. When α is a formula, it follows from two facts:

(i) that the free variables of the formulas treated in clauses B.1-7 are exactly those that are free in one or more of the next smaller parts; and

(ii) that the free variables of the formulas treated in clauses B.8-9 are all those except u which are free in the next smaller part and, moreover, the semantic value of the larger formula in B.8-9 is independent of what g assigns to u.)

C. We adopt the following truth definition for formulas of L_1 relative to M:

1. For any formula ϕ of L_1, $[\![\phi]\!]^M = 1$ if $[\![\phi]\!]^{M,g} = 1$ for all value assignments g.

2. For any formula ϕ of L_1, $[\![\phi]\!]^M = 0$ if $[\![\phi]\!]^{M,g} = 0$ for all value assignments g.

If a formula ϕ has one or more free variables then it may well be true with respect to some assignments and false with respect to others. In this case its truth or falsity with respect to M is left undefined by C. This last possibility is of no great consequence since it is really only for the *sentences* of L_1 that we are interested in knowing truth values independently of an assignment.[1]

To understand more clearly the workings of clauses B.8 and B.9, we will consider a few simple examples.

For the sake of brevity, we will choose a model for L_1 with a very small domain, *viz.*, the set $\{a, b, c\}$. We choose a set whose members are letters of the alphabet to facilitate the explanation that follows. It is of course somewhat odd to think of a language which can be used to talk about nothing but letters of the alphabet, so the reader may wish to think of this set as consisting of persons or objects of some other kind. However, as before, it is important to keep in mind that the things in the domain A are the *objects* of discourse themselves and not merely some auxiliary *names* of objects.

The *model M* will be the pair $\langle A, F\rangle$, where A is the set $\{a, b, c\}$ and F is as follows:

$$
\begin{aligned}
(3\text{-}1)\qquad F(j) &= a\\
F(d) &= b\\
F(n) &= c\\
F(m) &= a\\
F(M) &= \{a, b, c\}\\
F(B) &= \{b, c\}\\
F(K) &= \{\langle a, a\rangle, \langle a, b\rangle, \langle b, c\rangle\}\\
F(L) &= \{\langle a, c\rangle, \langle b, a\rangle, \langle c, a\rangle, \langle c, c\rangle\}.
\end{aligned}
$$

(Note that we have specified the semantic values of M, B, K, and L in the form of sets rather than as the corresponding functions.)

Suppose we pick as our initial value assignment g some function that assigns the object c to the variable x, assigns b to y, and assigns a to

z. We will not worry about what g assigns to the infinitely many other variables of L_1 since we will only be concerned with examples containing these three variables. Accordingly, we may represent (the initial part of) g as follows:

$$(3\text{-}2)\quad \begin{bmatrix} x \to c \\ y \to b \\ z \to a \\ \cdots \\ \cdots \\ \cdots \end{bmatrix}$$

Having now given semantic values for all the basic expressions of L_1, we can consider how the truth or falsity of a formula, say $\forall x M(x)$, will be determined with respect to M and g (and ultimately with respect to M alone) by the semantic rules of L_1. The formula in question is built up first by forming $M(x)$ by syntactic rule B.1 and then forming $\forall x M(x)$ by syntactic rule B.8. The semantic rule B.1 tells us that in this case $[\![M(x)]\!]^{M,g} = 1$ (i.e., $M(x)$ is true with respect to M and g) since $g(x) = c$ and $[\![M]\!]^{M,g} = \{a, b, c\}$ (more precisely, $[\![M]\!]^{M,g}$ is the characteristic function of the set $\{a, b, c\}$.) To determine the semantic value of $\forall x M(x)$, we must determine the semantic value of $M(x)$ not just with respect to g but also with respect to all value assignments *like g except for the value assigned to x.* Let us now introduce the following notational convention:

> Notational Convention 4: We use "g_u^e" to indicate the value assignment exactly like g except that it assigns the individual e to the variable u.

Thus in addition to g, we will have to consider the truth or falsity of $M(x)$ with respect to M, g_x^a and with respect to M, g_x^b. Since there are only three individuals in A, there can be only these three distinct variable assignments differing at most in the value assigned to x (g_x^c is identical to g itself). These other two are as follows (where the ellipsis represents exactly the *same* completions of g_x^a and g_x^b as in g.):

$$\text{(3-3)} \quad g_x^a: \begin{bmatrix} x \to a \\ y \to b \\ z \to a \\ \cdots \\ \cdots \\ \cdots \end{bmatrix} \qquad g_x^b: \begin{bmatrix} x \to b \\ y \to b \\ z \to a \\ \cdots \\ \cdots \\ \cdots \end{bmatrix}$$

Now we see that $M(x)$ is true with respect to M and any of these three assignments (since a, b, and c are all in $F(M)$), hence $\forall x M(x)$ is true with respect to M, g according to semantic rule B.8. It should also be clear that this sentence would have come out true with respect to a variable assignment g, no matter *which* variable assignment we had picked as g at the outset, since we systematically considered all other assignments assigning different values to x, which is the only variable appearing in the formula. Thus in accordance with clause C.1, we drop the reference to g and say simply that $\forall x M(x)$ is *true relative to M.*

Note also that for an existential formula, say $\exists x B(x)$, it likewise does not matter what g we pick originally. For the truth of this formula we require only that *some* value assignment like g (except possibly for the value assigned to x) make $B(x)$ true. It does not matter whether the g we initially pick happens to be one that makes $B(x)$ true or not, as long as there is one that does. Since all bound variables in all formulas will be interpreted through semantic rules B.8 or B.9 sooner or later, the initial choice of g turns out to be irrelevant for all formulas containing only bound variables, hence the possibility of using the definition in the semantic rules in C.

As we mentioned earlier, vacuous quantification will have no semantic consequences. Suppose we have a formula $\forall x M(x)$ and we vacuously quantify it by syntactic rule B.9, giving $\exists y \forall x M(x)$. By the semantic rule B.9, this will be true w.r.t. M, g just in case $\forall x M(x)$ is true w.r.t. M and to some assignment just like g except for the value assigned to y. Now y does not occur in $\forall x M(x)$, so what value y takes on can have no effect on the truth of it; rather, the truth value of $\exists y \forall x M(x)$ with respect to M and this last series of assignments will in every case be the same as the truth value of $\forall x M(x)$ with respect to M and g.

PROBLEM (3-1) Show that vacuous quantification of $B(x)$ by syntactic rule B.8 to yield $\forall y B(x)$ has no effect on the truth value of $B(x)$.

Now consider an example involving two quantifiers: $\forall x \exists y L(x, y)$, which is formed by using syntactic rule B.2, then B.9, then B.8. We note initially that

$L(x, y)$ is false w.r.t. M, g because $\langle c, b\rangle \notin F(L)$. But by semantic rule B.9, $\exists y L(x, y)$ will be true w.r.t. M, g iff we can find some assignment g' differing only in the value assigned to y that makes $L(x, y)$ true w.r.t. M, g'. We might first test g_y^a:

$$(3\text{-}4) \qquad g_y^a: \begin{bmatrix} x \rightarrow c \\ y \rightarrow a \\ z \rightarrow a \\ \cdots \\ \cdots \\ \cdots \end{bmatrix}$$

Here, $L(x, y)$ turns out to be true (since $\langle c, a\rangle \in F(L)$), so we know without any checking of further values for y that $\exists y L(x, y)$ is true w.r.t. M, g. Now we proceed to the full formula $\forall x \exists y L(x, y)$. By B.8 this formula will be true w.r.t. M, g just in case $\exists y L(x, y)$ is true w.r.t. M and to all g', where g' may differ from g in the value assigned to x. Now we have already checked $\exists y L(x, y)$ for one of the relevant assignments, namely g itself, and found that $\exists y L(x, y)$ is true for it. We then proceed to check g_x^a and g_x^b (exhibited above). To find out whether the formula $\exists y L(x, y)$ is true w.r.t. M, g_x^a, we must in turn ask whether $L(x, y)$ is true w.r.t. some assignment possibly differing from g_x^a in the value assigned to y. (Note that we earlier checked $L(x, y)$ with respect to assignments differing not from g_x^a but from g in the value assigned to y; the difference between the two kinds of assignments is crucial). That is, we will need to check $L(x, y)$ for g_x^a, $[g_x^a]_y^a$, and $[g_x^a]_y^c$ at this stage to see if it is true for at least one of them. These assignments are:

$$(3\text{-}5) \qquad g_x^a: \begin{bmatrix} x \rightarrow a \\ y \rightarrow b \\ z \rightarrow a \\ \cdots \\ \cdots \\ \cdots \end{bmatrix} \qquad [g_x^a]_y^a: \begin{bmatrix} x \rightarrow a \\ y \rightarrow a \\ z \rightarrow a \\ \cdots \\ \cdots \\ \cdots \end{bmatrix} \qquad [g_x^a]_y^c: \begin{bmatrix} x \rightarrow a \\ y \rightarrow c \\ z \rightarrow a \\ \cdots \\ \cdots \\ \cdots \end{bmatrix}$$

For the first two of these, $L(x, y)$ comes out false (since neither $\langle a, b\rangle$ nor $\langle a, a\rangle$ is in $F(L)$), but it comes out true for the third (since $\langle a, c\rangle \in F(L)$), so $\exists y L(x, y)$ is true w.r.t. M, g_x^a. Finally, we check the truth of $\exists y L(x, y)$ w.r.t. M, g_x^b, $[g_x^b]_y^a$, or $[g_x^b]_y^c$:

(3-6) $$g^b_x: \begin{bmatrix} x \to b \\ y \to b \\ z \to a \\ \dots \\ \dots \\ \dots \end{bmatrix} \quad [g^b_x]^a_y: \begin{bmatrix} x \to b \\ y \to a \\ z \to a \\ \dots \\ \dots \\ \dots \end{bmatrix} \quad [g^b_x]^c_y: \begin{bmatrix} x \to b \\ y \to c \\ z \to a \\ \dots \\ \dots \\ \dots \end{bmatrix}$$

The formula $L(x, y)$ is false with respect to the first (because $\langle b, b\rangle \notin F(L)$) but true for the second (because $\langle b, a\rangle \in F(L)$), so we need not bother with the third: we already know that $\exists y L(x, y)$ is true w.r.t. M, g^b_x.

Since we have now investigated $\exists y L(x, y)$ for all possible g' differing from g in the value assigned to x and found it true in these cases, we know by B.8 that $\forall x \exists y L(x, y)$ is true w.r.t. M, g. And since there are no free variables in the formula, we can be assured that it would come out true with respect to M and to any g, hence it is true with respect to M.

As a last example consider the formula $\exists y \forall x L(x, y)$ which is like the previous example but with the scope of the quantifiers reversed. We begin by noting that $L(x, y)$ is false w.r.t. M, g because $\langle c, b\rangle \notin F(L)$. Thus we know already at this point that $\forall x L(x, y)$ cannot be true w.r.t. M, g since there is at least one value assignment (namely, g itself) for which $L(x, y)$ is false. We next move to the question whether $\exists y \forall x L(x, y)$ is true w.r.t. M, g. By the semantic rule B.9, this will be the case iff there is some variable assignment like g except possibly for the value given to y for which $\forall x L(x, y)$ is true. We already know this desired assignment cannot be g itself, so we try others. Is $\forall x L(x, y)$ true w.r.t. g^a_y? If so, then $L(x, y)$ must be true for all assignments like g^a_y except for the individual assigned to x. $L(x, y)$ is true w.r.t. M, g^a_y because $\langle c, a\rangle \in F(L)$, but $L(x, y)$ is false w.r.t. M, $[g^a_y]^a_x$ because $\langle a, a\rangle \notin F(L)$. Therefore, $\forall x L(x, y)$ is false w.r.t. M, g^a_y, and we move on to yet another assignment. Is $\forall x L(x, y)$ true w.r.t. M, g^c_y? $L(x, y)$ is true w.r.t. M, g^c_y, because $\langle c, c\rangle \in F(L)$. Also, $L(x, y)$ is true w.r.t. M, $[g^c_y]^a_x$, because $\langle a, c\rangle \in F(L)$. However, $L(x, y)$ is false w.r.t. M, $[g^c_y]^b_x$ because $\langle b, c\rangle \notin F(L)$. Now we have exhausted all assignments differing from g in the value assigned to y (since g^b_y is g itself) and found $\forall x L(x, y)$ true for none of them. Therefore $\exists y \forall x L(x, y)$ is false w.r.t. M, g. Once again, we can see that this result depended in no way on the g chosen at the outset, so $\exists y \forall x L(x, y)$ is false w.r.t. M by C.2.

If it has not yet become intuitively clear how this procedure works and how it extends to more complex formulas with more quantifiers (or with complex formulas involving sentential connectives and quantifiers), then the reader is encouraged to form further examples and mechanically determine their truth or falsity with respect to M or other constructed finite models by the semantic rules for L_1. Fortunately, it is never necessary to carry out tedious computations of this sort in working with Montague's treatment of English – one's intuitive understanding of formulas in predicate logic is generally sufficient for seeing the point of the English examples. Nevertheless, it is important to keep in mind that a rigorous model-theoretic quantification theory underlies all the quantified formulas to be discussed throughout the rest of the book. This is not the place, however, to discuss mathematical proofs about quantification theory (the so-called *metatheorems* of first-order logic); for these the reader is referred to either Tarski's original treatment (Tarski 1935) or, what is perhaps preferable, to any logic textbook that treats formal semantics of first-order logic (e.g. Van Fraassen 1971, Church 1956, Quine 1951).

As a final comment to our presentation of L_1 we note that the definitions given in the preceding chapter of validity, entailment, etc. can be carried over directly to this new language. Since the dependence on a value assignment has been gotten rid of when we consider the truth values of sentences, we can continue to say that a valid sentence is one which is true with respect to every model, a contradictory sentence is false with respect to every model, and so on.

PROBLEM (3-2) Show by a detailed consideration of the relevant value assignments that the sentence $\forall x \forall y [L(x, y) \rightarrow L(y, x)]$ is false with respect to the given model M. Find a model $M' = \langle A, F' \rangle$ such that the sentence is true with respect to M'.

PROBLEM (3-3) Reformulate the syntactic and semantic rules of L_1 so that the logical connectives are assigned to basic categories rather than being introduced syncategorematically. What difficulties arise in attempting to make the same move with "$\forall$" and "$\exists$"?

PROBLEM (3-4) Show that the sentences $\forall x [B(x) \leftrightarrow B(x)]$ and $\exists x [M(x) \rightarrow \forall y M(y)]$ are valid.

II. THE LANGUAGE L_{1E}

Now that we have examined a logical language which allows quantification over individual variables, we next want to consider how our English-like fragment, L_{0E}, from the preceding chapter might be enlarged to accommodate similar syntactic and semantic processes. Languages L_0 and L_{0E} were virtually isomorphic syntactically, and they were deliberately chosen in this way to provide simple illustrations of the application of model-theoretic semantics to both natural and formal languages. When we consider quantification in natural language as opposed to a formal language such as L_1, however, we see that the two are different in important respects. Anyone who has taken a course in symbolic logic knows that some degree of skill is required to "translate" English sentences into first-order predicate logic. For example, an English sentence such as "Every man walks" is to be rendered in predicate logic as something like $\forall x [M(x) \rightarrow W(x)]$, a formula which contains a logical connective and three instances of a variable having no direct counterparts in the English sentence. Further, both the common count noun "man" and the intransitive verb "walks" have been represented in the logical formula by one-place predicates. If we then go on to reflect on the fact that there are many English quantifiers such as "most," "few," "many," and "much" which have no ready correspondents in predicate logic at all, it becomes clear that the syntax and semantics of quantification in English (or indeed of any other natural language) cannot be any simple isomorphism of L_1.

Quantificational phenomena in English (and in all other natural languages) are in fact so complex that there are still many problems in this area which have not been solved. Indeed, the importance of Montague's paper 'The Proper Treatment of Quantification in Ordinary English' lies in part in the fact that it represents an important advance in the direction of solving some of these problems. In the fragment that we will next construct, we will attempt to keep matters as simple as possible. For example, we will consider only the quantifiers "every," "some," and "the," and we will avoid entirely the problems raised by mass nouns, plural count nouns, relative clauses, and a host of other constructions. This fragment, however, will serve as an indication of one sort of approach to quantification in natural language, and in fact it is quite similar to the framework which Montague adopted in a paper which antedates PTQ, viz., 'English as a Formal Language.'

If we compare simple English quantificational statements with their translations into predicate logic, we note some obvious differences:

(3-7) a. Every student walks $\forall x [S(x) \rightarrow W(x)]$
b. Some student walks $\exists x [S(x) \wedge W(x)]$

While quantification in English is expressed by a determiner combined with a common noun to form a noun phrase, the effect in predicate logic is achieved by two syntactically independent devices: *variables,* which play the same syntactic role as names, and *quantification rules* which are later used to form a new formula from a formula. In the English examples above, however, nothing corresponding to a variable is evident. Nevertheless, there are at least some noun phrases in English that do seem to function as variables do in logic, namely certain pronouns, such as the underlined pronouns in (3-8):

(3-8) a. Every Englishman loves <u>himself</u>
b. Every Englishman loves <u>his</u> mother
c. Every Englishman believes that <u>he</u> is honorable

It has often been observed that from a semantic point of view at least, these pronouns do not merely serve as syntactic substitutes for their antecedents, for the sentences in (3-9) are not synonymous with their counterparts in (3-8):

(3-9) a. Every Englishman loves every Englishman
b. Every Englishman loves every Englishman's mother
c. Every Englishman thinks that every Englishman is honorable

Rather, we can paraphrase the meaning of (3-8a) correctly if we say that sentence (3-10a) below is true for every value of v_1 that is an Englishman (and similarly for (3-10b) and (3-10c)):

(3-10) a. v_1 loves v_1
b. v_1 loves v_1's mother
c. v_1 thinks that v_1 is honorable

Since this kind of paraphrase is obviously reminiscent of our semantic clause for $\forall x\phi$, these examples suggest the possibility that the sentences in (3-8) could be produced in an English-like formal language by using the quasi-sentences in (3-10) as an intermediate step, letting v_1 play the semantic role of a variable and letting the semantic rule corresponding to the syntactic conversion of (3-10) into (3-8) work like the semantic rule for $\forall x\phi$ in L_1. This syntactic "quantification" process that we will introduce into L_{1E} will have to do two things: the leftmost occurrence of the variable v_1 (or other variable) will have to be replaced by a full noun phrase such as *Every Englishman,* while the subsequent occurrence of v_1 in the sentence must be turned into a pronoun, such as *himself, his,* or *he.*

But now what of the simpler examples in (3-7)? Though we might treat them in a syntactically simpler way (and in fact, we will eventually see this possibility realized in the PTQ English syntax), note that this two-step process needed for (3-8) would work just as well for these. That is, we can produce *Every student walks* from v_1 *walks* by the same "replacement" operation (corresponding semantically to variable binding) as suggested above, the only difference here being that no second occurrence of the variable v_1 need be involved. Thus we will formulate our "quantification" rule for L_{1E} as replacing the first occurrence of a variable by a noun phrase containing a determiner *every* (or *some* or *the*) and at the same time replacing all subsequent occurrences of that variable, *if there are any,* with a pronoun (or, as we shall choose to do for simplicity in L_{1E}, a "pronoun substitute").

We specify the syntax of our English fragment L_{1E} as a set of formation rules rather than in the form of a phrase-structure grammar. The reader will also note that the syntax of our new English-like fragment contains "variables" v_1, v_2, etc. as basic expressions of category *N*. These are of course not really basic expressions of English, but they are essential to the approach to quantification we will assume here, and it will do no harm to include them so long as we distinguish, as we did in the case of L_1, between formulas and sentences. Thus, we will define the auxiliary concept of an "English formula" and then define in terms of this the notion of "English sentence."

In contrast to the distinction between formulas and sentences of L_1, however, English sentences will contain no occurrences of variables at all, while they may occur in English formulas. This reflects the different way in which variables will be treated in the English-like fragment – variables do not become *bound* in the way that the occurrence of *x,* for example, becomes bound when $B(x)$ is quantified by $\forall x$ or $\exists x$ in L_1; rather, the variables of L_{1E} will be *replaced* by lexical items of English. For example, by formation rule B5 below, we can form from the English formula v_1 *snores* and the common noun *man* the English sentence *Every man snores*. Similarly, from the formula v_1 *snores or* v_1 *is-boring* and the common noun *man* the same rule licenses the formation of the sentence *Every man snores or that man is-boring*.

Here is the formal specification of the syntax of L_{1E}:

1. *Syntax of* L_{1E}

A. The basic expressions of L_{1E} are as follows:
   1. *Hank, Liz, Sadie* are constants of category *N*.
   2. $v_1, v_2, v_3, \ldots$ are variables of category *N*.
   3. *sleeps, snores, is-boring* are constants of category V_i.
   4. *loves, hates, is-taller-than* are constants of category V_t.
   5. *man, woman, fish* are constants of category *CN* (common noun).

6. *it-is-not-the-case-that* is a (logical) constant of category *Neg*.
7. *and, or* are (logical) constants of category *Conj*.

B. The formation rules of L_{1E} are as follows:
1. If α is a V_t and β is an *N*, then $\alpha\beta$ is a V_i.
2. If α is a V_i and β is an *N*, then $\beta\alpha$ is a *For* (formula).
3. If α is a *Neg* and ϕ is a *For*, then $\alpha\phi$ is a *For*.
4. If α is a *Conj* and ϕ and ψ are *For*'s then $\phi\alpha\psi$ is a *For*.
5. If α is a *CN*, *u* is a variable, and ϕ is a *For* containing at least one occurrence of *u*, then ϕ' is a *For*, where ϕ' comes from ϕ by replacing the left-most occurrence of *u* by *every* α and each subsequent occurrence of *u* by *that* α.
6. If α is a *CN*, *u* is a variable, and ϕ is a *For* containing at least one occurrence of *u*, then ϕ' is a *For*, where ϕ' comes from ϕ by replacing the left-most occurrence of *u* by *some* α and each subsequent occurrence of *u* by *that* α.
7. If α is a *CN*, *u* is a variable, and ϕ is a *For* containing at least one occurrence of *u*, then ϕ' is a *For*, where ϕ' comes from ϕ by replacing the left-most occurrence of *u* by *the* α and each subsequent occurrence of *u* by *that* α.

C. If ϕ is a *For* by the rules in *A* and *B* above and contains no instances of any variable, then ϕ is an *S* (sentence).

Rules B5, 6, and 7, will, for example, allow us to form from the common noun *fish* and the formula *Hank loves* v_6 the sentences *Hank loves every fish, Hank loves some fish,* and *Hank loves the fish,* respectively. Note that the correct interpretation of these rules requires careful attention to the object language/meta-language distinction. In B5, for example, we are to replace the left-most occurrence of the variable not by the sequence "*every* α" to produce, say, "*Hank loves every* α"; rather, what is substituted for the variable occurrence is the sequence consisting of the word *every* followed by whatever word it is in the object language that is taken as the value of α.

Note how different the derivations are in L_{1E} of *Hank snores* and *Every man snores.* The former is derived in the way indicated by the following analysis tree:

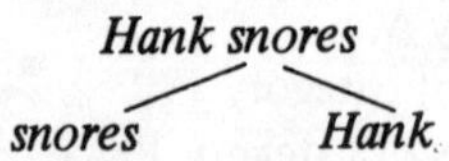

The derivation of the other sentence may be displayed in the following fashion:

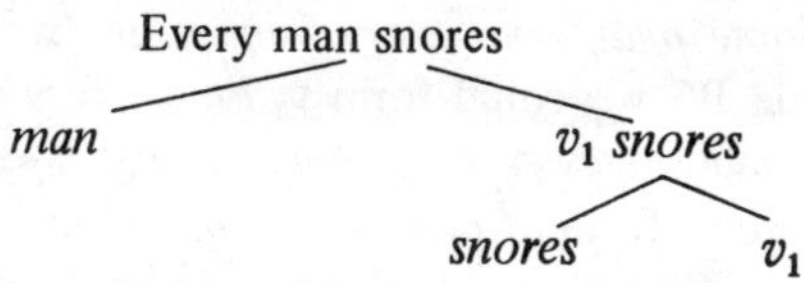

The grammar of L_{1E} has no category of noun phrases containing both *Hank* and *every man*. Indeed *every man* is not a phrase at all in L_{1E}! This is obviously a defect in our syntactic analysis of the language. Our reason for writing the grammar this way will become obvious when we state the semantic rules corresponding to syntactic rules B1-7.

Our syntax here follows Montague in using *that* plus another instance of the common noun to replace all but the first occurrence of a variable. This is a compromise which avoids the problems connected with personal vs. reflexive pronouns and with gender agreement. Thus, our fragment generates from *man* and v_1 *loves* v_1 the rather unnatural sentence *Every man loves that man* instead of *Every man loves himself,* and similarly from *man* and *Hank loves* v_1 *or Liz loves* v_1 we derive *Hank loves some man or Liz loves that man* rather than *Hank loves some man or Liz loves him.* In this connection, we should also point out another deficiency in our fragment vis-a-vis ordinary English. By our syntax, the sentence *Every man loves Hank and Liz loves that man* can only arise from a formula such as v_1 *loves Hank and Liz loves* v_1 (by rule B5). There is no possibility that the phrase *that man* could arise, as it were, as an epithet for Hank. Indeed, in our fragment we cannot generate sentences such as *Hank snores and that man is-boring* at all.

A comment is also in order concerning one peculiar formal property of our syntax: every sentence containing *every, some,* or *the* will have infinitely many distinct syntactic analyses. *Every man sleeps*, for example, could have been formed by rule B5 out of *man* and any one of the formulas v_1 *sleeps,* v_2 *sleeps,* v_3 *sleeps*, etc., etc. This may seem worrisome if one is accustomed to thinking that distinct syntactic derivations must receive distinct semantic interpretations, but as we shall see, this is not so in the semantics we give for L_{1E}. The sentence *Every man sleeps* will not turn out to be infinitely many ways ambiguous; it will turn out not to be even two ways ambiguous semantically. Thus, this proliferation of syntactic derivations need not bother us if we are willing to accept it as a harmless and trivial formal property of our system.

There will, however, arise sentences which will have genuinely nonequivalent syntactic derivations and to which we will want to assign semantic values in more than one way. For example, the formula v_1 *loves* v_2 can give rise to the sentence *Some man loves every woman* in two essentially different ways. First, by rule B5 we could form v_1 *loves every woman* and then by rule B6 form *Some man loves every woman*, or else we could apply these rules in the opposite order, forming first *Some man loves* v_2 and then the sentence in question. As we will see, the semantics will specify truth conditions for this sentence in two distinct ways corresponding to the two derivations just mentioned. The truth conditions will state that for the sentence derived in the first way it is true just in case there is someone who is a man and such that he loves every woman. The truth conditions for the sentence when derived in the second way will correspond to the other "reading" in which for each woman there is some man or other, not necessarily the same man for all women, who loves her. Thus, our fragment provides the means for capturing, at least for some sentences, differences in meaning that depend on the relative scope of quantifiers. We note also that our fragment allows nonequivalent derivations for sentences involving at least two connectives, just as the syntax of L_{0E} did; e.g., *Sadie sleeps or Liz is-boring and Hank snores.*

Thus in L_{1E} as in L_{0E} we will need to assign semantic values to analysis trees of the kind illustrated above. These structures, but not the expressions of which the trees are structural descriptions, contain enough information about syntactic derivations to permit the semantic rules to retrace them.

2. *Semantics of* L_{1E}

It is clear from the syntactic form of sentences containing quantifiers in L_{1E} that the truth conditions will have to be given in a form different from those for the quantifiers $\forall$ and $\exists$ in L_1. For example, in determining the truth value of a sentence such as *Every man sleeps* it will not do to say that it is true just in case the formula v_1 *sleeps* is true for all assignments of values to the variable v_1. That would give us the truth conditions for something like *Everyone sleeps* (i.e., every individual in the universe of discourse sleeps). What we want, rather, is something like "v_1 *sleeps* is true for every assignment of an individual to the variable v_1 such that that individual is a man." The semantic rules below thus treat quantification as "restricted" to a subdomain which is indicated by the common noun with which the quantifier is associated. This, in turn, indicates the sort of semantic values we will want to assign to common nouns, *viz.*, a function from individuals to truth values. This characteristic function of some set will thus represent the set of men, women, fish or whatever, just as the same sort of set indicates the set of snorers, sleepers, etc.

Here is the formal specification of the semantics of L_{1E}:

A model for L_{1E} is an ordered pair $\langle A, F\rangle$ such that A is a non-empty set and F is a function assigning a semantic value to each non-logical constant and which assigns to *it-is-not-the-case-that, and*, and *or* the semantic values appropriate to the logical connectives $\neg$, $\wedge$, and $\vee$ respectively. The domains of possible semantic values for expressions of each syntactic category are given in the following table:

Category	*Set of Possible Semantic Values*
N	A
For	$\{1, 0\}$
V_i	$\{1, 0\}^A$
CN	$\{1, 0\}^A$
V_t	$(\{1, 0\}^A)^A$

A value assignment g is a function assigning to each variable a semantic value of the appropriate sort (here, as in L_1, assigning an individual to each variable).

A. Semantic values of basic expressions:

1. If u is a variable, then $[\![u]\!]^{M,g} = g(u)$.
2. If α is a non-logical constant, then $[\![\alpha]\!]^{M,g} = F(\alpha)$.
3. If α is a logical constant (member of *Neg* or *Conj*) then $[\![\alpha]\!]^{M,g}$ is as follows:

$$[\![\textit{It-is-not-the-case-that}]\!]^{M,g} = \begin{bmatrix} 1 \to 0 \\ 0 \to 1 \end{bmatrix}$$

$$[\![\textit{and}]\!]^{M,g} = \begin{bmatrix} 1 \to & \begin{bmatrix} 1 \to 1 \\ 0 \to 0 \end{bmatrix} \\ 0 \to & \begin{bmatrix} 1 \to 0 \\ 0 \to 0 \end{bmatrix} \end{bmatrix} \qquad [\![\textit{or}]\!]^{M,g} = \begin{bmatrix} 1 \to & \begin{bmatrix} 1 \to 1 \\ 0 \to 1 \end{bmatrix} \\ 0 \to & \begin{bmatrix} 1 \to 1 \\ 0 \to 0 \end{bmatrix} \end{bmatrix}$$

B. Truth conditions of formulas of L_{1E} relative to M and g:

1. If α is a V_t and β is an N, then $[\![\alpha\beta]\!]^{M,g} = [\![\alpha]\!]^{M,g}([\![\beta]\!]^{M,g})$.
2. If α is a V_i and β is an N, then $[\![\beta\alpha]\!]^{M,g} = [\![\alpha]\!]^{M,g}([\![\beta]\!]^{M,g})$.
3. If α is a *Neg* and ϕ is a *For*, then $[\![\alpha\phi]\!]^{M,g} = [\![\alpha]\!]^{M,g}([\![\phi]\!]^{M,g})$.
4. If α is a *Conj* and ϕ and ψ are *For*'s, then $[\![\phi\alpha\psi]\!]^{M,g} = [[\![\alpha]\!]^{M,g}([\![\phi]\!]^{M,g})]([\![\psi]\!]^{M,g})$.
5. If α is a *CN*, u is a variable, and ϕ is a *For* containing at least one

occurrence of u, then for ϕ' as in syntactic rule B5, $[\![\phi']\!]^{M,g} = 1$ iff for all value assignments g_u^e such that $[\![\alpha]\!]^{M,g}(e) = 1$, $[\![\phi]\!]^{M,g_u^e} = 1$.

6. If α is a *CN*, u is a variable, and ϕ is a *For* containing at least one occurrence of u, then for ϕ' as in syntactic rule B6, $[\![\phi']\!]^{M,g} = 1$ iff for some value assignment g_u^e such that $[\![\alpha]\!]^{M,g}(e) = 1$, $[\![\phi]\!]^{M,g_u^e} = 1$.
7. If α is a *CN*, u is a variable, and ϕ is a *For* containing at least one occurrence of u, then for ϕ' as in syntactic rule B7, $[\![\phi']\!]^{M,g} = 1$ iff there is exactly one e in A such that $[\![\alpha]\!]^{M,g}(e) = 1$, and furthermore $[\![\phi]\!]^{M,g_u^e} = 1$.

As already noted, we need really to assign semantic values to analysis trees rather than directly to strings of basic expressions. The reader should understand the rules of A and B in that way. It is only to avoid the distraction of fussy details that we have formulated them in an oversimplified fashion. The same remark applies to C.

C. Truth conditions for sentences of L_{1E} relative to M:
1. For any sentence ϕ of L_{1E}, $[\![\phi]\!]^M = 1$ if for all value assignments g, $[\![\phi]\!]^{M,g} = 1$.
2. For any sentence ϕ of L_{1E}, $[\![\phi]\!]^M = 0$ if for all value assignments g $[\![\phi]\!]^{M,g} = 0$.

Let us now illustrate the workings of these rules by choosing a particular model and determining the semantic values of some sentences with respect to that model. We choose A as for L_{0E} in the preceding chapter, i.e., A = {Anwar Sadat, Queen Elizabeth II, Henry Kissinger}. Further, we let F assign to all the non-logical constants of L_{1E} which are in L_{0E} just the same values that we chose for those constants in model M_0 of the preceding chapter, i.e., F(*Hank*) = Henry Kissinger, etc. (pp. 26–33). To complete the assignment of values to the constants of L_{1E} we let the values of *man, woman,* and *fish* be as follows:

(3-8) $[\![\text{man}]\!]^{M,g} =$
Anwar Sadat → 1
Queen Elizabeth II → 0
Henry Kissinger → 1

(3-9) $[\![\text{woman}]\!]^{M,g} =$
Anwar Sadat → 0
Queen Elizabeth II → 1
Henry Kissinger → 0

(3-10) $[\![\textit{fish}]\!]^{M,g} =$
Anwar Sadat → 0
Queen Elizabeth II → 0
Henry Kissinger → 0

Let us also take as the value assignment g the following function:

$$(3\text{-}11)\quad g = \begin{bmatrix} v_1 \rightarrow \text{Anwar Sadat} \\ v_2 \rightarrow \text{Henry Kissinger} \\ v_3 \rightarrow \text{Queen Elizabeth} \\ \cdots\cdots\cdots\cdots \\ \cdots\cdots\cdots\cdots \end{bmatrix}$$

where the dots indicate some completion of the function whose exact nature we need not be concerned with. For concreteness, let us suppose that all other variables are assigned the value Queen Elizabeth II.

There is nothing new in sentences of L_{1E} that belong to L_{0E} also: their semantic values will be just as before. Therefore, let us consider straight off the semantic value of the sentence *Every man snores* with respect to this model and value assignment. Recall that syntactically this sentence is generated by first combining a variable, say v_2, with the intransitive verb *snores* to give the formula v_2 *snores*. Then by syntactic rule B5 the common noun *man*, the variable v_2, and the formula v_2 *snores* combine to yield *Every man snores*. Our semantic computations will then parallel these steps. First, semantic rule B2 says that $[\![v_2 \textit{ snores}]\!]^{M,g} = [\![\textit{snores}]\!]^{M,g}([\![v_2]\!]^{M,g})$; that is, the function given in (2-13) applied at the argument Henry Kissinger, the latter being $g(v_2)$. Thus, $[\![v_2 \textit{ snores}]\!]^{M,g} = 0$. Next we determine the semantic value of *Every man snores* (with respect to M and g) by semantic rule B5 on the basis of the semantic values of *man*, v_2, and v_2 *snores*. The semantic value of *man* with respect to M and any g' is given in (3-8) above. To apply semantic rule B5 we need first to find all e such that $[\![\textit{man}]\!]^{M,g}(e) = 1$, that is, all the individuals in A who are men according to this model and value assignment. By (3-8) we see that this is just Anwar Sadat and Henry Kissinger. Thus, we are to construct all value assignments which are like g except that the values assigned to v_2 are to range over the set {Anwar Sadat, Henry Kissinger}. Since g as it happens to have been chosen already assigns v_2 the value Henry Kissinger, we have only one other assignment to consider, namely:

$$(3\text{-}12)\quad g_{v_2}^{\text{Anwar Sadat}} = \begin{bmatrix} v_1 \rightarrow \text{Anwar Sadat} \\ v_2 \rightarrow \text{Anwar Sadat} \\ v_3 \rightarrow \text{Queen Elizabeth II} \\ \cdots\cdots\cdots\cdots \\ \cdots\cdots\cdots\cdots \end{bmatrix}$$

(where the dots indicate the same completion as for *g*). Now the rule tells us that *Every man snores* receives the value 1 iff v_2 *snores* receives the value 1 under *both* the above value assignments. Thus we see that we could have actually stopped after examining the value assignment *g* itself, since it makes v_2 *snores* false, and this would be sufficient for us to conclude that *Every man snores* is false (with respect to this model and value assignment). Since *Every man snores* contains no instances of free variables, it will be false in this model no matter which value assignment we start with. Thus, by rule C2 above, $[\![\textit{Every man snores}]\!]^M = 0$.

The reason we distorted English syntactic structure so much in the grammar of L_{1E} was to allow ourselves to formulate semantic rules B.5-7. If we had generated a category of noun phrases including *every man, some man, Hank, etc.,* then we would have found ourselves in a bind when trying to assign a suitable denotation to *some man,* for example. The requisite semantic value cannot be an individual. To see this, note that if it were, then what individual it is would have to depend only on the model and not on a value assignment – since *some man* does not contain any free variables. But then *Some man snores and it-is-not-the-case-that some man snores* (cf. the more colloquial "Some man snores and some doesn't snore") would have to be false in any model – for the same reason that *Hank snores and it-is-not-the-case-that Hank snores* must be. Nor would it help to assign a set of individuals as the semantic value of *some man*. An adequate semantic value will be developed in the next chapter. In the meantime, we have circumvented this particular semantic pitfall by providing a strange syntactic structure – merely for didactic purposes. It would be a good idea for the reader to verify that the problem sentence, *Some man snores and it-is-not-the-case-that some man snores*, is true (on one derivation) in the model under consideration.

In determining the semantic value of a quantified sentence, given a particular model and the value assignment, there is no need of course to go through such excruciating detail in practice as we did above. One can instead run quickly through a chain of reasoning like the following: What is the value of *man* according to the model: Answer: {Anwar Sadat, Henry Kissinger}. Are all the members of this set in the value of *snores*? Answer: No. Therefore, *Every man snores* is false in this model. Similarly, the truth value of *Some man snores* is easily seen to be true by determining that at least one of the members of the set {Anwar Sadat, Henry Kissinger}, namely Anwar Sadat, is in the semantic value of *snores*.

Now consider the example *Every fish snores*. According to the model we have chosen, there are no fish in the universe of discourse (the value of *fish* is the characteristic function of the null set). Thus, in applying semantic rule B5, there will be no value assignments g_u^e such that $[\![fish]\!]^{M,g}(e) = 1$. Thus, *Every fish snores* will be vacuously true (with respect to this model) since there are no e for which $[\![v_2 \ snores]\!]^{M, g^e_{v_2}}$ must be true. Alternatively, one can reason as follows: Are all the members of the set which is the value of *fish* also in the semantic value of *snores*? Answer: Yes, because there are no member in the former set.

Note, however, that semantic rule B6 requires for the truth of a sentence such as *Some fish snores* that there be some value assignment g_u^e such that $[\![fish]\!]^{M,g}(e) = 1$, etc, and since there is no such assignment, *Some fish snores* will receive the value 0 (in this model). This result and the one just mentioned are in accord with one traditional way of construing the meanings of English quantifiers; that is, "Every *X Y*'s" does not entail the existence of any individuals who are *X*, while "Some *X Y*'s" does. It is a consequence of this way of looking at these quantifiers that a sentence of the form "Every *X Y*'s" does not logically imply "Some *X Y*'s" since in case there are no individuals who are *X*, the former will be true but the latter false. In such a case also a sentence of the form "It-is-not-the-case-that every *X Y*'s" will be false. On an alternative view, "Every *X Y*'s" is taken to be false if there are no individuals who are *X*. Then such a sentence would logically imply "Some *X Y*'s", and the sentence "It-is-not-the-case-that every *X Y*'s" would be true. Another standard approach is to postulate a third value which is neither truth nor falsity and say that "Every *X Y*'s" has this third value (or equivalently, has no truth at all) when there is nothing in the semantic value of *X*; in some views one says the same of "It-is-not-the-case-that-every *X Y*'s." A discussion of all the alternatives would entangle us in various intricacies surrounding the notion (or notions) of "presupposition," and that would lead us too far afield at this point. For some references, see Chapter 9.

Similar considerations arise, however, in connection with the treatment of *the* in semantic rule B7. A sentence such as *The man snores* receives the truth value 1 just in case there is exactly one man and that man snores (with respect to the model and value assignment); otherwise, *The man snores* is false. Thus in the model chosen for our illustration, this sentence is in fact false since there are exactly two men. Similarly, *The fish snores* is false inasmuch as there is not, according to the model, exactly one fish who snores, there being no fish at all. We have thus implicitly adopted in semantic rule B7 Russell's theory of definite descriptions (Russell, 1905), according to which a sentence of the form "The *X Y*'s" logically implies that there is exactly one individual who is *X* and that individual *Y*'s. Thus, if there is not exactly one individual who is *X*, or if there is, but that individual does not *Y*, then "The *X Y*'s" is false. An alternative view – the one adopted for example, in (Strawson, 1950) – is that "The *X Y*'s" has no truth value in case there is not exactly one individual who is *X*. In giving the semantic rules as we have, we do not wish to be regarded as espousing a particular point of view on these rather complex issues. We have simply chosen one alternative for the sake of specificity; this alternative happens also to be the one adopted by Montague in PTQ, so the reader will be on a bit more familiar ground when we take up that system in Chapter 7.

PROBLEM (3-5): Determine the truth value of each of the following sentences according to the assumed model for L_{1E}. Which of them, if any, have truth values that differ according to the order in which syntactic rules have been applied?

a. Liz loves every man.
b. The woman hates Hank.
c. Some man sleeps and every woman is-boring.
d. Every man is-taller-than that man.
e. It-is-not-the-case-that some woman hates that woman.

In order to show that a sentence such as *Some man loves every woman* is, according to our system, a case of genuine ambiguity, we will have to choose a slightly more populous model. Let us add to the domain of discourse the individual Jacqueline Onassis, and let us choose the denotations of *man, woman* and *loves* in such a way that the men are, as before, just Henry Kissinger and Anwar Sadat, the women are Queen Elizabeth II and Jacqueline Onassis, and the semantic value of *loves* is now given (as shorthand for the appropriate function) as the following set of ordered pairs:

(3-13) ⟦*loves*⟧ = {⟨Henry Kissinger, Jacqueline Onassis⟩, ⟨Anwar Sadat, Queen Elizabeth II⟩}

(Recall that in this representation the first member of the ordered pair is taken as standing in the relation to the second member).

Now let us consider a syntactic derivation of the sentence *Some man loves every woman* which begins with v_1 and the transitive verb *loves*. We assume that the value assignment g is as in (3-11). Thus *loves* v_1 will receive the null set as semantic value (actually the characteristic function of this set) since $g(v_1)$ = Anwar Sadat and in this model no one loves Anwar Sadat. Next, we form v_2 *loves* v_1, and this receives the truth value 0, since $g(v_2)$ = Henry Kissinger and he does not love Anwar Sadat. We are now ready to insert the quantified expressions and show that the resulting sentence is assigned a different truth value depending on the order in which the phrases are inserted.

From *man* v_2, and v_2 *loves* v_1 we form by syntactic rule B6 the formula *Some man loves* v_1. This is assigned the truth value 0 since, according to our model and the value assignment g, there is no man who loves Anwar Sadat. Next, from *woman*, v_1, and *Some man loves* v_1 we form *Some man loves every woman.* To determine the truth value of this, we must find the truth value of *Some man loves* v_1 for every assignment in which the value of v_1 is a woman. When v_1 is assigned the value Queen Elizabeth II, *Some man loves* v_1 is true, since, by semantic rule B6, we determine that v_2 *loves* v_1 is true for at least one value of v_2 which is a man, namely, Anwar Sadat. When v_1 is assigned the value Jacqueline Onassis, *Some man loves* v_1 is true, since v_2 *loves* v_1 is true when v_2 takes on the value Henry Kissinger, who is a man. Thus, the semantic rules in connection with this syntactic derivatin of the sentence *Some man loves every woman* assign the sentence the semantic value 1. Note that the situation that was necessary to ensure this result can be described as "for each woman there is some man or other who loves her."

Now consider the different syntactic derivation in which we first form from *woman* v_1, and v_2 *loves* v_1 the formula v_2 *loves every woman* by syntactic rule B5. This is assigned the value 0 since Henry Kissinger does not love every woman; specifically, he doesn't love Queen Elizabeth II. Now we form *Some man loves every woman* from *man*, v_2, and v_2 *loves every woman* by syntactic rule B6. Here we must let v_2 take on successive values from the set of men and determine whether for any of these individuals it is true that he loves every woman. We already know that it is not true of Henry Kissinger, and when we let the value of v_2 be Anwar Sadat, we see that it is not true of him either (he doesn't love Jacqueline Onassis). Therefore, on this derivation the sentence *Some man loves every woman* is false, and the assumed situation that led to this being so can be expressed as "there is no man such that he loves every woman."

The sentence in question is intuitively ambiguous (at least for most speakers of English) in just the way countenanced by our semantics, so we might justifiably find some satisfaction in this approach to quantification in English. Of course it remains to be seen whether our good fortune will hold up as more complex syntactic constructions are added to the fragment. And one may very well wonder whether we should have to generate the sentence in two syntactically nonequivalent ways, as we did in order to provide a basis for the semantic ambiguity.[2] We will return to some of these questions in connection with our discussion of PTQ in Chapter 7.

A final point. In Chapters 2 and 3 we have repeatedly stressed that model-theoretic semantics proceeds by associating real-world objects with linguistic expressions. Our purpose has been to emphasize the important point that model theory capitalizes on the use of language to talk about things and incorporates the potential for this in a fundamental way. This characteristic of model theory tempts some people to think that the theory embodies too simplistic a notion of the way actual users of language connect expressions with real-world objects. Let us take this opportunity to head off such misapprehensions.

We illustrate one form of the error by formulating an objection someone might make. One might take the position that *every mammal suckles its young* could not possibly mean the truly universal proposition we have analyzed it as meaning, since

(a) human beings can mentally grasp its meaning;
(b) people can, moreover, have adequate grounds for asserting the sentence; but
(c) they may very well not know of the existence of some mammal and then could not be talking about mammals they were not aware of.

The fallacy in the objection lies in the falsity of point (c), which is clearly not a logical consequence of (a) and (b). Human beings certainly can grasp the meaning of universal sentences, and sometimes have adequate grounds for asserting them. But, "adequate" does not mean infallible here anymore than it does elsewhere. If there are mammals a speaker is unaware of, his ignorance of their existence does not excuse him of responsibility in case some of them turn out not to suckle their young – any more than if he were mistaken about the feeding habits of mammals he knew existed. If someone points out mammals he didn't know of which do not suckle their young, he would have to admit he had made a mistake and withdraw his assertion. This shows that this statement applies to all mammals, not only the ones he knew about at the time he asserted it. He could afterwards maintain at best that every mammal in a restricted set suckles its young, and only if the restriction in his statement excluded the nonsuckling mammals he has learned of could he have adequate grounds for this assertion. Thus it is correct to maintain that *every* makes truly universal statements. The mistake our objector made was in thinking that adequate grounds for asserting a sentence suffice to insure that the sentence is true.

Our human imperfections in correctly making the connection of our language to the world do not in any way negate the fact that our understanding of many words and phrases is grounded in exactly that connection. Precisely because this is so, it is appropriate to criticize speakers when they try to make the connections and do so incorrectly. But also because we intend to use language in terms of its real connections, it is possible for us to employ it in an entirely mental way when that is useful. Language can help us think about what it would be like if things were not as they really are. It can help us represent how things might be or might have been. This is important not only in every day activities like planning to make things different, but also in giving scientific explanation of the way things in fact are. Such "detached" uses of language do not reveal an inadequacy of model-theoretic semantics. If the world *were* as it is imagined, expressions *would* connect to objects just as the model has them do. Thus these imaginative uses of language actually illustrate a strength of model-theoretic semantics rather than a weakness.

EXERCISES

1. Reformulate the syntax and semantics of L_1, replacing the basic expression $\neg, \wedge, \vee$, etc. by the "Polish" connectives N, K, A, etc., treated as basic expressions (see Exercise 3, Chapter 2).

2. Show that in syntactic rules B5, 6, and 7 and also in the corresponding semantic rules for L_{1E} the condition that ϕ contain at least one occurrence of the variable u is essential in order to avoid absurd results for sentences such as *Hank snores* which contain no quantifiers.

3. What difficulties arise in attempting to specify the syntax of L_{1E} by means of a context-free phrase-structure grammar? Readers with sufficient background in mathematical linguistics may want to construct a proof that no context-free phrase-structure grammar generating this language is possible.

4. Construct a variant of the syntax and semantics of L_{1E} in which names as well as quantifiers + common nouns can be substituted for variables. For example, from *Hank* and v_1 *snores* one could form *Hank snores* (This sentence will also be generated in the usual way by syntactic rule B2). Write the syntactic rules in such a way that the phrase *that person* is substituted for all occurrences of a given variable other than the left-most; i.e., *Hank* + v_1 *loves* v_1 yields *Hank loves that person*, and *Hank* + v_1 *snores or Liz loves* v_1 yields *Hank snores or Liz loves that person*. Arrange the semantics in such a way that *Hank snores* has the same truth conditions under either derivation.

5. Show that under the syntax and semantics given for L_{1E} the sentences *Every man loves every man* and *Every man loves that man* have different truth conditions, and further, that the former logically entails the latter.

6. Show that under the syntax and semantics given for L_{1E} the sentence *Every man sleeps or that man snores* does not logically entail the sentence *Every man sleeps or every man snores.*

NOTES

[1] It is a technical consequence of this definition, C., that even certain formulas with free variables will count as true (in the unrelativized sense), namely those in which the formula comes out true no matter what values are assigned to its free variable(s). In other words, a formula with free variables that comes out true by this definition is one that would also be true just in case enough universal quantifiers were prefixed to it to bind all its free variables. Montague in fact exploited this technical consequence in PTQ by omitting universal quantifiers from some of his "meaning postulates": the intent is clearly that these postulates are to be read as if these additional universal quantifiers were present.

In his 'Universal Grammar,' however, Montague used the definition of *true relative to a value assignment g* in a different way. As we will explain in Chapter 8, the function *g* is there thought of as serving the additional purpose of supplying values for deictic pronouns (which are treated as free variables). That is, a formula like *He walks* (i.e. *x walks*) is considered now true, now false, depending on the context in which it is used (i.e. depending on which particular *g* is chosen as "context"). The interpretation of bound variables is unaffected by this new view of *g*. For a detailed analysis of non-anaphoric pronouns in English based on this idea, see Cooper (1979a).

[2] Linguists who consider syntax autonomous find it highly suspect to force syntactic rules to produce ambiguities that are motivated solely by semantic considerations. This particular problem about L_{1E} is not a result of the already noted syntactic inadequacy in that language of having no category of noun phrases; it will persist even after that has been remedied. The problem we face here is that, unlike the case of *Sadie sleeps or Liz is-boring and Hank snores,* there are no syntactic or prosodic correlates of the evident semantic ambiguity in the sentence. Montague, like the Generative Semanticists, chose to set up multiple syntactic representations anyway in such cases and to retain the policy of assigning just one semantic value to each syntactic representation. As Cooper (1975) demonstrated, however, there is an alternative compatible with the Principle of Compositionality. One can have a single syntactic representation of *Some man loves every woman* and assign as the semantic value of each phrase a set of things very like the semantic values Montague assigns. Then the sentence turns out semantically ambigous in the appropriate way, while being unambiguous syntactically.

CHAPTER 4

A HIGHER-ORDER TYPE-THEORETIC LANGUAGE

Our goal in this chapter is to describe a language, which we will call L_{type}, that is an extension of L_1 but contains an infinite number of syntactic categories. In order to smooth the transition to L_{type}, we first digress to make a slight notational reformulation of the syntactic rules of L_1, keeping the expressive power of the language the same as in L_1 but introducing some of the notational devices that will be needed for L_{type}.

I. A NOTATIONAL VARIANT OF L_1

The changes to be made in L_1 here involve a new system for naming the syntactic categories. The significance of the notation will, we hope, become clear in the course of the discussion.

1. The category of *terms* of L_1 (i.e., names and individual variables) will be designated by the symbol *e*.
2. The category of *formulas* of L_1 (including of course *sentence* as a special case) will be designated by the symbol *t*.
3. The category of *one-place predicates* of L_1 will be designated by the symbol $\langle e, t\rangle$.
4. The category of *two-place predicates* of L_1 will be designated by the symbol $\langle e, \langle e, t\rangle\rangle$.

Consider now the kinds of semantic values which are assigned to expressions of each of these categories. Terms (whether constants or variables) have as their semantic values individuals or entities in *A*, the universe of discourse. (The symbol *e* is Montague's mnemonic for "entity.") Formulas, including sentences, are assigned truth values; hence, the *t*. Expressions of the other two categories takes as values some sort of function; specifically, one-place predicates are assigned functions from individuals to truth values (which is suggested by the notation $\langle e, t\rangle$), and two-place predicates receive functions from individuals to functions from individuals to truth values (hence, $\langle e, \langle e, t\rangle\rangle$).

Let us, in fact, make this correspondence an official part of the model-theoretic intepretation of L_1 by using our new notation for syntactic categories in the definition of "possible semantic value for expressions of category so-an-so," or, to introduce another term for "semantic value" which is used equivalently in the sort of language we are considering here, "possible *denotation* for expressions of category so and so." First, some notation:

> Notational Convention 5: We use "D_x" for the set of possible denotations for expressions of syntactic category x.

Now the definition:

(4-1) 1. D_e is A.
2. D_t is $\{1, 0\}$.
3. For any syntactic categories a and b, $D_{\langle a, b \rangle} = D_b^{D_a}$ (i.e., the set of all functions from D_a to D_b).

This definition is obviously more general that it needs to be since we are here dealing with just four syntactic categories, and the possible denotations for those could be given, as we have done previously, as a list. But, as we have said, we have in mind a generalization to languages with an infinite number of syntactic categories, and of course in that instance we shall need some kind of recursive specification of the denotations appropriate to each.

Let us for the moment just assure ourselves that the definition given does indeed specify the sets of possible denotations we intended. Consider, for example, expressions of category $\langle e, t \rangle$ (one-place predicates). Clause 3 of (4-1) says that the set of possible denotations for this category, $D_{\langle e, t \rangle}$, is $D_t^{D_e}$. That, by clauses 1 and 2, is $\{1, 0\}^A$, i.e., the set of all functions from individuals to truth values, as required. It should now be easy to see that the definition also gives the intended result for $D_{\langle e, \langle e, t \rangle \rangle}$, since by clause 3 this is equal to $D_{\langle e, t \rangle}^{D_e}$, which, by clause 1 and the previous result, works out to $(\{0, 1\}^A)^A$.

Note that this definition is not intended to say *how* the denotations of expressions in the various categories are determined, and indeed we have seen that they are determined in different ways. An expression which is syntactically basic, e.g., a two-place predicate or a term, will have its denotation assigned by the function F in the model (if it is a constant) or by the value assignment g (if it is an individual variable). An expression which is syntactically derived, e.g., a formula, receives its denotation by means of the concerted operation of the semantic rules and the functions F and g. Definition (4-1) can thus be regarded as laying down a general principle which the model, the value assignment, and the semantic rules must all "conspire" to preserve.

Let us now re-examine the first two syntactic rules for L_1, i.e., B1 and B2, in light of our new notation. Rule B1 says that a one-place predicate can combine with a term to yield a formula. Using the new names for these categories, we might write, briefly: $\langle e, t\rangle + e = t$. Similarly, rule B2, which licenses the combination of a two-place predicate with two terms might be expressed: $\langle e, \langle e, t\rangle\rangle + e + e = t$. There is an obvious pattern here which suggests a kind of "cancellation" operation. A "complex" syntactic category of the form $\langle a, b\rangle$ combines with something of category a to yield something of category b. (In the case of $\langle e, \langle e, t\rangle\rangle$ we have carried out this "cancellation" twice – once with each of the e's.) Thus, our notation serves to make at least these syntactic processes look more like the correspondents of the semantic processes that go on in assigning denotations to complex expressions. And we could, in fact, make a small change in the formation rules of L_1 in the direction of preserving this general pattern; *viz.*, let a two-place predicate, i.e., an expression of category $\langle e, \langle e, t\rangle\rangle$ combine with *one* term to yield a one-place predicate, i.e. an expression of category $\langle e, t\rangle$. This is of course just the counterpart in L_1 of what we were led naturally to do in L_{0E} in Chapter 2: let transitive verbs combine with a name to yield a *VP*. The one-place predicates so formed will then combine with a term to yield a formula ($\langle e, t\rangle + e = t$), and so the form of the syntactic "cancellation" rules will be preserved exactly. There is one slight problem, however, and that is that we will, if we continue to insert parentheses by syntactic rule B1, arrive at formulas such as $L(b)(x)$ rather than $L(x, b)$. This need not trouble us so long as we agree that the former expression is to be taken as nothing more than a notational variant of the latter, more traditional expression. The order of the terms is of course reversed in the former, but it is arbitrary anyway whether we choose to regard the left-most term as the "subject" or "object," so to speak, in the logical formula.

Let us now reformulate the syntax and semantics of L_1 making the changes we have just discussed.

1. *Syntax*

A. The basic expressions of L_1 are as follows:

1. d, n, j, m are constants of category e.

2. $v_1, v_2, v_3, \ldots$ are variables of category e. (We continue to use x for v_1, etc.)
3. M, B are constants of category $\langle e, t\rangle$.
4. K, L are constants of category $\langle e, \langle e, t\rangle\rangle$.

B. The formation rules of L_1 are as follows:
1. If δ is a member of category $\langle e, t\rangle$ and α is a member of category e, then $\delta(\alpha)$ is a member of category t.
2. If γ is a member of category $\langle e, \langle e, t\rangle\rangle$ and α is a member of category e, then $\gamma(\alpha)$ is a member of category $\langle e, t\rangle$.

3.– 7. If ϕ and ψ are members of category t, then $\neg\phi$, $[\phi \wedge \psi]$, $[\phi \vee \psi]$, $[\phi \rightarrow \psi]$, and $[\phi \leftrightarrow \psi]$, are members of category t.

8. If ϕ is a member of category t and u is a variable of category e, then $\forall u\phi$ is a member of category t.
9. If ϕ is a member of category t and u is a variable of category e, then $\exists u\phi$ is a member of category t.

2. *Semantics*

A model for L_1 is an ordered pair $\langle A, F\rangle$ such that A is a non-empty set and F is a function assigning a denotation to each non-logical constant. The set of possible denotations for each category is defined in (4-1) above. A value assignment g is a function assigning to each variable a denotation of the appropriate sort (here, there are only variables of category e so each is assigned a member of A).

A. Semantic values of basic expressions:
1. If u is a variable, then $[\![u]\!]^{M,g} = g(u)$.
2. If α is a non-logical constant, then $[\![\alpha]\!]^{M,g} = F(\alpha)$.

B. Truth conditions for formulas of L_1 relative to M and g:
1. If δ is an expression of category $\langle e, t\rangle$ and α is an expression of category e, then $[\![\delta(\alpha)]\!]^{M,g} = [\![\delta]\!]^{M,g}([\![\alpha]\!]^{M,g})$.
2. If γ is an expression of category $\langle e, \langle e, t\rangle\rangle$ and α is an expression of category e, then $[\![\gamma(\alpha)]\!]^{M,g} = [\![\gamma]\!]^{M,g}([\![\alpha]\!]^{M,g})$.

3.– 7. If ϕ is an expression of category t, then $[\![\neg\phi]\!]^{M,g} = 1$ iff $[\![\phi]\!]^{M,g} = 0$; otherwise, $[\![\neg\phi]\!]^{M,g} = 0$. Similarly for $[\phi \wedge \psi]$, $[\phi \vee \psi]$, $[\phi \rightarrow \psi]$, and $[\phi \leftrightarrow \psi]$.

8. If ϕ is an expression of category t and u is a variable, then

$[\![\forall u\phi]\!]^{M,g} = 1$ iff for every value assignment g' such that g' is exactly like g except possibly for the individual assigned to u by g', $[\![\phi]\!]^{M,g'} = 1$.

9. (The truth condition for $[\![\exists u\phi]\!]^{M,g}$ is similar to that in 8. with "every" replaced by "some.")

C. Truth conditions for formulas relative to M:
1. For any expression ϕ of category t, $[\![\phi]\!]^M = 1$ if for all value assignments g, $[\![\phi]\!]^{M,g} = 1$.
2. For any expression ϕ of category t, $[\![\phi]\!]^M = 0$ if for all value assignments g, $[\![\phi]\!]^{M,g} = 0$.

We saw in the preceding chapters that the logical constants ¬, ∧, ∨, →, and ↔, which are here introduced syncategorematically, could also be treated as basic expressions and assigned semantic values (albeit *fixed* values which do not vary with choices of the function F). We have the same option here, and the categories to which these constants must be assigned will fit nicely into the scheme we have already developed.

The sentence operator ¬, as we saw, combines syntactically with a formula to yield a formula, and semantically its value is a function from truth values to truth values. Therefore, if we choose $\langle t, t\rangle$ as this category in our new notation, everything will work out exactly right. By definition (4-1), the appropriate denotation for expressions of this category is $D_t^{D_t}$, i.e., $\{1,0\}^{\{1,0\}}$, or the set of all functions from truth values to truth values. Synctactically, an expression of category $\langle t, t\rangle$ will combine with an expression of category t to yield an expression of category t, and thus we will have another instance of a syntactic rule in which the category of the "output" expression is determined by the "cancellation" operation on the categories of the "input" expressions. And of course the corresponding semantic rule will be another instance of functional application.

By similar reasoning, the sentence connectives ∧, ∨, →, and ↔ should belong to the category $\langle t, \langle t, t\rangle\rangle$, and each should be allowed to combine with an expression of category t to yield an expression of category $\langle t, t\rangle$. Note that when we say that one expression "combines" with another, we have not specified the precise way in which this combination is to be carried out. That is a part of each formation rule, and it will in general vary with the categories of expressions involved. The "mode of combination" in rules B1 and B2 (under either formulation above) is "first symbol + left parenthesis + second symbol + right parenthesis." When the negation operator combines with a formula, the syntactic rule directs us simply to concatenate the operator and the formula in that order. In order to get the desired expressions involving sentence connectives, we would have to arrange for the connective to stand to the right of the formula it combines with; i.e., "$\wedge$," for example, would combine with $B(j)$ to give the operator $B(j)\wedge$. There is a further problem in getting the punctuating brackets in the right places, and the easiest way around this is probably to allow them to be introduced by the rule which combines an operator with a formula. This yields formulas such as $[\neg[\neg B(j)]]$ which contain unnecessary brackets, but they are harmless if we are willing to ignore them. Accordingly, we could revise the syntax and semantics of L_1 further to incorporate these changes:

Add to the list of basic expressions:

5. $\neg$ is a logical constant of category $\langle t, t\rangle$.
6. $\wedge, \vee, \rightarrow, \leftrightarrow$ are logical constants of category $\langle t, \langle t, t\rangle\rangle$.

Replace formation rules 3.–7 by the following two rules:

3. If α is a member of category $\langle t, t\rangle$ and ϕ is a member of category t, then $[\alpha\phi]$ is a member of category t.
4. If β is a member of category $\langle t, \langle t, t\rangle\rangle$ and ϕ is a member of category t, then $\phi\beta$ is a member of category $\langle t, t\rangle$.

In the semantics we now have to insure that these logical constants are assigned the desired notations, and this is easily arranged by adding a clause to the definition of a model for L_1: A model for L_1 is an ordered pair $\langle A, F\rangle$ such that A is a non-empty-set, and F is a function which assigns a denotation to each non-logical constant and which assigns to the logical constant $\neg$ the denotation $\begin{bmatrix} 1 \rightarrow 0 \\ 0 \rightarrow 1 \end{bmatrix}$, etc. Semantic rules 3.–7. are then replaced by two rules of functional application.

PROBLEM (4-1): Write the semantic rules just referred to.

II. THE LANGUAGE L_{type}

The language we are now ready to consider, L_{type}, is called "type-theoretic" because its syntax is based on Russell's simple theory of types, probably most closely resembling the version of type theory found in Church (1940), the so-called *functional theory of types.* L_{type} will contain both constants and variables in every syntactic category, and it will allow quantification over variables of any category. Thus, L_{type} will have not only variables ranging over individuals (and the attendant quantification) which is characteristic of *first-order* languages, and variables ranging over predicates too, as does a *second-order* language, but variables ranging over *every* category defined in the type theory. Thus the language is known as a *higher-order* language.

The first step is to put to use the notational system we just introduced in connection with L_1 and let it fulfill its intended purpose of representing an infinite class of syntactic categories. Accordingly, we give the following recursive definition of the *set of types* (which is also called simply the set *Type*):

(4-2) (1) *e* is a type.
(2) *t* is a type.
(3) If *a* and *b* are any types, then $\langle a, b\rangle$ is a type.
(4) Nothing else is a type.

For example, since *t* and *e* are types by (1) and (2), so are $\langle e, t\rangle$, $\langle t, e\rangle$, $\langle t, t\rangle$ and $\langle e, e\rangle$ by rule (3); by (3) once again, the more complex symbols $\langle e, \langle e, t\rangle\rangle$, $\langle\langle e, t\rangle, t\rangle$, $\langle\langle e, t\rangle, \langle e, t\rangle\rangle$ etc. are also types, as are $\langle e, \langle e, \langle e, t\rangle\rangle\rangle$, $\langle\langle\langle e, t\rangle, \langle e, t\rangle\rangle, t\rangle$, and so on.

Following Montague, we will make a subtle terminological distinction here. The *syntactic categories* of a formalized language are most naturally thought of as *sets* of expressions – the set of all one-place predicates, the set of all formulas, etc. What is defined by the above recursive definition is obviously not a series of sets of expressions but rather a series of *names* or *labels* of sets of expressions. (In Montague's terms, the types serve to index the syntactic categories of the language.) Linguists typically do not make this distinction – for example, the symbol "NP" may be used indifferently to denote the label of a category (i.e., as a non-terminal symbol of a phrase structure grammar), the category itself (i.e., the set of all noun phrases of a language), or for that matter even as a variable over arbitrary expressions of this category (an arbitrary noun phrase of a language). Since the members of *Type* are technically *labels* of categories, we introduce the symbol ME_a (the *meaningful expressions* of type *a*) to denote sets of expressions themselves.

Clearly, all the category labels of L_1 (as reformulated using *e, t,* etc.) will appear in the set of types (and in fact, the language L_1 itself will be contained in L_{type}), but there will be an infinite number of other types besides. The thought of a language with an infinite number of categories is instantly apalling to a linguist, since surely no natural language has this many. By considering such a language we are not, however, suggesting that anything of this sort is characteristic of natural languages. Rather, Montague's interest in formal languages based on types lies in the systematic way that the categories are related and semantically interpreted. Note that the recursive definition of *possible denotation* that we gave in (4-1) for the simple language L_1 will serve equally well to define a possible denotation for each of the infinitely many categories of L_{type}. Further, as we will see in this and succeeding chapters, many syntactic rules of both natural and formal languages can be formulated in such a way that an expression of type $\langle a, b\rangle$ (for some types a and b) combines with an expression of type a to produce an expression of type b. (Thus, the type of the output expressions is determined by the "cancellation operation" referred to previously). And the corresponding semantic operation will be one of functional application in which the denotation of the expression of type $\langle a, b\rangle$ (a function) will be applied to the argument which is the denotation of the expression of type a, giving a semantic value appropriate to an expression of type b.

The point is that Montague thought that the syntax and semantics of English would turn out to require a variety of logical and semantic categories beyond those found in first-order logic, though of course only a finite number of them. Though he did not claim to know just which ones these would be (since he only attempted to formulate a grammar and semantics for what he called a small "fragment" of English, what linguists might call a "sample grammar"), he apparently saw in type theory a powerful system of categories and systematic interpretation which could be potentially extended at will to add (finitely many) new categories in a systematic way as soon as the need for particular futher categories became apparent. Thus, a type-theoretic system of syntactic categories should not be thought of as a theory of syntactic categories for a natural language, but rather as a syntactic and semantic framework in which to construct a theory of syntactic categories for a natural language.[1]

As for the non-logical constants of L_{type}, we will follow Montague in having a denumerably infinite supply of these in each category. Officially, each will be a symbol of the form $c_{n,\,a}$, where n is a natural number (positive integer or zero) and a is some member of the set of types. For example, $c_{0,\,e}$ is the first constant of type e; $c_{1,\,e}$ is the second constant of type e, $c_{0,\,\langle e,\,t\rangle}$ is the first constant of type $\langle e, t\rangle$, $c_{237,\,\langle e,\,\langle\langle e,\,t\rangle,\,\langle e,\,t\rangle\rangle\rangle}$ is the 238th constant of type $\langle e, \langle\langle e, t\rangle, \langle e, t\rangle\rangle\rangle$, etc. However, unofficially we will adopt as standard abbreviations for some of these unwieldy symbols the non-logical constant symbols we used in L_1. Thus j, d, m, n will stand for $c_{0,e}$, $c_{1,e}$, $c_{2,e}$ and $c_{3,e}$ respectively; M and B will stand for the first two constants of type $\langle e, t\rangle$, and K and L will stand for the first two constants of type $\langle e, \langle e, t\rangle\rangle$. Of logical constants we will retain in L_{type} just those in L_1.

Each category will also contain a denumerably infinite supply of variables. These will be designated by symbols of the form $v_{n,a}$, where n is a natural number and a is a member of the set of types. As before, we will let x, y and z stand for $v_{0,e}$, $v_{1,e}$, and $v_{2,e}$, respectively. Abbreviatory symbols for other variables will be introduced as needed. An assignment of values to variables is now a somewhat more complex affair than before, since for every type a and each natural number n it must assign to $v_{n,a}$ an appropriate denotation out of the set D_a of possible denotations of type a. However, the semantic and syntactic rules for variables and quantifiers will otherwise appear exactly as in L_1 except for being generalized to cover all possible types. We can make this generalization and still have a coherent semantics because our semantic interpretation is given entirely in terms of set theory. And it is always possible in set theory to go on indefinitely talking about sets containing other sets, sets which contain sets containing other sets, etc. (as long as we avoid the well-known set-theoretic paradoxes).

Now we can give the formal definitions of the syntax and semantics of L_{type}:

1. *Syntax of* L_{type}

A. The set of *types* of L_{type} is as given in (4-2) above.

B. The *basic expressions* of L_{type} consist of non-logical constants and variables:
 1. For each type a, the set of *non-logical constants of type a*, denoted Con_a, contains constants $c_{n,a}$, for each natural number n.
 2. For each type a, the set of *variables of type a*, denoted Var_a, contains variables $v_{n,a}$ for each natural number n.

C. *Syntactic rules of* L_{type}.
 The set of *meaningful expressions of type a*, denoted "ME_a", for any type a (which is simply the set of well-formed expressions of each type) is defined recursively as follows:
 1. For each type a, every variable and every non-logical constant of type a is a member of ME_a.
 2. For any types a and b, if $\alpha \in ME_{\langle a, b\rangle}$ and $\beta \in ME_a$, then $\alpha(\beta) \in ME_b$.

3.– 7. If ϕ and ψ are in ME_t, then so are each of the following:
3. $\neg\phi$
4. $[\phi \wedge \psi]$
5. $[\phi \vee \psi]$
6. $[\phi \rightarrow \psi]$
7. $[\phi \leftrightarrow \psi]$
8. If $\phi \in ME_t$ and u is a variable (of any type), then $\forall u\phi \in ME_t$.
9. If $\phi \in ME_t$ and u is a variable (of any type), then $\exists u\phi \in ME_t$.

PROBLEM (4-2) In the above rules what problems would we have if the logical constants were included among $ME_{\langle t, t\rangle}$ and $ME_{\langle t, \langle t, t\rangle\rangle}$?

2. *Semantics of L_{type}*

Given a non-empty set A (the domain of individuals, or entities), the set of possible denotations of expressions of each type a is given by the definition in (4-1).

A *model for L_{type}* is then an ordered pair $\langle A, F\rangle$ such that A is as above and F is a function assigning a denotation to each non-logical constant of L_{type} of type a from the set D_a.

An *assignment of values to variables* (or simply a *variable assignment*) g is a function assigning to each variable $v_{n,a}$ a denotation from the set D_a, for each type a and natural number n.

The *denotation of an expression of L_{type} relative to a model M and variable assignment g* is defined recursively as follows:

1. a. If α is a non-logical constant, then $[\![\alpha]\!]^{M,g} = F(\alpha)$.
   b. If α is a variable, then $[\![\alpha]\!]^{M,g} = g(\alpha)$.

2. If $\alpha \in ME_{\langle a, b\rangle}$ and $\beta \in ME_a$, then $[\![\alpha(\beta)]\!]^{M,g} = [\![\alpha]\!]^{M,g}([\![\beta]\!]^{M,g})$.

3.–7. If ϕ and ψ are in ME_t, then $[\![\neg\phi]\!]^{M,g}$, $[\![\phi \wedge \psi]\!]^{M,g}$, $[\![\phi \vee \psi]\!]^{M,g}$, $[\![\phi \rightarrow \psi]\!]^{M,g}$ and $[\![\phi \leftrightarrow \psi]\!]^{M,g}$ are as specified earlier for L_1.

8. If $\phi \in ME_t$ and u is in Var_a, then $[\![\forall u\phi]\!]^{M,g} = 1$ iff for all e in $D_a [\![\phi]\!]^{M,g^e_u} = 1$.

9. If $\phi \in ME_t$ and u is in Var_a, then $[\![\exists u\phi]\!]^{M,g} = 1$ iff for some e in $D_a [\![\phi]\!]^{M,g^e_u} = 1$.

As in L_1, the semantic value of an expression does not depend on variables that are not free in the expression. So we add the following definition.

The *denotation of an expression of* L_{type} *relative to a model M* is defined as follows:

1. For any expression ϕ in ME_t, $[\![\phi]\!]^M = 1$ iff $[\![\phi]\!]^{M,g} = 1$ for every value assignment g.
2. For any expression ϕ in ME_t, $[\![\phi]\!]^M = 0$ iff $[\![\phi]\!]^{M,g} = 0$ for every value assignment g.

We will now consider some examples of formulas of L_{type} not occurring in L_1 and how these formulas are interpreted semantically. As mentioned earlier, we can quantify not only over individuals but also over other sorts of things. Thus for example, we could write in L_{type} this second-order formula:

(4-3) $\forall v_{0, \langle e, t\rangle}[v_{0, \langle e, t\rangle}(j) \rightarrow v_{0, \langle e, t\rangle}(d)]$

which says that for all one-place predicates δ, if δ is true of j then δ is true of d. Semantically, this means that for all sets s consisting of members of A, if the individual denoted by j is in s, then so is the individual denoted by d. (Technically, the denotation involves the characteristic functions of these sets.) Of course, among these sets will be the unit set (set with only one member) containing $[\![j]\!]^{M,g}$, and since the above formula asserts that even this set contains $[\![d]\!]^{M,g}$, the formula says, in effect, that the names d and j denote the same individual.

But we can also write a parallel third-order formula in L_{type}:

(4-4) $\forall v_{0, \langle\langle e, t\rangle, t\rangle}[v_{0, \langle\langle e, t\rangle, t\rangle}(B) \rightarrow v_{0, \langle\langle e, t\rangle, t\rangle}(M)]$

This says in turn that for all predicates μ of predicates, if μ is true of the predicate B, then it is true of the predicate M. Here, the variable $v_{0, \langle\langle e, t\rangle, t\rangle}$ ranges over characteristic functions of sets of characteristic functions of sets of things in A, as the reader can determine by computing the possible denotation of expressions of type $\langle\langle e, t\rangle, t\rangle$. Thus this formula has the effect of saying that any set of characteristic functions (of sets of individuals) that contains the one denoted by B also contains the one denoted by M, and by reasoning parallel to that given for the first example, we see that this requires that B and M have the same denotation.

Such examples can obviously be extended to higher and higher types. What we *cannot* talk about in the language L_{type} is, for example, any set containing all sets that are not members of themselves, nor can we make any other such statement that would involve us in Russell's paradox. Such statements simply cannot be made in accord with the syntactic rules of L_{type}. To say that a set is not a member of itself would require a formula of the form

(4-5) $\neg c_{0,a}(c_{0,a})$

for some type a, and this cannot be a well-formed formula in L_{type}, no matter what a is.

PROBLEM (4-3) Consider the following formulas of L_{type}. For each formula, state in ordinary English what the formula asserts about the denotation of the constant $c_{0,\langle\langle e,t\rangle,t\rangle}$:

(i) $\forall v_{0,\langle e,t\rangle}[c_{0,\langle\langle e,t\rangle,t\rangle}(v_{0,\langle e,t\rangle}) \rightarrow \exists v_{0,e}[v_{0,\langle e,t\rangle}(v_{0,e})]]$

(ii) $\exists v_{0,e}\forall v_{0,\langle e,t\rangle}[c_{0,\langle\langle e,t\rangle,t\rangle}(v_{0,\langle e,t\rangle}) \rightarrow [v_{0,\langle e,t\rangle}(v_{0,e})]]$

In (iii) we use "$\exists!u\phi$" to mean "there is exactly one u such that ϕ"; we do not bother to give a precise semantic rule here.

(iii) $\exists!v_{0,e}\forall v_{0,\langle e,t\rangle}[c_{0,\langle\langle e,t\rangle,t\rangle}(v_{0,\langle e,t\rangle}) \leftrightarrow [v_{0,\langle e,t\rangle}(v_{0,e})]]$

The recursive definition of types in L_{type} also provides for other new categories besides those denoting sets of successively more complicated sets. To give the reader some feel for the possibilities of new categories and interpretations of expressions in these categories that are available in L_{type}, but not in first-order logic, we will consider a few illustrative examples.

First, we take the category $\langle\langle e,t\rangle,\langle e,t\rangle\rangle$. According to the syntactic rules of L_{type}, expressions of this category would combine with one-place predicates. Accordingly, we will call them ***predicate modifiers.*** If ζ is any expression of this category and δ is a one-place predicate, then the expression $\zeta(\delta)$ is a one-place predicate; consequently, if α is a term (member of ME_e), then $\zeta(\delta)(\alpha)$ is a formula. Semantically, predicate modifiers denote functions that (to speak in an intuitively natural metaphor for talking about functions) "take in a function in $\{0,1\}^A$ and spit out another function in $\{0,1\}^A$." Though we will eventually be most interested in non-logical constants of type $\langle\langle e,t\rangle,\langle e,t\rangle\rangle$, it will probably be easier for the reader to get an intuitive grasp of how the semantics for expressions of this type will work if we instead examine a logical constant of this type – that is, one for which the denotation is explicitly determined by a rule. Probably the only useful logical constant of this type that we would want to consider is one we will call **non** (after the English derivational prefix of this phonological shape which attaches to adjectives to form new adjectives as in *non-active* from *active, non-evident* from *evident,* etc.) It does not of course attach to true verbs, but in any case, we are simply using **non** for purposes of illustration and are not suggesting it as an analysis of an English morpheme. The denotation of **non** would be specified in the following way:

(4-6) $[\![\textbf{non}]\!]^{M,g}$ is that function h from $D_{\langle e,t\rangle}$ into $D_{\langle e,t\rangle}$ such that for any k in $D_{\langle e,t\rangle}$ and any individual e in A, $[h(k)](e) = 1$ iff $k(e) = 0$, and $[h(k)](e) = 0$ iff $k(e) = 1$.

This unwieldly definition simply says that the denotation of **non** is a function which takes any (characteristic function of a) set included in A and turns it into (the characteristic function of) the complement of that set relative to A. (Later in this chapter we will introduce lambda expressions, which provide a means for stating rules like (4-6) quite simply and concisely.)

In effect **non** is a new kind of "negation." (Some might prefer to call **non** "verb phrase negation" as opposed to "sentence negation," though this would be hazardous since people who use these terms are often not very explicit as to what the semantic consequences of this distinction are.)

PROBLEM (4-4) Assume a model in which there are just two individuals. How many members are there in $D_{\langle e,t\rangle}$? Write the function h (as in (4-6)) which is the semantic value of **non** with respect to this model.

PROBLEM (4-5) Define a logical constant of type $\langle\langle e, \langle e, t\rangle\rangle, \langle e, \langle e, t\rangle\rangle\rangle$ which "operates" on two-place predicates analogously to the way **non** works on one-place predicates; i.e., regarding the denotation of a two-place predicate as a set of ordered pairs, the new logical constant will operate on this predicate to produce the complement of that set of ordered pairs.

Would it be possible to do away with the negation operator $\neg$ in favor of the predicate modifier **non**? It would not, unless we are prepared to let *every* correspond sometimes to $\exists$ (as it would have to in *Not everyone is bald*, which is understood as equivalent to $\exists x \neg B(x)$) and sometimes to $\forall$ (as in *Everyone is bald*), since the meaning of $\neg\forall x B(x)$ cannot be represented with **non** and $\forall$. As both the negation operator and the rule for universal quantification make formulas from other formulas, the two "operations" can be performed on a formula in either order; consequently, the appropriate scope difference between the two formulas can be represented. Since **non** attaches only to predicates, it is not possible to represent this distinction with **non**; we can only have $\forall x\,\textbf{non}(B)(x)$ (corresponding to English "Everyone is non-bald"), which is semantically equivalent to $\forall x \neg B(x)$ by our rules. Neither $\textbf{non}(\forall x B)(x)$ nor $\textbf{non}(\forall x B(x))$ is syntactically well-formed and thus neither could be given meaningful interpretations by our semantic rules.

Despite the fact that **non** is somewhat less flexible than $\neg$, there are apparently situations in English where the category of predicate modifiers can be shown to be necessary on semantic grounds, just as $\neg$ was shown to be necessary to capture a distinction that English makes. Such cases have been discussed both by Thomason and Stalnaker (1973) and, with different examples, by Cresswell (1973). Discussion of these cases will involve us in some intricacies of English syntax, however, and is best postponed until later.

For further illustration of categories not found in first-order logic we present two constants which Richmond Thomason would call "relation reducers." These will illustrate the type $\langle\langle e, \langle e, t\rangle\rangle, \langle e, t\rangle\rangle$. Expressions of this type must by definition combine with expressions of type $\langle e, \langle e, t\rangle\rangle$ (which is the type of two-place predicates) to give expressions of type $\langle e, t\rangle$ (one-place predicates). Since two-place predicates denote *relations* (i.e, they denote ordered pairs of individuals, even though we may represent this alternatively through the use of functions), these new constants will "reduce" a relation to a predicate.

Consider now on the one hand the correspondence between English sentences of the form *x eats y* and sentences of the form *x eats,* and on the other the correspondence between *x loves y* and *y is loved.* Obviously, the second sentence form in each pair is parasitic on the first in some way, for *x eats* will be true for some value of *x* just in case there is some value of *y* for which it is true that *x eats y*; likewise, *y is loved* will be true for some value of *y* just in case *x loves y* is true for some value for *x*. In transformational grammar, the relations between these respective forms of sentences are treated by the transformation of *Indefinite Object Deletion* in the first case and by a combination of the *Passive Transformation* and a transformation deleting "*by*-phrases" in the second. However, let us temporarily ignore this analysis and consider for illustrative purposes how two logical constants might perform the "reduction" of a two-place predicate to a one-place predicate that these English sentences superficially seem to evidence. Accordingly, we introduce the two constants R_o and R_s of type $\langle\langle e, \langle e, t\rangle\rangle, \langle e, t\rangle\rangle$. ($R_o$ is so-named because it "knocks off" the "object" of a two-place predicate; R_s "knocks off" the "subject".) The denotations of these constants are specified as follows:

(4-7) $[\![R_o]\!]^{M,g}$ is that function h from $D_{\langle e, \langle e, t\rangle\rangle}$ into $D_{\langle e, t\rangle}$ such that for all functions k in $D_{\langle e, \langle e, t\rangle\rangle}$ and all individuals e in A,

$h(k)(e) = 1$ iff there is some individual e' in A such that $k(e')(e) = 1$.

(4-8) $[\![R_s]\!]^{M,g}$ is that function h from $D_{\langle e, \langle e, t\rangle\rangle}$ into $D_{\langle e, t\rangle}$ such that for all functions k in $D_{\langle e, \langle e, t\rangle\rangle}$ and for all individuals e in A, $h(k)(e) = 1$ iff there is some individual e' in A such that $k(e)(e') = 1$.

These definitions are a bit tedious to decipher at first, but they are nevertheless completely precise. (Once we have lambda expressions at our disposal, it will be quite easy to state such definitions.) These constants do, as promised, take a two-place predicate and produce from it a one-place predicate which will be true of an individual just in case the former two-place predicate would have been true of the individual and some other individual, where these two individuals were in the appropriate "subject-object" relation or "object-subject" relation specified by the two-place predicate. In terms of the denotations of the two-place predicates, each of these constants can be said to take a relation (set of ordered pairs) and form from it a set of individuals by taking all the individuals that appear as first member of one of the ordered pairs in the relation (in the case of R_o), or by taking all the individuals that appear as second member of one of the ordered pairs in the relation (in the case of R_s).

Thus a sentence $R_o(L)(j)$ will be logically equivalent to $\exists y L(y)(j)$, and a sentence $R_s(L)(j)$ will be logically equivalent to $\exists y L(j)(y)$.

PROBLEM (4-6) Assume (3-1) as a partial model for L_{type}. How many members are there in $D_{\langle e, \langle e, t\rangle\rangle}$? What are the values of $R_o(K)$, $R_o(L)$, $R_s(K)$, and $R_s(L)$ according to this model? What are the values of $[R_o(K)](j)$ and $[R_s(L)](m)$?

PROBLEM (4-7) The operators R_s and R_o were prompted by the observation of the relationship in meaning of the verbs in *Mary saw John* and *John was seen* and in *Mary ate lunch* and *Mary ate*, respectively. Yet a third kind of relationship among verbs can be seen by comparing the meaning of the verb in *The barber shaved John* with that in *The barber shaved* (which means that the barber shaved himself), or by comparing *John dressed the child* with *John dressed* (meaning John dressed himself). Suppose we were to introduce a constant R_r, also of type $\langle\langle e, \langle e, t\rangle\rangle, \langle e, t\rangle\rangle$, that would produce one-place predicates with this sort of meaning. Write the semantic rule for R_r.

III. LAMBDA ABSTRACTION AND THE LANGUAGE L_λ

We will now expand the language L_{type} by adding a new variable binder which we will call a *lambda operator* (or λ-operator). This "operator" is also known as an *abstraction operator, set abstractor,* or simply a *binder.*

The reader is probably familiar with the way sets are sometimes specified by the so-called *predicate notation,* as in the following examples:

(4-9) $\{x \mid x$ is a state of the U.S. having a Pacific coast.$\}$

(4-10) $\{x \mid 3 < x < 7\}$

(4-9) names a set containing California, Oregon, Washington, Alaska and Hawaii as members, while (4-10) is intended to represent the set of numbers greater than 3 but less than 7. The only requirements for this way of naming sets are that we have a sentence containing a variable in a language we understand clearly (English in the first example, the quasi-formal "language" of arithmetic in the second) and that we have a convention for marking which variable (in case there might be more than one in the sentence) is the key one for determining which set is to be indicated; in the above notation the variable written to the left of the vertical line indicates this. (Sometimes ":" replaces the vertical line.) Of course, there is no reason why we couldn't name sets in this way using formulas of a formalized artificial language in place of sentences of English, as long as we have already supplied an adequate interpretation of that language. In fact, we will do just this by adding the lambda operator to L_{type}. Instead of the notation above, we will write either

(4-11) $\lambda x[\ldots x \ldots]$

or equivalently

(4-12) $\hat{x}[\ldots x \ldots]$

for the expression specifying a set. Here, $\ldots x \ldots$ stands for the formula of L_{type} to which the lambda operator is attached. (Brackets will sometimes be omitted when no ambiguity can result and will sometimes be gratuitously inserted to aid perspicuity.) In L_{type} we are systematically identifying characteristic functions with sets, so we will continue this practice with the sets whose characteristic functions are denoted by expressions formed with the aid of the lambda operator. If ϕ is a formula, then $\lambda x\phi$ will denote a set – intuitively, this function will characterize the set specified by ϕ with respect to the variable x. (We would more properly refer to the symbol λ as a *functional abstractor* than as a *set abstractor*.) For example, with respect to a model in which L denotes the relation of loving and j denotes a (particular) individual John, the abstract

(4-13) $\lambda x[L(x)(j)]$

will denote (the characteristic function of) the set of individuals that John loves, whereas

(4-14) $\lambda x[L(j)(x)]$

will denote (the characteristic function of) the set of individuals that love John.

As abstracts of the sort illustrated above will have the same kinds of denotations as the one-place predicates of L_{type}, we will want to classify these abstracts syntactically as members of the type $\langle e, t\rangle$. This means that they will combine with terms to form formulas just as any other one-place predicate does; indeed, we may refer to them as *predicate abstracts.* The expression $\lambda x[L(j)(x)]$ can be read in English as "is an x such that $[L(j)(x)]$." Thus since $\lambda x[L(x)(j)]$ is a one-place predicate, then

(4-15) $\lambda x[L(x)(j)](m)$

will be a formula (member of ME_t) in our newly expanded language. This might be read as "m is an x such that $[L(x)(j)]$." Intuitively, this ought to be an equivalent but more complicated way of saying

(4-16) $L(m)(j)$,

and in fact it will turn out that these two formulas are logically equivalent by the formal semantic rules we will give for lambda operators. Likewise,

(4-17) $\lambda x[L(m)(x)](j)$

(which may be read "j is an x such that $[L(m)(x)]$") is another formula equivalent to these two formulas. The rule that a formula of the form

(4-18) $\lambda x[\ldots x \ldots](\alpha)$

may be converted to a logically equivalent formula of the form

(4-19) $[\ldots \alpha \ldots]$

(or vice versa) is called the principle of *lambda conversion* (following Church 1940, where a formal calculus containing lambda operators was first developed). Here, the second formula $[\ldots \alpha \ldots]$ must be understood as the result of replacing *all* free occurrences of the variable x in the first formula $[\ldots x \ldots]$ with α. Thus the formula

(4-20) $\lambda x[B(x) \wedge M(x)](j)$

becomes by lambda conversion

(4-21) $[B(j) \wedge M(j)]$

but not $[B(j) \wedge M(x)]$.

PROBLEM (4-8) Use λ-conversion to simplify the following and, where possible, classify the resulting expressions as true or false:

$\lambda x[2x + 3 = 13](5)$
$\lambda y[2x + 3y = 15](5)$
$\lambda x[4x^2 - 2x + 5 = 140](7)$
$\lambda x[\forall y[y < 7 \rightarrow x > (2y - x)](11)$

With this intuitive idea of the interpretation of lambda abstraction in mind, we now turn to the formal statement of the syntactic and semantic rules for the lambda operator. We will assume that all the syntactic and semantic definitions for L_{type} are to be repeated for L_λ, to which the following will be added:

(4-22) Syn C.10 If $\phi \in ME_t$ and $u \in Var_e$, then $\lambda u[\phi] \in ME_{\langle e,\, t\rangle}$.

(Note: as indicated earlier we will sometimes omit brackets in these formulas for convenience; e.g. we will write $\lambda u[\phi \wedge \psi]$ instead of $\lambda u[[\phi \wedge \psi]]$, etc.) Since the lambda operator, like the existential and universal quantifiers, serves to bind occurrences of a particular variable, the semantic rule will likewise make reference to an assignment of values to variables distinct from the basic assignment g relative to which denotation is being defined.

(4-23) Sem 10. If $\phi \in ME_t$ and $u \in Var_e$, then $[\![\lambda u \phi]\!]^{M,\, g}$ is that function h from A into $\{0, 1\}$ such that for all individuals e in A, $h(e) = 1$ iff $[\![\phi]\!]^{M,\, g^e_u} = 1$, and $h(e) = 0$ otherwise.

This definition might be a little hard to grasp on first reading but can be made clearer by examples. Suppose we want to find out the denotation of $\lambda x L(x)(j)$ with respect to M and some assignment g. Then we can understand the definition in (4-23), somewhat metaphorically, as an instruction concerning how to "construct" the function h (the denotation of the λ-expression) by systematically examining various variable assignments g_x^e and then evaluating $L(x)(j)$ with respect to each of these and M. Specifically, we want to go through the domain of individuals A one at a time and consider for each of these a variable assignment that assigns that individual to the variable x. For each such variable assignment g_x^e we evaluate $[\![L(x)(j)]\!]^{M,g_x^e}$; this truth-value will be the value of the function h for that member of A. From the model M which we specified in (3-1) we will need to recall only that $A = \{a, b, c\}$, $F(j) = a$, and $F(L)$ is:

(4-24)
$$\begin{bmatrix} a \rightarrow \begin{bmatrix} a \rightarrow 0 \\ b \rightarrow 1 \\ c \rightarrow 1 \end{bmatrix} \\ \\ b \rightarrow \begin{bmatrix} a \rightarrow 0 \\ b \rightarrow 0 \\ c \rightarrow 0 \end{bmatrix} \\ \\ c \rightarrow \begin{bmatrix} a \rightarrow 1 \\ b \rightarrow 0 \\ c \rightarrow 1 \end{bmatrix} \end{bmatrix}$$

Since the domain A contains only three individuals, we have to perform only three "computations". We check the variable assignment g' like g except that $g'(x) = a$ (i.e., g_x^a) and find that $[\![L(x)(j)]\!]^{M,g_x^a}$, which is equal to $F(L)(a)(a)$, is 0. Therefore $h(a) = 0$. We next check the assignment g' like g except that $g'(x) = b$ (i.e., g_x^b) and find that $[\![L(x)(j)]\!]^{M,g_x^b}$, which is $F(L)(b)(a)$, is also 0. Therefore $h(b) = 0$. Last we check the assignment g' like g except that $g'(x) = c$ (i.e., g_x^c) and find that $[\![L(x)(j)]\!]^{M,g_x^c}$, which is $F(L)(c)(a), = 1$. Therefore, $h(c) = 1$, and we now have the complete function h: it maps a into 0, b into 0, and c into 1.

PROBLEM (4-9) Assuming the model given in (3-1) for those constants of L_1 which are contained in L_{type}, show that the denotation of $\lambda x[B(x) \leftrightarrow L(j)(x)]$ is the function that maps each individual in A into 1.

A word is in order about "vacuous binding" with lambda operators. Given the very general way we have stated the syntactic rule for forming predicate abstracts, there is nothing to prevent the formation of abstracts such as $\lambda x[L(j)(m)]$ or $\lambda y[L(x)(j)]$, in which the lambda operator doesn't bind any variable. Moreover, such predicates can be combined with arguments to form formulas, e.g. $\lambda x[L(j)(m)](d)$ or $\lambda y[L(x)(j)](d)$. If we examine (4-23) carefully we see that $[\![\lambda x L(j)(m)]\!]^{M,g}$ should be a function depending on the denotation of $L(j)(m)$ as it varies according to the different values that can be assigned to x. But since x does not occur in $L(j)(m)$ at all, the values of this function will not "vary" in any way but will give the same value (namely, $[\![L(j)(m)]\!]^{M,g}$) no matter what is is applied to. It is thus the constant function which gives $[\![L(j)(m)]\!]^{M,g}$ for any argument. The same is true of a vacuously abstracted formula containing a free variable, such as $\lambda y[L(x)(j)]$, since (4-23) tells us for this expression to take into account assignments of values to variables that differ from the basic g *only* in the value assigned to y. Here again, whatever the function denoted by this expression is applied to, it will receive the same value (namely $[\![L(x)(j)]\!]^{M,g}$). This means that $\lambda x[L(j)(m)](d)$ will have the same denotation as $L(j)(m)$ for any model and assignment g, and $\lambda y[L(x)(m)](d)$ will have the same denotation as $L(x)(m)$ for any model and assignment g.

At this point we will make a two-fold generalization of lambda abstraction as defined above. Given the type-theoretic definition of the categories of our language and the kind of model-theoretic interpretation of lambda abstraction we have specified, there is no reason why we should limit ourselves to abstraction over formulas; we can just as well attach a lambda operator to expressions of *any* type. And given that we have a higher-order language with variables of all types and a means of interpreting them, there is no reason why we should not use a variable of any type in forming an abstract. The revised syntactic rule for the lambda operator will read like this:

(4-25) Syn C.10. If $\alpha \in ME_a$ and $u \in Var_b$, then $\lambda u[\alpha] \in ME_{\langle b, a\rangle}$.

The earlier lambda abstraction rule is an instance of this schema, since it took an expression of type t and a variable of type e to give an abstract of type $\langle e, t\rangle$. But now let us consider some other examples. Suppose we have a one-place predicate (an expression of type $\langle e, t\rangle$) containing a free variable – for example $L(x)$. By abstracting over it with a variable of type e we produce the expression $\lambda x L(x)$, which by (4-24) above is an expression of type $\langle e, \langle e, t\rangle\rangle$ – a "two-place predicate abstract." Or suppose we take a formula containing a variable of type $\langle e, t\rangle$ (a predicate variable), such as $[v_{0,\langle e,t\rangle}(j) \wedge M(b)]$, and abstract over it with respect to this variable. We get the expression $\lambda v_{0,\langle e,t\rangle}[v_{0,\langle e,t\rangle}(j) \wedge M(b)]$, which will be of type $\langle\langle e, t\rangle, t\rangle$ – a "predicate-of-predicates abstract". Moreover, there is no reason why we should not abstract over another abstract. If we take the formula

$L(x)(y)$ and do abstraction once we can get an expression $\lambda y[L(x)(y)]$ of type $\langle e, t\rangle$. (This expression will be equivalent to $L(x)$, as one can verify from Sem. 10, to be stated shortly.) Abstracting again, we can get $\lambda x[\lambda y[L(x)(y)]]$, which by (4-25) is of type $\langle e, \langle e, t\rangle\rangle$. Unlike single abstracts, there is not natural way of "reading" such a double abstract in English (though this one is equivalent to L), so these are a little harder to grasp intuitively. Nevertheless, they are perfectly cogent according to the rules given.

The revised semantic rule for this generalized lambda-abstraction rule will be this:

(4-26) Sem. 10. If $\alpha \in ME_a$ and $u \in Var_b$, then $[\![\lambda u[\alpha]]\!]^{M,g}$ is that function h from D_b into D_a such that for all objects k in D_b, $h(k)$ is equal to $[\![\alpha]\!]^{M,g_u^k}$.

(Note that the "objects" mentioned in this definition may be of various sorts depending on what D_b is: they might be members of A as in the case of the previous definition where we abstracted only over sentences – or they might be truth values or functions of some kind). Though this definition may be even harder to grasp intuitively than the previous semantic definition, we will not attempt to clarify it by examples. It should be sufficient for the reader to understand these more complicated abstracts by analogy to the special case of predicate abstracts discussed earlier.

In Frege's time, and in Frege's own writings, there was widespread confusion about expressions like $x^2 + 2$. This expression was considered on the one hand to be the name for the number obtained by squaring x and adding 2 to the result. But it was ambiguously taken also to name the function which maps any number x to the other number obtained in the fashion just described. Since this function is not the same thing as any one (or, for that matter, the set of all) of its outputs, the confusion obviously had the potential to cause considerable havoc. This it did in fact do.

Eventually it was realized that the source of the problems was simply equivocation between the number named by such an expression and the function canonically related to the expression by associating each number x with $x^2 + 2$. Church proposed a simple way of constructing a new name to stand for the function. He simply prefixed to the number-naming expression the symbols λx. Thus the function $\lambda x[x^2 + 2]$ maps any number x to the number $x^2 + 2$; it maps 3, for instance, to $3^2 + 2$, i.e., to 11. The beauty of this scheme lies in its generality as well as its simplicity. One can easily distinguish the function $\lambda x[x^2 + y]$, which maps 3 to $9 + y$, from the function $\lambda y[x^2 + y]$, which maps 3 to $x^2 + 3$. Furthermore, since $\lambda x[x^2 + y]$ names something, one can further prefix λy to obtain a name for a function whose values are other functions. This function $\lambda y[\lambda x[x^2 + y]]$ maps 3 to a function which maps 5 to $5^2 + 3$, and maps 5 to a function which maps 3 to $3^2 + 5$.

PROBLEM (4-10) Let $h(p, d)$ be the height of p on day d. Describe the following functions in words. (h: Persons × Days → Numbers).

(i) $\lambda p\ [h(p, \textit{April}\ 2, 1980)]$
(ii) $\lambda d\ [h(\textit{Mickey Mantle}, d)]$
(iii) $\lambda p\ [\lambda d\ [h(p, d)]](\textit{Mickey Mantle})$
(iv) $\lambda p\ [\lambda d\ [h(p, d](\textit{April}\ 2, 1980)]$
(v) $\lambda d\ [\lambda p\ [h(p, d)]](\textit{April}\ 2, 1980)$
(vi) $\lambda p\ [\lambda d\ [h(p, d)]]$
(vii) $\lambda d\ [\lambda p\ [h(p, d)]]$

PROBLEM (4-11) Describe in words $\lambda f[f(2) + 1]$, when f ranges over functions from integers to integers. (This problem may be somewhat challenging.)

By means of the lambda operator, we can not only define the constant **non** of (4-6) quite simply, but we can even heuristically discover the definition of this constant in L_λ. Recall that the type of **non** is $\langle\langle e, t\rangle, \langle e, t\rangle\rangle$ and that it maps any set of individuals to the complementary set; formally, this is just to say that **non** satisfies the following condition:

$$\forall x\, \forall v_{0, \langle e, t\rangle} [\mathbf{non}(v_{0, \langle e, t\rangle})(x) \leftrightarrow \neg v_{0, \langle e, t\rangle}(x)].$$

Thus

$$\forall v_{0, \langle e, t\rangle} [\lambda x [\mathbf{non}(v_{0, \langle e, t\rangle})(x)] = \lambda x [\neg v_{0, \langle e, t\rangle}(x)]],$$

which is equivalent to

$$\forall v_{0, \langle e, t\rangle} [\mathbf{non}(v_{0, \langle e, t\rangle}) = \lambda x [\neg v_{0, \langle e, t\rangle}(x)]]$$

since $\lambda x [\mathbf{non}(v_{0, \langle e, t\rangle})(x)]$ is equivalent to $\mathbf{non}(v_{0, \langle e, t\rangle})$. Hence

$$\lambda v_{0, \langle e, t\rangle} [\mathbf{non}(v_{0, \langle e, t\rangle})] = \lambda v_{0, \langle e, t\rangle} [\lambda x [\neg v_{0, \langle e, t\rangle}(x)]],$$

i.e.,

$$\mathbf{non} = \lambda v_{0, \langle e, t\rangle} [\lambda x [\neg v_{0, \langle e, t\rangle}(x)]].$$

This equivalence provides a completely satisfactory definition of **non**. If we use it, together with the principle of lambda-conversion, to calculate the value of say **non** (B), we find that **non** (B) =

$$\lambda v_{0,\langle e,t\rangle}[\lambda x[\neg v_{0,\langle e,t\rangle}(x)]](B) = \lambda x[\neg B(x)],$$

which denotes the set of individuals that do not belong to the set denoted by B – just as we desired.

PROBLEM (4-12) Show that the lambda expression

$$\lambda v_{0,\langle e,\langle e,t\rangle\rangle}[\lambda x[\exists y v_{0,\langle e,\langle e,t\rangle\rangle}(y)(x)]]$$

is equivalent to the "object-deletion" operator R_o defined in (4-7).

PROBLEM (4-13) Use lambda expressions to define the "subject-deletion" operator R_s of (4-8) and the "reflexive-object-deletion" R_r of Problem (4-7).

Let us state explicitly the principle of lambda conversion, which holds for the generalized definition of lambda-abstraction, using the notation $\phi(x/\alpha)$ to stand for the result of replacing all free occurrences of x in ϕ by α. The rule of lambda conversion states roughly that any expression $\lambda u[\phi](\alpha)$ is logically equivalent to $\phi(u/\alpha)$ (i.e. they have the same denotation in any possible model for L.) To be more precise, we must put further restrictions on this principle to insure that free variables do not, as it were, become "accidentally" bound in the process of lambda-conversion: $\lambda u[\phi](\alpha)$ will be logically equivalent to $\phi(u/\alpha)$ provided that any bound variables occurring in ϕ are distinct from any free variables that occur in α. Thus to take an example; $\lambda v_{0,\langle e,t\rangle}[\forall x v_{0,\langle e,t\rangle}(x)](L(x))$ cannot be converted to $\forall x[L(x)(x)]$, because the variable x which has now become bound in this last formula had occurred free in $L(x)$.[2] Also to be excluded by this restriction is the case of $\lambda u[\phi](\alpha)$ where α *is* a variable bound in ϕ; thus $\lambda y[\forall x L(y)(x)](x)$ may not be converted to $\forall x L(x)(x)$.

It should be noted that the principle of lambda conversion is in the present context not a primitive "rule of logical equivalence" or "rule of inference" in a deductive system (for we are not constructing such a system and indeed cannot construct a complete and sound one for higher order languages), but rather is a principle about the semantic interpretation of expressions that holds purely as a consequence of (4-26) and the other semantic rules of L_λ. Still less is it to be considered anything like a "meaning preserving transformation" operating somehow in the syntactic derivation of formulas of L_λ. It will be useful, however, to appeal to this principle to "reduce" complex expressions that result in the process of interpreting English to shorter, more perspicuous but nevertheless completely equivalent expressions. This is not the place to prove formally that lambda conversion follows from (4-26), though for the mathematically inclined it is not hard to see how such a proof can be constructed, and some readers may find it interesting to do so. (It would be necessary to do this by induction on the complexity of expressions of L_λ: that is, a metric of complexity would be defined for expressions of L_λ based on the recursive syntactic rules of L_λ. Then it would be shown that lambda conversion holds for the simplest expressions of L_λ and, furthermore, that if the principle holds for expressions of complexity n, then it holds for expressions of complexity $n + 1$.) For more complete discussion of lambda conversion the reader is referred to the discussion in Cresswell 1973, pp. 84-92 or to Church 1940.

Lambda expressions are a tool that can be used in discovering the semantic value one wants to assign to expressions. We saw simple examples of this in connection with **non**, R_o, etc.

Now we take up a more dramatic example – in fact, the very one that gave Montague's *Proper Treatment of Quantification in Ordinary English* its title. In the preceding chapter we had to distort the syntax of English drastically in order to assign correct truth conditions to sentences containing quantified *NPs* like *some man, every woman,* etc. In fact, we were unable to treat these collocations as *NPs* precisely because we did not know what semantic value could be assigned to them to yield correct results. Recall that the main difficulty in "translating" English into symbolic logic systematically is the fact that English sentences like the following have *NP* + *VP* syntactic structure, but their usual translations into ordinary predicate logic do no have this form at all and are not all parallel.

(4-27)	*English sentences:*	*Usual translation into logic:*
	(1) Every student walks	$\forall x[S(x) \rightarrow W(x)]$
	(2) Every student likes Mary	$\forall x[S(x) \rightarrow L(m)(x)]$
	(3) Some student walks	$\exists x[S(x) \wedge W(x)]$
	(4) Some student likes Mary	$\exists x[S(x) \wedge L(m)(x)]$
	(5) No student walks	$\neg\exists x[S(x) \wedge W(x)]$
	(6) No student likes Mary	$\neg\exists x[S(x) \wedge L(m)(x)]$

Strange as it may seem, it is an old idea in logic that perhaps the English sentences (1)-(6) *do* make parallel assertions of a subject-predicate form, though these assertions are not about individuals directly, but are rather assertions about the property of walking or of liking Mary: (1) says that the property of walking has the second-order property of being true of every student, (3) says that it has the property of being true of some student, and (5) says that it has the property of being true of no student. Lambda expressions can help in making this idea precise.

Let us abbreviate $v_{0, \langle e, t \rangle}$ as P, for convenience, and let P denote what the *VP* of sentence (1) or (2) denotes. Then clearly the sentence is true if and only if $\forall x[S(x) \rightarrow P(x)]$ is; the same holds true, in fact, of any sentence with *every student* as subject. So we can take the denotation of $\lambda P \forall x[S(x) \rightarrow P(x)]$ as the definition we seek of the semantic value of *every student*, provided that we interpret a sentence of the form *every student VP* as having the semantic value obtained by applying the semantic value of *every student* to that of the *VP*. This is so because lambda conversion guarantees that

(1′) $\lambda P \forall x[S(x) \rightarrow P(x)](W)$

(2′) $\lambda P \forall x[S(x) \rightarrow P(x)](L(m))$

are equivalent to the formulas in (1) and (2) of (4-27). Similarly we can define the semantic value of *some student* as $\lambda P \exists x[S(x) \wedge P(x)]$ and that of *no student* as $\lambda P \neg \exists x[S(x) \wedge P(x)]$.

If the semantic value of sentences of the form *NP* + *VP* is to be obtained by applying the semantic value of the *NP* to that of the *VP*, then what could we say about sentences (7) and (8)?

(4-28)

English sentences:	*Usual translation into logic:*
(7) John walks	$W(j)$
(8) John likes Mary	$L(m)(j)$

It will not do to define the semantic value of *NP John* as j, since the latter expression is of type e and thus does not denote a function of the type that we need to apply. A moment's reflection, however, shows that since a sentence of the form *John VP* whose *VP* denotes what P does is true iff $P(j)$ is, we can define the *NP John* as having the semantic value of $\lambda P[P(j)]$. This analyses (7) as saying, in effect, that the property of walking has the second-order property of being true of John, which is a complicated but completely equivalent way of saying that John walks. The flexibility of the higher-order language L_λ enables us to express these statements straightforwardly. And, crucially, by taking advantage of the lambda operators, we can express the second-order properties under discussion as abstracts. Now all of the sentences (1) through (8) can be seen to have a uniform subject-predicate form.

We can use lambda expressions further to analyze the semantic value of quantified *NP*s into a determiner meaning and a noun meaning, exactly paralleling the syntax of the phrases. Note that each of the *NP*s in (4-29) is to have the semantic value of the corresponding lambda expression.

(4-29)	*English NPs:*	*Lambda expressions:*
	(1) Every student	$\lambda P \forall x [S(x) \rightarrow P(x)]$
	(2) Every man	$\lambda P \forall x [M(x) \rightarrow P(x)]$
	(3) Some student	$\lambda P \exists x [S(x) \wedge P(x)]$
	(4) Some man	$\lambda P \exists x [M(x) \wedge P(x)]$
	(5) No student	$\lambda P \neg \exists x [S(x) \wedge P(x)]$
	(6) No man	$\lambda P \neg \exists x [M(x) \wedge P(x)]$

Note further that these lambda expressions are equivalent, by lambda conversion, to (1′) through (6′) – where Q abbreviates $v_{1,\langle e,t \rangle}$.

(1′) $\lambda Q [\lambda P \forall x [Q(x) \rightarrow P(x)]] (S)$

(2′) $\lambda Q [\lambda P \forall x [Q(x) \rightarrow P(x)]] (M)$

(3′) $\lambda Q [\lambda P \exists x [Q(x) \wedge P(x)]] (S)$

(4′) $\lambda Q [\lambda P \exists x [Q(x) \wedge P(x)]] (M)$

(5′) $\lambda Q [\lambda P \neg \exists x [Q(x) \wedge P(x)]] (S)$

(6′) $\lambda Q [\lambda P \neg \exists x [Q(x) \wedge P(x)]] (M)$

Thus we may define the semantic value of *every* as that of

$$\lambda Q [\lambda P \forall x [Q(x) \rightarrow P(x)]]$$

of *some* as that of

$$\lambda Q [\lambda P \exists x [Q(x) \wedge P(x)]]$$

and of *no* as that of

$$\lambda Q [\lambda P \neg \exists x [Q(x) \wedge P(x)]] .$$

This double abstract gives determiners the type $\langle\langle e, t\rangle, \langle\langle e, t\rangle, t\rangle\rangle$. They will combine with a noun expression of type $\langle e, t\rangle$ to give a noun phrase, of type $\langle\langle e, t\rangle, t\rangle$. Recalling that $\langle a, \langle a, t\rangle\rangle$ is the type of relations between two things of type a, we see that determiners are relations between two sets of individuals.

Every, for example, is the subset relation; i.e., *Every*$(Q)(P)$ holds true just in case Q is a subset of P.

Sentence (1), (3), and (5) in (4-27) might be represented by the formulas (1″), (3″), and (5″) respectively:

(1″) $\lambda Q[\lambda P \forall x[Q(x) \rightarrow P(x)]](S)(W)$

(3″) $\lambda Q[\lambda P \exists x[Q(x) \wedge P(x)]](S)(W)$

(5″) $\lambda Q[\lambda P \neg\exists x[Q(x) \wedge P(x)]](S)(W)$

When formulas of L_λ reach this complexity, their syntactic organization becomes a little hard to grasp at first sight. It might be helpful to draw "phrase markers" for such formulas, with the appropriate type entered as the node label of each sub-tree. Thus the overall structure of (1″) could be represented as the following tree:

(4-30)

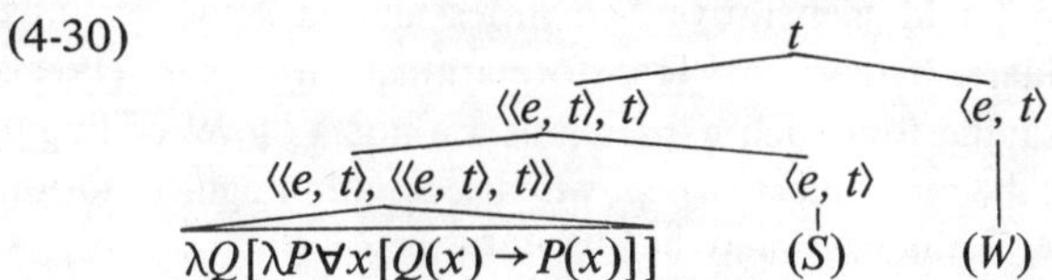

This reveals that (1″) indeed serves as a word-for-word and constituent-for-constituent representation of *Every student walks.* (An exact means for "translating" the sentence to this lambda expression has not been specified, of course.) If we wanted to represent in addition to this structure the internal structure of the determiner abstract in (1″), we would need the following more elaborate diagram:

(4-31)

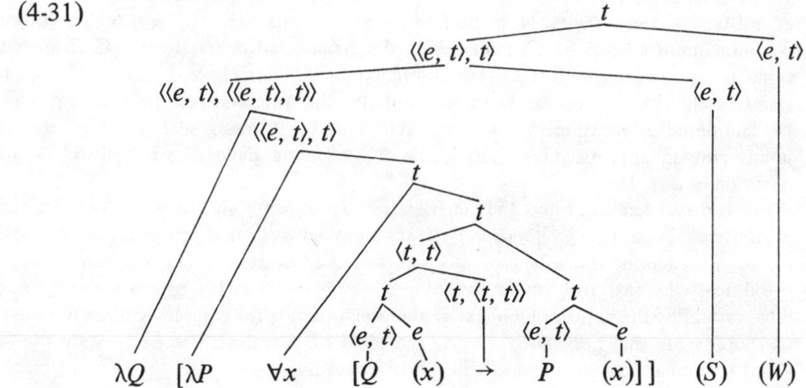

The reader might find it helpful occasionally to construct such phrase-markers for unusually complex expressions in order to be sure that their syntactic structure is correctly understood.

The usefulness of L_λ is obvious from this example. The lambda calculus can often be used to calculate what semantic values should be assigned to some syntactic constituent of a larger expression whose semantic value is known. The reader should not, however, carry away from this illustration the idea that in order to do this one needs to assign expressions of L_λ to natural language phrases as translations or logical forms in any official sense. Lambda expressions can be a very helpful way of giving the meaning of English words or phrases. But it is the semantic values of the lambda expressions, rather than the lambda expressions themselves, that we wish to identify with the semantic values of English expressions. Thus it is not necessary to regard L_λ as a level of linguistic representation, such as logical form is intended to be in Generative Semantics and in some versions of the Extended Standard Theory of Transformational Grammar. (Precisely what we mean by saying that such expressions are not a "level of linguistic representation" will become clear when we discuss Montague's notion of translation in Chapter 7 and especially in Chapter 8.)

EXERCISES

1. Assuming (3-1) as a partial model for L_λ, show that $\lambda P[\forall x[M(x) \rightarrow P(x)]](B)$ has the same semantic value as $\forall x[M(x) \rightarrow B(x)]$.

2. One approach to the model-theoretic treatment of English attributive adjectives assigns them to category $\langle e, t\rangle$ and thus makes their semantic values characteristic functions of sets of individuals. Then the semantic value of a complex common noun such as *red chair* would in effect be the intersection of the set of red entities with the set of entities that are chairs. Note that the syntactic rule used to form such a complex common noun cannot be an instance of the generalized syntactic rule C.2, since the types of the two expressions being combined here – namely $\langle e, t\rangle$ and $\langle e, t\rangle$ – do not stand in the relationship $\langle a, b\rangle$ to b. Similarly, the semantic rule here cannot simply be functional application. Write a syntactic rule for forming such complex common nouns and an appropriate semantic rule for assigning denotations to these complex common nouns.

3. It has been suggested that $\langle e, t\rangle$ is not an appropriate category for all English attributive adjectives, e.g., *good* and *clever*, inasmuch as a good pianist is not necessarily in the interaction of the set of pianists and the set of good entities. Show how one could deal with this problem by assigning such adjectives to the category $\langle\langle e, t\rangle, \langle e, t\rangle\rangle$. What would be the appropriate form of the semantic rule for complex common nouns of this sort? Note that necessarily every good pianist is a pianist. Use L_λ to state the fact about the semantic value of *good* which guarantees this.

4. Necessarily a fake gun is not a gun. Using the tools employed in Exercise 3, state the fact about the semantic value of *fake* which explains this observation. Note that a thing can be a fake gun and a piece of soap; in that case it cannot be a fake piece of soap. Why do these observations show that the semantic value of *fake* cannot be of type $\langle e, t\rangle$?

5. The syntactic rule that forms abstracts from an expression α and a variable u inserts brackets around α, thus, $\lambda u[\alpha]$. If the brackets had been omitted from this rule, the language L_λ would not be unambiguous.

(a) Demonstrate this by drawing two distinct tree diagrams in the manner of (4-31) for the expression $\lambda x \lambda y L(x)(y)(j)(m)$;

(b) Show that the expression in (a) reduces by lambda-conversion to two non-equivalent expressions depending on which tree structure is assigned;

(c) Show that by introducing brackets into the expression as we have done we get two unambiguous expressions corresponding to the two tree structures in (a).

NOTES

[1] Formally, one can take various positions on the status of the infinitely many "unused" types specified by (4-2). Cresswell (1973) takes the position that his formal language contains a infinite number of categories, of which all but a small finite number are simply *empty*. Montagûe uses a formal language that does have non-empty categories for all types, but as we shall see, it plays a rather indirect role in the semantics of English, while the syntax of English itself has expressions in only finitely many categories.

[2] Traditionally, lambda conversion is not *a* principle (or rule) but a *set* of principles (or rules) which include not only what we are calling lambda conversion but also a principle (or rule) of so-called *alphabetic variants.* This allows one to replace $\lambda u[\alpha]$ within any expression with $\lambda v[\alpha(u/v)]$, where u and v are variables of the same type, $\alpha(u/v)$ is the result of substituting v for all free occurrences of u, provided that v does not thereby become bound within α. This principle enables one to circumvent, in effect, the restriction on the first lambda conversion principle that no variable may be "accidentally" become bound in the process, since we can appeal to the principle of alphabetic variants to first convert a lambda expression into an equivalent one with a different variable, to which we then can *then* legitimately apply lambda conversion. Cf. Church (1940), Cresswell (1973) p. 89. The principle of alphabetic variants can easily be shown to follow from the semantic rules of L_λ. (Church, on the other hand, was constructing a "Lambda *Calculus,*" an uninterpreted formal system containing lambda operators. In his system, unlike ours, the principles of lambda conversion are primitive rules, not principles which are consequences of semantic definitions.)

CHAPTER 5

TENSE AND MODAL OPERATORS

I. TENSE OPERATORS AND THEIR INTERPRETATION

We are now ready to expand our semantic machinery in yet another way, this time in the direction of an *intensional* language – a language for which we provide a definition of denotation for all expressions not just for a single state of affairs but for many possible states of affairs. We will begin this expansion by considering the special case of tense operators and their interpretation. We choose to approach intensional languages via tense operators because the primitive model-theoretic notion needed to formalize the interpretation of these operators – namely, an ordered set which we will regard as the moments of time – is more intuitively natural than the primitive notions needed to formalize "possible states of affairs" in full generality. Tense operators, though, will illustrate the same formal techniques needed for the more general definitions.

Up to this point we have been assigning a truth value to a formula relative to a model "once and for all", thus ignoring the fact that many, if not most, sentences of natural languages may be now true, now false, as circumstances in the world change. Thus to understand a sentence such as *John is asleep*, it must be made clear to us implicitly or explicitly at what time it is intended to "apply," or else it gives us little useful information about the world. For a present tense sentence it suffices (generally) to know when the sentence was uttered, since present tense sentences (in one of their most common uses in English) are understood to describe the state of the world that obtains concurrent with the time of utterance. It will be most practical to begin by regarding all the existing formulas of our formal languages as "present tense" formulas and state their truth conditions relative to a moment of time. We first relativized the denotation (i.e., truth value) of formulas to an arbitrary model, then to a model and assignment of values to variables; now we will relativize their denotations to a model, value assignment, and to a *moment in time* (out of a given set of times). This given moment in time on which we base our definition can be intuitively regarded as analogous to the time of utterance of a natural language sentence, though of course we are not attempting to represent the process of uttering and of comprehending sentences, nor of any kinds of speech acts, in our semantic theory proper.

Accordingly, we will expand the definition of a model to include not only a domain of individuals A and an interpretation function F, but also a non-empty set I with a linear ordering imposed upon it (to be regarded intuitively as the set of moments in time of the model). We will use the symbol $<$ for this ordering, That is, $<$ is simply a *linear ordering* of the set I (i.e., a relation on I satisfying the conditions $\mathbf{i} \nless \mathbf{i}$, $[\mathbf{i}<\mathbf{j} \wedge \mathbf{j}<\mathbf{k}] \rightarrow \mathbf{i}<\mathbf{k}$, and $\mathbf{i}<\mathbf{j} \vee \mathbf{i}=\mathbf{j} \vee \mathbf{j}<\mathbf{i}$ for all $\mathbf{i}$, $\mathbf{j}$ and $\mathbf{k}$ in I). The expression $\mathbf{i}<\mathbf{i}'$ may be read "$\mathbf{i}$ is earlier than $\mathbf{i}'$" or equivalently, "$\mathbf{i}'$ is later than $\mathbf{i}$." Since we want to allow the truth values of formulas to come out different for different times, we must obviously allow the denotations of the non-logical constants to be different for various times. Thus the function F assigning a denotation to each non-logical constant "once and for all" will now become a function of two arguments, a constant and a member of I. For any constant α and any $\mathbf{i}$ in I, $F(\mathbf{i}, \alpha)$ is understood to be the denotation of α at the time $\mathbf{i}$. Of course, the denotation of certain non-logical constants may be allowed to be the same for all times in the model – in natural languages, names typically denote the same individual throughout time, but the denotation of predicates such as *is asleep* changes constantly.

Formally, we will define a *temporal model* for a language L as an ordered quadruple $\langle A, I, <, F\rangle$ such that A and I are any non-empty sets, $<$ is a linear ordering on I, and F is a function assigning to each pair consisting of a member of I and a non-logical constant of L an appropriate denotation (out of the set of possible denotations we allow for each category of non-logical constants in L). In the semantic rules we will uniformly replace each definition of $[\![\alpha]\!]^{M,g}$ with the definition $[\![\alpha]\!]^{M,\mathbf{i},g}$ – "the denotation of α relative to the model M, time $\mathbf{i}$, and value assignment g."

This kind of temporal model interpretation could be given for any of the languages we have discussed so far. To simplify discussion we will temporarily ignore the more complex languages and illustrate the discussion of time-relativized semantics (and tense operators below) with the simple language L_1.

For example, suppose we take $\langle A, I, <, F\rangle$ as a temporal model M for L_1, where $A = \{a, b, c\}$, $I = \{t_1, t_2, t_3\}$, $< = \{\langle t_1, t_2\rangle, \langle t_2, t_3\rangle, \langle t_1, t_3\rangle\}$, and F includes the following values:

$$F(t_1, d) = b \qquad F(t_2, d) = b \qquad F(t_3, d) = b$$

$$F(t_1, j) = a \qquad F(t_2, j) = a \qquad F(t_3, j) = a$$

$$F(t_1, M) = \{a, b, c\} \qquad F(t_2, M) = \{a, b\} \qquad F(t_3, M) = \{c\}.$$

Thus to illustrate, $[\![M(j)]\!]^{M,t_1,g} = 1$ (because $[\![j]\!]^{M,t_1,g}$ is in $[\![M]\!]^{M,t_1,g}$ and this in turn because $F(t_1, j)$ is in $F(t_1, M)$), while $[\![M(j)]\!]^{M,t_3,g}$ is 0 (because $F(t_3, j)$ is not in $F(t_3, M)$). That is, $M(j)$ is true at the earlier time t_1 (and "remains" true at t_2, as the reader can confirm) but becomes false later at t_3. Also, $[\![\forall x M(x)]\!]^{M,t_1,g} = 1$, but $[\![\forall x M(x)]\!]^{M,t_2,g} = 0$ and $[\![\forall x M(x)]\!]^{M,t_3,g} = 0$.

PROBLEM (5-1). Compute $[\![\forall x[M(x) \rightarrow M(j)]]\!]^{M,t_1,g}$. Do the same at t_2 and t_3.

The interesting thing about the temporal interpretations of natural languages is that all such languages have means for forming sentences that can be uttered at one time but are nevertheless about a situation that obtains at a different time, a time either earlier or later than the time of utterance. Perhaps the most obvious of these temporal indicators in a language like English – and the kind of temporal indicator which most logical studies have taken as a paradigm – are the *tenses*. The most common kind of *tense logic* is based on the assumption that the present tense can be taken as the starting point for sentences in all tenses. That is, a "present tense" formula is just a tenseless formula *simpliciter*, and other tenses – specifically, past, future, past perfect and future perfect – can be best explained as the application of a *tense operator* to a tenseless (i.e. present tense) formula. Thus to form a tensed language from L_1 we need to add only two operators: a *future tense operator* which we will symbolize as **F** and a *past tense operator* which we will symbolize as **P**. As for syntactic rules, we will simply say that if ϕ is any formula, then $\mathbf{F}\phi$ and $\mathbf{P}\phi$ are formulas. These are customarily read as "it will be the case that ϕ" and "it was the case that ϕ," respectively. (Actually, there is a slight problem in reading the formulas this way in English in that the English sequence-of-tense rules require that a past tense normally appear in the *that*- complement of these paraphrases whenever a past tense appears in the main clause, whereas we want to take ϕ to be a tenseless sentence. However, the literature on the sequence of tense phenomenon has made it clear that this tense in the complement clause is best regarded as a purely syntactic consequence of the tense in the higher clause; thus we take the sequence of tense problem to be a complex fact about English syntax that we will choose to ignore, not a deficiency in our construction of a tensed formal language per se.)

The semantic plausibility of this way of constructing pasts and futures out of presents comes from the fact that it is intuitively plausible to say that a sentence *John was asleep* is true relative to a time t (i.e., if it were uttered at t) just in case the present tense sentence *John is asleep* is true relative to some other time t', namely, relative to a time earlier than t. Likewise, a future tense sentence *John will be asleep* seems to be true relative to a time t just in case the present tense sentence *John is asleep* is true relative to a different t', but this time a t' later than t. Thus on this view the past and future tenses are construed as a means for "shifting" the ordinary truth conditions of a present tense (i.e. tenseless) sentence to a different point in time. This view leads to the following formal definitions, which we now add to the temporally interpreted L_1 to give the *tensed first-order language* L_{1t}:

Syn B.10. If ϕ is a formula, then $\mathbf{F}\phi$ is a formula.

Syn B.11. If ϕ is a formula, then $\mathbf{P}\phi$ is a formula.

Sem B.10. If ϕ is a formula, then $[\![\mathbf{F}\phi]\!]^{M,\mathbf{i},g} = 1$ iff there is some $\mathbf{i}'$ in I such that $\mathbf{i} < \mathbf{i}'$ and $[\![\phi]\!]^{M,\mathbf{i}',g} = 1$; otherwise, $[\![\mathbf{F}\phi]\!]^{M,\mathbf{i},g} = 0$.

Sem B.11. If ϕ is a formula, then $[\![\mathbf{P}\phi]\!]^{M,\mathbf{i},g} = 1$ iff there is some $\mathbf{i}'$ in I such that $\mathbf{i}' < \mathbf{i}$ and $[\![\phi]\!]^{M,\mathbf{i}',g} = 1$; otherwise, $[\![\mathbf{P}\phi]\!]^{M,\mathbf{i},g} = 0$.

(Note that these semantic definitions are exactly the same except that the first has $\mathbf{i} < \mathbf{i}'$ where the second has $\mathbf{i}' < \mathbf{i}$.) To illustrate these definitions we will take the temporal model M again and consider some tensed formulas. We saw that $[\![M(j)]\!]^{M,t_1,g} = 1$ (because $F(t_1, j) \in F(t_1, M)$); note now that $[\![\mathbf{F}M(j)]\!]^{M,t_1,g}$ is also 1 (because there is a time $\mathbf{i}$ later than t_1 for which $[\![M(j)]\!]^{M,\mathbf{i},g} = 1$ – namely t_2, since $[\![M(j)]\!]^{M,t_2,g} = 1$.) On the other hand, $[\![\mathbf{F}M(j)]\!]^{M,t_2,g} = 0$, since there is no time $\mathbf{i}$ later than t_2 for which $[\![M(j)]\!]^{M,\mathbf{i},g} = 1$. For examples of sentences with past tense operators, observe that $[\![\mathbf{P}M(j)]\!]^{M,t_2,g} = 1$, and likewise $[\![\mathbf{P}M(j)]\!]^{M,t_3,g} = 1$. The reader may be curious about the status of a future tense formula at the last moment in the set of times I in the model, or the status of a past tense formula at the first moment in time in the model. What, for example, is $[\![\mathbf{F}M(j)]\!]^{M,t_3,g}$? A careful, literal reading of Sem B.10 will convince us that $[\![\mathbf{F}M(j)]\!]^{M,t_3,g}$ must be 0, since there is no time $\mathbf{i}$ in I later than t_3 for which $[\![M(j)]\!]^{M,\mathbf{i},g} = 1$ for the simple reason that there is no time $\mathbf{i}$ in I which is later than t_3. In fact, for all formulas ϕ, $[\![\mathbf{F}\phi]\!]^{M,t_3,g} = 0$ for this reason, and for a similar reason, $[\![\mathbf{P}\phi]\!]^{M,t_1,g} = 0$ for all ϕ. In natural languages a parallel situation does not arise, since (real) time is either infinite or at least extends so far into the future and past that presumably, no human being has ever experienced its beginning or end (yet). In our models we may achieve this effect by requiring simply that for any **i** in I, there exist both **i**′ and **i**″ such that $\mathbf{i}' < \mathbf{i}$ and $\mathbf{i} < \mathbf{i}''$. Notice that such a set I must be infinite. Of course, we will not use such models with infinite I as examples, but the reader may keep in mind that they are possible models.

Since syntactic rules B.10 and B.11 make a formula from another formula, we can produce formulas with more than one tense operator by using these rules recursively. This will enable us to produce expressions that correspond more or less naturally to some of the compound tenses of English. A formula **PP**ϕ corresponds to an English sentence in the *past perfect tense*, and a formula **FP**ϕ corresponds to a *future perfect* sentence. The first type of formula will, by the semantic rules, "direct" us to some time preceding the time of utterance at which **P**ϕ is true, and this in turn "directs" us to some time preceding even this at which ϕ is true. The second formula similarly directs us to some future time at which **P**ϕ is true, and this in turn directs us back to some time preceding this future time at which ϕ is true. (This formal system does not, on the other hand, offer a natural way of treating the present perfect tense in English, nor the various progressive tenses, and the careful student of English grammar will know that even the future perfect and past perfect tenses of English interact crucially with implicit or explicit reference to *specific* points in time besides the moment of utterance and moment at which the "embedded" sentence is true, often by means of time adverbials.) These syntactic rules of L_{1t} will offer us other iterated tenses as well that do not correspond to any simple sentences in English, such as **PPP**ϕ, **PF**ϕ, **FF**ϕ, **FPF**ϕ, etc.

It will be interesting to note that certain formulas involving tense operators come out valid (true in all models with respect to all times in those models) as a consequence of our definitions. For example, if ϕ is any formula of L_{1t}, (5-1) and (5-2) will be true in any model for L_{1t}:

(5-1) $\mathbf{FF}\phi \rightarrow \mathbf{F}\phi$

(5-2) $\mathbf{PP}\phi \rightarrow \mathbf{P}\phi$

The validity of these formulas can easily be traced to the fact that $<$ is a transitive relation. That is, **FF**ϕ will be true at **i** just in case there is some **i**′ later than **i** at which **F**ϕ is true, and this in turn will be true at this **i**′ (whichever time this is) just in case there is some **i**″ later than **i**′ for which ϕ is true. Since it follows from the transitivity of $<$ that if $\mathbf{i} < \mathbf{i}'$ and $\mathbf{i}' < \mathbf{i}''$, then $\mathbf{i} < \mathbf{i}''$, it follows from the previous sentence that if **FF**ϕ is true at any **i**, then **F**ϕ will be true at that same **i**; hence (5-1) will be true in any model at any time **i**. A parallel argument shows that (5-2) is valid.

PROBLEM (5-2). Compute $[\![\forall x[\mathbf{F}M(x) \rightarrow \mathbf{P}M(x)]]\!]^{M, t_1, g}$ for the model used in Problem (5-1) (for arbitrary g). Do the same at t_2 and t_3.

PROBLEM (5-3). Show that each of the following formulas is valid in L_{1t}:

(i) $\mathbf{FP}\phi \rightarrow [\mathbf{F}\phi \vee \phi \vee \mathbf{P}\phi]$

(ii) $\mathbf{PF}\phi \rightarrow [\mathbf{F}\phi \vee \phi \vee \mathbf{P}\phi]$

PROBLEM (5-4). Show that the converses of (5-1) and (5-2), i.e., $\mathbf{F}\phi \rightarrow \mathbf{FF}\phi$ and $\mathbf{P}\phi \rightarrow \mathbf{PP}\phi$ are not valid. Could I and $<$ be constrained in such a way that these formulas would be true in all models so constrained?

Two tensed formula types of L_{1t} which are of some technical interest are $\neg\mathbf{F}\neg\phi$ and $\neg\mathbf{P}\neg\phi$. By the semantic rules of L_{1t}, the first makes the assertion that it is not the case that, for some future time **i**, ϕ is false at **i**. Awkward though this sounds in English, it is clear that this simply means that ϕ will always be true in the future (and indeed it is formally provable that the formula $\neg\mathbf{F}\neg\phi$ "means" this). The second formula makes the assertion that it is not the case that, for some time **i** in the past, ϕ is false at **i**. This is simply to say that ϕ has always been true in the past. These formulas are reminiscent of the quantified formula $\neg\exists x \neg M(x)$ and its logical equivalence to the formula $\forall x M(x)$ in first-order logic. Indeed, this parallel is not at all surprising when one recalls that the tense operators **F** and **P** in the *object language* are given a definition in the *meta-language* involving existential quantification over times. (In fact, some logicians have suggested that we might do away with tense operators entirely in the object language in favor of explicit quantification over times, representing a future tense sentence not as **F**ϕ but as something like $\exists t[now < t \wedge \phi$ is true at $t]$, where *now* is a contant denoting the "time of utterance". However, we will not pursue this approach here precisely because it is our purpose to show in this section how certain supposedly arcane concepts of natural language – such as "past" and "future" – can be treated in a formalized object language exactly (or almost exactly) as they appear in the syntax of natural language but can nevertheless be given an "explanation" in a meta-language that involves only the resources of first-order logic.) Thus since the universal quantifier of first-order logic can be given a definition in terms of the existential quantifier and negation, the parallel between tenses and quantification suggests the possibility of defining in terms of **F** and **P** and negation a pair of tense operators read as "it will always be true that" and "it has always been true that". It is customary in tense logic to use **G** and **H** respectively for these new tense operators, so we may accordingly introduce the following definitions:

(5-3) $\mathbf{G}\phi =_{\mathbf{def}} \neg\mathbf{F}\neg\phi$

(5-4) $\mathbf{H}\phi =_{\mathbf{def}} \neg\mathbf{P}\neg\phi$

(Alternatively, we could have begun by giving semantic rules for **G** and **H** in the obvious way parallel to Sem B.10 and Sem B.11 and then defined $\mathbf{F}\phi$ as $\neg\mathbf{G}\neg\phi$ and $\mathbf{P}\phi$ as $\neg\mathbf{H}\neg\phi$. That is, to say that it *was* the case that ϕ is to say that it has not always been the case that ϕ is (was) false, and to say that ϕ *will be* the case is to say that it will not always be the case that ϕ is (will be) false.) The operators **G** and **H** do not have direct parallels in the tenses of English as **F** and **P** do, since we express the equivalent English statements by a combination of tense and the adverb *always*; nevertheless, **G** and **H** have a technical interest for us that will become clear later.

The combination of tense operators with quantifiers introduces possibilities for scope distinctions unlike any we have seen so far. Since we can attach a quantifier to a formula either before or after adding a tense operator to it, we can produce syntactically distinct expressions like (5-5) and (5-6), or like (5-7) and (5-8):

(5-5) $\exists x\mathbf{G}M(x)$

(5-6) $\mathbf{G}\exists xM(x)$

(5-7) $\forall x\mathbf{F}M(x)$

(5-8) $\mathbf{F}\forall xM(x)$

To see that (5-5) and (5-6) are not semantically equivalent but rather make distinct assertions, consider the model M again. In particular, consider (5-5) and (5-6) with respect to t_1. By Sem B.9 of L_{1t} (i.e., the rule for existential quantification, which is the same as in L_1), $[\![\exists x\mathbf{G}M(x)]\!]^{M,t_1,g} = 1$ just in case we can find some g', possibly differing from g in the value assigned to x, for which $[\![\mathbf{G}M(x)]\!]^{M,t_1,g'} = 1$. Suppose we first try the g' that assigns a to x. (It is irrelevant whether this g' is the same as g, as long as we eventually consider *all* appropriate g'.) $[\![\mathbf{G}M(x)]\!]^{M,t_1,g^a_x}$ will be 1 by the definition of **G** just in case $[\![M(x)]\!]^{M,\mathbf{i},g^a_x}$ is true for all **i** later than t_1 (i.e., true for both the cases where $\mathbf{i} = t_2$ and $\mathbf{i} = t_3$). Though this denotation will be 1 for $\mathbf{i} = t_2$ (since a is a member of $F(t_2, M)$), it will be 0 for t_3. Therefore, $[\![\mathbf{G}M(x)]\!]^{M, t_1, g^a_x} = 0$. Next we do a similar computation for g^b_x. Here again we find that $[\![\mathbf{G}M(x)]\!]^{M, t_1, g^b_x} = 0$, since there is a time (t_3 again) where b fails to be in the denotation of the predicate M at that time. Finally, we perform the computation for g^c_x, and find here that though $[\![M(x)]\!]^{M, t_2, g^c_x} = 1$, still $[\![M(x)]\!]^{M, t_3, g^c_x} = 0$, so $[\![\mathbf{G}M(x)]\!]^{M, t_1, g^c_x} = 0$. Having exhausted all appropriate g' (since only a, b, and c are in A), we conclude that $[\![\exists x\mathbf{G}M(x)]\!]^{M, t_1, g} = 0$.

Now consider the formula (5-6). By definition of **G**, $[\![\mathbf{G}\exists xM(x)]\!]^{M, t_1, g} = 1$ iff for all $\mathbf{i}$ in I later than t_1, $[\![\exists xM(x)]\!]^{M, \mathbf{i}, g} = 1$. Thus we need to determine $[\![\exists xM(x)]\!]^{M, t_2, g}$ and $[\![\exists xM(x)]\!]^{M, t_3, g}$. Both of these computations will involve finding a g' for which $M(x)$ will be true at the appropriate time. However, there is nothing to require that the g' that makes $M(x)$ true for t_2 be the *same* g' that makes $M(x)$ true for t_3, and this is the essential difference between the truth conditions for $\mathbf{G}\exists xM(x)$ and those of the previous formula (5-5). It turns out that either g^a_x or g^b_x will make $M(x)$ true at t_2, while g^c_x makes $M(x)$ true at t_3. Thus the condition that $\exists xM(x)$ denote 1 at both t_2 and t_3 is satisfied, and thus $[\![\mathbf{G}\exists xM(x)]\!]^{M, t_1, g} = 1$.

In other words, the earlier formula (5-5) requires that there be *an* individual of whom M is always true, whereas (5-6) makes the weaker assertion that there will always be some individual *or other* of whom M is true. Any model in which (5-5) is true will be a model in which (5-6) is true (though not conversely), and in fact it can be proved that for any formula ϕ, any model in which $\exists u\mathbf{G}\phi$ is true is one in which $\mathbf{G}\exists u\phi$ is true. Thus (5-9) is a valid formula schema of L_{1t}:

(5-9) $\exists u\mathbf{G}\phi \rightarrow \mathbf{G}\exists u\phi$

Consider now the relationship between (5-7) and (5-8) informally. An inspection of the truth conditions for these formulas will show that (5-7) ($= \forall x\mathbf{F}M(x)$) requires only that for all individuals, there is some future time *or other* at which each individual is in the denotation of M, while (5-8) ($= \mathbf{F}\forall xM(x)$) has the stronger requirement that there be a *particular* time at which all individuals simultaneously appear in the denotation of M. For example, in the model M, $[\![\forall x\mathbf{F}M(x)]\!]^{M, t_1, g} = 1$, while $[\![\mathbf{F}\forall xM(x)]\!]^{M, t_1, g} = 0$, as the reader can confirm. Here again it turns out that the relationship between the two formulas is an instance of a general principle about L_{1t}: For any formula ϕ, any model in which $\mathbf{F}\forall u\phi$ is true will also be a model in which $\forall u\mathbf{F}\phi$ (though not conversely, as we have seen). Therefore (5-10) is also a valid schema of L_{1t}:

(5-10) $\mathbf{F}\forall u\phi \rightarrow \forall u\mathbf{F}\phi$

Considering that **F** and **G** are interpreted semantically like hidden existential and universal quantifiers over times, it is not surprising that (5-9) and (5-10) are valid, since these can both be seen to be analogous to the familiar quantifier law of first-order logic (5-11):

(5-11) $\exists u\forall v\phi \rightarrow \forall v\exists u\phi$

Considering also that (5-12) and (5-13) are valid in first order logic

(5-12) $\forall u\forall v\phi \leftrightarrow \forall v\forall u\phi$

(5-13) $\exists u\exists v\phi \leftrightarrow \exists v\exists u\phi$

(i.e., that $\forall u\forall v\phi$ is logically equivalent to $\forall v\forall u\phi$, and similarly for (5-13)), we are not surprised to find that (5-14) and (5-15) turn out to be valid formulas of L_{1t}.[1]

(5-14) $\forall u\mathbf{G}\phi \leftrightarrow \mathbf{G}\forall u\phi$

(5-15) $\exists u\mathbf{F}\phi \leftrightarrow \mathbf{F}\exists u\phi$

We will leave it to the reader, however, to demonstrate the validity of (5-14) and (5-15). Because of the "symmetry" between **F** and **G** on the one hand and **P** and **H** on the other, the valid formulas (5-9), (5-10), (5-14) and (5-15) will have valid counterparts in which **P** systematically replaces **F** and **H** systematically replaces **G**. Thus parallel to (5-9) we have the valid formula $\exists u\mathbf{H}\phi \rightarrow \mathbf{H}\exists u\phi$, etc.[2]

PROBLEM (5-5). Show that the following formulas are valid in L_{1t} for any sentence ϕ:

(i) $\exists u\mathbf{H}\phi \rightarrow \mathbf{H}\exists u\phi$

(ii) $\mathbf{P}\forall u\phi \rightarrow \forall u\mathbf{P}\phi$

(iii) $\forall u\mathbf{H}\phi \leftrightarrow \mathbf{H}\forall u\phi$

(iv) $\exists u\mathbf{P}\phi \leftrightarrow \mathbf{P}\exists u\phi$

PROBLEM (5-6). Show that the converses of (i) and (ii) in Problem (5-5) are not valid by constructing a model in which $\mathbf{H}\exists u\phi$ is true but $\exists u\mathbf{H}\phi$ is false, and similarly for the second formula.

PROBLEM (5-7). Let ϕ be a valid sentence of L_1. Show that **H**ϕ and **G**ϕ are valid sentences of L_{1t}, but that **P**ϕ and **F**ϕ are not valid in general.

II. THE OTHER VARIETIES OF MODAL LOGIC; THE OPERATORS □ AND ◇

We have observed that the truth value of sentences like

(5-16) Jimmy Carter has been elected President of the U.S.

can vary as a function of the time with respect to which we evaluate their truth. Obviously their truth value can vary with respect to factual contingencies also. It is easy to imagine a different outcome of the 1976 presidential election which would have made (5-16) false rather than true at the time of writing – false because the facts would have been that Gerald Ford was elected in 1976. We now take up some considerations relating to this kind of variation in truth value. For the present we set aside the dependence of denotation on time in order both to simplify the discussion and to bring out more clearly some formal parallels between variation of denotation with the passage of time, on the one hand, and with change of factual circumstances, on the other. Later in this chapter we will treat the two together.

In addition to sentences like (5-16), some phrases of other categories have varying denotations as a function of factual contingencies. Consider, for instance, those in (5-17).

(5-17) 1. The President of the U.S.
2. holds the winning poker hand.

We have no difficulty in imagining that, at the time John Kennedy was assassinated, the situation might have been slightly different in that he would have recovered from his wounds (or the assassin's shots would have missed). In that case (5-17)1. would have referred to John Kennedy when it in fact referred to Lyndon Johnson. Similar observations can be made about (5-17)2.

In contrast to these expressions, those in (5-18) could not change denotation if some fact about the world were different than what it actually is. (We exclude from consideration here change of facts concerning what English phrases and sentences mean).

(5-18) 1. The President of the U.S. is the President of the U.S.
2. The set that is included in every set.
3. is a number that is not identical to itself.

In this chapter we introduce one kind of syntactic/semantic device for dealing with change in the denotation of expressions as a function of change in facts: the *modal operators*. To interpret these operators we will require a new kind of model-theoretic primitive, so-called *possible worlds*. In the next chapter we greatly generalize these methods to apply them to expressions of all the syntactic categories of L_{type}, more fully exploiting the power of a semantics based on possible worlds.

A sentence like (5-18)1. is a necessary truth in the sense that it could not possibly have been false. This sense of necessity is recognizable from the preceding sentence as the dual of possibility, in the sense of logical possibility. That is, for a sentence ϕ, it *is necessary that* ϕ is equivalent to *it is not possible that it is not the case that* ϕ. Some necessarily true sentences are not, like (5-18)1., true solely because of the logical words they contain, but in part because of nonlogical words whose denotations necessarily stand in certain relationships to one another. For example,

(5-19) All bachelors are unmarried men

is necessarily true because of the fact that it is logically impossible for the denotation of *bachelor* not to be a subset of both the denotation of *man* and also that of *unmarried*. We will eventually see how these necessary truths can be captured.

It is customary to divide the set of all true statements into the *contingently true* (those that are true as a matter of fact, though they might have been otherwise had the world been different, e.g., *Paris is the capital of France*) and the *necessarily true* (those that could not be denied without contradiction or departure from the normal meanings of words of the language, such as mathematical and logical truths and analytic statements). Likewise, the false statements are divided into the *contingently false* (e.g., *Vincennes is the capital of France*) and the *necessarily false* (e.g., $2 + 2 = 5$). This division is most easily visualized by the following traditional diagram (Figure 5-1):

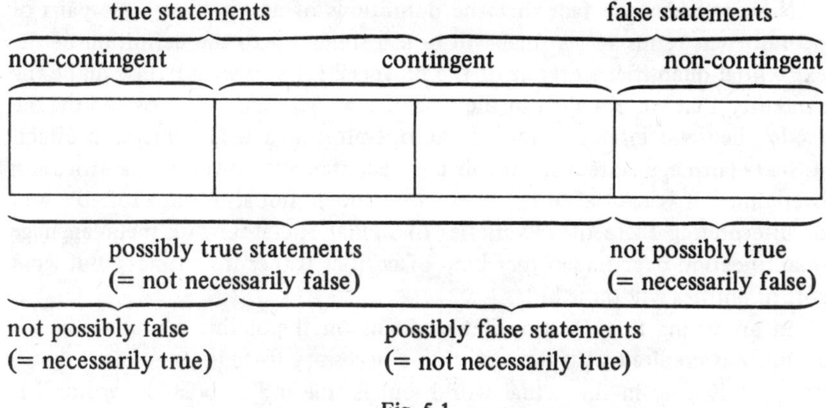

Fig. 5-1

Of course, we already have in effect such a four-way distinction among statements, if we take into account the distinction between formulas that are logically valid (true in every possible model) and those that are "merely" true (true in the particular model under consideration), and also the distinction between formulas that are "merely" false (false in the model under consideration) and those that are contradictory (true in no possible model). However, we certainly want also to countenance some statements that are necessarily true even though they are not logically valid, and similarly some statements are necessarily false yet not logically contradictory.

Now it is reasonable that one might construct a formal language with the pairs of concepts *possible/necessary* treated as sentence operators, just as **F** and **G** or **P** and **H** were treated in L_{1t}. Only one of the operators in the pair would have to be taken as basic; the other could be defined in terms of it with the aid of the negation operator. Indeed, such formal languages have been constructed and studied quite extensively.[3] A system with operators for *it is possible that* (in the sense of logical possibility) and *it is necessary that* has recently been called an *alethic logic* (a term which is apparently due to G. H. von Wright). Because of the inevitable formal similarities among such systems, the study of all of them (including tense logic) is interrelated to a great extent, and the term *modal logic* is sometimes used as a cover term for the study of all such systems. The last of these, the alethic modalities, are the oldest and best established of the lot, and the term *modal logic* is also commonly used in a narrower sense to refer to the study of alethic modalities alone.

Now consider the fact that the definitions of any one of these pairs of operators in terms of its dual will bear a similarity to the definition of the existential quantifier in terms of the universal (or vice-versa); this will be the similarity that we observed in the case of **F** and **G**. Since we showed how the model-theoretic interpretation of the operators **F** and **G** reduces, in effect, to meta-language statements involving existential and universal quantification over times, it is natural to ask whether we should not also find a suitable way of interpreting these other varieties of modal operators with meta-language quantification over some other kind of entities (other than times). But what sort of entities will these be?

In answering this question, let us focus on the alethic modalities alone. Leibnitz is credited with the idea that a necessary truth is a statement that is not merely true in the actual world, but is true in "all possible worlds." If we were to attempt to follow up on Leibnitz' idea in constructing a formal interpretation for modal operators parallel to the one for tense operators just given, this would mean taking *it is necessary that* ϕ as true in the actual world if and only if ϕ is true in all possible worlds. If possibility is to be the dual of necessity, then this commits us to the truth of *it is possible that* ϕ in the actual world whenever ϕ is true in at least one possible world. Would this be an enlightening way of analyzing the semantics of necessity and possibility? Many philosophers of language have unequivocally answered "no" to this question; they have contended that since "possible worlds" are surely vague and ill-understood entities (if not entities that should be banned from serious discussion of semantics altogether on philosophical grounds), it cannot help to explain one mysterious semantic concept (necessity) in terms of an even more mysterious one (possible worlds).[4] However, this conclusion does not automatically follow. Rather, it would seem that the value of any model-theoretic analysis involving possible worlds will depend on (1) how successfully it can be carried out technically, and (2) whether it results in definitions of validity and entailment among sentences of the formal language that reasonably match our intuitions about entailment and validity among the corresponding English sentences (taking into account the syntactic limits of the formal language). Any reasonably simple model-theoretic analysis of a semantic problem of natural language that satisfies these two requirements merits our serious attention (at least until a better model-theoretic analysis of the same problem is available), even if the primitive entities required in the model theory appear somewhat mysterious at first. If such an analysis meeting these requirements but involving some mysterious entity such as possible worlds is presented, then it behooves us to try to elaborate on the analysis and to try to further elucidate the mysterious entity involved. We are *not* entitled to reject such an analysis out of hand because we dislike the entities involved.

Thus though the reader will probably agree that the analysis of tenses in terms of a model theory involving an ordered set of moments of time is at the very least enlightening to our understanding of how temporal expressions of natural language work, entities called "moments of time" are surely not above metaphysical question themselves and are deserving of close philosophical scrutiny. In fact, one of the most important scholars of tense logic, A. N. Prior, has consistently held to axiomatic study of tense logics (deductive systems in which **F**, **P**, **G** and **H** appear in axioms) and has tried to avoid model-theoretic explanations of tense primarily because he regards "moments in time" as having dubious philosophical status (cf. Prior 1967). But even for someone who would raise metaphysical questions about moments in time, it would seem rather pointless to avoid explicit reference to moments in time when discussing tenses in view of the very tight structural connections between tenses and the kind of model theory of them we have sketched above and in view of our intuitions that there "are" past and future moments. What we hope to suggest in the discussion of the modal operators *necessarily* and *possibly* below (and in the later discussion of allied intensional concepts such as *propositions* and *properties*) is that an equally tight structural connection exists beween these operators (and intensional concepts) and a model theory involving things called "possible worlds", a connection which is quite workable and useful in analyzing semantics of natural languages – so much so that we cannot afford to ignore it, even though our pre-theoretic intuitions about the connections between modal operators and possible worlds do not parallel our more salient intuitions about the connection between tenses and things we call "moments in time." Accordingly, we will first see what can be accomplished with a possible-worlds-based theory, and afterwards return to the question of the proper status of the primitive notion "possible world" on which it is based.

At this point the importance of completely explicit formalization of such model-theoretic analyses cannot be overemphasized. If in the course of our research we have a need for theoretical entities that we have only vague pre-theoretical intuitions about, then absolutely rigorous formalization of the theory involving these entities will insure that only the properties we explicitly assign to them can play a role in the theory proper, and any problems that arise with them should be noticed immediately. If, on the other hand, we do not formalize our analysis completely, then certain of our vague, unspoken assumptions about such theoretical entities may inadvertently play a role in the subsequent development of our theory. This role may be hard to detect and may easily lead to confusion and misunderstanding. Chomsky has repeatedly emphasized this point in developing his theory of transformational syntax, and it is no less relevant, perhaps even more so, for a theory of semantics.

We will now turn to the question of just how this idea for the interpretation of the modal operators is to be formalized. Again, we will take L_1 as our basis and simply add two new operators to it to give the *first-order modal language* L_{1m}. For "necessarily" we will use the symbol $\Box$, so that $\Box\phi$ may be read "it is necessary that ϕ" or "necessarily, ϕ". Its dual will be $\Diamond$, so that $\Diamond\phi$ is read "it is possible that ϕ", or "possibly, ϕ." (In the literature on modal logic the symbol **L** is often used for necessity, together with **M** for possibility.) We will write rules for both operators, though of course either will be definable in terms of the other. The new syntactic rules will read as follows:

Syn B.10. If ϕ is a formula, then $\Box\phi$ is a formula.

Syn B.11. If ϕ is a formula, then $\Diamond\phi$ is a formula.

Now just how do we formally describe the entities we are to quantify over (the so-called "possible worlds") in giving the semantics for these two operators? In the earliest attempt to give a model-theoretic semantics for the modal notions, Rudolf Carnap (Carnap 1947) identified necessary truth (what he called *L-truth*) with truth in all possible models, hence $\Box\phi$ was to be true just in case ϕ was true in any possible model. While this approach is to some extent natural, it is too inflexible to permit as many things to be necessarily true as our intuition requires. A breakthrough was provided by Kripke's work on the semantics of modal operators (Kripke 1959, 1963), where it was pointed out that the difficulties could be circumvented by a new notion of model, namely an indexed set of old models, say $\{M_{i_1}, M_{i_2}, M_{i_3}, \ldots\}$. One can then think of the indices $i_1, i_2, i_3, \ldots$ as possible worlds and the model M_{i_n} as the denotations of expressions in the world i_n. Formally, this parallels the way we treated moments of time earlier in this chapter. In this approach the definition of a model and the semantic rules will look almost exactly like those for the tensed language L_{1t}. One difference will be that the possible worlds do not have a natural order defined upon them as the moments of time do (i.e., the "earlier-than" relation among moments), so the model will be simpler in that respect. In the most straightforward interpretation of modal operators a formula $\Box\phi$ will simply be true with respect to the actual world in case ϕ is true with respect to *all* possible worlds, not just those standing in a certain relation to the actual one (whereas $\mathbf{G}\phi$ was true at t if ϕ was true at those times *which are latter than t*). Another difference is that we have only two operators, not four: we don't need a second set of operators that form the "mirror image" of $\Diamond$ and $\Box$ (in the way that the past operators **P** and **H** formed the "mirror image" of **F** and **G** with respect to the direction of time).

Just as we relativized the temporal definitions of denotation to a moment in time which was intuitively regarded as "now", the moment of utterance, we will relativize the definition of denotation in L_{1m} to an arbitrary member of the set of possible worlds which we will regard as the "actual" world. Thus the definitions themselves do not single out any particular world as the actual ones; we may alternately choose one or the other of them as the "actual" world, all other worlds becoming possible but not actual worlds relative to this choice. (Alternatively, we could change the definition of a model to include the designation of one particular world as the actual one – in fact, Kripke's original treatment followed this procedure. But with his approach there will still be alternative models differing only in the choice of which world is so designated. Thus the definition of validity in our approach as truth in every world in every model is equivalent to the definition of validity in Kripke's approach as truth in every model.) Thus the formal definitions needed are these:

A *model* for the modal language L_{1m} is an ordered triple $\langle A, I, F \rangle$ such that A and I are any non-empty sets and F is a function assigning to each pair $\langle \mathrm{i}, \alpha \rangle$ consisting of a member of I and a non-logical constant of L_{1m} an appropriate denotation (out of the set of possible denotations we allow for each category of non-logical constants of L_{1m}).

The semantic rules of L_{1m} will be the same as for L_1 except for uniformly defining $[\![\alpha]\!]^{M,\mathrm{i},g}$ instead of $[\![\alpha]\!]^{M,g}$. To these rules we add the new rules:

Sem B.10. If ϕ is a formula, then $[\![\Box\phi]\!]^{M,\mathrm{i},g} = 1$ iff for all i' in I, $[\![\phi]\!]^{M,\mathrm{i}',g} = 1$.

Sem B.11. If ϕ is a formula, then $[\![\Diamond\phi]\!]^{M,\mathrm{i},g} = 1$ iff for some i' in I, $[\![\phi]\!]^{M,\mathrm{i}',g} = 1$.

Since these definitions are simpler than either the semantic rules for quantifiers or the semantic rules for the tense operators, though they are parallel to both sets of rules, we will not bother to give sample models and compute truth conditions for specific formulas.

PROBLEM (5-8). Reinterpret the temporal model given earlier in this chapter as a modal model for L_{1m} in the following way. Let $I = \{t_1, t_2, t_3\}$ be a set of possible worlds rather than a set of times, and ignore $<$ entirely. Given this understanding of the model M, compute the following (for arbitrary g):

(i) $[\![\Diamond M(d)]\!]^{M, t_3, g}$

(ii) $[\![\forall x[M(x) \to \Box M(x)]]\!]^{M, t_1, g}$

(iii) $[\![\Box[M(d) \to M(j)]]\!]^{M, t_1, g}$

(iv) $[\![\exists x \Box M(x)]\!]^{M, t_3, g}$

(v) $[\![\Box \exists x M(x)]\!]^{M, t_3, g}$

We want to call attention to some of the more obvious valid types of formulas of L_{1m}. If ϕ is any formula, then the following will be true in any world in any model:

(5-20) $\Box\phi \to \phi$

(5-21) $\phi \to \Diamond\phi$

Formulas of the form of (5-20) are valid for the obvious reason that if a formula ϕ is true for all i in I, then it is true in any one of them, in particular, it is true in whichever one we choose to call the actual wor' 1. This formula schema, called the *Law of Necessity*, is therefore the meta-la"guage analogue of *Universal Instantiation* in first-order logic, the rule that allows us from $\forall x P(x)$ to infer $P(a)$. Formulas of the form of (5-21) are valid because if ϕ is true in the actual world in any model, then there is trivially at least one member of I for which ϕ is true (namely, the actual world), so $\Diamond\phi$ is therefore true.[5] Again, this is the analogue of the inference from $P(a)$ to $\exists x P(x)$ in first-order logic. The fact that (5-22) and (5-23) are valid formulas according to the semantic rules of L_{1m} shows that we have achieved the desired interdefinability of $\Box$ and $\Diamond$ in our language:

(5-22) $\Box\phi \leftrightarrow \neg\Diamond\neg\phi$

(5-23) $\Diamond\phi \leftrightarrow \neg\Box\neg\phi$

Also, the validity of (5-24) and (5-25) show that the impossible is that which is necessarily false in our system, and that the possibly false is that which is not necessary:

(5-24) $\neg\Diamond\phi \leftrightarrow \Box\neg\phi$

(5-25) $\Diamond\neg\phi \leftrightarrow \neg\Box\phi$

In view of our semantic rules the following formulas will also be valid:

(5-26) $\forall u \Box\phi \leftrightarrow \Box\forall u \phi$

(5-27) $\exists u \Diamond\phi \leftrightarrow \Diamond\exists u \phi$

However, it is somewhat controversial whether the last two biconditionals should be formally valid. It has been suggested that $\forall u \Box\phi$ ought to mean "every individual u that *actually* exists is necessarily such that ϕ," whereas $\Box\forall u \phi$ ought to mean "in any possible world, anything that exists in that world is such that ϕ." Similarly, $\exists u \Diamond\phi$ might be suggested to mean that "some individual u that actually exists is in some world such that ϕ", whereas $\Diamond\exists u \phi$ should mean that "in some world it is the case that some individual which exists in that world is such that ϕ." To make these pairs of formulas semantically distinct would require a model theory in which each possible world has its own domain of individuals over which quantifiers range (though the domains would, in general, overlap partially). In this way, there could be "possible individuals" that are not actual individuals, and perhaps actual individuals that do not "exist" in some other possible worlds. The question whether there are such individuals has, not surprisingly, been the subject of considerable philosophical debate.[6] It is possible to construct a satisfactory model theory on this approach (and in fact Kripke's early treatment in Kripke 1963 adopted it), but it is technically more complicated than the approach we have taken here, and it was not adopted by Montague (for discussion see Hughes and Cresswell 1968, pp. 170–184). The analogous problem for tense logic (i.e., quantifying over individuals that exist at the present time, versus quantifying over the set of all individuals that either have existed, exist, or will someday exist) was first studied extensively by Nino Cocchiarella in his dissertation (Cocchiarella 1966). Moreover, there are many sentences of natural language that suggest the need for quantification over the set of possible individuals (or the set including individuals existing at other times), such as *No two presidents of the U.S. ever looked alike*, or *There is a letter I have to write today*, or *John often dreams about a certain large purple anteater*. Thus Montague and most others in the field of intensional logic followed Dana Scott's advice (Scott, 1970) in assuming a single domain A of quantification for all possible worlds – (or in tense logic, for all possible times). If it is necessary to express quantification over the actual individuals, this can be accomplished within the simpler model theory by including among the non-logical constants an *existence predicate* E, whose denotation may of course vary from one world to the next. With this predicate and a fixed A the alleged reading of $\forall u \Box \phi$ as "every actual individual is necessarily such that ϕ" can be expressed by the formula $\forall u[E(u) \rightarrow \Box \phi]$ and the alleged reading of $\Box \forall u \phi$ as "it is necessary that any (possibly) existing individual is such that ϕ" can be expressed as $\Box \forall u[E(u) \rightarrow \phi]$. The formulas $\forall u \Box \phi$ and $\Box \forall u \phi$ remain equivalent, and both can be thought of as saying "every possible-or-actual individual is necessarily such that ϕ."[7]

Associated with this question about differing sets of individuals in different worlds is the so-called "cross-world identity problem," the problem of how we are to know when an individual in one possible world is the "same" as an individual in a different possible world. This problem is discussed at length by Quine (cf. Quine 1953, 1960). There is a huge literature on this problem which we cannot begin to do justice to here. Suffice it to say that with the model theory presented here in which the set I is primitively given and in which the domain A is, as it were, fixed once and for all for all possible worlds in I, the problem simply does not arise (at least, as a technical problem within the theory). This will be made clearer later on in the discussion of "quantifying in". There remains of course the important *epistemic* problem of how we might recognize an individual as the same individual as one we know in the actual world if that individual had quite different properties from those he actually has, but this question is independent of the setting up of the kind of model theory for modal operators that we have discussed here.[8] There were, on the other hand, significant technical problems of so-called "cross-world identification" with the early attempts at semantics for modal logic based on Carnap's idea of identifying a possible world with a possible model for the language. The criticism by Quine and others of these technical problems with pre-Kripke modal logic should not be confused with their later criticism of the revised model theory of modal logic based not on technical problems but entirely on metaphysical objections to the notion of possible worlds. An alternative to the method of having A fixed for all worlds is David Lewis' "counterpart" theory of cross-world identification (cf. Lewis 1968) in which the domain is different for each world but every individual in each domain is tied to objects in the domains of other worlds (generally to a single object for each other world) that resemble it in the most important respects by a *counterpart relation*.

Note finally that if ϕ is a valid formula (e.g., if ϕ is a formula of the form $[\psi \vee \neg \psi]$), then it follows that $\Box \phi$ is a true formula and in fact a valid one. That is, if it follows from the syntactic form of ϕ and the semantic rules that ϕ will turn out to be true at any possible world in any possible model, then

$\Box\phi$ will likewise be true at any possible world in any model, hence valid. Similarly, if ϕ is contradictory, then $\Diamond\phi$ is also contradictory (and $\Box\neg\phi$ is valid). On the other hand, $\Box\phi$ can be true in some particular model even though ϕ is not valid, and $\Diamond\phi$ can be false even though ϕ is not a contradiction. This means we have achieved in L_{1m} the desideratum (mentioned earlier) of distinguishing logical validity from necessary truth: any logical truth is a necessary truth, but not every necessary truth is a logical truth. (Likewise, every logical contradiction is necessarily false, but not every necessary falsehood is logically contradictory.)

It turns out that there is not a single "classical" system of modal logic (as there is a single universally accepted system of first-order logic), but rather a huge variety of alternative systems. (The reader is referred to Hughes and Cresswell 1968 for a survey of these.) The system just presented (known in the literature on modal logic as the system S5) has the simplest model-theoretic interpretation and is the closest to a standard modal logic there is; it is essentially the one used by Montague in PTQ.

III. LANGUAGES CONTAINING BOTH TENSE AND MODAL OPERATORS: COORDINATE SEMANTICS

We have now seen two ways of interpreting operators relative to a model consisting of a domain of individuals A and a set of "other things" I; we thought of these first as times, then as "possible worlds". Now we will consider a language that contains *both* tense and modal operators. For the interpretation of this language we will need a model with *two* sets besides the set of individuals. We will designate these as the set W (which is to be thought of as the set of worlds) and the set T (which is to be thought of as the set of times); $<$ will be the ordering of the set T. (I and J are the letters chosen by Montague in PTQ, and thus they appear also in subsequent literature based on PTQ. It is unfortunate that Montague did not pick the more mnemonically obvious symbols W, for the worlds, and T for the times.) Thus we can think of our "semantic space" as expanded to two dimensions. We have, as it were, differing worlds as we move along one axis and differing times as we move on the other axis. Any particular point on this plane can be metaphorically thought of as being a pair of *coordinates* $\langle w, t \rangle$ for some w in W and t in T; that is, as a point whose location is determined by which world it is in on the one hand, and by what time it is on the other hand. We will call such a pair an *index* (hence Montague's original use of the letter i). Any one of these can represent "the actual world now", and our definitions of denotation will now be relativized to a choice of some arbitrary index $\langle \mathbf{w}, \mathbf{t} \rangle$. Thus our semantic rules will now give a definition of $[\![\alpha]\!]^{M, \mathbf{w}, \mathbf{t}, g}$ for each expression α, i.e., "the denotation of α relative to a model M, possible world $\mathbf{w}$, time $\mathbf{t}$, and assignment of values to variables g." Suppose we have a simple model in which W contains two worlds $\mathbf{w}_1$ and $\mathbf{w}_2$ and T contains three times $\mathbf{t}_1$, $\mathbf{t}_2$ and $\mathbf{t}_3$ (with the temporal ordering appropriate to their subscripts, i.e., $\mathbf{t}_1 < \mathbf{t}_2 < \mathbf{t}_3$). We could diagram this tiny metaphysical "universe" as follows:

$$\begin{array}{ll} \text{World } \mathbf{w}_2: & \langle \mathbf{w}_2, \mathbf{t}_1 \rangle - \langle \mathbf{w}_2, \mathbf{t}_2 \rangle - \langle \mathbf{w}_2, \mathbf{t}_3 \rangle \\ & \quad\;\; | \qquad\qquad\quad | \qquad\qquad\quad | \\ \text{World } \mathbf{w}_1: & \langle \mathbf{w}_1, \mathbf{t}_1 \rangle - \langle \mathbf{w}_1, \mathbf{t}_2 \rangle - \langle \mathbf{w}_1, \mathbf{t}_3 \rangle \\ & \xrightarrow[\text{time}]{\hspace{14em}} \end{array}$$

As we move horizontally to the right, we move from one time to a later time in the same possible world; as we move vertically we move from one possible world to another but remain at the same point in time.

We will give the semantics for tense operators so that they "shift" us to an earlier or later time but leave us in the same possible world (or more accurately, they have the effect of asserting that a sentence is true at an earlier or later time in the same world.) Thus, we will specify that $\mathbf{F}\phi$ is true at an index $\langle \mathbf{w}, \mathbf{t} \rangle$ just in case there is some other index $\langle \mathbf{w}, \mathbf{t}' \rangle$ with $\mathbf{t} < \mathbf{t}'$ such that ϕ is true at $\langle \mathbf{w}, \mathbf{t}' \rangle$, and similarly for the other tense operators.

Modal operators, on the other hand, will involve shifting the world coordinate, but now we have a choice. Do we interpret $\Box\phi$ so that it means "necessarily always ϕ", or just "necessarily now ϕ"? Selecting the former interpretation means saying that $\Box\phi$ is true at a particular $\langle \mathbf{w}, \mathbf{t} \rangle$ just in case ϕ is true at all $\langle \mathbf{w}', \mathbf{t}' \rangle$, for all $\mathbf{w}'$ in W and all $\mathbf{t}'$ in T. Choosing the latter interpretation means saying that $\Box\phi$ is true at an index $\langle \mathbf{w}, \mathbf{t} \rangle$ just in case ϕ is true at $\langle \mathbf{w}', \mathbf{t} \rangle$ for all $\mathbf{w}'$ in W (i.e., at all indices with the same time coordinate but possibly differing world coordinate). Disregarding for now the question of which interpretation is closer to the English word *necessarily*, we will choose the former interpretation ("necessarily always") because there will be technical advantages to having an operator $\Box$ which is defined this way, and because Montague also used this interpretation of the necessity operator in PTQ. We can always add later a second operator with the other interpretation if needed.

The definitions for this language will be based on the definitions of L_1 for simplicity, hence we will call it L_{1mt} (for *1st order modal tensed language*).

The *syntax of* L_{1mt} contains all the syntactic rules of L_1, plus the following:

Syn B.10. If ϕ is a formula, then $\Box\phi$ is a formula.

Syn B.11. If ϕ is a formula, then $\Diamond\phi$ is a formula.

Syn B.12. If ϕ is a formula, then $\mathbf{F}\phi$ is a formula.

Syn B.13. If ϕ is a formula, then $\mathbf{P}\phi$ is a formula.

(We will not add separate rules for **G** and **H** – these could be introduced by definition in terms of **P** and **F** if necessary; the operator $\Diamond$ could on the other hand be introduced by definition in terms of $\Box$ if desired.)

The *semantics of* L_{1mt} is as follows:

A *model for* L_{1mt} is an ordered quintuple $\langle A, W, T, <, F\rangle$, where A, W, and T are any non-empty and mutually disjoint sets, $<$ is a linear ordering of the set T, and F is a function that assigns an appropriate denotation to each non-logical constant of L_{1mt} relative to each pair $\langle \mathbf{w}, \mathbf{t}\rangle$ for $\mathbf{w}$ in W and $\mathbf{t}$ in T. (Thus "$F(\langle \mathbf{w}, \mathbf{t}\rangle, \alpha) = \gamma$" is to be understood as asserting that the denotation of the constant α in the possible world $\mathbf{w}$ at the time $\mathbf{t}$ is the object γ.)

The *semantic rules of* L_{1mt} recursively define the denotation of each expression α of L_{1mt} with respect to a model M, a world $\mathbf{w}$, time $\mathbf{t}$ and value assignment g. (This is symbolized $[\![\alpha]\!]^{M,\mathbf{w},\mathbf{t},g}$.) These rules consist of all the rules for L_{1t} (with $[\![\alpha]\!]^{M,\mathbf{w},\mathbf{t},g}$ substituted for $[\![\alpha]\!]^{M,\mathbf{i},g}$ throughout), plus the following:

Sem B.10. If ϕ is a formula, then $[\![\Box\phi]\!]^{M,\mathbf{w},\mathbf{t},g} = 1$ iff $[\![\phi]\!]^{M,\mathbf{w}',\mathbf{t}',g} = 1$ for all $\mathbf{w}'$ in W and $\mathbf{t}'$ in T.

Sem B.11. If ϕ is a formula, then $[\![\Diamond\phi]\!]^{M,\mathbf{w},\mathbf{t},g} = 1$ iff $[\![\phi]\!]^{M,\mathbf{w}',\mathbf{t}',g} = 1$ for some $\mathbf{w}'$ in W and some $\mathbf{t}'$ in T.

Sem B.12. If ϕ is a formula, then $[\![\mathbf{F}\phi]\!]^{M,\mathbf{w},\mathbf{t},g} = 1$ iff $[\![\phi]\!]^{M,\mathbf{w},\mathbf{t}',g} = 1$ for some $\mathbf{t}'$ in T such that $\mathbf{t} < \mathbf{t}'$.

Sem B.13. If ϕ is a formula, then $[\![\mathbf{P}\phi]\!]^{M,\mathbf{w},\mathbf{t},g} = 1$ iff $[\![\phi]\!]^{M,\mathbf{w},\mathbf{t}',g} = 1$ for some $\mathbf{t}'$ in T such that $\mathbf{t}' < \mathbf{t}$.

Consider briefly part of a simple model for L_{1mt} and the interpretation of some formulas relative to it. Let *the model M* be $\langle A, W, T, <, F\rangle$ where

$$A = \{a, b, c\}$$

$$W = \{\mathbf{w}_1, \mathbf{w}_2\}$$

$$T = \{\mathbf{t}_1, \mathbf{t}_2, \mathbf{t}_3\}$$

$$< \; = \{\langle \mathbf{t}_1, \mathbf{t}_2\rangle, \langle \mathbf{t}_2, \mathbf{t}_3\rangle, \langle \mathbf{t}_1, \mathbf{t}_3\rangle\}$$

and F includes values to be specified in a moment. This time we will include for variety not only names that denote the same individual at each index – what Kripke calls ***rigid designators*** – but also a name m that designates a different person at different indices – a ***non-rigid designator***, or perhaps a flaccid designator. We may think of this as analogous in natural language to a title that different individuals hold at different times. In English most of these are of the form of definite descriptions – *The President of the U.S.*, *the Pope*, etc. – but David Lewis has suggested the example of *Miss America* as a non-rigid designator most closely resembling a name; hence we may think of m as this "name".

Values of F:

j	t_1	t_2	t_3
w_1	a	a	a
w_2	a	a	a

d	t_1	t_2	t_3
w_1	b	b	b
w_2	b	b	b

n	t_1	t_2	t_3
w_1	c	c	c
w_2	c	c	c

m	t_1	t_2	t_3
w_1	a	b	c
w_2	c	c	b

B	t_1	t_2	t_3
w_1	$\{a, b\}$	$\{a, c\}$	$\{b, c\}$
w_2	$\{b, c\}$	$\{a\}$	$\{a, b, c\}$

Let us evaluate formulas relative to the index $\langle w_1, t_2 \rangle$; that is, we will consider w_1 to be the actual world and t_2 to be "now." Relative to this index in this model, $B(j)$ is true. (We will here use informal locutions like that of the previous sentence, rather than precise statements such as $[\![B(j)]\!]^{M, w_1, t_2, g} = 1$.) Notice now how formulas involving the non-rigid designator m will be evaluated. $B(m)$ is false at this index (because $F(\langle w_1, t_2 \rangle, m)$ is not in the set $F(\langle w_1, t_2 \rangle, B)$, i.e. $b \notin \{a, c\}$). The formulas $\mathbf{F}B(m)$ and $\mathbf{P}B(m)$ are both true at this same index, but they are, so to speak, true for different reasons. $\mathbf{F}B(m)$ is true here because the denotation of B at the "future index" $\langle w_1, t_3 \rangle$ (i.e. the set $\{b, c\}$) contains the denotation of m at that same index (i.e., the individual c). However, $\mathbf{P}B(m)$ is true at the original index $\langle w_1, t_2 \rangle$ because the denotation of B at the "past index" $\langle w_1, t_1 \rangle$ (this time the set $\{a, b\}$) contains the denotation of m at the same index (i.e. the individual a). Consider now some formulas involving quantification, evaluated with respect to the same index $\langle w_1, t_2 \rangle$. The formulas $\forall x \mathbf{F}B(x)$ and $\forall x \mathbf{P}B(x)$ are both false here (since neither the denotation of B at $\langle w_1, t_3 \rangle$ nor its denotation at $\langle w_1, t_1 \rangle$ contains the entire domain A), consequently the formula $[\forall x \mathbf{F}B(x) \vee \forall x \mathbf{P}B(x)]$ is also false here. But contrast this last formula with the formula $\forall x[\mathbf{F}B(x) \vee \mathbf{P}B(x)]$, which is true (because everything in the domain A is such that it appears in *either* the denotation of B at $\langle w_1, t_3 \rangle$ *or* in its denotation at $\langle w_1, t_1 \rangle$). The formula $\forall x \Diamond B(x)$ is true (everything in A appears in the denotation of B at some index or other), and so is the stronger formula $\Diamond \forall x B(x)$ (there is a particular index, namely $\langle w_2, t_3 \rangle$ at which everything in the domain appears in the denotation of B all at once). On the other hand, the formula $\Box \exists x B(x)$ is true (at every index there is at least one individual in the denotation of B) but the stronger formula $\exists x \Box B(x)$ is false (it is not true that there is a particular individual that appears in the denotation of B at all indices). Therefore the even stronger formula $\forall x \Box B(x)$ (and its logical equivalent $\Box \forall x B(x)$) must also be false.

Notice that the definition of $\Box$ as "necessarily always" makes it "stronger" than any of the tense operators, in the sense that the following formulas will be true in any model in which time (i.e., the members of T) extends without end into the future and past:

(5-28) $\Box\phi \rightarrow \mathbf{F}\phi$

(5-29) $\Box\phi \rightarrow \mathbf{P}\phi$

If we introduced **G** and **H** by definition, the formulas corresponding to (5-28) and (5-29) in which **G** and **H** replace **F** and **P**, respectively, would be true in all models. This fact about $\Box$ renders tense operators preceding $\Box$ otiose, in the sense that the following will be true in any model in which time has no beginning or end:

(5-30) $\mathbf{F}\Box\phi \leftrightarrow \Box\phi$

(5-31) $\mathbf{P}\Box\phi \leftrightarrow \Box\phi$

The following conditionals are also valid in all such "eternal" models, although the converses are not.

(5-32) $\Box\phi \rightarrow \Box\mathbf{F}\phi$

(5-33) $\Box\phi \rightarrow \Box\mathbf{P}\phi$

And the following are true in any models, even if time is finite:

(5-34) $\mathbf{F}\phi \rightarrow \Diamond\phi$

(5-35) $\mathbf{P}\phi \rightarrow \Diamond\phi$

PROBLEM (5-9). Assuming the model M just given for L_{1mt}, compute the following (for arbitrary g):

(i) $[\![[B(m) \wedge \mathbf{F}B(j)]]\!]^{M, \mathbf{w}_1, \mathbf{t}_2, g}$

(ii) $[\![[\Diamond \mathbf{P} \neg B(d)]]\!]^{M, \mathbf{w}_1, \mathbf{t}_2, g}$

(iii) $[\![\Box[\mathbf{F}B(m) \rightarrow \mathbf{P}B(m)]]\!]^{M, \mathbf{w}_1, \mathbf{t}_2, g}$

(iv) $[\![\Box[[\neg B(m) \wedge \mathbf{F}B(m)] \rightarrow \mathbf{P}B(m)]]\!]^{M, \mathbf{w}_1, \mathbf{t}_2, g}$

(v) $[\![\exists x \Box[B(x) \vee B(d)]]\!]^{M, \mathbf{w}_1, \mathbf{t}_2, g}$

PROBLEM (5-10). Show that (5-30) is not valid in the right-to-left direction for models in which time has an end.

PROBLEM (5-11). Construct infinite models in which the converses of (5-28) and (5-29) do not hold.

PROBLEM (5-12). Show that (5-34) and (5-35) would not be valid if **G** and **H** replaced **F** and **P**, respectively.

Tenses are but one of a class of linguistic phenomena that linguists generally refer to as *deictic expressions* (from Greek *deiktos*, 'able to show directly'), more or less the same class of expressions which philosophers call *indexical expressions* or *demonstratives*. These are all expressions whose "meaning" in some way or other depends on the context in which the expression is used. Tenses, obviously, depend on the time of the utterance for their meaning. Other obvious examples of deictic expressions are first and second person pronouns, various temporal expressions (*recently*, *soon*, *now*, *then*, *yesterday*, *tomorrow*, etc.), locative expressions (*here*, *there*, *nearby*, *over there*, etc.) and "true" demonstratives (*this*, *that*, *these*, *those*, etc.). There are a multitude of more subtle cases, which are discussed in Charles Fillmore's *Lectures on Deixis* (Fillmore, 1975). The treatment of the semantics of tense operators naturally raises the question whether other kinds of deictic expressions could be given an analogous model-theoretic analysis. We have, in effect, treated alethic modality as deictic (since we relativized the definition of denotation to an arbitrary **w** out of the set W), though the semantics of $\Box$ and $\Diamond$ (in the S5 system) make this somewhat trivial insofar as the denotation of $\Box\phi$ and $\Diamond\phi$ do not really depend on the choice of a particular **w** within a particular model. But there is no reason why we should not expand the notion of an index to provide what Fillmore would call the "deictic anchorage" for other context-dependent expressions as well. Suppose we think of an index as a triple $\langle \mathbf{w}, \mathbf{t}, \mathbf{s} \rangle$ where **w** and **t** are respectively thought of as the possible world and time of an utterance, but s, a member of A, is to represent the speaker of the utterance. We could then treat the pronoun *I* in English as an individual term just like any other whose denotation, relative to any model, world, time, speaker and value assignment, is given by a semantic rule like the following:

$$[\![I]\!]^{M,w,t,s,g} = s.$$

Thus we have in effect expanded our two-dimensional semantic space to a three-dimensional one. We can of course go on adding other coordinates to our indices. If we wanted to treat *here* and *there*, we would need not only a place coordinate, but something like a "closeness relation" on places (parallel to $<$ on T), so that relative to a place p, *here* would denote all those places "close" to p, *there* would denote other places. David Lewis suggests (in Lewis 1972) that an index include a possible-world coordinate, a time coordinate, a place coordinate (in view of such sentences as *Here there are tigers*), a speaker coordinate, an audience coordinate (in view of such sentences as *You are Porky*, an indicated objects coordinate (in view of such sentences as *That pig is Porky*) and a previous discourse coordinate (in view of such sentences as *The aforementioned pig is Porky*). Such a septuple can be though of as specifying a *context* relative to which an expression is to be given a denotation (or at least, all the features of a context relevant to interpreting the deictic expressions). No doubt other coordinates would be needed besides these in a full treatment of a natural language, but the method is extendable to any finite number of coordinates (see Lewis 1972, Appendix, for further discussion). The fact that such a complete expansion of an index would be exceedingly complex is of course no objection to the method in itself; however, some people have worried that the number of ways expressions of possible human languages may depend upon context is not only complex but in principle unlimited. A proposal by Cresswell is to take contexts as simple, primitive entities, but entities which may have an unlimited number of *properties* (in the technical sense of property to be explained shortly), such as the property of having a certain speaker, a certain hearer, a certain time, etc. Interpretations of expressions would then depend not on the constituents of a context (i.e. an index), but rather on the properties the context has. See Cresswell 1972, pp. 109–119 for discussion. David Kaplan has pointed out the advantages of a two-step process which first maps these added components of context to a sense, where that in turn maps possible worlds and moments of time to denotations (Kaplan 1970, 1971, 1973). Since the coordinate method is adopted by Montague in PTQ, we will not elaborate on the alternatives to it here.

A word is in order at this point on terminology. In dealing with tenses and other contextual coordinates we are now in a sense no longer dealing purely with the relation between sentences of the language and the world, but also to some degree with the relation among the world, the sentences of the language, the speakers of the language, and the contexts in which they use them. Thus it would seem that in dealing with deictic or indexical expressions we have crossed the boundary into pragmatics. In fact, Bar-Hillel (1954) has suggested that the study of indexical expressions *is* the subject of the field of pragmatics, and Montague followed this terminological lead. Thus the kind of formal language that Montague called 'pragmatics', the name of which appears in the title of two of his papers 'Pragmatics' (Montague 1968) and 'Pragmatics and Intensional Logic' (Montague 1970), is simply a first-order language that may contain arbitrary sentence operators interpreted in the context-dependent way that we have just illustrated with tense and modal operators. However, Richmond Thomason has suggested (in comments to the 1973 MSSB Workshop on Formal Pragmatics and elsewhere) that we reserve the term *pragmatics* for the study of direct and indirect speech acts, presuppositions (if such are needed in a theory of natural language), conventional and conversational implicature, and the like. Whereas these latter problems may involve quite a different methodology from that of formal semantics (given the model theoretic approach to natural language semantics), the analysis of indexical expressions in the manner just illustrated is a rather straightforward extension of Tarski's original model theory. It is Thomason's use of the term *pragmatics*, not Montague's, that we will adopt here. Though the linguist's use of the term *pragmatics* is far from standardized, Thomason's use seems to be more in accord with that of linguists in any case. (We could still make a terminological distinction between *indexical semantics* and *non-indexical semantics* if necessary.)

Note also that in dealing with the interpretation of indexical expressions in this way we are still not dealing with the notions of *sentence utterance* and *sentence use* in an essential way. For example, we have suggested that the pronoun *I* be interpreted relative to an index containing an arbitrary individual s thought of as "the speaker" in that context. The sentence *I feel ill* would be true at an index containing s as speaker whenever s feels ill at the time and place of that index. However, this could count as true whether or not s actually utters a token of the sentence *I feel ill* at that index; s might actually be saying *Snow is green* or any other sentence at that index, or he might be silent. Though this result may seem strange at first, it is a natural and harmless consequence of our decision to abstract the study of semantics (including indexical semantics) from the more general study of pragmatics, and could be easily modified in a theory which includes language use.

EXERCISES

1. Suppose the definition of an index is expanded to make them ordered quadruples $\langle w, t, s, h \rangle$, where $w \in W$ is a possible world, $t \in T$ is the time of utterance, $s \in A$ is the speaker, and $h \in A$ is the hearer. Suppose further that we add a second individual constant Y (in addition to the individual constant I introduced on p. 137), which is to behave like the English pronoun "you." Give formal definitions of the denotations of I and Y relative to a model and an index $\langle w, t, s, h \rangle$. Assuming that the two-place predicate L is thought of as "loves," show formally in terms of these definitions and the other semantic rules of L_{1mt} (suitably expanded of course to give $[\![\alpha]\!]^{M, w, t, s, h, g}$ for all basic expressions α) how the following informally stated observation holds:

> "The sentence *I love you* when spoken by A to B is true in a given situation just in case the sentence *You love me* would be true in a situation that is exactly the same except that B is speaking to A."

2. Show that (i) entails (ii) in L_{1t}:

(i) $[F\phi \wedge F\psi]$

(ii) $[F[\phi \wedge \psi] \vee F[F\phi \wedge \psi] \vee F[\phi \wedge F\psi]]$

Determine which property or properties of the relation $<$ are crucial in proving this entailment, and show how the entailment fails if $<$ cannot be assumed to have it (them).

3. Show that each of the following formula schemata is valid in L_{1m}.

(i) $\Box[\phi \rightarrow \psi] \rightarrow [\Box\phi \rightarrow \Box\psi]$

(ii) $\Box\phi \rightarrow \Box\Box\phi$

(iii) $\phi \rightarrow \Box\Diamond\phi$

(iv) $\Diamond\phi \rightarrow \Box\Diamond\phi$

NOTES

[1] The formula (5-14) in one implicational direction is in fact the tense-logical analogue of a controversial modal formula known as the *Barcan* formula. This is discussed on pp. 129-130 and the comments there apply *mutatis mutandis* to (5-14) as well.

[2] There is an extensive literature on tense logic. The "standard" work on tense logic is said to be Prior (1967), but it is based entirely on axiomatic, not semantic, treatments. An excellent survey article is Burgess (1979). The relationship between tense logic and tenses in natural language has been the subject of recent works such as Bull (1960) and Clifford (1975). Since tense logic and its semantics are formally quite similar to modal

logic and its semantics. Hughes and Cresswell (1968) is also to be recommended in this connection.

[3] Hughes and Cresswell (1968) is a thorough introduction to modern modal logic and its semantics, and a source of bibliography on the subject.

[4] This is not the place to review the long philosphical debate about possible worlds as a basis of modal semantics. The reader may be referred to the articles in Copi and Gould (1967) for a survey of the topic. Scott's 'Advice on Modal Logic' (Scott 1970) has had a major influence on more recent developments.

[5] The formula (5-21), when translated into English, makes for peculiar sounding utterances, e.g. "If it is raining, then it is possible that it is raining," The strangeness of this sentence, however, should not be taken to suggest that there is anything wrong with a system of modal logic that makes (5-21) valid, but rather can be traced to rules of conversation and to the fact that *possible* and *must* in ordinary language tend to be interpreted as epistemic (or deontic) modals, not alethic modals; cf. Karttunen (1972).

[6] See also Hughes and Cresswell (1968), Chapter 10, and for the philosophical issues involved in identifying an object in one world with an object in another, Chisholm (1967), Purtill (1968), and Hintikka (1967).

[7] Likewise, we will still be able to capture scope distinctions in which definite descriptions are involved or in which more than one predicate is involved. For example, we will be able to represent in tense logic the two readings of *The president of the United States will always be a Republican*: one which asserts that a particular individual will remain a Republican all his life, the other which asserts that at any future time whoever is president of the U.S. will be a Republican at that time. These cases will be discussed in Chapter 6; see also Thomason and Stalnaker (1969).

[8] See Scott (1970) for a discussion of alternative ways of relating individuals across worlds, possibly via their properties, but compare these with the appendix to that paper and with Kaplan (1970).

CHAPTER 6

MONTAGUE'S INTENSIONAL LOGIC

I. COMPOSITIONALITY AND THE INTENSION-EXTENSION DISTINCTION

Up to this point we have treated tense and other modal operators syncategorematically, i.e., we have not defined a denotation for the symbol **F** directly, but only a denotation of the whole expression **F**ϕ in terms of the interpretation of the expression ϕ. Now let us consider the question whether we can assign a denotation separately to **F** in such a way that the denotation of **F**ϕ can be determined entirely on the basis of the denotation of **F** and the denotation of ϕ. (This would parallel the way in which we gave a denotation for *it-is-not-the-case-that* in L_{0E} in such a way that the denotation of *it-is-not-the-case-that* ϕ was the result of applying the function denoted by *it-is-not-the-case-that* to the denotation of ϕ.) However, this simply cannot be done for **F** because the denotation of ϕ is a truth value, yet the truth value of **F**ϕ is independent of the truth value of ϕ. **F**ϕ may be true at a given time whether or not ϕ is true at that time; the same is true of formulas of the form **P**ϕ. To bring the point home for natural languages, consider (6-1) and (6-2) versus (6-3) and (6-4) (examples cited by Thomason 1974a, to establish the same point):

(6-1) Iceland is covered with a glacier.

(6-2) Africa is covered with a glacier.

(6-3) Iceland was (once) covered with a glacier.

(6-4) Africa was (once) covered with a glacier.

Though (6-1) and (6-2) are both false at the present time, (6-3) is now true but (6-4) is now false. Obviously, the denotations of **F**ϕ and **P**ϕ at a time **t** will depend on other things besides the denotation (i.e. truth values) of ϕ at **t**; specifically, they will depend on the denotation of ϕ at other times. This contrasts with negation, since the denotation of $\neg\phi$ at any time depends merely on the denotation (truth value) of ϕ at that same time. For this reason, negation is said to be a *truth-functional* operator, while the tense operators (and modal operators) are said to be *non-truth-functional.* But how can this fact about the interpretation of tenses be reconciled with our principle that the semantic value of a whole expression be a function of the semantic values of its parts? The answer would seem to be that we cannot consider the semantic value of **F**ϕ to be merely a function of the *denotations* of **F** and ϕ, but it must be a function of something other than the denotation (as we have defined it) in the case of ϕ. The question is, what else?

The first philosopher to confront this issue directly was Gottlob Frege (Frege 1893), and all subsequent discussion (and in particular, Montague's) seems to have been influenced one way or another by what he said about it. Frege noticed the problem with modal operators, not tenses. One of his examples (which has become a standard example for discussions of the problem) was as follows: Most systems of logic with an identity predicate contain a law (the so-called *Leibnitz' Law*) that the result of substituting in any formula one name for another name denoting the same individual results in a formula that is true if and only if the original formula was true. Thus to take a natural language example, the phrase *The Morning Star* denotes the same entity as the phrase *The Evening Star* (i.e. both denote the planet Venus), so the sentence *The Morning Star is not visible now* is true just in case the sentence *The Evening Star is not visible now* is true. However, contrast sentence (6-5) and (6-6):

(6-5) Necessarily, the Morning Star is the Morning Star.

(6-6) Necessarily, the Morning Star is the Evening Star.

Sentence (6-5) is true because *The Morning Star is the Morning Star* is a logically true sentence, an instance of the axiom $a = a$ (for any name a) in predicate logic with identity. (As with most simple logical truths, it is hard to imagine this sentence being uttered as a sentence of English, since it could hardly convey any useful new information to anyone.) However, (6-6) is not true according to Frege, since it is a matter of contingent fact that the Morning Star is the same as the Evening Star, not a matter of logical necessity. Yet the truth of (6-6) should follow from the truth of (6-5) by Leibnitz' Law, since (6-6) merely substitutes for a name in (6-5) another name denoting the same individual. Apparently, the operator $\Box$ produces another case where the denotation of the whole expression is not strictly a function of the denotation of the parts. (In fact, the reader will recall that in the rules we gave, the denotation of $\Box\phi$ at a given index did not depend just on the denotation of ϕ at that index but on ϕ's denotation at other indices as well.)

Another case discussed by Frege involves the complements of verbs like *believe.* Sentence (6-7) would seem to follow from (6-8) by Leibnitz' Law again, yet (6-7) might be true though (6-8) is false if the individual named *John* here is a perfectly rational person when it comes to principles of identity, but is nevertheless somewhat benighted astronomically:

(6-7) John believes that the Morning Star is the Morning Star.

(6-8) John believes that the Morning Star is the Evening Star.

Such syntactic constructions (sentences with modals and the complements of verbs like *believe, think, imagine, suppose, say,* etc.) are sometimes called *oblique constructions* or *referentially opaque constructions* (since they are "opaque" to the substitution of co-designative names while preserving truth values) as opposed to the more "ordinary" *referentially transparent* constructions (those for which Leibnitz' Law holds). Once such constructions are noticed, they are not hard to find in natural languages. Another frequently discussed "opaque" position (in fact, possibly the only one in non-modal, non-embedded sentences having no adverbs) is the object position of transitive verbs like *want, seek, need,* etc. Thus (6-9) can be true, in one reading at least, even though there is no single individual whose name could be substituted for *a friend* in (6-9) while preserving truth value:

(6-9) John is seeking a friend.

The reading of (6-9) in question is what linguists call the *non-specific* reading of (6-9), the reading in which there is no *particular* friend that John is seeking. To make the point even more strongly, (6-10) can be true even in a world (as the actual world is) where there are no unicorns:

(6-10) John is seeking a unicorn.

Cases where the denotation of a whole phrase cannot be explained in terms of the denotation of its parts include other sorts of constructions where the notion of "referential opacity" is not applicable; in particular, certain adjectives and adverbs. In many instances, it seems natural to think of an adjective as having a set as its denotation, just as intransitive verbs and nouns do. For example, given our model-theoretic treatment of subject-predicate sentences, it is natural to take the sentence *John's house is blue* as true (at an index) just in case the object denoted by *John's house* (at that index) is in the set of things denoted by the adjective *blue* (at that index). In attributive position, adjectives of this sort can still be taken to have a set as denotation without endangering the principle of compositionality. It is possible to take the combination of adjective and noun as having as its denotation the set of things that are in both the set denoted by the adjective and the set denoted by the noun (or to say the same thing, the combination has as its denotation the *intersection* of the set denoted by the adjective with the set denoted by the noun). Thus *Some blue house is rentable* can be said to be true just in case there is an individual that is a member of the set of blue things and of the set of houses, and that individual is also in the set denoted by *rentable.* (Essentially the same semantic analysis would obtain if we were to derive the phrase *some blue house* transformationally from the relative clause *some house which is blue*.) However, adjectives such as *former* and *alleged* (as in *former senator* and *alleged communist*) cannot have as denotation (at an index) the intersection of any such sets: e.g. *former senator* cannot be analyzed as the intersection of the set of senators with the set of "things that are former" (at that index), since the latter phrase is meaningless. In fact, no analysis of the denotation of *former senator* (at an index) in terms of the denotation of *senator* at that same index will be adequate; rather, what is obviously required for the denotation of *former senator* at a given index is the denotation of *senator* at indices with earlier time coordinates. This case is semantically similar to the problem with tenses.

Frege's solution to this sort of problem lay in his distinction between the *sense* of an expression (German *Sinn*) and its *reference* or *denominatum* (German *Bedeutung*). (The term *intension* later came to be used for sense, and the term *extension* for reference). The *reference* of an expression for Frege corresponded to what we have uniformly termed the denotation of an expression (e.g. a truth value in the case of sentences, a set in the case or predicates, etc.). The sense corresponded to what we might intuitively think of as the "meaning" of the expression as distinct from its denotation. (Frege referred to the sense of a sentence as the "thought" (*Gedanke*) expressed by the sentence, what is now often called the *proposition* expressed by the sentence.) The sense of an expression is supposed to determine what its reference is in any possible state of affairs.

Armed with this distinction, Frege attempted to solve the problem of non-referential contexts (modal contexts, belief contexts, etc.) by saying that expressions of natural language have a kind of "ambiguity" in that sometimes an expression has a "normal" denotation (i.e., the kind of denotation we have been assigning to expressions of our formal language), but in certain circumstances an expression "denotes" what is ordinarily its sense. For example, in isolation the sentences *The Morning Star is the Morning Star* and *The Morning Star is the Evening Star* have the same denotation (the truth value 1), but when preceded by a modal, these sentences "denote" the sense of the respective sentences, i.e., the propositions expressed by these sentences. Since the senses of the two sentences are clearly not the same, it follows from this position that the truth conditions for *necessarily* ϕ need not violate the principle that the denotation of a complex expression be a function of the "denotations" of its parts. Of course, the usefulness of this idea for formal semantics depends on whether a satisfactory way of formalizing the notion of *sense* can be found, as well as a systematic way of predicting when an expression will have its "normal" denotation and when it will "denote" its sense.

The first attempt to formalize the notion of sense was made by Rudolf Carnap (1947). Since the meaning of an utterance is supposed to determine its extension, Carnap suggested that the sense of an expression (for which he substituted the term *intension* of an expression) is simply a function from possible states of affairs which gives, for any particular state of affairs, the denotation of the expression (which Carnap called the *extension* of the expression) at that state of affairs. In other words, the intension of an expression is nothing more than all the varying extensions (denotations) the expression can have, put together and "organized", as it were, as a function with all possible states of affairs as arguments and the appropriate extensions arranged as values.

With the advent of Kripke's semantics for modal logic (taking *possible worlds* as indices), it became possible for the first time to give an unproblematic formal definition of *intension* for formalized languages. When we have done this for a formal language resembling English, we will have produced a theoretical construct (*intension* of an expression) that "does what a meaning does", insofar as a meaning of an expression is something that determines, for any time, place and possible situation, the denotation of the expression in that time, place and situation (or in the case of a sentence, the truth value of the sentence in that time, place and situation).

For our formal languages that employ coordinate semantics, we will want to take an intension as a function from *indices* to extensions; in this way we will be able to treat the "meanings" of indexical expressions uniformly with that of all other expressions. It will be helpful to give explicit names (based on traditional terms) to certain kinds of intensions. We assume, for simplicity, that indices are just ordered pairs consisting of a possible world and a time (as in L_{1mt}).

A *name* denotes an individual at each index. Hence, the intension of a name is a function from indices to individuals (intuitively, a function which gives for each context the person denoted by the name at that context). It is traditional to call such an intension an *individual concept* or *the concept of* a particular name. For example, if *Miss America* (or simply *m*) is a name, then *the concept of Miss America* is that function which for each index (i.e. for each world and time) gives the person picked out by the name at that world and time. For the actual world these are, for each time, the persons who actually were, are, or will be Miss America, and for different world coordinates, these are persons who would be or would have been Miss America had the world been different in various ways from the way it actually is. Since "ordinary" names (unlike *Miss America*) denote the same individuals at various times (and according to some philosophical views on naming would denote the same individual even in different worlds), it has been a matter of some philosophical dispute whether names should have an intension as well as an extension (cf. Kripke (1972) and references therein). This is not the place to review that discussion, but it is pertinent to note that even if ordinary names denote the same individual at all indices, they will nevertheless have an intension at least in the trivial sense that there will be a well-defined function on indices giving the extension of the name at each index, though it will be a *constant function.*

Let us illustrate individual concepts by taking the model *M* for L_{1mt} given in the preceding chapter. There are six distinct indices for this model (two worlds and three times for each world), and the denotations of the names *m* and *d* are fully determined for each of these by the interpretation function *F.* Thus the intensions of the names *m* and *d* in the model *M* are the following functions (cf. notational convention on the next page):

(6-11a) $[\![m]\!]^{M,g}_{\text{¢}} = \begin{bmatrix} \langle w_1, t_1\rangle \rightarrow a \\ \langle w_2, t_1\rangle \rightarrow c \\ \langle w_1, t_2\rangle \rightarrow b \\ \langle w_2, t_2\rangle \rightarrow c \\ \langle w_1, t_3\rangle \rightarrow c \\ \langle w_2, t_3\rangle \rightarrow b \end{bmatrix}$ (6-11b) $[\![d]\!]^{M,g}_{\text{¢}} = \begin{bmatrix} \langle w_1, t_1\rangle \rightarrow b \\ \langle w_2, t_1\rangle \rightarrow b \\ \langle w_1, t_2\rangle \rightarrow b \\ \langle w_2, t_2\rangle \rightarrow b \\ \langle w_1, t_3\rangle \rightarrow b \\ \langle w_2, t_3\rangle \rightarrow b \end{bmatrix}$

> Notational Convention[6]: For any expression α and for any model M and value assignment g, we use $[\![\alpha]\!]_{¢}^{M,g}$ for the intension of α with respect to M and g.

Note that since we do not need to relativize the definition of intension to a particular index, we need not add subscripts **w** and **t** to $[\![\alpha]\!]_{¢}^{M,g}$.

A *one-place predicate* denotes a set of individuals (or equivalently, the characteristic function of a set of individuals) at each index. Thus the intension of a predicate will be the function that gives, for each index, the set (or characteristic function thereof) denoted at that index. Such an intension will be called a *property*. Thus the property corresponding to the English *is asleep* can be thought of as the function which gives, for each possible situation, the set of individuals that are asleep in that situation. In the model M for L_{1mt}, $[\![B]\!]_{¢}^{M,g}$ can be reconstructed from $F(B)$ just as the above intensions were:

(6-12) $$[\![B]\!]_{¢}^{M,g} = \begin{bmatrix} \langle w_1, t_1\rangle \rightarrow \{a, b\} \\ \langle w_2, t_1\rangle \rightarrow \{b, c\} \\ \langle w_1, t_2\rangle \rightarrow \{a, c\} \\ \langle w_2, t_2\rangle \rightarrow \{a\} \\ \langle w_1, t_3\rangle \rightarrow \{b, c\} \\ \langle w_2, t_3\rangle \rightarrow \{a, b, c\} \end{bmatrix}$$

A *formula* denotes a truth value at each index. Hence the intension of a formula is a function from indices to truth values, and such an intension will be called a *proposition*. Since a function from any set into {0, 1} is the characteristic function of some subset of that set, a proposition as just defined "characterizes" a set of indices; i.e. a proposition maps all the indices at which a formula is true into 1, and maps all other indices into 0. Thus it characterizes the set of indices at which the formula is true, and on this view it is common to equate a proposition with a set of indices (in the same way as the function denoted by a predicate is equated with the set of individuals that function characterizes). In the literature on possible world semantics it is also common to see propositions described as "sets of possible worlds"; this locution is based on essentially the same idea except that indexical expressions are ignored; hence in place of functions on indices, a proposition is thought of as a function on possible worlds only.

As an illustration, consider the formulas $B(m)$ and $B(n)$ with respect to the model M. In this model their intensions (i.e., the respective propositions expressed by these formulas) will be the following functions:

(6-13) $[\![B(m)]\!]_{¢}^{M,g} = \begin{bmatrix} \langle w_1, t_1\rangle \to 1 \\ \langle w_2, t_1\rangle \to 1 \\ \langle w_1, t_2\rangle \to 0 \\ \langle w_2, t_2\rangle \to 0 \\ \langle w_1, t_3\rangle \to 1 \\ \langle w_2, t_3\rangle \to 1 \end{bmatrix}$ (6-14) $[\![B(n)]\!]_{¢}^{M,g} = \begin{bmatrix} \langle w_1, t_1\rangle \to 0 \\ \langle w_2, t_1\rangle \to 1 \\ \langle w_1, t_2\rangle \to 1 \\ \langle w_2, t_2\rangle \to 0 \\ \langle w_1, t_3\rangle \to 1 \\ \langle w_2, t_3\rangle \to 1 \end{bmatrix}$

Thus the proposition $[\![B(m)]\!]_{¢}^{M,g}$ may be thought of as the set $\{\langle w_1, t_1\rangle, \langle w_2, t_1\rangle, \langle w_1, t_3\rangle, \langle w_2, t_3\rangle\}$, and the proposition $[\![B(n)]\!]_{¢}^{M,g}$ as the set $\{\langle w_2, t_1\rangle, \langle w_1, t_2\rangle, \langle w_1, t_3\rangle, \langle w_2, t_3\rangle\}$. How were these intensions determined? By simply determining the denotation of each formula at each index (and this was determined in each case by whether the denotation of the name at that index was a member of the denotation of the predicate at that index), and then writing out the result of this computation as a function giving for each index the appropriate truth value at that index. Clearly, then, the intension of any expression of L_{1mt} relative to a model is determined by the interpretation of the basic expressions and the semantic rules: For any expression α, if α is a non-logical constant, then $[\![\alpha]\!]_{¢}^{M,g}$ can be computed by inspecting the denotation that F assigns to α at each index, and if α is a complex expression, then $[\![\alpha]\!]_{¢}^{M,g}$ can be computed from the semantic rules by the steps needed to determine the denotation of α for each index $\langle w, t\rangle$. What we have been calling "denotation" is of course just what we now mean by "extension." What we have just said about computing intensions from the definition of "extension" means that *intension* and *extension* will be notions that are interdefinable relative to a (completely specified) model. From the extension of an expression at all indices we can determine the intension by just assembling these extensions in the form of a function; conversely, from the intension of any expression we can determine the extension of the expression at any index by just applying the intension (as function-to-argument) to the index we are interested in: the value of $[\![\alpha]\!]_{¢}^{M,g}$ for this argument will be the extension we want. Thus the following equivalence will hold for any model M, any assignment g, any w in W and t in T, and any expression of the language:

(6-15) $[\![\alpha]\!]_{¢}^{M,g}(\langle w, t\rangle) = [\![\alpha]\!]^{M,w,t,g}$

Of course, the intension of an expression is a stronger notion than the extension of that expression at a *particular* index alone; knowing the intension of α implies knowing the extension of α at any particular index, sinse any extension of α is, as it were, contained within the extension of α. But simply knowing the extension of α at a *single* index is in general not sufficient for figuring out the intension, since one still needs to know the extension of α at all other indices as well. The "interdefinability" of intension and extension obtains only when one has, so to speak, the entire model in view.

Notice also that variables, as well as constants, are supposed to be provided with intensions by this definition. But recall that the extension (i.e. denotation) of a variable is always supplied by the value assignment g and thus does not differ from one index to the next. Thus the intension of a variable will be a constant function on indices (as were the intensions of the "ordinary" names *j, d* and *n* in *M*), in particular, one that gives at any index whatever g assigns to that variable. Formally stated, if u is any variable, then for all w and t, $[\![u]\!]_{¢}^{M,g}(\langle w, t\rangle) = g(u)$.

We can summarize these new technical terms in the form of a chart describing the intension and extension of the three main categories of expressions (Table 6-1):

TABLE 6-1

Category of expression of the language	Extension	Intension	
		Name of Intension	Description of Intension
Individual terms (constant or variable)	individuals in *A*	individual concepts	functions from indices to individuals in *A*
One-place predicates	sets of individuals in *A*	properties (of individuals)	functions from indices to sets of individuals in *A*
Formulas (including sentences)	truth values	propositions	functions from indices to truth values ("sets" of indices)

A couple of words of warning are in order to forestall possible confusions about these intensional notions.

First, the terms *individual concept, property of an individual, proposition,* and the other intensional notions to be introduced later must be treated as technical terms which mean just what their definitions say they mean and no more. The choice of terminology is, of course, deliberate in that each formal set-theoretic construct is intended to stand as an analysis for the more elusive philosophical concept to which it corresponds. How successful these analyses are is an important question, but it is not of immediate concern to us here.

A second point, related to the first, is that individual concepts, properties of individuals, propositions and the like are not expressions of any formal or natural language (nor elements of abstract deep structures of any formal or natural language), but are set-theoretic constructs and thus entirely independent of any language. These intensions will be correlated systematically with expressions of formal and natural language by semantic rules, but the intensions themselves are extra-linguistic semantical objects constructed by set-theoretic means entirely out of the basic sets A, W, T, and $\{0, 1\}$ of some model.

Third, on this view a proposition which is the intension of some English sentence need not consist of a *single* possible world, but is rather a *set* of worlds – possibly a large set. Sometimes one reads in the linguistic literature that a sentence such as *John dreamed that he visited Alaska* "creates (or describes) *a* possible world in which John visited Alaska." By our account it is not necessarily one possible world but conceivably many that comprise the proposition expressed by *John visited Alaska.* This proposition may include possible worlds in which John visited Alaska in the summer and worlds in which he visited it only in the winter; it may include worlds in which he made a long visit and worlds in which he made only a short visit. It may include worlds in which made a visit to Alaska and Sam Smith of Detroit, Michigan, had Wheaties for breakfast on Christmas in 1944, and worlds similar to these except that Smith had not Wheaties but scrambled eggs for breakfast on that day. What this proposition does not contain are any of those (perhaps infinitely) many worlds in which John did not visit Alaska at all. Thus what from an intuitive point of view is a simple proposition (such as that expressed by the sentence *it is raining*) may in this theory be a very large set of possible worlds (or indices) since this proposition is indifferent to so many details about the way things might have been. What is to us an intuitively complex proposition is just a more specific one, that is, one that rules out more possible situations and consequently constitute a smaller set of worlds. The more specific a proposition, the smaller the set of worlds it contains. But even the incredibly specific proposition expressed by the sentence formed by conjoining all the true

English sentences in all the books in all the world's libraries would not be so specific as to single out a set containing only one world (i.e. the actual world) since even this proposition would leave various details undetermined and thus would contain distinct worlds differing in these respects.

This brings us to the fourth point: in a possible-world semantics for a natural language (and for most formal languages also) there will in general be propositions which are not the intensions of any sentence of the language, in addition to those propositions that *are* intensions of sentences of the language. In a model, any collection of the possible worlds, no matter how motley, counts as a well-defined proposition. A similar comment applies to properties and other intensional objects: any function from worlds to sets of individuals is a well-defined property in our sense, etc.

Finally, this leads to the observation that even for those properties which *are* to be the intensions of basic one-place predicates of the language, any function from indices to sets of individuals whatsoever counts as a well-defined property. Within the semantic theory developed so far, there is thus no requirement that all the members of the various sets which serve as the extensions of some property at each possible world have "something in common," though of course we intuitively feel that the extensions of nouns and verbs of natural languages in various situations are not determined haphazardly. We have this feeling not only about physical properties (e.g., *is green, is spherical, is alive,* etc.), but even such anthropocentric and individually subjective properties such as those expressed by *is beautiful, is amusing,* etc. Montague and other practitioners of possible worlds semantics apparently do not view this overbroadness of the technical notion *property* as a defect or inadequacy of their theories by any means. Rather, they seem to view the tasks of narrowing such concepts appropriately as a problem for various empirical physical sciences, and for psychology, but not for a theory of semantics. On the other hand, the linguist – even one who adopts the basic model-theoretic definition of property proposed here – will be interested in asking whether the notion "property expressible by a word of a possible human language" can be distinguished in a substantive way from "properties" in the wide, set-theoretic sense.

We are now almost ready to show how Montague formally treated the puzzles of oblique constructions that concerned Frege, but we first need one more technical device. Notice that the distinction we have made between intension and extension is so far confined entirely to the meta-language. That is, we have shown how both $[\![\alpha]\!]^{M,g}_{\text{¢}}$ and $[\![\alpha]\!]^{M,w,t,g}$ can be defined for any expression α, but the syntax of L_{1mt} has not been changed in any way, nor have we changed the way in which the semantic rules compute the extension (denotation) of a complex phrase in terms of the extensions of the parts. However, to carry through with Frege's suggestion that the interpretation of $\Box\phi$ must involve $[\![\phi]\!]_{\phi}^{M,g}$ and not just $[\![\phi]\!]^{M,w,t,g}$, we must do one of two things: Either we must (1) change the semantic rules so that in the right circumstances they can use intensions as well as the extensions in determining the semantic value of a complex expression (that is, in effect, what we did surreptiously with the semantic rules for $\Box\phi$ and $F\phi$ in the language of L_{1mt}), or else we must (2) modify the object language to include expressions which "denote" (have as extension) the intensions of certain other expressions. The latter would seem to follow in a rather direct way Frege's idea that expressions in oblique contexts denote their senses. Thus, on this approach we would need for each sentence ϕ a second expression ϕ' which denotes the intension of ϕ. Then if we combined an operator *Necessarily* with ϕ' syntactically, the corresponding semantic rule would define the extension of *Necessarily* ϕ' in terms of the extensions of *Necessarily* and of ϕ'.

Either approach to intensional analysis is workable, and Montague used them both in various papers in which he analyzed English. The second approach is the one he adopted in PTQ, however, and it is therefore the one we will pursue here.

The first attempt to develop a formal logic which contained expressions "denoting" intensions as well as extensions was Church's "A Formulation of the Logic of Sense and Denotation" (Church 1951), though this was an axiomatic, not a semantic treatment. David Kaplan in his dissertation (Kaplan 1964) attempted to construct a semantic analysis for Church's system, but this attempt was hampered by the fact that he adopted Carnap's notion of an intension as a function from possible models to extensions. It remained for Montague, in a series of papers (Montague 1968, 1970a, 1970b), to fully develop an intensional language and its model-theoretic interpretation based on the ideas of Kripke's semantics for modal logic, and to apply this formal language systematically to the analysis of intensional phenomena in English.

In Montague's intensional logic, as in Church's, there is the means for forming from any expression α a second expression denoting the intension of α. Since the expressions of the language are infinite in number, it is convenient to form these intension-naming expressions syntactically out of the expressions whose intention they name. Montague's device for doing this is quite simple:

(6-16) If α is any expression, then $^\wedge\alpha$ is an expression which denotes $[\![\alpha]\!]_{\not{c}}^{M,g}$.

For example, since $B(m)$ is a formula in L_{1mt}, the expression $^\wedge B(m)$ will be an expression of the expanded, intensional language corresponding to L_{1mt}, and its denotation at any **w** and **t**, i.e., $[\![{}^\wedge B(m)]\!]^{M,\mathbf{w},\mathbf{t},g}$ will be the proposition $[\![B(m)]\!]_{\not{c}}^{M,g}$. With respect to the model M discussed earlier, $[\![{}^\wedge B(m)]\!]^{M,\mathbf{w},\mathbf{t},g}$ for any **w** and **t**, is the function shown in (6-13), i.e., $[\![B(m)]\!]_{\not{c}}^{M,g}$.

Since the notion of intension is defined for *every* expression of the language, expressions like $^\wedge\alpha$ will themselves have an intension as well as an extension. Moreover, we can form a second expression $^\wedge\alpha$ from any expression α whatsoever, and thus from $^\wedge\alpha$ itself we can form yet another expression denoting the intension of $^\wedge\alpha$, namely $^{\wedge\wedge}\alpha$. And from this we can form $^{\wedge\wedge\wedge}\alpha$, and then $^{\wedge\wedge\wedge\wedge}\alpha$, and so on. In fact, all such expressions count as well-formed in Montague's intensional language and are assigned a well-defined intension and extension by the principles we have already outlined. But these higher-order intensions turn out to be rather uninteresting in the long run. Observe that $[\![{}^\wedge\alpha]\!]^{M,\mathbf{w},\mathbf{t},g}$ will be the same for all indices $\langle\mathbf{w},\mathbf{t}\rangle$; the reason is that there is one and only one $[\![\alpha]\!]_{\not{c}}^{M,g}$. Therefore the intension of this intension, i.e. $[\![{}^\wedge\alpha]\!]_{\not{c}}^{M,g}$, will be a *constant function* on indices which gives for any index the value $[\![\alpha]\!]_{\not{c}}^{M,g}$. Likewise, the intension of the intension of this intension, i.e. $[\![{}^{\wedge\wedge}\alpha]\!]_{\not{c}}^{M,g}$, will be yet another constant function which gives for any index the constant function $[\![{}^\wedge\alpha]\!]_{\not{c}}^{M,g}$, and similarly for the more complex iterated intentions. (To paraphrase the famous little old lady cited in the *Fragestellung* to J. R. Ross' dissertation (Ross 1967), "It's constant functions all the way down".) The puzzled reader may take comfort in the fact that only "first-order" intensions are ever involved in the interpretation of English in PTQ, so the others can be safely ignored.

Montague introduced a second syntactic device into his intensional language as a sort of converse to the intension operator "$^\wedge$". This is the extension operator "$^\vee$", which can be applied to any expression α which denotes an intension $[\![\alpha]\!]_{\not{c}}$ to give a new well-formed expression "$^\vee\alpha$." For any index $\langle\mathbf{w},\mathbf{t}\rangle$ the expression "$^\vee\alpha$" denotes whatever the value of $[\![\alpha]\!]_{\not{c}}^{M,g}$ is at $\langle\mathbf{w},\mathbf{t}\rangle$. Stated formally, if α denotes an intension, then for any index $\langle\mathbf{w},\mathbf{t}\rangle$ $[\![{}^\vee\alpha]\!]^{M,\mathbf{w},\mathbf{t},g}$ is defined as $[\![\alpha]\!]_{\not{c}}^{M,g}(\langle\mathbf{w},\mathbf{t}\rangle)$. The result of combining $^\vee$ with an expression of the form $^\wedge\alpha$ has the effect of "cancelling" out the two operators $^\vee$ and $^\wedge$. That is, it turns out that for all expressions α, and all models M and all **w**, **t**, and g,

$$(6\text{-}17)\quad [\![{}^{\vee}{}^{\wedge}\alpha]\!]^{M, w, t, g} = [\![\alpha]\!]^{M, w, t, g}$$

This equation licenses a rule of "down-up cancellation" which will play an important role in the simplification of complex expressions of intensional logic produced as translations of English phrases. We will return to this later, but we may as well note here that the opposite "cancellation rule" is not valid; i.e., it is not always the case that $[\![{}^{\wedge}{}^{\vee}\alpha]\!]^{M, w, t, g} = [\![\alpha]\!]^{M, w, t, g}$.[1] The reader may have also noticed that whereas $[\![{}^{\wedge}\alpha]\!]^{M, w, t, g}$ has, as we have seen, the same value at every index, $[\![{}^{\vee}\alpha]\!]^{M, w, t, g}$ may differ from index to index, just as $[\![\alpha]\!]^{M, w, t, g}$ may.[2]

These operators $^{\wedge}$ and $^{\vee}$ and their associated definitions are admittedly perplexing to anyone who encounters them for the first time, and this is true of logicians and philosophers of language as well as of linguists. But rather than dwell on the problem here it is probably best to defer it until a later section, where the function of these operators will, we hope, become clearer. Let us proceed then to the formal definitions of the full intensional logic that Montague employed in PTQ.

II. THE INTENSIONAL LOGIC OF PTQ

Montague's *intensional logic* ("IL") is a formal system that combines all the syntactic and semantic resources we have been gradually developing. This system therefore employs a type hierarchy (with expressions for each of the denumerably infinite set of types), higher-order quantification (variables and quantifiers for each type), lambda-abstraction for all types, tenses, modal operators, and finally, means for forming ${}^{\wedge}\alpha$ from any expression α and ${}^{\vee}\beta$ from any intension-denoting expression β.

Probably because of their familiarity, Montague employed the usual syncategorematic definitions for expressions with the logical operators $\neg$, $\wedge$, $\vee$, $\rightarrow$, $\leftrightarrow$, **F**, **P** and $\Box$. The only additional syncategorematic logical symbol is $=$ for "identity", whose semantic interpretation is relatively unproblematic.

The syntactic definitions begin, as in L_{type}, with the recursive definition of the set of types. Since we will now be dealing with expressions denoting intensions as well as extensions for the various types, the definition of the set of types will include a new recursive clause to define for each type a, a new type $\langle s, a\rangle$ for the intensions (or senses) corresponding to each type a. These new types will be explained more fully when the semantic definitions are introduced.

1. *Syntax of IL*

Let t, e, and s be any fixed objects (for technical reasons they should not be ordered pairs or triples). Then the set of *types* is defined recursively as follows:

1. t is a type
2. e is a type
3. If a and b are any types, then $\langle a, b\rangle$ is a type.
4. If a is any type, then $\langle s, a\rangle$ is a type.

A. *Basic Expressions*

1. For each type a, *IL* contains a denumerably infinite set of *non-logical constants* (or simply *constants*) $c_{n,a}$, for each natural number n. The set of all (non-logical) constants of type a is called Con_a.
2. For each type a, *IL* contains a denumerably infinite set of *variables* $v_{n,a}$ for each natural number n. The set of all variables of type a is called Var_a.

(Note that no logical constants are listed here, since these are introduced syncategorematically by the syntactic rules. Notice also that s is not a type.)

B. *Syntactic rules of IL* [3]

The set of *meaningful expressions of type a*, called ME_a, is defined recursively as follows:

1. Every variable of type a is in ME_a.
2. Every constant of type a is in ME_a.
3. If $\alpha \in ME_a$ and u is a variable of type b, then $\lambda u\alpha \in ME_{\langle b, a\rangle}$.
4. If $\alpha \in ME_{\langle a, b\rangle}$ and $\beta \in ME_a$, then $\alpha(\beta) \in ME_b$.
5. If α and β are both in ME_a, then $\alpha = \beta \in ME_t$.

6.–10. If ϕ and ψ are in ME_t, the the following are also in ME_t:

6. $\neg\phi$

7. $[\phi \vee \psi]$

8. $[\phi \wedge \psi]$

9. $[\phi \rightarrow \psi]$

10. $[\phi \leftrightarrow \psi]$

11. If $\phi \in ME_t$ and u is a variable of any type, then $\forall u\phi \in ME_t$.

12. If $\phi \in ME_t$ and u is a variable of any type, then $\exists u\phi \in ME_t$.

13. If $\phi \in ME_t$, then $\Box\phi \in ME_t$.

14. If $\phi \in ME_t$, then $\mathbf{F}\phi \in ME_t$.

15. If $\phi \in ME_t$, then $\mathbf{P}\phi \in ME_t$.

16. If $\alpha \in ME_a$, then $\hat{}\alpha \in ME_{\langle s, a\rangle}$.

17. If $\alpha \in ME_{\langle s, a\rangle}$, then $\check{}\alpha \in ME_a$.

PROBLEM (6-1) We will use the following abreviations for constants and variables in this problem:

Type	*Variables*	*Constants*
e	x, y, z	j, d, m, n, 0, 1, 2, . . .
$\langle s, e\rangle$	r	–
$\langle e, t\rangle$	X, Y	walk′, B, M
$\langle\langle s, e\rangle, t\rangle$	Q	rise′, change′
$\langle s, \langle e, t\rangle\rangle$	P	–
$\langle e, e\rangle$	–	Sq
$\langle e, \langle e, t\rangle\rangle$	R	Gr, K, L
$\langle s, t\rangle$	p	–
$\langle e, \langle e, e\rangle\rangle$	–	Plus

Give the *type* of each of the following expressions of *IL*:

1. $\text{walk}'(j)$
2. $\text{change}'(\hat{}j)$
3. $\lambda x[\text{walk}'(x)]$
4. $\lambda r[\text{rise}'(r)]$
5. $\lambda Q[Q = \text{rise}']$
6. $\lambda P[P = \hat{}\text{walk}']$
7. $\check{}P(\check{}\hat{}j)$
8. $\lambda P[\check{}P(j)]$
9. $\lambda x[\text{Sq}(x)]$
10. $\hat{}[\lambda x[\text{Gr}(3)(x)]]$
11. $\lambda p[\hat{}p = \Box\text{rise}'(\hat{}j)]$
12. $\lambda x[\lambda p[\check{}p = \text{change}'(\hat{}x)]]$
13. $\hat{}\check{}r$
14. $\check{}\hat{}\text{rise}'$
15. $\lambda x[R(x)(\text{Sq}(x))]$

2. *Semantics of IL*

A. A *model for IL* is an ordered quintuple $\langle A, W, T, <, F\rangle$ such that A, W and T are any non-empty sets, $<$ is a linear ordering on the set T, and F is a function whose domain is the set of all non-logical constants of *IL* and whose range is described below. The set of *possible denotations* of type a is defined as follows (where a and b are any types):

1. $D_e = A$
2. $D_t = \{0, 1\}$
3. $D_{\langle a, b\rangle} = D_b^{D_a}$
4. $D_{\langle s, a\rangle} = D_a^{W \times T}$

(Recall that the notation "$W \times T$" stands for the set of all ordered pairs whose first member is in W and whose second member is in T, i.e., the set of all indices $\langle w, t\rangle$. Clause 4 simply says that the possible denotations of type $\langle s, a\rangle$ will be the set of all functions from indices into D_a.)

The set of *senses of type a*, denoted S_a, is defined as $D_{\langle s, a\rangle}$. The function F will assign to each non-logical constant of *IL* of type a a member of S_a. Here Montague introduces a subtle and not particularly important distinction between *sense* and *intension*. The set of senses of type a is simply the set of "possible intensions" out of which the intensions of expressions of type a are to be chosen. Thus all intensions of expressions will be senses, but not necessarily all senses will be intensions of some expression or other. To say that F assigns a member of S_a to each constant of type a (i.e., assigns an intension to each constant) involves only a trivial reformulation of our treatment of L_{1mt} where F assigned a denotation to each *pair* consisting of an index and an expression. Here we have simply changed F from a function of two arguments – an index and an expression – to a function of one argument – an expression. The value assigned to each expression is another function, namely an intension – a function from indices to appropriate denotations. As will be seen, the definitions of intension and extension for non-logical constants will parallel those for L_{1mt} exactly, except that we now have a larger variety of categories of non-logical constants.

An *assignment of values to variables* g is a function having as domain the set of all variables and giving as value for each variable of type a a member of D_a. Note that g assigns to each variable an *extension*, whereas each (non-logical) constant is assigned an *intension* by F.

B. Semantic rules of IL: The semantic rules of *IL* define recursively for any expression α, *the extension of α with respect to model M,* $w \in W$, $t \in T$ *and value assignment g,* denoted $[\![\alpha]\!]^{M,w,t,g}$, as follows:

1. If α is a non-logical constant, then $[\![\alpha]\!]^{M,w,t,g} = [F(\alpha)](\langle w, t\rangle)$. (i.e., the extension of α at $\langle w, t\rangle$ is simply the result of applying the intension of α, which is supplied by F, to the argument $\langle w, t\rangle$.)

2. If α is a variable, then $[\![\alpha]\!]^{M,w,t,g} = g(\alpha)$.

3. If $\alpha \in ME_a$ and u is a variable of type b, then $[\![\lambda u\alpha]\!]^{M,w,t,g}$ is that function h with domain D_b such that for any object x in that domain, $h(x) = [\![\alpha]\!]^{M,w,t,g'}$ where g' is that value assignment exactly like g with the possible difference that $g'(u)$ is the object x.

4. If $\alpha \in ME_{\langle a,b\rangle}$ and $\beta \in ME_b$, then $[\![\alpha(\beta)]\!]^{M,w,t,g}$ is $[\![\alpha]\!]^{M,w,t,g}([\![\beta]\!]^{M,w,t,g})$ (i.e., the result of applying the function $[\![\alpha]\!]^{M,w,t,g}$ to the argument $[\![\beta]\!]^{M,w,t,g}$).

5. If α and β are in ME_a, then $[\![\alpha = \beta]\!]^{M,w,t,g}$ is 1 if and only if $[\![\alpha]\!]^{M,w,t,g}$ is the same as $[\![\beta]\!]^{M,w,t,g}$.

6. If $\phi \in ME_t$, then $[\![\neg\phi]\!]^{M,w,t,g}$ is 1 if and only if $[\![\phi]\!]^{M,w,t,g}$ is 0, and $[\![\neg\phi]\!]^{M,w,t,g}$ is 0 otherwise.

7.–10. If ϕ and ψ are in ME_t, then $[\![[\phi \wedge \psi]]\!]^{M,w,t,g}$ is 1 if and only if both $[\![\phi]\!]^{M,w,t,g}$ and $[\![\psi]\!]^{M,w,t,g}$ are 1. (The definitions for the other truth-functional connectives of $[\phi \vee \psi]$, $[\phi \rightarrow \psi]$, and $[\phi \leftrightarrow \psi]$ are the usual ones, paralleling this definition.)

11. If $\phi \in ME_t$ and u is a variable, then $[\![\forall u\phi]\!]^{M,w,t,g}$ is 1 if and only if $[\![\phi]\!]^{M,w,t,g'}$ is 1 for all g' exactly like g except possibly for the value assigned to u.

12. If $\phi \in ME_t$ and u is a variable, then $[\![\exists u\phi]\!]^{M,w,t,g}$ is 1 if and only if $[\![\phi]\!]^{M,w,t,g'}$ is 1 for some value assignment g' exactly like g except possibly for the value assigned to u.

13. If $\phi \in ME_t$, then $[\![\Box\phi]\!]^{M,w,t,g}$ is 1 if and only if $[\![\phi]\!]^{M,w',t',g}$ is 1 for all w′ in W and all t′ in T..

14. If $\phi \in ME_t$, then $[\![\mathbf{F}\phi]\!]^{M,w,t,g}$ is 1 if and only if $[\![\phi]\!]^{M,w,t',g}$ is 1 for some t′ in T such that $t < t'$.

15. If $\phi \in ME_t$, then $[\![P\phi]\!]^{M,w,t,g}$ is 1 if and only if $[\![\phi]\!]^{M,w,t',g}$ is 1 for some t′ in T such that t′ < t.

16. If $\alpha \in ME_a$, then $[\![{}^\wedge\alpha]\!]^{M,w,t,g}$ is that function h with domain $W \times T$ such that for all ⟨w′, t′⟩ in $W \times T$, h(⟨w′, t′⟩) is $[\![\alpha]\!]^{M,w',t',g}$.

17. If $\alpha \in ME_{\langle s,a\rangle}$, then $[\![{}^\vee\alpha]\!]^{M,w,t,g}$ is $[\![\alpha]\!]^{M,w,t,g}$(⟨w, t⟩) (i.e., the result of applying the function $[\![\alpha]\!]^{M,w,t,g}$ to the argument ⟨w, t⟩).

C. Further definitions.

1. If ϕ is a formula (i.e., a member of ME_t) then ϕ is *true with respect to M and to* ⟨w, t⟩ if and only if $[\![\phi]\!]^{M,w,t,g}$ is 1 for all value assignments g.

2. If α is any expression, then the *intension of* α *with respect to M and g*, denoted $[\![\alpha]\!]_{\not{c}}^{M,g}$, is that function h with domain $W \times T$ such that for all ⟨w, t⟩ in $W \times T$, h(⟨w, t⟩) is $[\![\alpha]\!]^{M,w,t,g}$. (It follows as a direct consequence of this definition and of B.16 that for any α and for any w in W and t in T, $[\![\alpha]\!]_{\not{c}}^{M,g} = [\![{}^\wedge\alpha]\!]^{M,w,t,g}$, and moreover, $[\![\alpha]\!]_{\not{c}}^{M,g}(\langle w, t\rangle) = [\![\alpha]\!]^{M,w,t,g}$.)

A few comments on this language are now in order. First, note that the new symbol "=" can be used to assert the identity of the denotations of two expressions of any type whatsoever (as long as both expressions have the same type). Thus we can assert that two names have the same extension, or that two predicates have the same extension. The reader should bear in mind that intensions are set-theoretically defined entities, hence identity among intensions is no more mysterious a notion than identity among any other kinds of entities. Two intensions are identical if they are, in fact, the same function (i.e., if they give the same value for each index in $W \times T$). To assert that ${}^\wedge\alpha = {}^\wedge\beta$, is, in most cases, a stronger assertion than $\alpha = \beta$, of course. The formula $\alpha = \beta$ is true at an index whenever α and β have the same extension at that index, but ${}^\wedge\alpha = {}^\wedge\beta$ is true at an index only if α and β have the same extension at every index in $W \times T$. Another instance where = may be used is the case where the two expressions that flank it are formulas, i.e., members of ME_t. In this case, $\phi = \psi$ simply says that ϕ and ψ denote the same truth value and this formula is logically equivalent to the formula $\phi \leftrightarrow \psi$. Thus the symbol $\leftrightarrow$ is actually redundant and could have been eliminated if desired. (Of course, Montague was making no attempt to construct this language with the smallest possible number of primitive symbols, but rather included all the familiar symbols from first-order and modal logic to increase the perspicuity of translations of English expressions. Actually, *all* of the logical operators $\neg$, $\wedge$, $\vee$, $\rightarrow$, $\leftrightarrow$, $\Box$, and universal and existential quantification can be defined within *IL* in terms of $=$, λ, and $\hat{}$ with the aid of variables of various types. For these definitions see Montague's Universal Grammar (Montague 1970b, p. 236).)

Consider now the types that will correspond to the intensions we have already discussed. Since individuals are denoted by expressions of type *e*, *individual concepts* will be denoted by expressions of type $\langle s, e\rangle$. Expressions of this type will include variables, constants, and also expressions formed by prefixing the intension operator to expressions of type *e*. E.g., if *d* is a name, $\hat{}d$ is of type $\langle s, e\rangle$ and denotes an individual concept. Other intensional types will have expressions of a similar syntactic heterogeneity. As one-place predicates of individuals are of type $\langle e, t\rangle$, expressions of type $\langle s, \langle e, t\rangle\rangle$ will denote *properties* of individuals. Since formulas are expressions of type *t*, propositions (the intensions of formulas) will be denoted by expressions of type $\langle s, t\rangle$. There will be many other kinds of intensional "semantic objects" besides these three that we will use in interpreting English, so it will be useful to have a general procedure for referring to these various kinds of semantical objects in the metalanguage. We have already implicitly adopted the convention that the denotation of an expression of type $\langle a, t\rangle$ can be called a *set of* whatever things are denoted by expressions of type *a*; for example expressions of type $\langle e, t\rangle$ denote sets of individuals, those of type $\langle\langle e, t\rangle, t\rangle$ denote sets of sets of individuals, and now we can also say that those of type $\langle\langle s, e\rangle, t\rangle$ denote sets of individual concepts, those of type $\langle\langle s, t\rangle, t\rangle$ denote sets of propositions, etc.

We will therefore extend the term *property* in the same way, saying that an expression of type $\langle s, \langle a, t\rangle\rangle$ denotes a *property of* whatever sort of things are denoted by expressions of type *a*. For example, expressions of type $\langle s, \langle e, t\rangle\rangle$ denote *properties of individuals*, those of type $\langle s, \langle\langle s, t\rangle, t\rangle\rangle$ denote *properties of propositions*, and those of type $\langle s, \langle\langle s, \langle e, t\rangle\rangle, t\rangle\rangle$ denote *properties of properties of individuals*. We earlier said that expressions of type $\langle e, \langle e, t\rangle\rangle$ (i.e. two-place predicates) denoted *relations between individuals* (in that a function from individuals to characteristic functions of sets of individuals in effect specifies a two-place relation between individuals). Now we will call the intensional notion corresponding to such a relation (following Montague) a *relation-in-intension between individuals*, and these semantical objects will be denoted by expressions of type $\langle s, \langle e, \langle e, t\rangle\rangle\rangle$.

Generalizing this term, we will call the denotations of expressions of type $\langle s, \langle a, \langle b, t\rangle\rangle\rangle$ (for any types a and b) *relations-in-intensions between* whatever things expressions of type b denote and whatever things expressions of type a denote. Thus expressions of type $\langle s, \langle\langle s, t\rangle, \langle e, t\rangle\rangle\rangle$ will denote *relations-in-intension between individuals and propositions* and expressions of type $\langle s, \langle\langle s, \langle e, t\rangle\rangle, \langle\langle e, t\rangle, t\rangle\rangle\rangle$ denote *relations-in-intension between sets of individuals and properties of individuals.* Fortunately, very few types of this degree of complexity are actually used in Montague's system.

Note that the type-theoretic distinction between "intensional" and "non-intensional" types must be strictly observed when expressions are combined by the functional application rule (B.4). This rule takes an expression of type $\langle a, b\rangle$ and an expression of type a and yields an expression of type b. For example, we can combine an expression α of type $\langle e, t\rangle$ with an expression β of type e to give the expression $\alpha(\beta)$ of type t. We are also allowed to combine δ of type $\langle\langle s, e\rangle, t\rangle$ with γ of type $\langle s, e\rangle$ to give $\delta(\gamma)$ of type t. However, we could not combine α of type $\langle e, t\rangle$ with γ of type $\langle s, e\rangle$ by this rule, nor are we allowed to combine δ of type $\langle\langle s, e\rangle, t\rangle$ with β of type e. Such combinations would count as ill-formed by B.4, and indeed they ought to be since the semantic interpretation of such combinations would require that a function be applied to an argument that is not in its domain. In fact, any expression of any type $\langle s, a\rangle$ cannot directly serve as a functor to apply to anything. This follows from the fact that s alone is not a type according to the recursive definition of types; rather, types involving the symbols s are *all* of the form $\langle s, a\rangle$. Semantically, this means that no expressions of *IL* denote indices directly but can only denote functions from indices to something else. In this respect *IL* was deliberately designed to resemble intensionality in natural languages, since natural languages do not make explicit reference to "indices"; cf. Gallin 1972, p. 83.

The operators $\hat{}$ and $\check{}$ provide a great deal of flexibility in such cases, however. For example, we could first form from β (of type e) the expression $\hat{}\beta$ (which will be of type $\langle s, e\rangle$) and then combine that with δ (of type $\langle\langle s, e\rangle, t\rangle$) to give $\delta(\hat{}\beta)$. This asserts that the concept corresponding to β is in the extension of δ. Or we could first form from γ (of type $\langle s, e\rangle$) the expression $\check{}\gamma$ (of type e) and then combine that with α (of type $\langle e, t\rangle$) to give $\alpha(\check{}\gamma)$, which asserts that the extension of the concept denoted by γ is in the extension of α. A case that arises frequently in PTQ is the one in which we have an expression ζ of type $\langle s, \langle e, t\rangle\rangle$ (denoting a *property* of individuals) and a second expression α of type e (denoting an individual) and we want to combine these to make the apparently innocent assertion that "α has the property ζ." However, we may not do this directly, since a property is a function from indices to functions from individuals to truth values, and what we really have to say is "α is in the extension of property ζ at the present index." This we *can* assert by writing $^{\vee}\zeta(\alpha)$. Probably because of the naturalness of saying that an individual "has" a property and of similar assertions involving properties of higher types, Montague introduces a special notational abbreviation for $^{\vee}\zeta(\alpha)$, which is $\zeta\{\alpha\}$. Formally,

(6-18) If $\gamma \in ME_{\langle s, \langle a, t\rangle\rangle}$ and $\alpha \in ME_a$ for some type *a*, then the expression $\gamma\{\alpha\}$ is to be the expression $[^{\vee}\gamma](\alpha)$, which asserts that the object denoted by α has the property denoted by γ.

The brace notation is thus really inessential and could be eliminated without any reduction in the expressive power of the language.

PROBLEM (6-2) Let the model $M = \langle A, W, T, <, F\rangle$ be as in Chapter 5, pp. 133–134, except that the interpretation function F is assumed to have undergone the notational changes described on pp. 146–147. We will use variables of the types indicated in Problem (6-1). Compute the following (for arbitrary g):

(i) $[\![\lambda x B(x)]\!]^{M, w_1, t_1, g}$

(ii) $[\![\lambda x B(x)]\!]_{\not{c}}^{M, g}$

(iii) $[\![^{\wedge}\lambda x B(x)]\!]_{\not{c}}^{M, g}$

(iv) $[\![[B(m) \wedge \neg B(j)]]\!]_{\not{c}}^{M, g}$

(v) $[\![^{\wedge}[B(m) \wedge \neg B(j)]]\!]^{M, w_2, t_2, g}$

(vi) $[\![m = n]\!]^{M, w_2, t_2, g}$

(vii) $[\![^{\wedge}m = {}^{\wedge}n]\!]^{M, w_2, t_2, g}$

PROBLEM (6-3) How would the answers to (i), (ii), and (iii) above have changed if $\lambda x B(x)$ had been replaced by B in each case?

III. EXAMPLES OF 'OBLIQUE CONTEXTS' AS REPRESENTED IN *IL*

Let us now consider how some of the troublesome oblique constructions can be treated in this language along the lines that Frege first envisioned.

First note that sentences of the form *Necessarily* ϕ could indeed be given an analysis in which the extension of the whole is a function of the extensions of the parts if we treated the word *Necessarily* as a functor which combined not with ϕ but rather with $\hat{}\phi$. This means that the operator in *IL* corresponding to *necessarily* would be treated not as an expression of type $\langle t, t\rangle$ but rather of type $\langle\langle s, t\rangle, t\rangle$. Let us call such an operator Nec. Its denotation would be a function in the set

$$\{0, 1\}^{(\{0, 1\}^{W \times T})}$$

i.e., functions from propositions to truth values. We could give the semantic rule for **Nec** by saying that at any index ⟨w, t⟩, $[\![\mathbf{Nec}]\!]^{M, \mathbf{w}, \mathbf{t}, g}$ is that function from propositions into truth values that gives the value 1 when applied to any proposition *p* just in case *p* itself maps every index ⟨w, t⟩ into 1: otherwise *p* will be mapped into 0. The fact that Montague in PTQ did not exactly treat □ as such a functor on propositions but rather introduced it by forming □ϕ from ϕ syncategorematically is probably a bow to tradition. There is of course nothing illegitimate in introducing □ syncategorematically; it is merely less "Fregean" than treating it as a functor. The reader who is bothered by this apparent inconsistency may think of □ϕ as merely a notational abbreviation for Nec($\hat{}\phi$). (This is, in fact, similar to the way □ϕ is introduced in Montague's 'Universal Grammar.')

Consider now the oblique context formed by adjectives such as *former*. The extension of phrases like *former senator* can now be defined in terms of the extensions of its parts if we combine *former* not with an expression denoting a predicate, but one denoting a property. (This idea was developed by J. A. W. Kamp and also by Montague and Terence Parsons.) That is, we introduce **For** as an expression of type $\langle\langle s, \langle e, t\rangle\rangle, \langle e, t\rangle\rangle$, whose extension will therefore be in the set

$$(\{0, 1\}^{A})^{((\{0, 1\}^{A})^{W \times T})}$$

Thus, $[\![\mathbf{For}]\!]^{M, \mathbf{w}, \mathbf{t}, g}$ is a functor which, so to speak, has "access" not only to the "current" extension of the one-place predicate it combines with, but also "access" to the extension of that predicate at other indices as well. In particular, it has access to the extension of that predicate at indices with earlier time coordinates. Thus $[\![\mathbf{For}]\!]^{M, \mathbf{w}, \mathbf{t}, g}$ may be thought of as a function which takes as input a property (say, the property of being a senator) and then gives as output the set of individuals that are not now but were at earlier times in the extension of that property, i.e., the set of former senators. Correspondingly, $[\![\mathbf{For}]\!]_{¢}^{M, g}$ is a function which indicates how this is to be done at any index; in fact this "procedure" does depend systematically on which index it is carried out at, in the sense that the set of former senators at the present index will depend not only on the sets of senators at various indices but the temporal relation in which these indices stand to whichever is the present one. It is thus possible to give a fairly simple description of $[\![\mathbf{For}]\!]_{¢}^{M,g}$: it is that function h on $W \times T$ which gives for any index $\langle w, t\rangle$ a function on properties of individuals that in turn gives for any property k the set of individuals which are in the extension of k at an earlier index in the same world. Equivalently, we could define $[\![\mathbf{For}]\!]_{¢}^{M,g}$ as that function h such that for any property k, the set $h(\langle w, t\rangle)(k)$ is the set $k(\langle w, t'\rangle)$ for all $t' < t$. Stated yet another way, for any individual x, $[[h(\langle w, t\rangle)](k)](x)$ is 1 iff $k(\langle w, t'\rangle)(x) = 1$ for some $t' < t$.

Next consider the treatment of verbs like *believe.* It was Montague's view that such verbs could be successfully treated as denoting a relation between individuals (specifically, persons) and propositions. Thus in intensional logic we would treat a constant **Bel** as an expression of type $\langle\langle s, t\rangle, \langle e, t\rangle\rangle$. A sentence like *John believes that Miss America is bald* would then be rendered in intensional logic as $\mathbf{Bel}({}^\wedge[B(m)])(j)$. Since the so-called "relational notation" $\gamma(\alpha, \beta)$ is familiar for stating that "α stands in the relation γ to β", Montague introduces $\gamma(\alpha, \beta)$ as an alternative notation for $\gamma(\beta)(\alpha)$. Thus $\mathbf{Bel}({}^\wedge[B(m)])(j)$ is also written as $\mathbf{Bel}(j, {}^\wedge[B(m)])$. Now let us see how Frege's puzzle about substituting names in belief contexts is treated. In the model M given toward the end of Chapter 5 the formula $B(m)$ was true at index $\langle w_2, t_1\rangle$ (because the individual denoted by m at that index – namely c – is in the set denoted by B at that index – namely $\{b, c\}$. The name n denotes the same individual as the name m at that index, and so it will follow by the semantic rules of IL that since $B(m)$ is true at that index, so is $B(n)$. That is, the fact that $[\![B(m)]\!]^{M, w_2, t_1, g}$ is equal to $[\![B(n)]\!]^{M, w_2, t_1, g}$ is a logical consequence of the fact that $[\![m]\!]^{M, w_2, t_1, g}$ is equal to $[\![n]\!]^{M, w_2, t_1, g}$. In this sense Lebnitz' Law holds in IL; substituting another name for the same individual in the expression $B(m)$ preserves truth value. However, it does not follow from this fact that the proposition denoted by ${}^\wedge B(m)$ is identical to the proposition denoted by ${}^\wedge B(n)$ at this index (or at any other index in M), and in fact these two propositions are not identical in M, since there are some indices at which one of these formulas is true and the other is false (e.g. at the index $\langle w_1, t_2\rangle$ the formula $B(m)$ is false while $B(n)$ is true). Hence we can construct a perfectly consistent model along the lines of M such that $\mathbf{Bel}(j, {}^\wedge B(m))$ is true at $\langle w_2, t_1\rangle$ while $\mathbf{Bel}(j, {}^\wedge B(n))$ is false at the same index. We might translate these expressions into ordinary English (using *Norma* as the name *n*) and say that it can be true that *Norma is Miss America* even though the sentence *John believes that Miss America is bald* is true while the sentence *John believes that Norma is bald* is false. These sentences are similar to Frege's examples with *the Morning Star* and *the Evening Star.*

What we have also illustrated in effect is that the following formula schema is not valid in intensional logic, even though it is valid in ordinary predicate logic with identity:

(6-19) $\alpha = \beta \rightarrow [\phi \leftrightarrow \phi^{\alpha}_{\beta}]$

(Here, ϕ^{α}_{β} is understood as the result of substituting β for all occurrences of α in ϕ; to exclude "accidental" binding and unbinding of variables we should say "all *free* occurrences of α in case α might be a variable.) A restricted version of this formula *is* valid in intensional logic, however. The formula is valid just in cases where α does not stand in an "oblique context", and in *IL* these will be cases where α stands within the scope of any of the operators $\hat{}$, $\Box$, **F** or **P**. Thus the valid restricted version of the above formula for *IL* is

(6-20) $\alpha = \beta \rightarrow [\phi \leftrightarrow \phi^{\alpha}_{\beta}]$, where α does not stand within the scope of $\hat{}$, $\Box$, **P**, or **F**.

Another restricted version of this formula that is valid in *IL* is the case where α and β not only have the same extension as the current index but have the same intension as well. If two expressions (of any type) have the same intension, then we may indeed freely substitute one for the other in any syntactic context whatsoever while preserving the extension (and even the intension) of the original expression:

(6-21) $\hat{}\alpha = \hat{}\beta \rightarrow [\phi \leftrightarrow \phi^{\alpha}_{\beta}]$

This feature of *IL* preserves a principle of Frege's that the sense of a complex expression would always be a function of the senses (though not of the reference) of its parts.

It has been noted by many linguists as well as philosophers that belief sentences like our example *John believes that Miss America is bald* can be understood in two ways, though so far we have treated only one of them. This example might be understood to assert that John has a belief about a certain individual who happens to be Miss America at the "current" index, the belief being that this individual is bald. On this reading the example could describe a true belief of John's about a certain person even if John does not know that she is Miss America, does not know any name for that individual, or is mistaken about her name. Among philosophers this reading is commonly referred to as the "*de re*" reading. Linguists have sometimes described this reading as one in which the name *Miss America* is the "speaker's description" of the person in question. The other reading, called the *de dicto* reading, is the one in which John believes that whoever is named by the name *Miss America* is bald, and on this reading the sentence can describe a belief of John's even though he does not know which individual the name actually denotes and thus there is no specific person *of whom* he can be said to hold any such belief. This reading is sometimes described as the one in which Miss America is "John's description" of the person in question. It is this second reading, the *de dicto reading,* which we have formalized by the formula $\mathbf{Bel}(j, \,^{\wedge}[B(m)])$.

The *de re* reading can also be formalized in *IL,* with the aid of the lambda-abstraction operator, as

(6-22) $\lambda x[\mathbf{Bel}(j, \,^{\wedge}[B(x)])](m)$.

We can read this formula as asserting that "the individual denoted by m is such that John believes the proposition that that individual is bald." Let us examine carefully the interpretation of this formula by the semantic rules of *IL* to see how its interpretation differs from that of the previous formula. Since this formula is the result of combining a lambda expression with the term m by rules B.3 and B.4, the formula will be true at an index $\langle \mathrm{w}, \mathrm{t} \rangle$ just in case the formula $\mathbf{Bel}(j, \,^{\wedge}[B(x)])$ is true at that index when x takes on the value $[\![m]\!]^{M, \mathrm{w}, \mathrm{t}, g}$. This will be the case if $[\![j]\!]^{M, \mathrm{w}, \mathrm{t}, g}$ stands in the "belief relation" to the proposition denoted by $^{\wedge}B(x)$ where x takes on the appropriate value. The important thing to notice is that this latter proposition is not in general the same proposition as the one denoted by $^{\wedge}B(m)$, for in "computing" this second proposition we will need to check the denotation of m at each index as well as the denotation of B at the same index to determine whether $B(m)$ is true at each of these indices, and both of these denotations may in general vary from index to index. On the other hand, in "computing" the proposition $^{\wedge}B(x)$ (where x takes on the value $[\![m]\!]^{M, \mathrm{w}, \mathrm{t}, g}$) we check the denotation of B at each index but, as it were, hold the value of x constant for all indices; its value remains at whatever m denotes at $\langle \mathrm{w}, \mathrm{t} \rangle$. This is why one formula involves a belief about a particular individual, while the other involves a belief about "whoever m is". That this "computation" should be carried out this way is a formal consequence of the fact that in *IL* the denotation of a variable will not vary from one index to the next in the way that the denotations of non-logical constants do; rather, the denotation of a variable depends only on the value assignment *g*. Thus the crucial difference between $\mathbf{Bel}(j,\ {}^\wedge[B(m)])$ and $\lambda x[\mathbf{Bel}(j,\ {}^\wedge[B(x)])](m)$ is that the "non-rigid designator" *m* stands within the scope of the oblique-context-creating operator $^\wedge$ in the first formula, but outside the scope of it in the second formula.

Note that if lambda conversion were applied to the second formula, the first would result. This shows that the principle of lambda conversion does not hold with full generality in *IL*. In fact it is subject to the same restriction as Leibnitz' Law is subject to. Thus, we have:

(6-23) $\lambda u[\phi](\alpha) \leftrightarrow \phi^u_\alpha$, provided that *u* does not stand within the scope of $^\wedge$, $\Box$, **P** or **F** in ϕ (and no variable free in α becomes bound when α is substituted for *u* in ϕ).

(As before, we could drop the restriction on intensional operators where α has a constant intension, e.g. where α is $^\wedge\beta$ or where α is itself a variable).[4] (In manipulating the translations of the English sentences of PTQ it turns out that the opportunity to violate these restrictions on lambda conversion does not actually arise, since the PTQ fragment does not contain non-rigid names like this *m*.)

Though non-rigid names such as *Miss America* are not common in natural language, there are a number of *de dicto/de re* ambiguities involving quantified noun phrases, and *IL* is capable of representing these as well. For example, (6-24) involves this ambiguity with respect to the phrase *a Republican:*

(6-24) John believes that a Republican will win.

On the *de re* reading, this example asserts that John believes of some particular person (who is in fact a Republican) that he will win. On the *de dicto* reading it asserts that John's belief is simply that, regardless of who the winner turns out to be, it will be a Republican. The *de re* reading is formalized as (6-25), the *de dicto* as (6-26): (Here, *R* and *W* are to be constants of type $\langle e, t\rangle$ understood as "Republican" and "win" respectively.)

(6-25) $\exists x[R(x) \wedge \mathbf{Bel}(j,\ {}^\wedge[\mathbf{F}W(x)])]$

(6-26) $\mathbf{Bel}(j,\ {}^\wedge\mathbf{F}\exists x[R(x) \wedge W(x)])$

As before, the crucial difference is that in the first formula the existensial quantifier and the constant *R* occur outside the scope of $^\wedge$. Here, what John believes is the proposition that some particular individual who now actually is a Republican will win. In the second formula the quantifier and constant R occur within the scope of ˆ, and here what John believes is the logically weaker proposition that it will be the case that some Republican or other will win. (For simplicity we ignore the possibility of change of party affiliation across time, since this introduces a further distinction, though one which is in fact representable in *IL*.)

Formulas such as (6-25) and (6-22) involve what is known as "quantifying into" an oblique context, inasmuch as a quantifier (or in the second case, a lambda operator) that is "outside" an oblique context binds a variable that is within one. This has been the subject of much discussion in the logical literature; in particular Quine (in Quine 1943, 1947, and 1960) raised serious questions about the meaningfulness of quantification into intensional contexts, based on the "pre-Kripke" state of modal logic and on the previous attempts to construct an intensional logic by Carnap and Church. Quine also pointed out numerous examples where sentences of natural languages seemed to require a "quantifying in" analysis, and he concluded that natural languages as they stood were in this respect not fit vehicles for conducting philosophical and scientific discourse, but should be subjected to "regimentation" to circumvent in one way or another quantifying into oblique contexts. Montague's intensional logic, in fact, differs from its predecessors in being the first system capable of treating the quantifying-in problem with full generality. Though Kaplan's system allowed for quantifying in, it could not treat so-called "iteration" of beliefs (as exhibited in English sentences such as *John believes that Bill believes that Miss America is bald.*) Montague's system, on the other hand, treats both "quantifying in" and iteration of belief satisfactorily. (This point is made in Montague 1960, 1968 and 1970).

In Montague's view the analysis of intensional entities within his intensional logic only begins with the treatment of propositional attitude verbs (like *believe*), modal operators and intensional adjectives. In his paper "On the Nature of Certain Philosophical Entities" (Montague 1960) he indicated how this method of analysis might be extended to phrases which he believed to denote such intensional entities as properties, events, tasks, "sense-data" relations (as in *John sees a unicorn*), experiences and obligations. For example, he held that an extensional semantic analysis of a predicate *is red* is not by itself adequate to analyze the phrase *the property of being red* (he might have equivalently cited the derived noun *redness*, an example of what linguists often call "abstract nouns"), since the extensional predicate *is red* applies only to actual, currently existing individuals, whereas *the property of being red* (or *redness*) denotes something much more comprehensive than this. Perhaps this can be made intuitively clearer by pointing out that the sentence *John admires honesty* should not be analyzed as asserting that a certain relation holds between John and, so to speak, whatever is shared in common by the set of actual, existing individuals x of which *x is honest* is true. Rather, insofar as the denotation of *honesty* has to do with honest individuals, it has equally to do with all individuals who ever were, are, will be, might be, or might have been honest. Thus the noun *honesty* would, in Montague's view, denote that property which is the intension of the one-place predicate *is honest* (in the technical sense of *property* and *intension* that we have just developed in this chapter).

It should be pointed out that Montague did not claim to have completely analyzed "the meaning" of verbs like *believe* or abstract nouns like *honesty*. That is, he claimed that belief should be analyzed as a relation between individuals and propositions, but made no attempt to *define* belief or say *which* relations of this sort correspond to propositional attitude verbs of some language and which do not. Rather, his goal should be described as constructing a semantic framework which in principle appears capable of giving a Tarski-style analysis of these words (as distinct from all previous semantic frameworks which appear incapable in principle of such analyses.) For more comment on this point see Montague 1960 and the review Cresswell 1976.

PROBLEM (6-4) For each of the following pairs of formulas of *IL*, determine whether they are logically equivalent. If not, construct a partial model in which they have different values. Constants and variables are as in Problem (6-1). Square brackets have occasionally been inserted for perspicuity.

(i)	j,	$\check{}\hat{}j$
(ii)	$B(j)$,	$[\lambda x B(x)](j)$
(iii)	$\Box B(m)$,	$[\lambda x \Box B(x)](m)$
(iv)	$[\lambda P\, \check{}P(j)](\hat{}\mathrm{walk}')$,	$\mathrm{walk}'(j)$
(v)	$\exists r\, \mathrm{walk}'(\check{}r)$,	$\exists x\, \mathrm{walk}'(x)$
(vi)	$\exists r\, \mathrm{change}'(r)$,	$\exists x\, \mathrm{change}'(\hat{}x)$
(vii)	$L(j)(m)$,	$L(m, j)$
(viii)	$[\lambda x[\lambda y \mathrm{Gr}(y, x)](3)](2)$,	$[\lambda x[\lambda y \mathrm{Gr}(y, x)]](3)(2)$

(ix) $[\lambda p \Box {}^{\vee}p](^{\wedge}\text{change}'(^{\wedge}m))$, $\Box\text{change}'(^{\wedge}m)$

(x) $[\lambda P\, {}^{\vee}P(m)](^{\wedge}\lambda x[\text{walk}'(x)])$, $\text{walk}'(m)$

(xi) $[\lambda Q\, Q(^{\wedge}m)](\lambda r[\text{change}'(r)])$, $\text{change}'(^{\wedge}m)$

(xii) $[\lambda X\, X(m)](\lambda x[\text{walk}'(x)])$, $\text{walk}'(m)$

PROBLEM (6-5) Using the new constant **For** ('former') introduced on p. 163, evaluate the following with respect to the model M as specified in Problem (6-2):

(i) $[\![\mathbf{For}(^{\wedge}B)]\!]_{¢}^{M,g}$

(ii) $[\![\forall x[\mathbf{For}(^{\wedge}B)(x) \leftrightarrow \mathbf{P}B(x)]\,]\!]^{M,w_2,t_2,g}$

(iii) $[\![\forall x[\mathbf{For}(^{\wedge}B)(x) \leftrightarrow \mathbf{P}B(x)]]\!]_{¢}^{M,g}$

(iv) $[\![^{\wedge}\forall x[\mathbf{For}(^{\wedge}B)(x) \leftrightarrow \mathbf{P}B(x)]]\!]^{M,w_2,t_2,g}$

IV. SOME UNRESOLVED ISSUES WITH POSSIBLE WORLDS SEMANTICS AND PROPOSITIONAL ATTITUDES

This is perhaps the best place to point out that there are still certain unresolved difficulties with an analysis that treats propositions (sets of indices, or sets of possible worlds) as the objects of belief and other propositional attitudes (i.e. the relations expressed by verbs such as *believe, know, wonder, desire, deny,* etc.). If two sentences ϕ and ψ are logically equivalent (i.e. have the same intension, and thus are true at exactly the same indices), then it will always be a logically valid inference from $\mathbf{Bel}(\alpha, {}^{\wedge}\phi)$ to $\mathbf{Bel}(\alpha, {}^{\wedge}\psi)$, for any believer denoted by α. Yet this is a curious and undesirable result, since there are always instances where a person fails to realize that one sentence is equivalent to another, hence believes one without believing the other.

A particularly striking case of this problem arises with necessarily true sentences. Since there is one and only one necessarily true proposition (i.e. the proposition true at every index in a model), it follows that if a person believes one necessarily true sentence (say, one expressing a mathematical truth, an analytic sentence, or other such non-contingent truth), he then believes all necessarily true sentences. It is thus impossible for a person to discover any "new" necessarily true sentences.

Note that this problem is apparently not just one of finding an appropriate logical type for the objects of belief and other propositional attitudes with

Montague's semantics, i.e. a type other than $\langle s, t\rangle$. For since Montague's semantics for *IL* allows substitution of logical equivalents no matter what their type (in the generalized sense of logical equivalence, in which any two expressions count as equivalent if they have the same intension, no matter what the type of that intension), then $\mathbf{Bel}(\alpha, \beta)$ will follow from $\mathbf{Bel}(\delta, \gamma)$ whenever γ and β are logically equivalent, no matter what types β and γ denote.

A closely related further problem arises if one adopts the position that proper names (and maybe some other expressions) should be rigid designators, that is, have the same denotation in all possible worlds and times. For reasons we cannot go into in detail at this point, it is arguable that proper names should be taken to have such rigid denotations; cf. Putnam (1973), Kripke (1972), Donellan (1974), or the articles reprinted in Schwartz (1977). One of the reasons for this position involves the explanation of how people can use names to "refer" to individuals they do not know personally and cannot identify by first-hand knowledge, e.g. the name Frege. This so-called *causal theory of proper names* holds that we simply intend to refer, with such a name, to the individual other speakers have traditionally referred to by this name. Thus our "reference" to such individuals with these names really depends on a causal chain of other speakers' use of the same name, a chain that ultimately goes back to a dubbing of the actual person with this name, rather than depending upon our own "grasping" of an intension that picks out a person (maybe a different one) in each possible world (via his or her "attributes", as it were). Thus the intension (in our technical sense) of a name must be a constant function.

Given this position, it ought to follow from the truth of *The ancients believed that Hesperus was Hesperus* that the sentence *The ancients believed that Hesperus was Phosphorus* is likewise true. For, given the fact that the names *Hesperus* and *Phosphorus* do in fact name the same thing (the planet Venus), the sentences *Hesperus is Hesperus* and *Hesperus is Phosphorus* do and always have had the same intension, even though there was a time that this was not realized.

Kripke, Putnam and others have extended this position to names of natural kinds (e.g., names of chemical elements and compounds, biological species, etc.); that is, these names can be argued to be rigid designators as well. But now it will follow that if *John does not doubt that woodchucks are woodchucks* is true, then *John does not doubt that woodchucks are groundhogs* is true; given that *woodchucks* are *groundhogs* denote the same species.

The distinction Putnam draws (Putnam 1973, Dowty 1979, ch. 9) between a theory of understanding and a theory of reference is only of limited help for these two problems. From considerations noted by Putnam, it is arguable that a referential theory of semantics is probably not best thought of as a theory of any one speaker's psychological grasp of the meanings of expressions of his language, but rather as a theory of the relation between expressions and the external world(s) that explains what a language is good for. Given this position, it is perfectly reasonable to say that no person really completely "knows" the meanings (intensions) of all expressions of his language, despite the fact that he uses the language in a normal way. With this view of our semantic theory, we can of course see why a person may not realize that a sentence ϕ means the same as a sentence ψ, even though our formal semantics for English gives them the same intension. Thus he may believe one but not the other. (This distinction between a theory of referential semantics and a theory of the psychology of semantics is in some ways analogous to the competence/performance distinction drawn by linguists.)

But this apparent avenue out of our dilemma is really only helpful as long as we are dealing with an object language that has no belief sentences and are speaking of a person's beliefs only in the metalanguage, as it were. As soon as we add sentences such as $\mathbf{Bel}(\alpha, \hat{}\phi)$ to our object language, our formal semantics runs into problems even when construed as a "non-psychological" theory. For even from an "idealized" point of view (as Partee (1979c) says, "a semantics for English as spoken and understood by God"), we do not want to treat $\mathbf{Bel}(\alpha, \hat{}\phi)$ equivalent to $\mathbf{Bel}(\alpha, \hat{}\psi)$ just because ϕ and ψ are equivalent, for it seems odd to say that an "idealized" speaker would make the mistake of assuming that all other persons who hold beliefs are similarly logically infallible (and nearly omniscient) as well. In other words, our semantics for propositional attitude verbs is really only appropriate for sentences ascribing beliefs to a community of individuals who are themselves all "idealized believers." (Cf. Linsky (1977), Partee (1979c).)

The approaches to this dilemma which have been considered and/or extensively explored are numerous and varied and continue to be developed in new ways up to the present day. We can only take the space to outline some of the important lines of development here.

One can of course maintain that an analysis of belief such as Montague's (as presented in this chapter) *is* adequate for at least a highly idealized conception of belief and leave it to others to produce other theories for other purposes. As far as we can tell, this was Montague's position at the time of his death (though we suspect that he would not remain so sanguine about it if he were alive today).

Another set of developments can be characterized as the "impossible worlds" approach. On this view, the possible worlds (or indices) in a model are divided into two sets, one of which consists of the "classical" possible worlds (or "really possible worlds"), the others are "non-classical" (or "impossible worlds"). While the customary rules of logic and values for logical connectives hold for the classical worlds, they do not hold for the non-classical ones. Thus even though ϕ and $\neg\neg\phi$ would have the same values in all classical worlds, they would differ in value in some of the non-classical worlds. And the proposition that there is a round square would be true in some non-classical worlds if false in all the classical ones. A particularly complex version of the "impossible worlds" approach is given in Cresswell (1973). While these approaches do in principle allow us to distinguish propositions (and thus beliefs) that are otherwise logically equivalent, it leaves us with the problem of deciding just what values to give to the logical connectives and semantic rules for the various non-classic worlds, and critics have pointed out that it is not at all clear how to approach this task in a revealing and interesting way that captures our intuitions about the ways people hold propositional attitudes.

Another set of attempts are based in one way or another on Carnap's idea of *intensional isomorphism*. Lewis (1972) gives a well-known statement of this tactic. Lewis defines *intension* essentially as we have defined it but adds a second technical notion which he calls a *meaning*. In a meaning one has, as it were, the intension of the whole sentence *and* the intensions of each of its subconstituents arranged in correspondence to the syntactic structure of the sentence. A meaning (in this sense) of a sentence is something like a linguist's phrase marker for a sentence except that where the node labels of the tree would be, one finds instead the intensions of the sub-tree that each node dominates. Though the top nodes of the meanings of two logically equivalent sentences will be the same, the meanings of the lower nodes need not be, hence equivalent sentences can have technically distinct meanings. If the objects of belief are meanings rather than intensions, then a solution to the propositional attitude problem seems available. (See Cresswell (1975) for an explicit semantics along these lines.) Two problems with this approach can immediately be noted. First, this approach does not help distinguish a pair of belief sentences where the embedded clauses have the same syntactic structure and differ only in that one has a synonym of the corresponding word in the other (e.g. *John believes that a woodchuck is in the garden* vs. *John believes that a groundhog is in the garden*), since the meanings of the embedded clauses (in this technical sense) will still be the same. Second, it is not immediately clear how "quantifying into" a belief context is to be handled in this approach. For two different treatments along this line which do incorporate a means for quantifying in, see Bigelow (1978a) and Bigelow (1978b).

Another approach to the semantics of belief with a longer history is to consider the objects of belief to be sentences (or the names of sentences) rather than intensions, meanings, or some other semantic entity. This is the so-called *quotational* theory. A variant of this is Davidson's (1968) *paratactic* theory, which is to treat a sentence such as *John believes that unicorns exist* as if it were "*John believes that. Unicorns exist*", the demonstrative *that* referring to the following sentence. For a variety of arguments against the quotational theory, see Partee (1973b), Thomason (1977) and Bigelow (1978b).

Yet another avenue toward solving this problem (considered by Partee (1979c), along with other approaches) is to confront head-on the problem that sentences attributing beliefs to various persons behave strangely in part because each person may understand the meanings of the words expressing his beliefs in ways that differ from the ways other speakers understand those same words. From this point of view, a reasonable tactic might be to let an interpretation function assign to each basic expression a function that gives for each person an intension for the word, possibly a different intension for each speaker. The values given by the semantic rules must then be relativized to a given speaker. However, for sentences of the form $\mathbf{Bel}(\alpha, \hat{}\phi)$, the proposition determined by ϕ will be computed not on the basis of the speaker's understanding of the words in ϕ, but rather on the understanding of these words for the individual denoted by α, the believer. For example, *John believes that woodchucks are not groundhogs* would assert in effect simply that John's understanding of *woodchucks* is not the same as his understanding of *groundhogs*. One of the problems Partee notes with this approach is that an inference like the following would not seem to come out valid: *John believes that clouds are alive; Mary believes everything that John believes; therefore Mary believes that clouds are alive*. Note that the proposition expressed by *clouds are alive* will not be the same in premise and conclusion. For an approach somewhat related to this, see Rantala (1975).

Partee concludes from her survey of various problems and attempted solutions to the belief problem that a crucial difficulty lies in the strict separation of the psychological and referential aspects of semantics that Montague's program (and others like it) presupposes. She suggests that an ultimate solution to the belief problem may involve reuniting these two sides of semantics, though as yet she proposes no such explicit analysis. For discussion see Partee (1979c, 1979d, forthcoming) and also Johnson-Laird (forthcoming).

A final line of development which is similar to the preceeding one but does not specifically involve psychological factors is to relativize the assignment of semantic values of expressions to a specific context of utterance in a more drastic way than has been done so far. One of the most promising treatments of this sort is found in Stalnaker (1978) and other as yet unpublished work by Stalnaker. This may be particularly helpful in treating the problem created by the assumption that names are rigid designators (e.g. in sentences such as *Aristotle didn't exist*, which would seem to come out either necessarily true or necessarily false in the customary "rigid designator" approach, yet nevertheless seem to be informative.) See also Kaplan (1977) and other work by Kaplan.

We must acknowledge that the problem of propositional attitude sentences is a fundamental one for possible worlds semantics, and for all we know, could eventually turn out to be a reason for rejecting or drastically modifying the whole possible worlds framework. Since new ways of attacking this problem appear virtually every day, it would be inappropriate for us to take a stand as to which, if any, of these may turn out to be successful. But it seems safe to say that the great amount of energy being devoted to solving this problem within the possible worlds framework shows that a great many workers have been so impressed by the dramatic success achieved by possible worlds semantics in other areas (and, to a limited degree, with propositional attitude sentences, e.g. the solution to the quantifying-in problem where descriptions rather than names are quantified in) that they are prepared to exercise their utmost ingenuity to try to solve this problem in a way that is compatible with these successes of the present framework.

NOTES

[1] These are cases where α is a constant denoting an intension, i.e., α is of type $\langle s, a\rangle$, for some a (see section II for this notation). Suppose k is a constant of type $\langle s, e\rangle$, a constant denoting an individual concept. The intension of this constant, therefore, will be a function that assigns an individual concept to α at each index, perhaps a different one at each index, and this function depends only on the interpretation function F. Suppose in a particular model M the intension of k is as follows:

$$[\![k]\!]_{\not c}^{M,g} = \begin{bmatrix} \langle w_1, t_1\rangle \to & \begin{bmatrix}\langle w_1, t_1\rangle \to a \\ \langle w_1, t_2\rangle \to a \\ \langle w_2, t_1\rangle \to a \\ \langle w_2, t_2\rangle \to a\end{bmatrix} \\ \langle w_1, t_2\rangle \to & \begin{bmatrix}\langle w_1, t_1\rangle \to a \\ \langle w_1, t_2\rangle \to b \\ \langle w_2, t_1\rangle \to c \\ \langle w_2, t_2\rangle \to d\end{bmatrix} \\ \langle w_2, t_1\rangle \to & \begin{bmatrix}\langle w_1, t_1\rangle \to c \\ \langle w_1, t_2\rangle \to b \\ \langle w_2, t_1\rangle \to d \\ \langle w_2, t_2\rangle \to a\end{bmatrix} \\ \langle w_2, t_2\rangle \to & \begin{bmatrix}\langle w_1, t_1\rangle \to c \\ \langle w_1, t_2\rangle \to d \\ \langle w_2, t_1\rangle \to a \\ \langle w_2, t_2\rangle \to b\end{bmatrix} \end{bmatrix}$$

Thus, for example, $[\![k]\!]^{M, w_1, t_2, g}$ is straightforward to determine:

$$[\![k]\!]^{M, w_1, t_2, g} = \begin{bmatrix}\langle w_1, t_1\rangle \to a \\ \langle w_1, t_2\rangle \to b \\ \langle w_2, t_1\rangle \to c \\ \langle w_2, t_2\rangle \to d\end{bmatrix}$$

But what is $[\![{}^{\wedge\vee}k]\!]^{M, w_1, t_2, g}$? By the definition of $^\wedge$, it is that function which gives at any particular index the extension of $^\vee k$ at that index. That is, this function gives at $\langle w_1, t_1\rangle$ the extension of $^\vee k$ at $\langle w_1, t_1\rangle$, it gives at $\langle w_1, t_2\rangle$ the extension of $^\vee k$ at $\langle w_1, t_2\rangle$, etc. In other words, by looking at the above chart of $[\![k]\!]_{\not c}^{M,g}$ taking at each index the function given and applying it to that same index, we arrive at the following:

$$[\![{}^{\wedge\vee}k]\!]^{M, w_1, t_2, g} = \begin{bmatrix}\langle w_1, t_1\rangle \to a \\ \langle w_1, t_2\rangle \to b \\ \langle w_2, t_1\rangle \to d \\ \langle w_2, t_2\rangle \to b\end{bmatrix}$$

Thus the two extensions are not the same. On the other hand, $^{\wedge\vee}\alpha$ and α will always have the same extension if α itself is a complex expression of the form $^\wedge\beta$, i.e., $^{\wedge\vee\wedge}\beta$ and $^\wedge\beta$ have the same extension.

This failure of the equivalence of $^{\wedge\vee}\alpha$ and α can be ignored for two reasons: (1) in interpreting English, constants of type $\langle s, a\rangle$ are never used – though there will be plenty of *expressions* of type $\langle s, a\rangle$ in the treatment of English, there are always complex expressions of the form $^\wedge\alpha$; (2) expressions of the form $^{\wedge\vee}\alpha$ never arise in translating English.

[2] Another way of thinking of the operators $^\wedge$ and $^\vee$ (suggested by Daniel Gallin in his dissertation, Gallin 1972) is that $^\wedge$ works as a kind of hidden functional abstractor (or lambda operator) on indices. It is hidden in the sense that variables denoting

indices do not appear in the object language itself, but ˆ nevertheless acts as if it takes an expression α and forms from it an expression denoting a function on indices which gives as value for any index the extension of α at that index. Of course this "functional abstract" is not normally applied to any argument (because there are no expressions denoting indices in the object language). The operator ˇ, however, acts as a kind of hidden "functional application" operation on indices: it takes the function denoted by α and "applies" it to whatever index $^{\vee}\alpha$ is being evaluated at. Thus in a certain sense, the equivalence of $^{\vee\wedge}\alpha$ with α is a consequence of the prinicple of lambda conversion. (In § 8 of Gallin (1972) this suggestion is exploited by the construction of a language similar to Montague's intensional logic except that variables over indices are included; then $^{\wedge}\alpha$ can be explicitly defined in the object language in terms of abstraction over indices.)

[3] Our notation differs slightly from that in PTQ. We use "∀" and "∃" instead of "⋀" and "⋁", respectively and our tense operators are "F" and "P" instead of Montague's "W" and "H", respectively. Furthermore, we use w and t instead of Montague's *i* and *j* for possible world and moment in time.

[4] To give a complete statement of the cases where the principles of lambda conversion and substitution hold for *IL*, it is necessary to give a recursive characterization of all those expression of *IL* whose extension does not vary from index to index. This characterization is given by Gallin (1972) for a tenseless version of *IL*, where the set of expressions in question is called the class of *modally closed* expressions. The definition is as follows:

(1) $v_{n,a}$ is modally closed for every variable $v_{n,a}$ of every type *a*.

(2) $^{\wedge}\alpha$ is modally closed for every expression α of every type *a*.

(3) $\Box\phi$ is modally closed for every formula ϕ.

(4) If α of type $\langle a, b\rangle$ and β of type *a* are modally closed, then so is $\alpha(\beta)$.

(5) If α is modally closed, then so is $\lambda u\alpha$, for any variable *u*.

(6) If α and β are modally closed expressions of any type *a*, then so is $\alpha = \beta$.

(7) If ϕ and ψ are modally closed formulas, then so are $\Box\phi$, $[\phi \wedge \psi]$, $[\phi \vee \psi]$, $[\phi \rightarrow \psi]$, $[\phi \leftrightarrow \psi]$, $\forall u\phi$, and $\exists u\phi$.

In effect, (1)-(3) correspond to the base of the recursive definition: any variable, any expression denoting an intension, and any formula $\Box\phi$ have extensions that do not vary across indices. (4)-(6) are recursive clauses saying that any expression formed by the syntactic rules illustrated is modally closed if its parts are. What these definitions exclude is thus any expression of *IL* containing a non-logical constant not within the scope of ˆ or □. It would appear, then, that it is only necessary to exclude Fϕ and Pϕ from the recursive clauses because of the case of models in which time has a beginning or an end. For example, ϕ might be modally closed yet Fϕ could differ in truth value according to whether the index it is evaluated at contains the last moment in time or not. However, Fϕ and Pϕ could be added to the recursive definition of modally closed formula as in the above for the restricted class of models for which for any **t** in *T*, there exist $\mathbf{t}'$ and $\mathbf{t}''$ such that $\mathbf{t}' < \mathbf{t} < \mathbf{t}''$. Armed with this definition, we can say that the following are valid formulas of *IL* if either (1) α and u do not stand within the scope of ˆ, □, F or P in ϕ, *or* (2) ϕ and α are modally closed.

$$\alpha = \beta \rightarrow [\phi \leftrightarrow \phi^{\alpha}_{\beta}]$$

$$\lambda u[\phi](\alpha) \leftrightarrow \phi^{u}_{\alpha}.$$

CHAPTER 7

THE GRAMMAR OF PTQ

I. THE OVERALL ORGANIZATION OF THE PTQ GRAMMAR

The reader, having patiently waded through pages of discussion of intensions, types, and lambda operators, will now be rewarded by being able to see Montague's syntactic treatment of English with a maximum understanding of the semantic motivation behind each part of the analysis. The grammar of PTQ, which Montague referred to as a "fragment" of English, is deliberately restricted for expository purposes. Nevertheless, it illustrates the treatment of a variety of problems involving quantifier words and their interaction with pronouns and conjunctions that have puzzled linguists as well as philosphers of language for some time (cf. Lakoff 1970, Partee 1970, 1972); it also treats all the "intensional constructions" discussed in the previous chapter and others besides. In many cases it is clear how Montague's fragment could be extended to deal with other English constructions, but in many other cases the possibility of a simple or straightforward treatment within his framework is problematic. References to the literature on both sorts of cases can be found in Chapter 9.

The syntax of the English fragment is formulated like the syntax of the languages of the previous chapters in that complex expressions are built up "from the inside out," i.e., by means of recursive definitions specifying how complex phrases are to be formed out of simpler ones. This procedure makes for a "Fregean" semantic treatment of English parallel to that we have given for the languages of the previous chapters. As with the language L_{1E} of Chapter 3, the syntactic rules will not only *concatenate* input expressions, possibly with other symbols added as well, but may also perform transformation-like manipulations on the inputs. In fact, this syntax can be fairly easily converted into an equivalent grammar with a phrase structure and a simple transformational component. Such a reformulation is in fact carried out in Cooper and Parsons (1976), along with proofs that this transformational "metamorphosis" is syntactically and semnatically equivalent to the PTQ grammar.

In contrast to his earlier treatment in 'English as a Formal Language,' Montague in the PTQ grammar did not give a direct model-theoretic interpretation of English parallel to the model-theoretic interpretations of the languages of the previous chapters. Instead, he proceeded indirectly, first translating each English expression into an expression of the intensional logic just presented in Chapter 6. The given model-theoretic interpretation of *IL* thus serves indirectly as the interpretation of the English fragment. Doing things in this apparently roundabout way is motivated in part by convenience in exposition and in part by aspects of Montague's overall program as outlined in 'Universal Grammar.' We will return to this matter in the next chapter.

Translating from English into *IL* follows a rigorously formalized procedure, unlike the unsystematic way in which English is "translated" into first-order predicate calculus in introductory logic courses. It is also rather unlike translation between natural languages, where there is much less regularity in the correspondences between types of syntactic constructions. Montague's translation procedure, in contrast, follows exactly the syntactic structure of each English sentence and furthermore must satisfy the following requirements (which are not in fact given in PTQ but are found in UG, p. 232):

1. Each basic expression of English is translated into one and only one expression of *IL*. Thus, there are no ambiguous basic expressions. The translation of an English basic expression, however, need not be a basic expression of *IL*. For example, we saw earlier that the name *John* translates into the complex expression $\lambda P[P\{j\}]$, where P is a variable over properties of individuals and j is an individual constant.

2. There is a uniform correspondence between the categories of English and the types of *IL*; that is, if an English expression of category x translates into an *IL* expression of type a, then *all* English expressions of category x must translate into expressions of type a.

3. For each syntactic rule of English there is a corresponding translation rule which specifies the translation of the output of the syntactic rule in terms of the translations of the input(s) to it. These translation rules must be written so as to "obey" the correspondence between English categories and logical types set up in 2. That is, if the English syntactic rule forms an expression of category x out of one or more input expressions, the corresponding translation rule must give a well-formed expression of *IL* of the type corresponding to category x, this expression of *IL* being formed out of the translations of the input expression(s) of English. Thus the correspondence in 2. holds for all derived as well as for all basic expressions of English.

These requirements insure that the translation procedure obeys a kind of compositionality principle of its own: the translation of the whole English expression is determined by the translation of its parts and the syntactic rules used in forming it. And since the expressions of *IL* are themselves given a compositional model-theoretic interpretation, it turns out that the indirect model-theoretic interpretation that results from the translation procedure is likewise compositional. (In UG Montague states a theorem to the effect that the translation procedure induces a unique, compositional model-theoretic interpretation of the base language, provided that his stated requirements are met).

It will probably be tempting for the reader approaching Montague Grammar for the first time to think of the *IL* translation of an English sentence as its "semantic representation" or its "logical form." Indeed, it may be helpful at first to make this association in order to get a better intuitive grasp of the system, but one must ultimately come to realize that this translation plays quite a different and, in many ways, less significant role in Montague's program than does the concept of logical form within certain linguistic theories. For Montague, the translation is in fact a completely dispensible part of the theory. The "real" semantic interpretation of an English sentence is simply its model-theoretic interpretation, however arrived at, and nothing else. (For a discussion of the differences between the use of logical formulas in Montague Grammar and Generative Semantics, see Dowty (1979)).

1. *The Syntactic Categories of English in the PTQ Grammar*

The specification of the English fragment begins with the recursive definition of an infinite set of syntactic categories. To the linguist, this may seem a curious preliminary step, but it was certainly not motivated by any belief on Montague's part that natural languages actually employed an infinite number of such categories; rather, this way of characterizing them offers certain advantages in the way of generality and elegance. On the one hand, the system thus specified is guaranteed to be comprehensive enough to contain whatever categories turn out actually to be needed in a full treatment of English or any other natural language. At the same time, the "construction" of complex categories out of elementary ones in his system proceeds in a particularly simple manner which permits a direct correspondence to be established between syntactic categories and the logical types of

IL, and ultimately with the kinds of semantic objects in the model-theoretic interpretation.

Here is the recursive definition:

(7-1)
1. *t* is a syntactic category.
2. *e* is a syntactic category.
3. If *A* and *B* are any syntactic categories, then A/B and $A//B$ are syntactic categories.

This system is based on the *categorial grammars* developed years ago by Ajdukiewicz (1935).[1] In a categorial grammar an expression of category A/B (or of $A//B$; we will return to the difference in a moment) typically combines with an expression of category *B* to give an expression of category *A*. The notation is consciously chosen to suggest a kind of algebraic cancellation operation (cf, $x/y \cdot y = x$), and the result is that the specification of what categories combine with what others is implicit in the category labels themselves. As an example, in the PTQ grammar expressions of category $t/(t/e)$ (so-called *term phrases* such as *John* and *Mary*) combine with expressions of category t/e (intransitive verb phrases such as *walk* and *seek a unicorn*) to yield expressions of category *t* (sentences).

The reader must be cautioned at this point that the complex English category symbols are, as it were, "read right to left," whereas the complex types of *IL*, to which they bear an obvous resemblance, are "read left to right." Note that a logical expression of *type* $\langle a, b \rangle$ combines with an expression of type *a* to give an expression of type *b*, whereas an expression of *category* A/B combines with an expression of category *B* to give an expression of category *A*. It is unfortunate that Montague chose to inflict on us such a confusing divergence in notation.

The parallelism between categories of English and the types of *IL* makes the correspondence between the two systems rather easy to state. There is one complicating factor, however. Montague observed that there would be certain cases where syntactically distinct categories of English would correspond to the same logical type, and to make this distinction he introduced the notational device of the "double slashes." Thus, A/B and $A//B$ are distinct categories but are to correspond to the same logical type. In the PTQ grammar, for example, intransitive verbs are given the category label t/e, while common nouns are classified as $t//e$, and both are translated into one-place predicates in *IL*. Other categories denoted $t///e$, $t////e$, etc. could also have been introduced had they been needed,

TABLE 7-1

Category Name	Categorial Definition of Name	Nearest Transformational Equivalent	Basic Expressions
e		None	None
t		Sentence	None
IV	*t/e*	Verb Phrase *and* Intransitive Verb (*IV* is mnemonic for "Intransitive Verb Phrase")	**run, walk, talk, rise, change**
T	*t/IV*	Noun Phrase *and* Proper Name (*T* is mnemonic for "Term Phrase")	**John, Mary, Bill, ninety, $\mathbf{he_0}$, $\mathbf{he_1}$, $\mathbf{he_2}$, . . .**
TV	*IV/T*	Transitive Verb	**find, lose, eat, love, date, be, seek, conceive**
IAV	*IV/IV*	Verb Phrase Adverb (*IAV* is mnemonic for "Intransitive Adverb")	**rapidly, slowly, voluntarily, allegedly**
CN	*t//e*	Common Noun	**man, woman, park, fish, pen, unicorn, price, temperature**
t/t		Sentence Adverb	**necessarily**
IAV/T		Preposition (one that forms a *VP*-modifying prepositional phrase)	**in, about**
IV/t		Sentence-complement Verb	**believe, assert**
IV//IV		Infinitive-complement Verb	**try, wish**
DET[2]	*T/CN*	Determiner	**every, the, a(n)**

provided that they too were translated into one-place predicates of *IL*. In reality, the PTQ grammar contains no category labels with more than two slashes.

Since the slash notation becomes cumbersome for the more complex categories, Montague introduced mnemonic abbreviations for them. The categories actually used in the PTQ grammar are summarized in Table 7-1, which gives for each category (1) its definition, if there is one, in terms of more fundamental categories, (2) the nearest transformational equivalent, and (3) the basic expressions, if any, which are members of that category.

All syntactic categories other than those listed are empty in the PTQ grammar. (We will need to press some of the unused categories into service later on.) In the table we note that the category *IV* contains both basic expressions (one-place predicates) and expressions formed by combining other kinds of verbs with appropriate complements (either direct objects, sentences, or infinitives); hence *IV* corresponds to both the lexical category verb and to the non-lexical category *VP*. Though this state of affairs may strike linguists as unappealing, it seems to have no particularly malign consequences. Note also that many of these categories correspond to sub-categories in a transformational grammar, e.g., intransitive verbs, transitive verbs, sentence-complement verbs, etc. This situation is a consequence of the fact that each syntactic category must correspond to one and only one logical type, and it should now be abundantly clear to the reader why we are forced to treat, say, transitive and intransitive verbs as corresponding to different logical types. One could of course simply stipulate that all of the "sub-categories" of verbs are to comprise a "super-category" (call it *Verb*) and thereby honor this syntactic generalization, if only in the breach, but it is nevertheless the "sub-categories" *IV*, *TV*, etc. which are relevant for semantic interpretation and not *Verb*.

The category *e* is devoid of basic expressions because Montague treated proper names such as *John* as denoting not an individual, John, but the set of John's properties. This move assimilates names to the same logical type as quantified noun phrases such as *every man* – both belong to the syntactic category *T* – so there is no longer any need for a syntactic category *e* which would denote individuals directly. The details of this procedure will be explained shortly.

The "subscripted pronouns" $\mathbf{he}_0$, $\mathbf{he}_1$, $\mathbf{he}_2$, . . . play the role of individual variables in formal languages. They undergo a kind of "binding" by antecedents in the course of certain syntactic rules and thereupon lose their subscripts and acquire the gender of their antecedents. (Cf. the use of the individual variables v_1, v_2, etc. in L_{1E}, Chapter 3.) Thus $\mathbf{he}_0$, etc. are in fact genderless, despite appearances, and are the only basic expressions of the fragment which are not full-fledged English words.

2. *The Correspondence Between Categories of English and Types of IL*

As we take up each syntactic rule of Montague's fragment, we will present the corresponding translation rule. We must therefore first establish the precise correspondence between syntactic categories and logical types, and this involves us again in a discussion of intensions. Consider once more the cases of intensional constructions discussed in the previous chapter and the categories of the corresponding English expressions in the PTQ syntax.

1. *Modal operators*: **Necessarily** is treated as a member of t/t, and so it combines with a sentence to give a new sentence. However, we found that we needed the intension of this constituent sentence, not just its extension, in order to satisfy Frege's principle in the interpretation of the combination **Necessarily** ϕ.
2. *Belief-contexts:* **Believe** is treated as a member of IV/t, so it combines with a sentence to give an IV-phrase; again, we need the intension of this embedded sentence, not its extension, to satisfy Frege's principle.
3. *Intensional transitive verbs*: We noted that the noun phrase **a unicorn** in the sentence **John seeks a unicorn** is in an oblique construction. Though we have not yet shown how to represent such a sentence in intensional logic, it is clear that we need some sort of intensional semantic object for the denotation of **a unicorn** if Frege's principles are to be satisfied. **Seek** is categorized as TV, which is defined as IV/T.
4. *Intensional adjectives*: Adjectives are omitted from the PTQ grammar, but it is clear that at least adjectives such as *former* would be put in a category CN/CN in Montague's system, so as to combine with a common noun to give a derived common noun phrase. We noted that we need the intension, not the extension, of the noun *senator* in order to obtain the extension of the phrase *former senator*.
5. *Intensional verb-phrase adverbs*: Though we did not discuss such examples, it should be readily apparent that examples like *John was formerly a senator*, *John is allegedly a communist* exhibit exactly the same intensionality as *John is a former senator*, *John is an alleged communist*. Verb phrase adverbs are categorized as IAV, which is IV/IV.
6. *Intensional Prepositions*: Though Montague's example in this category may be less convincing than the other cases, he thought that the preposition *about* in the sentence *John is talking about a unicorn* formed an oblique context. That is,

> this sentence can supposedly be true even though there is no particular uniforn that John is talking about, and can even be true if unicorns do not exist. Prepositions are classified as members of the category *IAV/T*; thus they will combine with term phrases to form verb-phrase modifiers.

What all of these oblique constructions have in common, given Montague's characterization of their constituent syntactic categories, is that an "oblique-context creating element" of a category *A/B* combines with an expression of category *B* to give an expression of category *A*. Thus in each such case, we must take the intension of the expression of category *B*, and not merely its extension, to determine the extension of the whole expression. (How this is done will become clearer as we discuss the individual cases (1) though (6) below.)

Montague apparently found this pattern striking and sufficiently widespread in English to warrant its being incorporated as a general principle of semantic interpretation in English.[3] Expressions of category *A/B*, whatever the *A* and *B* in question, are in general to denote functions applying to the *intensions* of expressions of category *B*, rather than to their extensions. For example, **necessarily** is of category *t/t*, but denotes a function applying to the intension, rather than the extension, of expressions of category *t*. The reader may confirm that all the cases (1)–(6) above fit this pattern.

To be sure, there will be some expressions in each of these functor categories for which the extension of the argument-expression would suffice. Contrast, for example, the "intensional" verb **seek** with the "extensional" verb **find**, as in the sentences **John seeks a unicorn** versus **John finds a unicorn**. In the second example an extensional relation between two actual, existing individuals is asserted, so the sentence can only be true for worlds and times at which unicorns exist. Yet **seek** and **find** are both interpreted as functions applying to the intensions of term phrases, in accord with Montague's principle that every member of a given syntactic category is to be treated in fundamentally the same way semantically. We will see in Section VI how the semantic distinction between verbs like **seek** and verbs like **find** is reintroduced in the semantics in a way that does not disturb the overall correspondence between syntactic categories and logical types. The reader might merely note here that, as we mentioned previously, intension is a "stronger" notion than extension, in that the extension of an expression at a certain index is determined by the intension, but not conversely. Thus, confronted with a syntactically homogeneous class of words, e.g., transitive verbs, that are semantically heterogeneous, e.g., requiring sometimes the intension, sometimes merely the extension of their objects, Montague chose to unify them by assimilating the extensional class to the intensional class. This makes a treatment of the extensional subclass more complicated, but it is at least possible. On the other hand, assimilating the intensional subclass to the extensional subclass would not result in an adequate semantics for the truly intensional members, since the intension of an expression is *not* in general recoverable from the extension of that expression at a given index.

With this background, we can now state the correspondence between the categories of English and the types of intensional logic. It is in the form of a recursive definition of a function f which maps English categories into types.

(7-2)
1. $f(t) = t$
2. $f(e) = e$
3. For all categories A and B, $f(A/B) = f(A//B) = \langle\langle s, f(B)\rangle, f(A)\rangle$.

Table 7-2 lists some examples of correspondences defined by this function, along with the names of the semantical objects denoted by expressions of each logical type (cf. Chapter 6, Section I):

TABLE 7-2

Category Name	Categorial Definition of Name	Corresponding Type by Rule (7-2)	Name of Semantical Object Denoted by this Type
e	e	e	individual
t	t	t	truth value
IV	t/e	$\langle\langle s, e\rangle, t\rangle$	set of individual concepts
T	t/IV (= $t/(t/e)$)	$\langle\langle s, \langle\langle s, e\rangle, t\rangle\rangle, t\rangle$	set of properties of individual concepts
CN	$t//e$	$\langle\langle s, e\rangle, t\rangle$	set of individual concepts
t/t	t/t	$\langle\langle s, t\rangle, t\rangle$	set of propositions
etc.	etc.	etc.	etc.

PROBLEM (7-1). Complete the specification of Table 7-2 for all the remaining syntactic categories listed in Table 7-1.

Definition (7-2) introduces "intensional" types in cases where they are not motivated by oblique constructions of English that we have discussed so far. Intransitive verbs and common nouns, for example, will translate into expressions denoting sets of *individual concepts* rather than the expected sets of *individuals*; yet we have observed no examples so far that seem to require this analysis. Montague thought that certain oblique constructions did in fact motivate this feature of his system, but it now appears that he was mistaken about the best way to analyze them. (These cases, such as *The temperature is ninety and rising* are discussed in Appendix III.) Moreover, Bennett (1974) observed that a great deal of semantic complexity in the system can be avoided if intransitive verbs and common nouns simply denote sets of individuals rather than sets of individual concepts, and he found a way to make this simplification without disturbing the rest of the recursively defined correspondence between categories and types. Bennett's innovation starts with IV and CN as basic syntactic categories of English instead of defining them as t/e and $t//e$, respectively. The syntactic category e can now be eliminated altogether since it is not otherwise used in the grammar. (Don't confuse the syntactic category e with the logical type e; the latter will still be used for the type of expressions of IL denoting individuals.) So for Bennett the basic syntactic categories are t, IV, and CN, and any A/B formed recursively out of these is also a category. The correspondence between categories and logical types is now stated by the following revised definition of f:

(7-3)
1. $f(t) = t$
2. $f(CN) = f(IV) = \langle e, t\rangle$
3. For all categories A and B, $f(A/B) = f(A//B) = \langle\langle s, f(B)\rangle, f(A)\rangle$.

We will adopt Bennett's simplified system in the remainder of this book. Accordingly, Table 7-2 should be revised as shown in Table 7-3. Note that the entries are identical except that $\langle s, e\rangle$ in Table 7-2 is uniformly replaced by e in Table 7-3. (The reader need not try to make sense out of the more complicated semantical objects at this point; they will be much more easily understood later on.)

Before going on to discuss the syntactic rules of the PTQ fragment, we must say a word about the translations of basic expressions of English. A function g (not to be confused with the function g which assigns values to variables in IL; Montague apparently failed to notice this notational collision) assigns a translation to each of the (finitely many) basic expressions of English. Thus, g plays much the same role in the translation procedure as the

TABLE 7-3

Category Name	Categorial Definition of Name	Corresponding Type by Bennett's Rule (7-3)	Name of Semantical Object Denoted by this Type
t	t	t	truth value
CN	CN	$\langle e, t\rangle$	set of individuals
IV	IV	$\langle e, t\rangle$	set of individuals
T	t/IV	$\langle\langle s, \langle e, t\rangle\rangle, t\rangle$	set of properties of individuals
IAV	IV/IV	$\langle\langle s, \langle e, t\rangle\rangle, \langle e, t\rangle\rangle$	function from properties of individuals to sets of individuals
TV	IV/T $(= IV/(t/IV))$	$\langle\langle s, \langle\langle s, \langle e, t\rangle\rangle, t\rangle\rangle, \langle e, t\rangle\rangle$	function from properties of properties of individuals to sets of individuals
T/CN	$(t/IV)/CN$	$\langle\langle s, \langle e, t\rangle\rangle, \langle\langle s, \langle e, t\rangle\rangle, t\rangle\rangle$	function from properties of individuals to sets of properties of individuals
t/t	t/t	$\langle\langle s, t\rangle, t\rangle$	set of propositions
IV/t	IV/t	$\langle\langle s, t\rangle, \langle e, t\rangle\rangle$	function from propositions to sets of individuals
$IV//IV$	$IV//IV$	$\langle\langle s, \langle e, t\rangle\rangle, \langle e, t\rangle\rangle$	function from properties of individuals to sets of individuals
IAV/T	$(IV/IV)/T$	$\langle\langle s, \langle\langle s, \langle e, t\rangle\rangle, t\rangle\rangle, \langle\langle s, \langle e, t\rangle\rangle, \langle e, t\rangle\rangle$	function from properties of properties of individuals to functions from properties of individuals to sets of individuals

function F does in a model in assigning interpretations to the basic expressions. In many cases, g simply translates a basic expression of English into a non-logical constant of IL (of the appropriate type prescribed by f). For example, the basic expression **man** of category CN is translated into some constant of IL of type $\langle e, t\rangle$. Montague chose to designate each constant of IL that translates a word of English by a primed variant of the English word, e.g., *g*(**man**) = **man**′, *g*(**fish**) = **fish**′, etc. (Strictly speaking, this is a meta-language convention. The actual constant of *IL* corresponding to **man** might be $c_{273,\langle e,t\rangle}$, or some such constant; **man**′ is merely our meta-language name for it. This technicality can safely be ignored, however.) A few basic expressions of English, such as names and logical words like *every* and *necessarily*, are given special translations which are not simply constants of *IL*, though of course they must be expressions of the appropriate type. These will be discussed one by one as we come to the syntactic rules involving them. In any case, the basic expressions of English are finite in number, and so the values of *g* can be specified as a finite list.

II. SUBJECT-PREDICATE AND DETERMINER-NOUN RULES

The *set of basic expressions of category A*, denoted B_A, has already been described for each of the ten non-empty basic categories (see Table (7-1)). These may be thought of as simply the "lexical entries" of each category. The *set of phrases of category A*, denoted P_A, includes the basic expressions for each category together with any complex expressions of that category that are formed by the syntactic rules. The first syntactic rule of PTQ takes care of the basic expressions:

(7-4) S1. $B_A \subseteq P_A$, for every category A.

The remaining rules take care of the complex expressions.

A syntactic rule forming a complex expression contains three sorts of information: (1) the category or categories of expression(s) that serve as "input" to the rule, (2) the category of the complex expression that is the "output" of the rule, and (3) the *structural operation* for the rule, i.e., a specification of how the input expression(s) must be combined and/or transformed to give the output. (We should note here that the expressions produced by the PTQ grammar are *strings* of symbols. Among the modifications of the PTQ grammar that have been proposed is one in which the syntactic rules operate on phrase markers instead of strings and produce phrase markers as output. Thus, syntactic rules forming complex expressions have the following general form:

(7-5) S_n. If $\alpha \in P_A$, and $\beta \in P_B$, then $F_m(\alpha, \beta) \in P_C$, where $F_m(\alpha, \beta)$ is . . .

Here, n is the number of the syntactic rule, A and B are the syntactic categories of the "input expressions," C is the syntactic category of the new expression formed by the rule, F_m is the name of the structural operation of the rule, and in place of the ellipsis is a description of just what this operation does. The structural operations have numerical subscripts, e.g. F_0, F_1, F_2, etc., and this numbering is independent of the numbering of the syntactic rules themselves. If the same operation is used in more than one syntactic rule, it is described in the first rule that uses it and is thereafter referred to by number. For example, the operation F_6 which merely concatenates two input expressions α and β to form $\alpha\beta$ is used in rules S7, S8, and S9. (Montague's reasons for numbering the structural operations independently of the syntactic rules in which they appear has to do with the algebraic formulation of his theory in UG; for the purposes of PTQ, a syntactic rule and its associated operation might just as well be treated as a single, indivisible combination.) Though we have described the general form of a syntactic rule as having two input categories, such a rule might equally well have only one input or more than two inputs.

As an example of a syntactic rule, consider S4, the so-called "subject-predicate" rule:

(7-6) S4. If $\alpha \in P_T$ and $\delta \in P_{IV}$, then $F_4(\alpha, \delta) \in P_t$, where $F_4(\alpha, \delta) = \alpha\delta'$, and δ' is the result of replacing the first *verb* (i.e., member of B_{IV}, B_{TV}, $B_{IV/t}$, or $B_{IV//IV}$) in δ by its third person singular present form.

This rule thus takes a term phrase (member of P_T) and a verb phrase (member of P_{IV}) and combines them to form a sentence (member of P_t), performing "subject-verb agreement" in the process. (The PTQ fragment does not contain plural noun phrases; if it did, this structural operation would have to be even more complicated.[4]) As an example of how a sentence is formed by this rule, take **John** $\in B_T$ (hence **John** $\in P_T$ by S1), **walk** $\in B_{IV}$ (hence **walk** $\in P_{IV}$), and thus **John walks** $\in P_t$ by S4.

The way in which a sentence or other phrase is constructed syntactically can be displayed in the form of an *analysis tree*. The analysis tree for **John walks** as we have just constructed it is shown in (7-7):

(7-7)
```
        John walks, 4
       /             \
   John               walk
```

All the terminal nodes of an analysis tree are basic expressions. Any node dominating a node or nodes is labeled with the expression formed from its daughter node(s) by some syntactic rule. The number of the structural operation of this rule is written to the right of the higher node (in this analysis tree the only number is 4).[5] Such analysis trees bear a superficial resemblance to phrase-structure trees in transformational grammar, but these trees really indicate the "derivational history" of a sentence, hence they are more like the "T-markers" of early transformational grammar than "P-markers". Analysis trees will come to be of particular interest when we consider semantically ambiguous sentences of English.

Each syntactic rule S_n has associated with it a translation rule T_n with the same numerical subscript. The translation rule associated with S4 is the following:

(7-8) T4. If $\alpha \in P_T$ and $\delta \in P_{IV}$, and α, δ translate into α', δ' respectively, then $F_4(\alpha, \delta)$ translates into $\alpha'({}^\wedge\delta')$.

As promised, this rule specifies the translation of any expression formed by S4 (i.e., any complex English phrase $F_4(\alpha, \delta)$) in terms of the translations of the inputs to rule S4 (i.e., the logical expressions α' and δ').

The rule S4, together with the translation rule T4, happens to be an instance of the most common kind of syntactic rule/translation rule combination of PTQ, a *rule of functional application*. A syntactic rule of functional application is any rule with input categories whose names have the form A/B and B (for some A and B), and whose output category is A. The rule S4 counts as such a rule because it combines a phrase of category T, which is defined as t/IV, with a phrase of category IV to give a phrase of category t. The translation rule for a rule of functional application is always of exactly the same form: It is an instruction to take the translation α' of the A/B-expression and combine it with the intension of the translation β' of the B-expression to give $\alpha'({}^\wedge\beta')$. Hence we need not bother to describe the translation rule of such a syntactic rule once it has been so identified.

As noted in the previous section, all rules giving rise to cases of "oblique constructions" will turn out to be rules of functional application in this sense; it is for this reason that the whole system is set up to allow the general form of the translation of such rules to be $\alpha'({}^\wedge\beta')$ rather than $\alpha'(\beta')$. That is, the correspondence between syntactic categories and logical types assures that an expression of category A/B will be assigned as its translation an expression of IL of type $\langle\langle s, f(B)\rangle, f(A)\rangle$ and for this reason, $\alpha'({}^\wedge\beta')$ is well-formed in each such case.

We will illustrate T4 by translating our example **John walks** into IL, but we must first ascertain the translations of the basic expressions **John** and **walk**. The second of these translates into the IL constant **walk**$'$. Since **walk** is in the category IV and since $f(IV) = \langle e, t\rangle$, we know that **walk′** is a constant of this type. As we already indicated in the previous chapter, names are treated as if they denoted sets of properties of individuals. Thus **John** will translate into an expression denoting the set of properties of some particular person. (Indeed, it follows from the fact that **John** $\in P_T$ that it must translate into some expression denoting a set of properties, for T is t/IV, and $f(t/IV) = \langle\langle s, f(IV)\rangle, f(t)\rangle = \langle\langle s, \langle e, t\rangle\rangle, t\rangle$, and expressions of IL of this type do, by definition, denote sets of properties of individuals.) The translations of the three names **John**, **Bill** and **Mary** that occur in PTQ are given in (7-9). Here, P is, by convention, the variable $v_{0, \langle s, \langle e, t\rangle\rangle}$, which ranges over properties of individuals, and j, b, and m are non-logical constants of type e, which we may think of as denoting the persons John, Mary and Bill respectively. (If there were other names in the PTQ fragment, their translations would be exactly parallel to these.)

(7-9) **John** translates into $\lambda P[P\{j\}]$
Mary translates into $\lambda P[P\{m\}]$
Bill translates into $\lambda P[P\{b\}]$.

Recall that $\alpha\{\beta\}$ by convention stands for $\check{}\alpha(\beta)$ (we will refer to this as the *brace convention*), so the translation of **John** is equivalently written as $\lambda P[\check{}P(j)]$, etc. As mentioned before, we must have $\check{}P(j)$ (or $P\{j\}$) and *not* simply $P(j)$ in these expressions, since P denotes a property (function from indices to functions from individuals to truth values) and thus cannot be combined *directly* with j.

Now, given the translations of **John** and **walk**, the sentence **John walks** must have, by T4, the translation

(7-10) $\lambda P[P\{j\}](\hat{}\mathbf{walk}')$

Since $\hat{}\mathbf{walk}'$ is of type $\langle s, \langle e, t\rangle\rangle$ and $\lambda P[P\{j\}]$ is of type $\langle\langle s, \langle e, t\rangle\rangle, t\rangle$, this expression is well-formed, and in fact is of type t. By the principle of lambda conversion, this formula is logically equivalent to the formula

(7-11) $\hat{}\mathbf{walk}'\{j\}$.

By the brace convention this last formula is alternatively written as

(7-12) $\check{}\hat{}\mathbf{walk}'(j)$,

and since it is a principle of IL (cf. Chapter 6, p. 154) that $\check{}\hat{}\alpha$ is always equivalent to α, this in turn is equivalent to

(7-13) $\mathbf{walk}'(j)$.

It turns out that all translations of English sentences into *IL* yield rather complex formulas which can be converted to simpler logically equivalent formulas by appeal to principles such as lambda-conversion, conversion of $^{\vee\wedge}\alpha$ to α, and other such rules, just as we have here converted $\lambda P[P\{j\}](^\wedge\mathbf{walk}')$ to $\mathbf{walk}'(j)$. Learning to perform such simplifications is, in fact, an important step in learning to "understand" Montague Grammar, since the complex formulas that result directly from the translation rules are often much too complicated to be grasped intuitively as they stand. However, it is also important to realize that the process of performing such a simplification is not a crucial part of the "derivation" or "interpretation" of an English sentence as far as the theory itself is concerned. For example, $\lambda P[P\{j\}](^\wedge\mathbf{walk}')$ is logically equivalent to $\mathbf{walk}'(j)$, so the former has exactly the same model-theoretic interpretation as the latter and thus "represents the meaning" of the English sentence **John walks** in exactly the same way. The same is true of the even more complicated cases we will encounter later on.

The second rule we will consider is S2, the "Determiner-Noun" rule:[6]

(7-14) S2. If $\delta \in P_{T/CN}$ and $\zeta \in P_{CN}$, then $F_2(\delta, \zeta) \in P_T$, where $F_2(\delta, \zeta) = \delta'\zeta$, and δ' is δ except in the case where δ is **a** and the first word in ζ begins with a vowel; here, δ' is **an**.

For example, this rule combines **every** with **woman** to give **every woman**, and **the** with **fish** to give **the fish**. (If one were willing to relegate the choice between **a** and **an** to a "morphology component", the operation F_2 could be reduced to simple concatenation.) As S2 is a rule of functional application, its associated translation rule is predictable:

(7-15) T2. If $\delta \in P_{T/CN}$ and $\zeta \in P_{CN}$, then $F_2(\delta, \zeta)$ translates into $\delta'(^\wedge\zeta')$.

As an example of a sentence using this rule, consider **Every man talks**, constructed according to the analysis tree shown in (7-16):

(7-16)

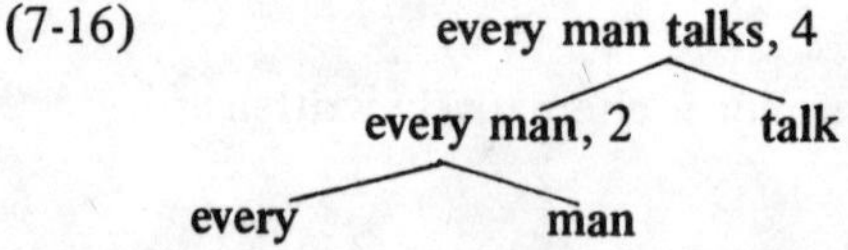

For the translation of this sentence, we will need to know the translations of the determiners. These are not translated into constants of *IL* but are instead treated in effect as "logical words," assigned the once-and-for-all translations shown in (7-17). (These translations were hinted at near the end of Chapter 4 but differ slightly here in that they take into account intensions in the appropriate places.) P is, as before, $v_{0,\langle s,\langle e,t\rangle\rangle}$, and Q is $v_{1,\langle s,\langle e,t\rangle\rangle}$.

(7-17) **every** translates into: $\lambda P[\lambda Q \forall x[P\{x\} \rightarrow Q\{x\}]]$
the translates into: $\lambda P[\lambda Q \exists y[\forall x[P\{x\} \leftrightarrow x = y] \wedge Q\{y\}]]$
a translates into: $\lambda P[\lambda Q \exists x[P\{x\} \wedge Q\{x\}]]$

Though these expressions are complex, the reader can confirm by examining them carefully that they are well-formed and are expressions of the appropriate type to serve as translations of English expressions of category T/CN; i.e., determiners must translate into expressions of IL of type $f(T/CN)$, and this is $f((t/IV)/CN) = \langle\langle s, f(CN)\rangle, f(t/IV)\rangle = \langle\langle s,\langle e,t\rangle\rangle, \langle\langle s, f(IV)\rangle, f(t)\rangle\rangle, = \langle\langle s,\langle e,t\rangle\rangle, \langle\langle s,\langle e,t\rangle\rangle, t\rangle\rangle$. To see that the translations are of this type, note that, for example, $\forall x[P\{x\} \rightarrow Q\{x\}]$ (which appears as part of the translation of **every**) is obviously a formula, or expression of type t; since Q is a variable of type $\langle s,\langle e,t\rangle\rangle$, the expression $\lambda Q \forall x[P\{x\} \rightarrow Q\{x\}]$ is of type $\langle\langle s,\langle e,t\rangle\rangle, t\rangle$; since P is a variable of the same type as Q, $\lambda P[\lambda Q \forall x[P\{x\} \rightarrow Q\{x\}]]$ is of type $\langle\langle s,\langle e,t\rangle\rangle, \langle\langle s,\langle e,t\rangle\rangle, t\rangle\rangle$.

In writing out translations and their simplifications from this point on, we will adopt two conventions from Partee (1975) which have since been used by others as well. First, the steps will be written out in the form of a "proof", listing expressions of IL by number in the left-hand column and giving in the corresponding line of the right-hand column the translation rule, notational convention (e.g. "brace convention") or principle of intensional logic (e.g., "lambda-conversion") which justifies it. The second convention is the use of the symbol "$\Rightarrow$" for "translates into"; thus anything written to the left of this symbol is an expression of English, anything to the right is an expression of IL. Any line which does not contain the symbol "$\Rightarrow$" is understood to be a simplification of the line just above it, i.e. an expression of IL that is logically equivalent to the preceding line according to the principle named on the right. (The principle that $^{\vee\wedge}\alpha$ is logically equivalent to α (cf. pp. 153–4) has come to be known as "Down-up cancellation", after the practice of reading $^{\wedge}\alpha$ aloud as "up α" or "up of α" and α as "down α" or "down of α.")

In computing the translation of the sentence generated in (7-16), one must begin with the "terminal" nodes of the analysis tree, first determining the translations of these basic expressions and then determining the translation of each "non-terminal" node by using the appropriate translation rule and the translations of its daughter nodes.

In computing the translation of a complex analysis tree, *the reader is strongly advised to make all the simplifications possible in the translation of a given node before going on to the translation of a higher node*. For example, in the derivation below, the translation of **every man** is simplified in steps 4–6 before it is combined with **talk**′ in step 8. In theory, such a procedure is unnecessary; one could just as well write out the translation of the entire sentence before beginning to perform simplifications. In practice, the chances of making a clerical error are very great if one does not simplify as soon as possible, and much time and paper will be wasted by failure to do so in any case.

(7-18) Translation for analysis tree (7-16):

1. $\mathbf{every} \Rightarrow \lambda P[\lambda Q \forall x[P\{x\} \rightarrow Q\{x\}]]$	Basic expression (logical word)
2. $\mathbf{man} \Rightarrow \mathbf{man}'$	Basic expression (non-logical constant)
3. $\mathbf{every\ man} \Rightarrow \lambda P[\lambda Q \forall x[P\{x\} \rightarrow Q\{x\}]]({}^{\wedge}\mathbf{man}')$	From 1, 2 by T2.
4. $\lambda Q \forall x[{}^{\wedge}\mathbf{man}'\{x\} \rightarrow Q\{x\}]$	Lambda conversion
5. $\lambda Q \forall x[{}^{\vee\wedge}\mathbf{man}'(x) \rightarrow Q\{x\}]$	Brace convention
6. $\lambda Q \forall x[\mathbf{man}'(x) \rightarrow Q\{x\}]$	Down-Up cancellation
7. $\mathbf{talk} \Rightarrow \mathbf{talk}'$	Basic expression
8. $\mathbf{every\ man\ talks} \Rightarrow \lambda Q \forall x[\mathbf{man}'(x) \rightarrow Q\{x\}]({}^{\wedge}\mathbf{talk}')$	From 6, 7 by T4
9. $\forall x[\mathbf{man}'(x) \rightarrow {}^{\wedge}\mathbf{talk}'\{x\}]$	Lambda conversion
10. $\forall x[\mathbf{man}'(x) \rightarrow {}^{\vee\wedge}\mathbf{talk}'(x)]$	Brace convention
11. $\forall x[\mathbf{man}'(x) \rightarrow \mathbf{talk}'(x)]$	Down-Up cancellation

The formula in line 11 above, like the translation of our first example, **walk**′(j), appears to be a "completely extensional first-order formula," in the sense that it could occur as a formula of a first-order language such as L_1 and could receive the same sort of model-theoretic interpretation in such a language as it receives in *IL* – provided, of course, that we confine our attention to a particular index $\langle \mathbf{w}, \mathbf{t} \rangle$ in *IL*. The interpretation of such a formula in *IL* differs from that in a first-order language in that for a given *IL* model, the truth value of the formula may vary from index to index. Thus, with respect to an *IL* interpretation, the formula asserts that at a given index everything that has the *property* of being a man also has the *property* of talking. In a first-order extensional system, the formula would be interpreted as making the simpler once-and-for-all statement that everything in the (once-and-for-all) set of men is also in the (once-and-for-all) set of talking things.

Incidentally, Montague presumably intended **Every man talks** to be interpreted more or less as we would normally interpret the English progressive sentence *Every man is talking* (*right now*), rather than with the "habitual" or "dispositional" interpretation normally associated with such examples in the simple present tense. This is a detail which Montague probably ignored for the sake of simplicity. For further discussion see Dowty (1979).

A word is in order about the translation of the definite determiner **the** in (7-17). If we translate the sentence **The fish walks**, as generated in (7-19), simplifying the translation, we arrive at the formula shown in (7-20):

(7-19)

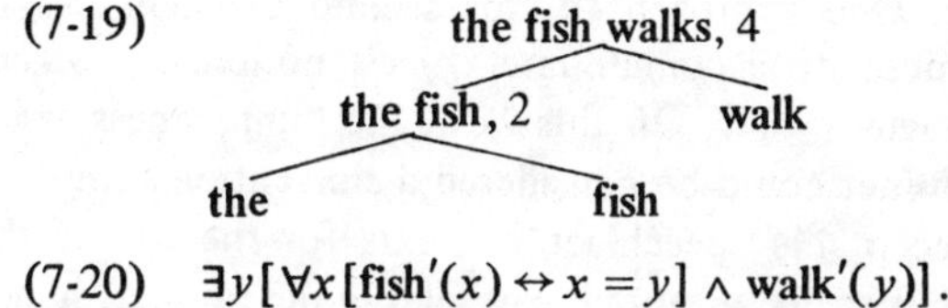

(7-20) $\exists y[\forall x[\text{fish}'(x) \leftrightarrow x = y] \wedge \text{walk}'(y)]$.

(We will not bother to write out the steps in the translation and simplification, since these correspond exactly to the eleventh steps in the previous translation, except for the different basic expressions involved.)

The formula (7-20) will be familiar to readers who are acquainted with Russell's analysis of definite descriptions (Russell, 1905) (cf. pp. 77–78). According to this view, the role of the definite determiner in (7-19) is to make two assertions: (1) that there is one and only one individual that has the property of being a fish, and (2) that this individual also has the property of walking. The advantages and disadvantages of Russell's theory of definite descriptions have been much discussed (cf., for example, Strawson 1950, Donnellan 1955, Kaplan 1970, and Mates 1973, among many other articles, for a variety of reactions to Russell's view.) We will briefly mention only the two most obvious difficulties. First, it is clear that the "one and only one" part of the assertion must somehow be relativized to a context of utterance. Example (7-19) would probably never be intended by a speaker of English to imply that only one fish exists in the entire world, but rather would be used where a certain fish is uniquely identifiable to the hearer in the immediate surroundings or at least in the context of the immediately preceding discourse. The technique of indexical semantics adopted in PTQ offers at least a potential framework for providing this relativization. The truth of formula (7-20) of *IL* requires only that there be a unique fish at the index at which the formula is being evaluated, that the formula be true at this index, and that the formula is compatible with a model in which there are no fish or more than one fish at other indices besides this one. If the notion of an index is expanded to include a place coordinate and possibly a "previous discourse coordinate" (as suggested by Lewis (1970)), then it may be possible to approach the use of **the** in natural language rather closely in Montague's system.

The second problem arises with the negation of formulas such as (7-20) (which would appear as the translation of **The fish doesn't walk**), since such a negated formula would be true not only when a unique fish does not walk, but would also be true when there is simply no unique fish. This problem, of course, underlies much of the discussion of presupposition in recent linguistic and philosphical literature. One approach to this second problem lies in Karttunen and Peters' proposal to accommodate Grice's notion of *conventional implicature* in Montague's PTQ. On this view, the "uniqueness assertion" of the definite determiner could be considered a conventional implicature (i.e., condition on acceptable speech-act contexts for the use of the definite determiner) rather than as an entailment of the determiner, hence this aspect of the "meaning" of the determiner would be unaffected by negation. The reader is referred to Karttunen and Peters (1975, 1979) for details.

PROBLEM (7-2). Give an analysis tree and the corresponding step-by-step translation for the sentence **A unicorn walks**, following the example of (7-16) and (7-18).

III. CONJOINED SENTENCES, VERB PHRASES AND TERM PHRASES

The rule for producing sentences conjoined with **and**, both in its syntactic rule S11 and its associated translation rule T11, is simple and transparent:

(7-21) S11a. If $\phi, \psi \in P_t$, then $F_8(\phi, \psi) \in P_t$, where $F_8(\phi, \psi) = \phi$ **and** ψ.

(7-22) T11a. If $\phi, \psi \in P_t$ and ϕ, ψ translate into ϕ', ψ' respectively, then $F_8(\phi, \psi)$ translates into $[\phi' \wedge \psi']$.

Note that S11a is the first rule discussed which is *not* a rule of functional application, since the two input categories, t and t, do not stand in the relation of A/B to B. The translation rule nevertheless does obey the prescribed category-to-type correspondence, since this rule takes two logical expressions of type $f(t)$ (= t) and produces a well-formed expression of *IL* of type $f(t)$.

A completely analogous pair of rules produces sentences conjoined with **or** and their translations:

(7-23) S11b. If $\phi, \psi \in P_t$, then $F_9(\phi, \psi) \in P_t$, where $F_9(\phi, \psi) = \phi$ **or** ψ.

(7-24) T11b. If $\phi, \psi \in P_t$ and ϕ, ψ translate into ϕ', ψ' respectively, then $F_9(\phi, \psi)$ translates into $[\phi' \vee \psi']$.

To illustrate the first conjunction rule, we can take our first two example sentences **John walks** and **Every man talks** and combine them by S11 to give **John walks and every man talks**. The translation of this example will be (7-25), produced by T11a from the translations we derived earlier for these examples:

(7-25) $[\mathbf{walk}'(j) \wedge \forall x[\mathbf{man}'(x) \rightarrow \mathbf{talk}'(x)]]$

Note that the rules S11a and S11b treat the English words **and** and **or** syncategorematically. We could of course modify the syntax of English to include a category of coordinating conjunctions which would have the basic expressions **and** and **or** and perhaps other connectives (e.g., **but**, **nor**, **yet**, etc.) as its members. The single rule replacing S11 and S11a in this treatment would then combine any two sentences with any conjunction to give a derived sentence. This is a case where two different treatments would produce exactly the same English sentences with exactly the same interpretations.

It may come as a slight surprise to linguists that there are also rules for combining two *IV*-phrases directly to form a conjoined verb phrase, as well as rules combining two term phrases:

(7-26) S12a. If $\delta, \gamma \in P_{IV}$, then $F_8(\delta, \gamma) \in P_{IV}$.

(7-27) S12b. If $\delta, \gamma \in P_{IV}$, then $F_9(\delta, \gamma) \in P_{IV}$.

(7-28) S13. If $\alpha, \beta \in P_T$, then $F_9(\alpha, \beta) \in P_T$.

Here, the syntactic operations F_8 and F_9 are the same as those used earlier in the sentence conjunction rules (namely, the operation that combines the two inputs with **and** in between, and the operation that combines the inputs with **or**), although the categories of the inputs and outputs happen to be different. The only rule for combining two term phrases is the one that combines them with the conjunction **or**. Conjoined term phrases with **and** are omitted from the PTQ grammar purely for the sake of simplicity, since these would require plural rather than singular verb forms. As we mentioned earlier, plurals have been omitted from this grammar entirely.

The translation rules are the following:

(7-29) T12a. If $\delta, \gamma \in P_{IV}$ and δ, γ translate into δ', γ' respectively, then $F_8(\delta, \gamma)$ (i.e. δ **and** γ) translates into $\lambda x[\delta'(x) \wedge \gamma'(x)]$.

(7-30) T12b. If $\delta, \gamma \in P_{IV}$ and δ, γ translate into δ', γ' respectively, then $F_9(\delta, \gamma)$ (i.e. δ **or** γ) translates into $\lambda x[\delta'(x) \vee \gamma'(x)]$.

(7-31) T13. If $\alpha, \beta \in P_T$ and α, β translate into α', β' respectively, then $F_9(\alpha, \beta)$ translates into $\lambda P[\alpha'(P) \vee \beta'(P)]$.

Linguists may initially question the advisability of these rules, since it is widely held that greater syntactic generality can be achieved by taking sentence conjunction as basic and by deriving instances of verb phrase and noun phrase conjunction (and conjunction of other constituents) from conjoined sentences by deletion transformations. For example, **John walks and talks** is derived from the underlying sentence **John walks and John talks**. However, it is also well-known that certain semantic problems arise with this approach (cf. Partee 1970, Lakoff 1970). Reduced sentence conjunctions involving quantifiers are not always synonymous with the sentence conjunctions that would be their underlying sources in this analysis. For example, **Every man walks or talks** is not synonymous with **Every man walks or every man talks**. The former sentence could be true in a situation in which some subset of the men in question walk but do not talk, while all the remaining men talk but do not walk. The second sentence would be false in this situation because it is neither true that every man in the group walks, nor is it true that every man in the group talks. (Analogous points can be made with sentences containing the determiner a and verb phrases conjoined with **and**. The semantic principles involved in this distinction should be familiar to any student of first-order logic.) It has been suggested by Generative Semanticists that such pairs of sentences come from different deep structures, these underlying structures having approximately the form of the representation of these two sentences in first-order logic (i.e. $\forall x[man(x) \rightarrow [walk(x) \vee talk(x)]]$ for the first and $[\forall x[man(x) \rightarrow walk(x)] \vee \forall x[man(x) \rightarrow talk(x)]]$ for the second). Such an analysis requires complicated constraints on the quantifier lowering transformation to insure a meaning-preserving derivation from underlying to surface structure in every case.

It is thus of considerable interest that the PTQ rules given above predict just the correct distinction in meaning between these two sentences (while at the same time accounting for the fact that no such semantic difference arises when proper names replace the quantified noun phrases – **John walks or talks** is predicted to be synonymous with **John walks or John talks**). The reason for this has to do with the fact that conjoined verb phrases are translated with the aid of lambda abstraction over individual variables; **walk or talk** is translated as $\lambda x[\text{walk}'(x) \vee \text{talk}'(x)]$, "the property of being an x such that x walks or x talks." In the translation of **Every man walks or talks**, the two occurrences of x will be bound by a single quantifier, not by two separate quantifiers. The best way to make this clear is to exhibit the two sentences and their derivations:

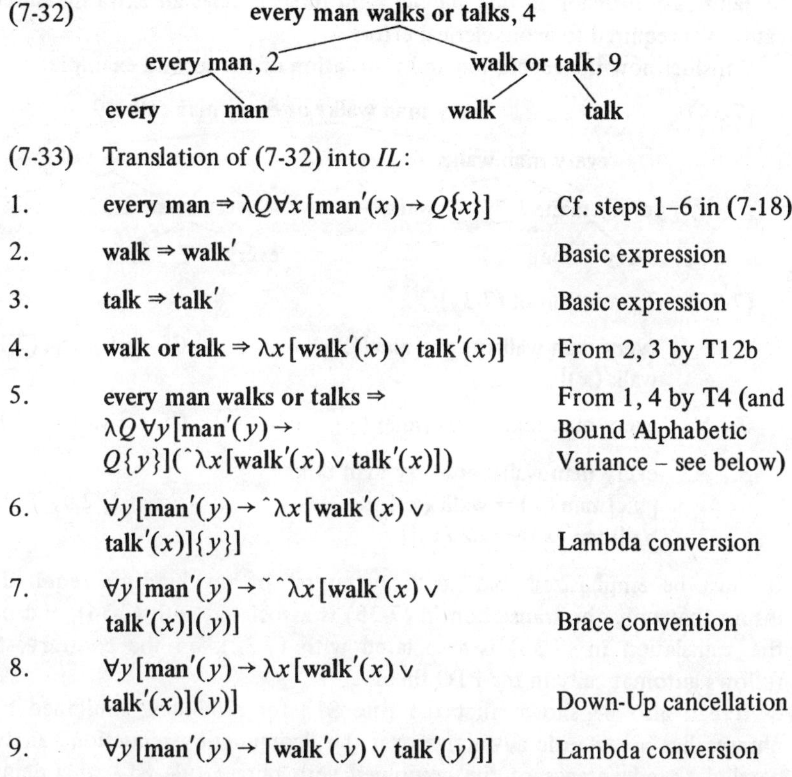

(7-33) Translation of (7-32) into *IL*:

1. **every man** $\Rightarrow \lambda Q \forall x[\text{man}'(x) \rightarrow Q\{x\}]$ — Cf. steps 1–6 in (7-18)
2. **walk** $\Rightarrow$ **walk**$'$ — Basic expression
3. **talk** $\Rightarrow$ **talk**$'$ — Basic expression
4. **walk or talk** $\Rightarrow \lambda x[\text{walk}'(x) \vee \text{talk}'(x)]$ — From 2, 3 by T12b
5. **every man walks or talks** $\Rightarrow$ $\lambda Q \forall y[\text{man}'(y) \rightarrow Q\{y\}](\hat{\ }\lambda x[\text{walk}'(x) \vee \text{talk}'(x)])$ — From 1, 4 by T4 (and Bound Alphabetic Variance – see below)
6. $\forall y[\text{man}'(y) \rightarrow \hat{\ }\lambda x[\text{walk}'(x) \vee \text{talk}'(x)]\{y\}]$ — Lambda conversion
7. $\forall y[\text{man}'(y) \rightarrow \check{\ }\hat{\ }\lambda x[\text{walk}'(x) \vee \text{talk}'(x)](y)]$ — Brace convention
8. $\forall y[\text{man}'(y) \rightarrow \lambda x[\text{walk}'(x) \vee \text{talk}'(x)](y)]$ — Down-Up cancellation
9. $\forall y[\text{man}'(y) \rightarrow [\text{walk}'(y) \vee \text{talk}'(y)]]$ — Lambda conversion

In copying the translation of **every man** from line 1 to line 5, we have systematically replaced variable x with the variable y to avoid confusion of this variable with the variable x that occurs in the expression copied in line 5 from line 4.[7] This is a legitimate change since, as mentioned in chapter 4, for any formula ϕ and any variables u and v, $\forall u\phi$ is logically equivalent to $\forall v\phi'$ in *IL*, where ϕ' is the result of substituting v for all free occurences of u in ϕ, provided that v is not a variable originally occurring in ϕ. This is sometimes called a principle of *alphabetic variants*. It might also be pointed out that in the lambda-conversion of 5 to 6, the whole expression $\hat{}\lambda x[\mathbf{walk}'(x) \vee \mathbf{talk}'(x)]$ was substituted for the property variable Q in $\forall y[\mathbf{man}'(y) \rightarrow Q\{y\}]$. There is of course nothing wrong with this, as both expressions are of the same type (i.e. $\langle s, \langle e, t\rangle\rangle$) and in the proper configuration in 5 for lambda-conversion to be applicable. It is not unusual in simplifying translations of complex English sentences to see rather lengthy expressions "moved around" by lambda-conversion in this manner, and in such cases an extra measure of caution is required to avoid clerical errors.

Consider now the generation and translation of the second example:

(7-34)

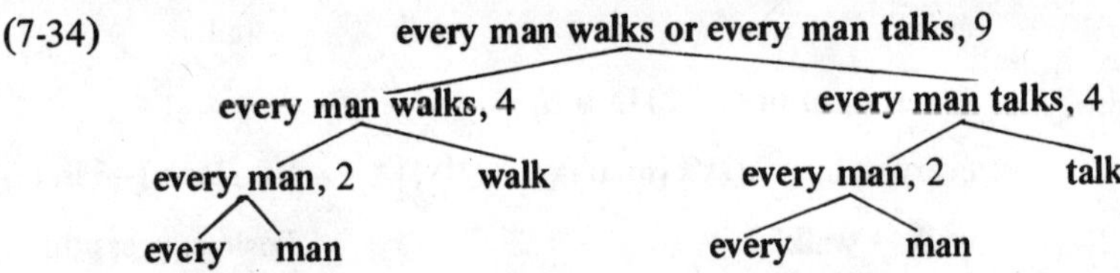

(7-35) Translation of (7-34):

1. **every man walks** ⇒ $\forall x[\mathbf{man}'(x) \rightarrow \mathbf{walk}'(x)]$ — Cf. derivation (7-18)

2. **every man talks** ⇒ $\forall x[\mathbf{man}'(x) \rightarrow \mathbf{talk}'(x)]$ — Cf. derivation (7-18)

3. **every man walks or every man talks** $[\forall x[\mathbf{man}'(x) \rightarrow \mathbf{walk}'(x)] \vee \forall x[\mathbf{man}'(x) \rightarrow \mathbf{talk}'(x)]]$ — From 1, 2 by T11b.

It must be emphasized that no "constraints" of any kind are required to insure that only the translation in (7-35) is associated with (7-34), and only the translation in (7-33) is associated with (7-32); on the contrary, this follows automatically in the PTQ theory.

It can also be shown that the rule S13 for producing conjoined term phrases has a semantic advantage over the "conjunction reduction" analysis parallel to advantages of the conjoined verb phrase rule S12; this demonstration would involve examples such as **A man or a woman found every fish** versus **A man found every fish or a woman found every fish**, but we will forego discussion of this case.[8]

PROBLEM (7-3). Construct analysis trees and the corresponding translations for **John walks or talks** and **John walks or John talks** and show that the translations are equivalent.

PROBLEM (7-4). Do the translations of **A unicorn walks and talks** and **A unicorn walks and a unicorn talks** turn out to be equivalent? What about the translations of **Every unicorn walks and talks** and **Every unicorn walks and every unicorn talks?**

PROBLEM (7-5). Give an analysis tree and step-by-step translation for the sentence **A man or a woman talks.** Is the translation equivalent to that for **A man talks or a woman talks?**

PROBLEM (7-6). Give an analysis tree and translation for the sentence **A fish or a unicorn walks and talks.** Does the relative scope which the PTQ fragment assigns to **and** and **or** in this case agree with your intuitions about the sentence? Would a conjunction-reduction analysis yield the same results as the PTQ fragment?

IV. ANAPHORIC PRONOUNS AS BOUND VARIABLES; SCOPE AMBIGUITIES AND RELATIVE CLAUSES

We have mentioned that among the basic term phrases (members of P_T) are the subscripted pronouns **he**$_0$, **he**$_1$, **he**$_2$, . . . , which serve roughly as free variables in the English syntax. These play a role in the production of anaphoric pronouns, scope ambiguities in sentences with more than one term phrase, *de dicto/de re* ambiguities, and relative clauses. These pronouns do not translate directly into the individual variables $v_{0,e}$, $v_{1,e}$, etc. of *IL* but, like all other term phrases, translate into expressions denoting sets of properties of individuals: The schema for their translations is (7-36):

(7-36) **he**$_n$ translates into $\lambda P[P\{x_n\}]$

Here, x_n stands for a variable of type *e* having the same subscript as the pronoun it translates, e.g. **he**$_0$ translates into $\lambda P[P\{x_0\}]$, **he**$_1$ translates into $\lambda P[P\{x_1\}]$, etc.[9]

In the PTQ fragment the subscripted pronouns behave much as the variables v_1, v_2, etc. did in the language L_{1E} of Chapter 3. They are "bound" by the operation of *replacing* a variable with a term phrase, thus making the operation of variable binding a kind of invisible one with respect to the "surface" form of the sentence. However, the semantic effect of the operation is exactly like that of the familiar variable binding operation in formal languages, as we will see below in the translation rule. If there is more than one occurrence of a certain free variable in a sentence, then only the first of these is replaced by the "quantifying" term phrase, and the remaining instances of this variable becoming anaphoric pronouns. For example, the quantification rule S14 (to be discussed below) can combine the term phrase **Mary** with the sentence **he$_3$ walks and he$_3$ talks** to give the derived sentence **Mary walks and she talks**, the first variable having been replaced with **Mary** and the second having been turned into a "real" (i.e., non-subscripted) pronoun of the appropriate gender.

Each of the four rules performing such "quantifications" – S14, S15, S16 and S3 – does not really involve a *single* structural operation as do the other rules, but rather each involves an infinite *schema* of structural operations, each of which replaces only instances of pronouns with a particular subscript. The operation schema of S14, S15 and S16 is called $F_{10,n}$; one operation of this schema would be $F_{10,0}$ (which replaces only the variables **he$_0$** and **him$_0$**), another would be $F_{10,5}$ (which replaces only **he$_5$** and **him$_5$**), etc. If we attempt to apply the "wrong" operation to a string, no substitutions or changes result. For example $F_{10,4}$(**Mary, he$_4$ walks and he$_4$ talks**) = **Mary walks and she talks**, but $F_{10,5}$(**Mary, he$_4$ walks and he$_4$ talks**) = **he$_4$ walks and he$_4$ talks.**[10] (Dividing up the operation in this way is required by the general theory in UG and by the requirement of getting a unique translation for each distinct syntactic operation.)

Finally, the definition of these operation schemata is divided into two cases; one in which the "quantifying" term phrase is not itself a subscripted pronoun, and a second case in which this term phrase *is* another subscripted pronoun. Including this second case makes each $F_{10,n}$ a total function on the sets P_T and P_t – i.e., each is well-defined for *any* P_T and P_t, no matter whether the first is a subscripted pronoun or not.

The quantification rule S14 reads as follows:

(7-37) S14. If $\alpha \in P_T$ and $\phi \in P_t$, then $F_{10,n}(\alpha, \phi) \in P_t$, where either (i) α does not have the form **he$_k$**, and $F_{10,n}(\alpha, \phi)$ comes from ϕ by replacing the first occurrence of **he$_n$**, or **him$_n$** by α and all other occurrences of **he$_n$** or **him$_n$** by $\left\{\begin{matrix}\textbf{he}\\\textbf{she}\\\textbf{it}\end{matrix}\right\}$ or $\left\{\begin{matrix}\textbf{him}\\\textbf{her}\\\textbf{it}\end{matrix}\right\}$ respectively, according as the gender of the first B_{CN} or B_T in α is $\left\{\begin{matrix}\text{masc.}\\\text{fem.}\\\text{neuter}\end{matrix}\right\}$, or (ii) α = **he$_k$**, and $F_{10,n}(\alpha, \phi)$ comes from ϕ by replacing all occurrences of **he$_n$** or **him$_n$** by **he$_k$** or **him$_k$**, respectively.

The translation rule likewise differs in its effect according to which instance of $F_{10,n}$ is employed:

(7-38) T14. If $\alpha \in P_T$, $\phi \in P_t$, and α, ϕ translates into α', ϕ' respectively, then $F_{10,n}(\alpha, \phi)$ translates into $\alpha'(\hat{}\lambda x_n \phi')$.

This is understood to mean that $F_{10,0}(\alpha, \phi)$ translates into $\alpha'(\hat{}\lambda x_0 \phi')$, $F_{10,1}(\alpha, \phi)$ translates into $\alpha'(\hat{}\lambda x_1 \phi')$, etc. Intuitively, this translation rule may be thought of as taking the translation of a sentence ϕ' (in particular, one containing the free variable x_i), forming from this a property abstract – "the property of being an x_i such that ϕ'" – and finally asserting that this property is in the set of properties denoted by the translation α' of the term phrase α. For example, the sentence formed in the last step of the analysis tree (7-39)

(7-39)

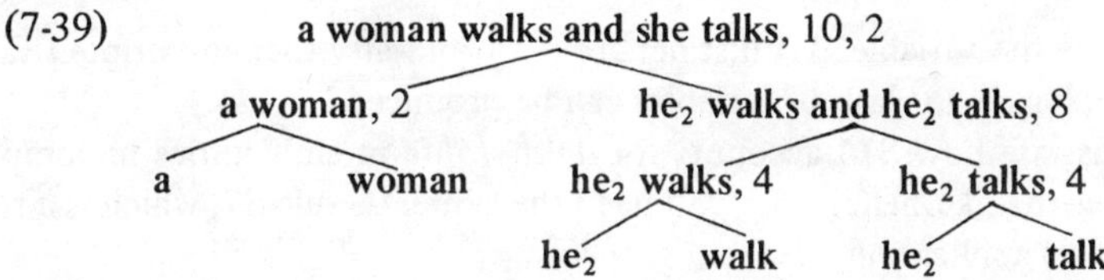

is translated by T14 as asserting, intuitively, that "the property of being an x_2 such that x_2 walks and x_2 talks is among the properties that a woman has" (i.e. ". . . that a certain woman has". Here "a woman" is not intended to be interpreted generically. Rather, (7-39) is interpreted like the more idiomatic English sentence "A woman is walking and she is talking.") To see how this works out in detail, consider the translation and simplification for (7-39), given in (7-40) below, especially steps 12–16:

(7-40)

1.	**he$_2$** $\Rightarrow \lambda P[P\{x_2\}]$	Basic expression
2.	**walk** $\Rightarrow$ **walk**$'$	Basic expression
3.	**talk** $\Rightarrow$ **talk**$'$	Basic expression
4.	**he$_2$ walks** $\Rightarrow \lambda P[P\{x_2\}](\hat{}\mathbf{walk}')$	From 1, 2 by T4
5.	$\hat{}\mathbf{walk}'\{x_2\}$	Lambda conversion
6.	$\check{}\hat{}\mathbf{walk}'(x_2)$	Brace convention
7.	$\mathbf{walk}'(x_2)$	Down-Up cancellation
8.	**he$_2$ talks** $\Rightarrow \lambda P[P\{x_2\}](\hat{}\mathbf{talk}')$	From 1, 3 by T4
9.	$\mathbf{talk}'(x_2)$	Cf. Steps 5–7
10.	**he$_2$ walks and he$_2$ talks** $\Rightarrow$ $[\mathbf{walk}'(x_2) \wedge \mathbf{talk}'(x_2)]$	From 7, 9 by T13

11. **a woman** ⇒ $\lambda P \exists x[\text{woman}'(x) \wedge P\{x\}]$ (Cf. earlier examples)
12. **a woman walks and she talks** ⇒ $\lambda P \exists x[\text{woman}'(x) \wedge P\{x\}](\hat{}\lambda x_2[\text{walk}'(x_2) \wedge \text{talk}'(x_2)])$ From 10, 11 by T14
13. $\exists x[\text{woman}'(x) \wedge \hat{}\lambda x_2[\text{walk}'(x_2) \wedge \text{talk}'(x_2)]\{x\}]$ Lambda conversion
14. $\exists x[\text{woman}'(x) \wedge \check{}\hat{}\lambda x_2[\text{walk}'(x_2) \wedge \text{talk}'(x_2)](x)]$ Brace convention
15. $\exists x[\text{woman}'(x) \wedge \lambda x_2[\text{walk}'(x_2) \wedge \text{talk}'(x_2)](x)]$ Down-Up cancellation
16. $\exists x[\text{woman}'(x) \wedge [\text{walk}'(x) \wedge \text{talk}'(x)]]$ Lambda conversion

(Recall that the variable x is distinct from x_2 and all other subscripted variables here, hence no clash of variables can be produced by T14.)

To illustrate how S14 accounts for *de dicto/de re* ambiguities in complements of verbs like **believe**, we will need the syntactic rule S7, which is a rule of functional application:

(7-41) S7. If $\alpha \in P_{IV/t}$, $\phi \in P_t$, then $F_{11}(\alpha, \phi) \in P_{IV}$, where $F_{11}(\alpha, \phi) =$ α **that** ϕ.

(7-42) T7. If $\alpha \in P_{IV/t}$, $\phi \in P_t$, and α, ϕ translate into α', ϕ' respectively, then $F_{11}(\alpha, \phi)$ translates into $\alpha'(\hat{}\phi')$.

The *de dicto* reading of **John believes that a fish walks** (i.e., the one in which he believes that there is at least one walking fish, but does not necessarily have this belief about any particular fish) is produced simply as in (7-43):

(7-43)

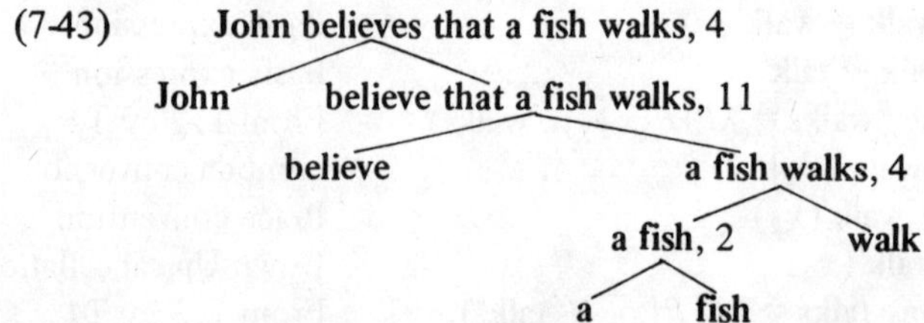

The translation of (7-43) is shown in (7-44). In this and subsequent translations we will compress steps involving familiar operations into one step and gloss over many details.

(7-44)

1. **a fish walks** $\Rightarrow \exists x[\text{fish}'(x) \wedge \text{walk}'(x)]$ — (Cf. earlier examples)
2. **believe** $\Rightarrow$ **believe**$'$ — Basic expression
3. **believe that a fish walks** $\Rightarrow$ $\text{believe}'(\hat{}\exists x[\text{fish}'(x) \wedge \text{walk}'(x)])$ — From 1, 2 by T7
4. **John believes that a fish walks** $\Rightarrow$ $\lambda P[P\{j\}](\hat{}\text{believe}'(\hat{}\exists x[\text{fish}'(x) \wedge \text{walk}'(x)]))$ — From 3 by T4
5. $\text{believe}'(\hat{}\exists x[\text{fish}'(x) \wedge \text{walk}'(x)])(j)$ — Lambda conversion, Brace notation, and Down-Up cancellation
6. $\text{believe}'(j, \hat{}\exists x[\text{fish}'(x) \wedge \text{walk}'(x)])$ — Relational notation (Cf., Ch. 6, p. 164).

Here, John stands in the "believe" relation to the proposition (expression of *IL* of type $\langle s, t\rangle$) that there is a walking fish. The *de re* reading is produced when the term phrase **a fish** is inserted into the analysis tree by the quantification rule S14, rather than being introduced "directly," as in the above analysis tree.

(7-45)

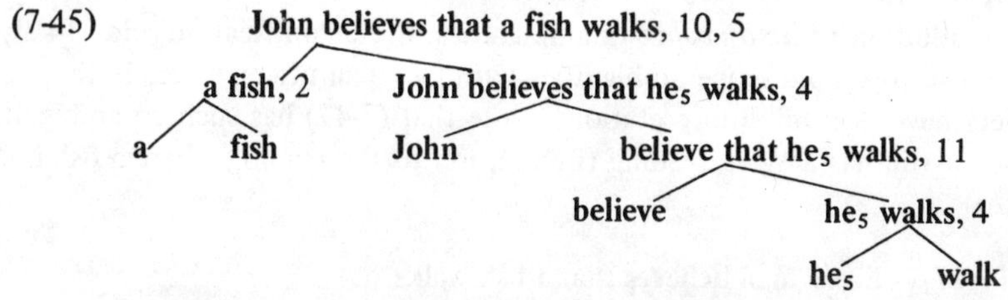

Note that unlike (7-39), no pronouns remain in the sentence of (7-45) after S14 has applied. This happens because there was only one occurrence of the prescribed subscripted pronoun in the tree, this pronoun being replaced by the quantifying term phrase. The translation for analysis tree (7-45) is (7-46):

(7-46)

1. **he$_5$ walks** $\Rightarrow \text{walk}'(x_5)$ — (Cf. (7-40))
2. **believe that he$_5$ walks** $\Rightarrow$ $\text{believe}'(\hat{}[\text{walk}'(x_5)])$ — From 1 by T7
3. **John believes that he$_5$ walks** $\Rightarrow$ $\lambda P[P\{j\}](\hat{}\text{believe}'(\hat{}[\text{walk}'(x_5)]))$ — From 2 by T4
4. $\text{believe}'(\hat{}[\text{walk}'(x_5)])(j)$ — Lambda conversion, Brace notation, Down-Up cancellation

5.	**believe**$'(j, \hat{}[\mathbf{walk}'(x_5)])$	Relational notation
6.	**a fish** $\Rightarrow \lambda P \exists x [\mathbf{fish}'(x) \wedge P\{x\}]$	(Cf. (7-18))
7.	**John believes that a fish walks** $\Rightarrow$ $\lambda P \exists x [\mathbf{fish}'(x) \wedge P\{x\}](\hat{}\lambda x_5[\mathbf{believe}'(j, \hat{}[\mathbf{walk}'(x_5)])])$	From 5, 6 by T14
8.	$\exists x [\mathbf{fish}'(x) \wedge \lambda x_5[\mathbf{believe}'(j, \hat{}[\mathbf{walk}'(x_5)])](x)]$	Lambda conversion, Brace notation, Down-Up cancellation
9.	$\exists x [\mathbf{fish}'(x) \wedge \mathbf{believe}'(j, \hat{}[\mathbf{walk}'(x)])]$	Lambda conversion

Here there is some fish such that John stands in the "believe" relation to the proposition that the fish walks. By comparing the last lines of (7-44) and (7-46), the reader can see that this *de dicto/de re* ambiguity of the English sentence is appropriately accounted for by the translation procedure, since these two formulas are exactly parallel to the formulas of *IL* cited in our discussion of this ambiguity and its representation in *IL* in Chapter 6, pp. 167–168, where we discussed the two readings of *John believes that a Republican will win.*

In addition to *de dicto/de re* ambiguities, the quantification rule S14 also gives rise to simple scope ambiguities with two quantifiers, where both quantifiers have "*de re*" interpretations. Note that (7-47) has such an ambiguity when **a fish** has a *de re* reading (in addition to the reading where **a fish** is *de dicto*):

(7-47) **Every man believes that a fish walks.**

This sentence might involve a belief about one particular fish shared by every man, or else beliefs about possibly different (though specific) fish for each man. The former reading will be produced if the sentence is generated as in (7-48), the latter reading if the sentence is generated as in (7-49):

(7-48)

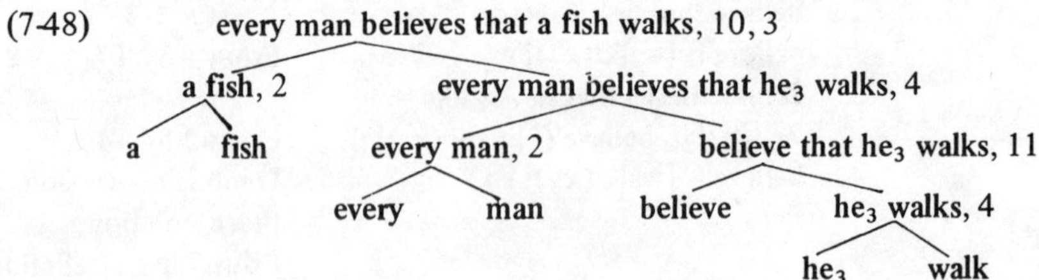

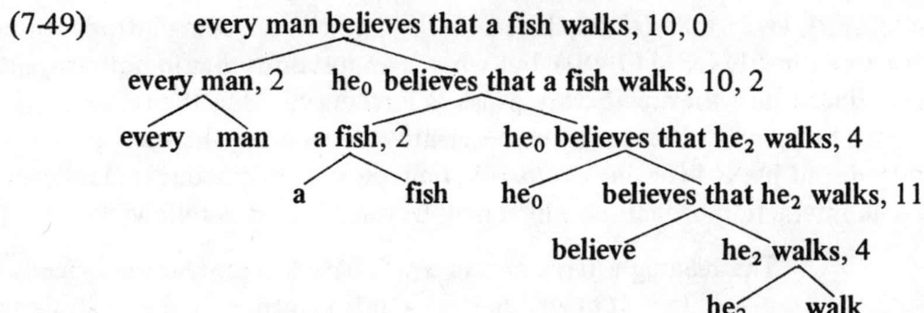

The translations of (7-48) and (7-49) are, in simplified form, (7-50) and (7-51) respectively:

(7-50) $\exists x[\mathbf{fish}'(x) \wedge \forall y[\mathbf{man}'(y) \rightarrow \mathbf{believe}'(y, \hat{}[\mathbf{walk}'(x)])]]$

(7-51) $\forall y[\mathbf{man}'(y) \rightarrow \exists x[\mathbf{fish}'(x) \wedge \mathbf{believe}'(y, \hat{}[\mathbf{walk}'(x)])]]$

(We do not give the step-by-step translations and reductions of these two formulas since they do not involve any steps not already illustrated.)

PROBLEM (7-7). Verify that the translations of (7-48) and (7-49) do in fact reduce to the formulas in (7-50) and (7-51), respectively. (You may arrive at bound alphabetic variants of the given formulas, which are of course equivalent.)

It may now become apparent to the reader that S14 gives rise to syntactically distinct derivations even where no semantic ambiguity appears. For example, even as simple a sentence as **John walks** can be produced either directly by S4 alone, or by S14 from **John** plus **he$_1$ walks**, yet these two derivations result in logically equivalent translations.[11] Or again, the sentence (7-47) can also be derived as in (7-52), though the translation for this analysis tree is equivalent to that of (7-49) (i.e., (7-51)):

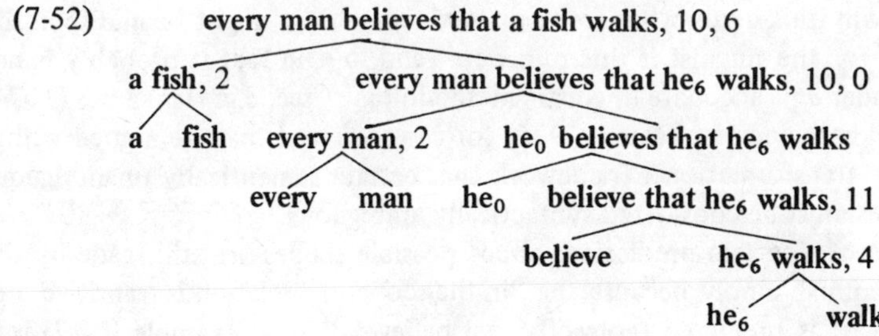

In (7-52), **every man** is introduced by S14 rather than being introduced into the tree directly (as in (7-48)), but what is important is that in both cases it is introduced into the tree before **a fish** is introduced. Thus the reading a given term phrase will have does not necessarily depend on whether or not it is introduced by S14 (or one of the other quantifying rules), but rather depends on an interaction of factors, which may be summarized as follows:

> The reading a term phrase α will have in a sentence ϕ depends on two things: (1) whether it is introduced into the analysis tree before or after an oblique-context-creating element (such as **believe**); this determines whether it has a *de dicto* or *de re* reading; (2) whether it is introduced into the tree before or after any other given term phrase β, regardless of whether α and β each happen to be introduced directly or by a quantification rule; this determines whether α will be interpreted as having narrower or wider scope than β. (When we have introduced the rules for tense and negation in Section VIII below, we will see that the interpretation of a term phrase α also depends on (3) whether it is introduced into the tree before or after the tense and/or negation; this determines whether it has scope narrower or wider than the tense and/or negation.)

PROBLEM (7-8). Do the derivation and translation for **John walks** using quantification rule S14 and the corresponding translation rule T14.

The fact that the PTQ theory allows, in effect, for a sentence to be syntactically ambiguous in ways that correspond to no semantic ambiguity flies in the face of what seems to be an implicit dictum of transformational grammar – that any sentence that is semantically unambiguous is *ipso facto* syntactically unambiguous as well. However, there seems to be no really good reason why this dictum has to be maintained. Things might be methodically simpler for the linguist if this rule were valid, but in fact it probably is not valid under *any* adequate linguistic methodology – see, e.g. Hankamer (1974) and Pinkham and Hankamer (1975) for cases where it can be argued within a purely transformational framework that certain semantically unambiguous sentences must be considered syntactically ambiguous.

Of course, certain predictions about possible scopes are still made by the PTQ grammar simply because the "in-the-scope-of" relation is transitive. For example, it is predicted (correctly, we believe) that in example (7-47) it is impossible for **a fish** to have a *de dicto* reading and at the same time to have wider scope than **every man**. This is because **a fish** must be within the scope of **believe** in order to receive a *de dicto* interpretation, but **believe** must necessarily be introduced into the tree before **every man**, no matter whether **every man** is introduced by a quantification rule or not. Hence it follows that **every man** must have wider scope than **a fish** (i.e., be introduced into the tree after **a fish**) whenever this latter term phrase has a *de dicto* reading. Any theory of grammar which treats scope relations as they are traditionally handled in formal logic would probably make the same prediction, but perhaps theories which attempted to distinguish such readings by means of semantic features like [±SPECIFIC] would not.

A syntactic operation involving the "binding" of subscripted pronouns is also used in the rule for forming relative clauses, so a discussion of the relative clause rule belongs in this section. Linguists are well aware that normal relative clauses in English formed with the "WH-pronouns" (i.e., **who, whom, whose, which**) must involve at least (1) marking of a term phrase within the relative clause as a WH-pronoun with gender and number matching that of the head noun and case determined by its syntactic position within the clause, (2) movement of this term phrase to the beginning of the relative clause, and (3) provision for "Pied-Piping" (cf. Ross 1967), i.e., optional movement of the preposition (and other material) preceding the noun phrase within the clause along with that noun phrase. But for reasons of expository simplicity, Montague did not choose to include these familiar relative clauses in the PTQ grammar (e.g. *the man whom Mary loves*) but instead included relative clauses formed with *such that* (e.g. *the man such that Mary loves him*) which are characteristic of mathematical jargon, but hardly a part of colloquial English. Note that these relative clauses are simpler than the normal ones in that they involve neither WH-pronouns nor movement of the embedded noun phrase. (Moreover, they are not subject to Ross' Complex *NP* Constraint.) The linguist will no doubt be able to imagine how Montague's rule might be modified along traditional transformational lines to produce the more normal relative clause, if desired. The inputs to the relative clause rule are a common noun and a sentence, and the output is a new phrase of the category common noun (*CN*):

(7-53) S3: If $\zeta \in P_{CN}$ and $\phi \in P_t$, then $F_{3,n}(\zeta, \phi) \in P_{CN}$, where $F_{3,n}(\zeta, \phi) = \zeta$ **such that** ϕ', and ϕ' comes from ϕ by replacing each occurrence of $\mathbf{he}_n$ or $\mathbf{him}_n$ by $\left\{\begin{matrix}\mathbf{he}\\ \mathbf{she}\\ \mathbf{it}\end{matrix}\right\}$ or $\left\{\begin{matrix}\mathbf{him}\\ \mathbf{her}\\ \mathbf{it}\end{matrix}\right\}$

respectively, according as the first B_{CN} in ζ is of $\left\{\begin{matrix}\text{masc.}\\ \text{fem.}\\ \text{neuter}\end{matrix}\right\}$ gender.

Note that this rule combines a common noun and a clause to give another common noun; it does *not* combine a term phrase (i.e., linguist's noun phrase) with a clause to give another term phrase. Thus as Partee (1975) points out, the analysis parallels linguistic analyses of relative clauses such as (7-54), not the perhaps more common analyses like (7-55):

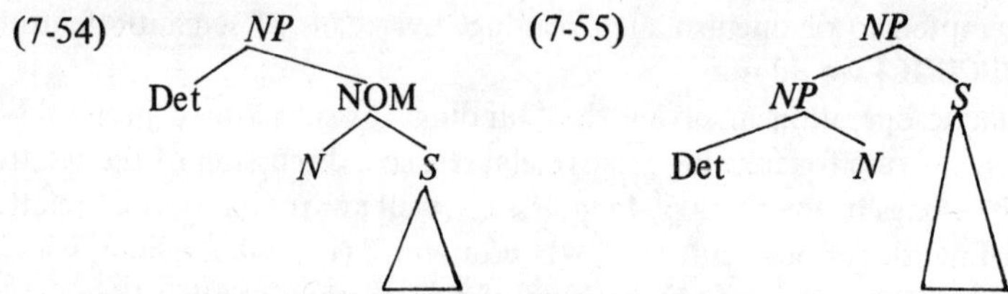

The reason for this choice is semantic: the requirement of producing the correct meaning of a relative clause structure (i.e., determiner, noun and clause) from the meanings of its parts in a way consistent with the analysis of determiner-noun constructions elsewhere requires an analysis like (7-54), not (7-55). As Partee notes, this can probably best be appreciated by comparing the meaning of *the fish* with that of *the fish which walks*. The meaning of *the* in *the fish* is analyzed so as to require that there is one and only one fish. But in *the fish which walks* it is clearly not intended that there be one and only one fish (or a unique fish identifiable to the hearer in the context of the utterance), but merely that there be a unique individual that is *both* a fish *and* is something which walks. But if *fish which walks* is a constituent interpreted as denoting the set of things which are both fish and are things which walk, then the meaning of *the* in the full phrase *the fish which walks* is exactly the same as that of *the* in all other constructions. In a parallel way, *a* plus *fish which walks* will require that there is at least one thing which is both a fish and a thing which walks. Finally, *every fish which walks* will involve every individual that is *both* a fish *and* a thing which walks (but not necessarily everything that is a fish, nor everything which walks). Thus we will get correct semantic results for relative clauses in each case if the combination of a noun ζ and a sentence ϕ (containing a free variable x) is interpreted as denoting the intersection of the set denoted by ζ with the set of all x such that ϕ. (This observation about the semantics of relative clauses seems to stem from Quine 1960.) Montague's translation rule for S3 has this effect:

(7-56) T3: If $\zeta \in P_{CN}$ and $\phi \in P_t$, and ζ and ϕ translate into ζ', ϕ' respectively, then $F_{3,n}(\zeta, \phi)$ translates into $\lambda x_n[\zeta'(x_n) \wedge \phi']$.

Note that S3, like S14, is a rule schema; each instance operates on subscripted pronouns with a particular subscript n, and it is this same subscript which is to appear on the variable x in the corresponding instance of the translation. For example, if the pronoun **he**$_7$ is "relativized" in a sentence ϕ, then the translation of the resulting relative clause must be $\lambda x_7[\zeta'(x_7) \wedge \phi']$, insuring that the lambda operator will bind one or more occurrence of x_7 in ϕ'. The best way to understand the details of this rule is by an example:

(7-57)

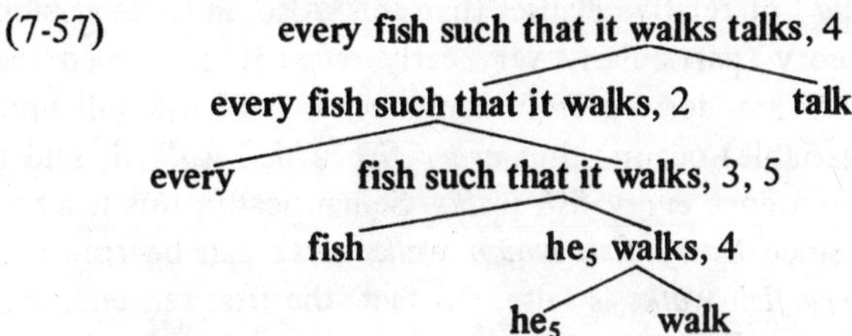

The translation and simplification is sketched in (7-58):

(7-58)

1. **he**$_5$ **walks** $\Rightarrow$ $walk'(x_5)$ — (Cf. earlier examples)
2. **fish such that it walks** $\Rightarrow$ $\lambda x_5[fish'(x_5) \wedge walk'(x_5)]$ — From 1 by T3
3. **every fish such that it walks** $\Rightarrow$ $\lambda P\lambda Q\forall x[P\{x\} \rightarrow Q\{x\}](\hat{}\lambda x_5[fish'(x_5) \wedge walk'(x_5)])$ — From 2 by T2
4. $\lambda Q\forall x[\hat{}\lambda x_5[fish'(x_5) \wedge walk'(x_5)]\{x\} \rightarrow Q\{x\}]$ — Lambda conversion
5. $\lambda Q\forall x[\lambda x_5[fish'(x_5) \wedge walk'(x_5)](x) \rightarrow Q\{x\}]$ — Down-Up cancellation, Brace convention
6. $\lambda Q\forall x[[fish'(x) \wedge walk'(x)] \rightarrow Q\{x\}]$ — Lambda conversion
7. **every fish such that it walks talks** $\Rightarrow$ $\lambda Q\forall x[[fish'(x) \wedge walk'(x)] \rightarrow Q\{x\}](\hat{}talk')$ — From 6 by T4
8. $\forall x[[fish'(x) \wedge walk'(x)] \rightarrow talk'(x)]$ — Lambda conversion, Brace convention Down-Up cancellation

It might also be noted that Montague's rule predicts the existence of so-called "stacked relative clauses" (such as **Every unicorn such that it walks such that**

it talks loves Mary, though less awkward examples occur in colloquial English) and assigns a correct interpretation to them.

It is perhaps instructive to compare the semantic side of Montague's relative clause rule with the treatment of relative clauses in transformational grammar. Little is customarily said about the "meaning" of relative clauses beyond an assignment of a "logical structure" to relative clauses that looks something like (7-54) or (7-55). This may be a satisfactory analysis from the point of view of "structural semantics" in that this kind of structure is distinct from all other "logical deep structures" representing different semantic relationships, but the reader should now be able to see clearly why more needs to be said about the "meaning" of relative clauses than this. Also, in some versions of transformational theory (particularly very early ones) it is claimed that relative clause structures are derived from sentences in which a full noun phrase (rather than a variable) occurs; thus *every fish which walks* is said to involve an underlying sentence *every fish walks*. Semantically, this is a very strange claim indeed, since *Every fish which walks talks* can be true even when the sentence *Every fish walks* is false. (In fact, the first sentence happens to conversationally implicate that the second is false.) It is hard to see how the meaning of this second sentence is useful at all in giving a compositional semantic analysis of the first. A little thought about this should convince the reader that the sentential function "x walks" is the most obviously relevant embedded-sentence source for a compositional analysis of such a relative clause, just as Quine and Montague suggested.

The relative clause rule S3 is unfortunately not protected from forming relative clauses in which no appropriate subscripted variable occurs. Thus S3 forms derived CNs such as **man such that a fish walks** and **woman such that he$_3$ runs** (the latter example formed by $F_{3,n}$ where n is any integer *other* than 3). These could of course be avoided by "filtering out" such structures along the lines suggested by Chomsky (1965) (cf. also footnote 10), but it is not clear how such filtering should best be accomplished within the theoretical framework of UG.

Though the PTQ grammar is simplistic and awkward in its syntactic treatment of relative clauses, the same compositional semantic interpretation of relative clauses that Montague demonstrated in PTQ can be – and has been – incorporated into a variety of more elegant and comprehensive syntactic treatments of relativization. The earliest of these, Rodman (1976), not only produced the "normal" English relative clauses introduced by **who**, **which**, etc. and **that**, but also showed how non-restrictive relative clauses are most naturally distinguished from restrictive relatives (syntactically and semantically) in a Montague Grammar. Furthermore, Rodman hypothesized that Ross's (1967) Complex *NP*-constrain and Coordinate Structure Constraint can be formulated in this framework in such a way as to make observably correct predictions about semantic interpretation that go beyond the syntactic facts observed by Ross. (For further discussion of Rodman's hypothesis, see Cooper (1979a).) In a series of papers (Cooper, 1975, 1978, 1979b), Robin Cooper has presented varying syntactic analyses of relative clauses based on his system for interpreting noun phrases that does not require quantification rules like S14. Gazdar (to appear) offers a radically different syntactic approach to relative clauses which is still compatible with Montague's semantic program.

It might be assumed from our discussion that an adequate compositional semantic analysis of relative clauses can only be based on the "Determiner-Nom" syntactic analysis (as in (7-54)), not on the "*NP–S*" analysis (as in (7-55)), but this is not the case. While it may be true that the more simple and straightforward treatment of English relies on this "Det–Nom" constituent grouping, Cooper and Bach (1978) have shown that by giving a more complicated semantic treatment to the "*NP*" of the "*NP–S*" analysis, this grouping too can be given a satisfactory semantic interpretation. Moreover, this more complicated semantic analysis is the only one that will suffice for languages like Hittite and Walbiri which have so-called "correlative" clauses (relative clauses which always appear at the beginning or ends of sentences and do not form a constituent with their "head" *NP*).

PROBLEM (7-9). Give an analysis tree and a step-by-step translation for the sentence **A woman such that she talks walks.**

PROBLEM (7-10). What ambiguities does the PTQ fragment attribute to the sentence **Every man such that he believes that a woman walks runs**? Do these accord with your intuitions about what the sentence means?

V. Be, TRANSITIVE VERBS, MEANING POSTULATES AND NON-SPECIFIC READINGS

We now come to the rule for combining a transitive verb with a term phrase to give an IV-phrase. This is an ordinary concatenation rule, except for the provision that if the object term phrase is a subscripted pronoun, it is changed to the objective form (**he**$_n$ becomes **him**$_n$):

(7-59) S5. If $\delta \in P_{TV}$ and $\beta \in P_T$, then $F_5(\delta, \beta) \in P_{IV}$, where $F_5(\delta, \beta) = \delta\beta$ if β does not have the form $\mathbf{he}_n$, and $F_5(\delta, \mathbf{he}_n) = \delta\ \mathbf{him}_n$.

As this is a rule of functional application (note the relationship of the categories involved, recalling that *TV* is *IV*/*T*), the translation rule is predictable and we will not write it out (it will give $\delta'(\hat{}\beta')$).

We will consider four kinds of examples that involve this rule: first, the non-specific (or *de dicto*) reading of **John seeks a unicorn**, then the *de re* reading of this same example, then the case of extensional verbs (**John finds a unicorn**), which have no non-specific readings, and then finally examples with the verb **be**. The non-specific reading with **seek** is produced as in (7-60):

(7-60)

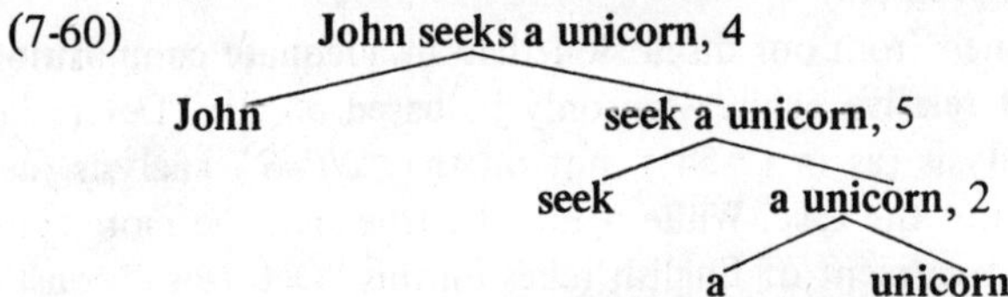

The verb **seek** and all other transitive verbs (except **be**) translate into simple constants of *IL* (i.e., **seek** translates into **seek**′, etc.), so the translation works out as follows:

(7-61)
1. **seek** ⇒ **seek**′ — Basic expression
2. **a unicorn** ⇒ $\lambda Q \exists x[\mathbf{unicorn}'(x) \wedge Q\{x\}]$ — (Cf. earlier examples)
3. **seek a unicorn** ⇒ $\mathbf{seek}'(\hat{}\lambda Q \exists x[\mathbf{unicorn}'(x) \wedge Q\{x\}])$ — From 1, 2 by T5
4. **John seeks a unicorn** $\lambda P[P\{j\}](\hat{}\mathbf{seek}'(\hat{}\lambda Q \exists x[\mathbf{unicorn}'(x) \wedge Q\{x\}]))$ — From 3 by T4
5. $\hat{}\mathbf{seek}'(\hat{}\lambda Q \exists x[\mathbf{unicorn}'(x) \wedge Q\{x\}])\{j\}$ — Lambda conversion
6. $\mathbf{seek}'(\hat{}\lambda Q \exists x[\mathbf{unicorn}'(x) \wedge Q\{x\}])(j)$ — Brace, Down-Up
7. $\mathbf{seek}'(j, \hat{}\lambda Q \exists x[\mathbf{unicorn}'(x) \wedge Q\{x\}])$ — Relational notation

At this point, no more simplifications of line (7) are possible in the PTQ system. The formula in line (7) of (7-61) asserts that John (the individual denoted by j) stands in the "**seek**-relation" to, as it were, the property of being a property that some unicorn has. We must now try to understand exactly what the interpretation of this formula is. This interpretation is undoubtedly one of the most arcane aspects of the entire PTQ system, but also one of the most fascinating and ingenious.

Why does this semantical object that John stands in the **seek**-relation to have to be such an incredibly abstract thing as a property of properties of individuals? To answer this, it is best to approach the question indirectly, by starting with simpler semantic analyses of (the non-specific reading of) **John seeks a unicorn** and seeing why, within the framework of referential semantics, each of these simpler analyses is inadequate in one way or another.

First, note that we cannot analyze this sentence (on the non-specific reading) as a simple relation between two individuals as we did with transitive verbs in the formal languages in the earlier chapters, because this fails to capture the fact that John can be seeking a unicorn (or a friend, or a penny, etc.) without there being any *particular* unicorn (or friend, or penny, etc.) that he is seeking. Furthermore, **John seeks a unicorn** can even be true in a world in which unicorns do not exist (as in our actual world).

Next, we can consider Quine's suggestion (in Quine 1960) that we consider the phrase **seek a unicorn** as a basic, one-place predicate; thus we might understand this sentence as paraphrased by "John is unicorn-seeking." But notice that in place of *a unicorn* we can substitute an unlimited number of other "non-specific" noun phrases, e.g. *seek a unicorn*, *seek a large unicorn*, *seek a unicorn with a golden mane*, *seek a unicorn with a gold mane and a bushy tail*, etc. All of these are semantically distinct, so Quine's analysis apparently leads us to the conclusion that all these phrases are distinct basic one-place predicates. As Montague observed, this solution "raises the psychological problem of explaining how a natural language containing infinitely many primitive predicate constants can be learned" (Montague, 1960, p. 155).

It might next be suggested, within the framework of intensional analysis developed here, that **John seeks a unicorn** be analyzed as a relation between John and the property of unicornhood (where *property* has our technical sense). This seems to circumvent the difficulty about their being no unicorns in the actual world, since a property is a function from indices to sets. Though the property denoted by $^\wedge$**unicorn**$'$ may have the null set as extension for all indices in the actual world, there will be many indices (e.g., those in the propositions expressed by all the medieval stories about unicorns) where this property has non-null extensions. However, this solution still leaves open the question of how we are to distinguish **John seeks a unicorn** from **John seeks every unicorn** (or for that matter, from *John seeks two unicorns*, etc.), since all of these seem to involve the property of unicornhood in exactly the same way.

When we take this problem with quantifiers into consideration, it seems natural to suggest that a *set* of properties might be involved, since we have already seen how quantifier phrases are successfully treated as sets of properties in extensional contexts. (In fact, logicians since Frege have recognized that quantifiers are really second-order properties in a sense.) This will help, because the set of properties that every unicorn has is clearly distinct from the set of properties that some unicorn or other has. (Consider, for example, a situation in which there are exactly three unicorns, u_1, u_2, and u_3. Here the set of properties that some unicorn or other has will include the property of being identical with u_1, the property of being identical with u_2 and the property of being identical with u_3. However, the set of properties that every unicorn has[12] will not contain any of these properties, since it is false that every unicorn is identical with u_1, or that every unicorn is identical with u_2, etc.

However, it won't quite work to treat **seek** as a relation between individuals and sets of properties of individuals, because of the following problem. In the actual world, no unicorns exist. Thus the set of properties that some unicorn or other has is, in this world, the null set.[13] But so is the set of properties that some centaur or other has, since there are no centaurs in the actual world either. It ought to follow from this observation that **John seeks a unicorn** is true in the actual world if and only if **John seeks a centaur** is true, which is clearly wrong.

Thus we must go one more step and consider the semantical object of the *seek*-relation to be not a set of properties, but a function from indices to sets of properties, or in other words, a *property of properties.*[14] Thus the property of being a property that some unicorn has is a function which gives the empty set of properties when applied to indices in the actual world, but for other indices in other worlds where there are unicorns, this function will give non-null sets of properties. By looking at these indices, we can distinguish the property of being a property that some unicorn has from the property of being a property that some centaur has.

To summarize, the analysis of the object of the *seek*-relation as a property of properties of individuals allows us to (1) account for the "non-specific" character of this relation, (2) distinguish between **seek a unicorn** and **seek every unicorn**, and at the same time (3) handle those cases where the object of **seek** denotes a non-existent being in some worlds. Thus it appears that the semantic analysis of intensional transitive verbs like **seek** must, in a possible-worlds semantic framework, involve entities at least as abstract as properties of properties of individuals. Of course one cannot rule out the possibility that a simpler solution may some day be found, but at present this analysis seems to stand as a *tour de force* of intensional semantic analysis, in that it captures such an elusive meaning as the "non-specific" reading of **seek a unicorn** in a semantic theory based on the notion of reference.

Note also that we are now in a position to see a "payoff" of Montague's insistence upon a uniform correspondence between syntactic category and logical type, for it follows automatically from (1) the general principle of correspondence between categories and logical types given by the function f, (2) the categorization of term phrases as t/IV (i.e., as denoting sets of properties), and (3) the categorization of transitive verbs as IV/T, that transitive verbs MUST be treated as functions applying to properties of properties of individuals – i.e., this is what $f(TV)$ (or $f(IV/T)$) turns out to give. But though this fact would appear to produce unmotivated semantic complexity for "extensional" transitive verbs, this complex semantical object is just what is needed for verbs like **seek**. (We will see shortly how the extensional cases are handled.) In this sort of situation, some enthusiasts might claim that Montague's system here captures a "significant generalization" about natural language which can hardly be a result of chance. We refrain from such grandiose claims here, but merely note this as an apparently pleasant consequence of Montague's general principles which is interesting enough to deserve further scrutiny.

There is another well-known analysis of the *seek*-problem (cf. McCawley (1970), Bach (1968), and Quine (1960)), which is to derive **seek** syntactically from a structure involving **try to find**. This preserves an otherwise seemingly valid principle that "intensional contexts" are restricted to embedded clauses. Quine even goes so far as to suggest that **John seeks a unicorn** be paraphrased as "John endeavors that he find a unicorn." (Of course Quine is not suggesting a program involving syntactic "lexical decomposition" in a transformational grammar, but rather a program of "reconstructing" natural languages into a more workable, unproblematic form.) Montague seems to be suspicious of this analysis because (1) it departs from the apparent surface syntactic form of English, and (2) he thought it very damaging that there was no obvious "paraphrase" available for certain other allegedly intensional transitive verbs such as **worship** and **conceive (of)**. Whether these verbs really have "non-specific" readings comparable to those of **seek, want, owe**, etc. is hard to say, however; cf. Bennett (1974: 82ff.) for an extensive discussion. Montague nevertheless seems to have thought the "definition" of **seek** as **try to find** might be correct, and he showed how this "definition" could be incorporated into the PTQ system (we will see below how this is accomplished).

There is a second reading of **John seeks a unicorn** (the "specific reading") which does mean that there is some particular but unnamed unicorn that

John is looking for. This reading can be produced in PTQ by a "quantifying in" derivation such as (7-62).

(7-62)

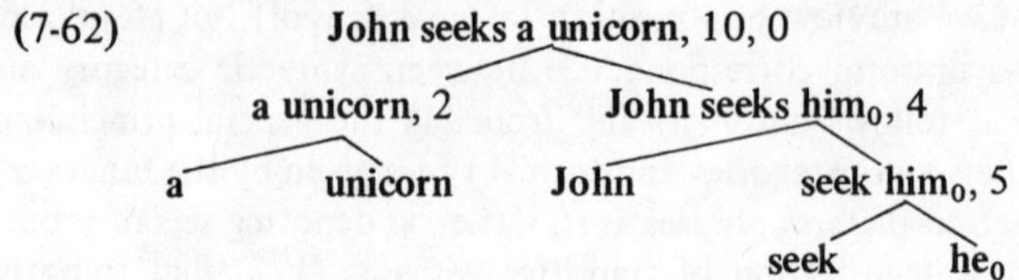

The translation proceeds as in (7-63).

(7-63)		
	1. **he**$_0$ $\Rightarrow \lambda P[P\{x_0\}]$	Basic expression
	2. **seek** $\Rightarrow$ **seek**$'$	Basic expression
	3. **seek him**$_0$ $\Rightarrow$ **seek**$'({}^\wedge\lambda P[P\{x_0\}])$	From 1, 2 by T5
	4. **John seeks him**$_0$ $\Rightarrow$ $\lambda P[P\{j\}]({}^\wedge$**seek**$'({}^\wedge\lambda P[P\{x_0\}]))$	From 4 by T4
	5. ${}^\wedge$**seek**$'({}^\wedge\lambda P[P\{x_0\}])\{j\}$	Lambda conversion
	6. **seek**$'(j, {}^\wedge\lambda P[P\{x_0\}])$	Brace, Down-Up, Relational notation
	7. **a unicorn** $\Rightarrow \lambda Q\exists x[$**unicorn**$'(x) \wedge Q\{x\}]$	(Cf. earlier examples)
	8. **John seeks a unicorn** $\Rightarrow$ $\lambda Q\exists x[$**unicorn**$'(x) \wedge Q\{x\}]({}^\wedge\lambda x_0[$**seek**$'(j, {}^\wedge\lambda P[P\{x_0\}])])$	From 6, 7 by T14
	9. $\exists x[$**unicorn**$'(x) \wedge {}^\wedge\lambda x_0[$**seek**$'(j, {}^\wedge\lambda P[P\{x_0\}])]\{x\}]$	Lambda conversion
	10. $\exists x[$**unicorn**$'(x) \wedge \lambda x_0[$**seek**$'(j, {}^\wedge\lambda P[P\{x_0\}])](x)]$	Down-Up, Brace
	11. $\exists x[$**unicorn**$'(x) \wedge [$**seek**$'(j, {}^\wedge\lambda P[P\{x\}])]]$	Lambda conversion

Note that in line 11 the quantifier binding x is in "extensional" position (not within the scope of ${}^\wedge$), as is **unicorn**$'(x)$, so this formula entails that a unicorn exists. It turns out that line 11 of (7-63) is in fact equivalent to a first-order formula. To see why this is so, we should begin by distinguishing two kinds of sets of properties. We will refer to certain sets of properties as *sublimations* (a term which Montague is said to have used, although it does not appear in his published writings. Lewis 1972 uses the term *character* for the same purpose.) The set of properties that a particular individual has (at some index) will be called the *sublimation of* that individual, an *individual sublimation*. An individual sublimation must be a *maximally consistent* set of properties:

it is consistent in that there is one individual that possesses all the properties in the set, and it is maximal in that it is the largest such consistent set possible – adding even one more property would render it inconsistent (in this sense of *inconsistent*). In contrast, the set of properties that "some unicorn or other" has need not (and usually will not) be consistent; for example, it can simultaneously be true that some unicorn or other is asleep and that some unicorn or other is not asleep, so this set of properties will contain both the property of being asleep and the property of not being asleep (though no single *individual* is both asleep and not asleep). On the other hand, other sets of properties can be consistent but fail to single out just one individual; for example, the set of properties that every unicorn has (in situations in which there are more than one unicorn). Any set of properties that fails to be an individual sublimation (either by having "too many" or "too few" properties) will be called a *generic sublimation*. Among generic sublimations, we will introduce terms for two kinds of sublimations: for a given noun α, we will call the set of properties that some α or other has the *existential sublimation* of α, and we will call the set of properties that every α has the *universal sublimation* of α.

The intuitive difference between existential sublimations, individual sublimations and universal sublimations might better be appreciated from the diagram in Fig. 7-1. In each case, the large circle represents the denotation of a term phrase (a set of properties of individuals), the circles or ovals within the large circle represent the properties that are members of that property set, and dots represent individuals that possess these properties. (The diagrams cannot represent the difference between intensional and extensional types, however.)

Instances of truly "non-specific" seeking are always relations between individuals and (the intensions of) generic sublimations.

On the other hand, there is exactly one individual sublimation of any individual at any index. Thus, individuals and their sublimations stand in one-to-one correspondence at any index, i.e., the following is a valid formula:

(7-64) $\forall x \forall y \Box[x = y \leftrightarrow \lambda P[P\{x\}] = \lambda P[P\{y\}]]$

Likewise, individuals and the concepts of their individual sublimations stand in one-to-one correspondence:

(7-65) $\forall x \forall y \Box[x = y \leftrightarrow {}^\wedge\lambda P[P\{x\}] = {}^\wedge\lambda P[P\{y\}]]$

But where a and b are arbitrary individual constants $\Box[a = b \leftrightarrow {}^\wedge\lambda P[P\{a\}] = {}^\wedge\lambda P[P\{b\}]]$ does not hold, unless for some reason a and b are known to have the same denotation at every index (more on that point later).

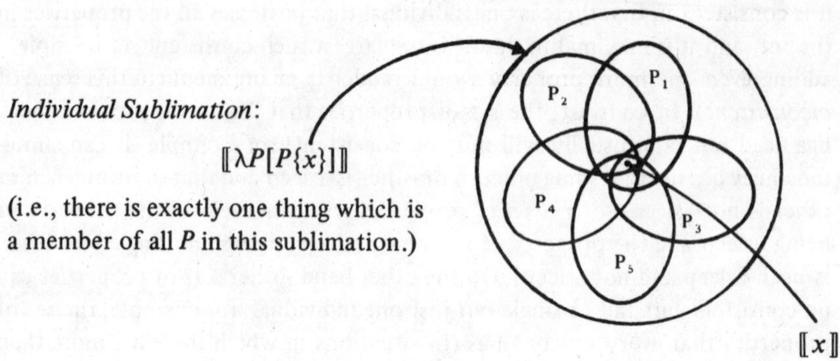
Individual Sublimation:
$[\![\lambda P[P\{x\}]]\!]$
(i.e., there is exactly one thing which is a member of all P in this sublimation.)
P_1
P_2
P_4
P_3
P_5
$[\![x]\!]$

Fig. 7-1a

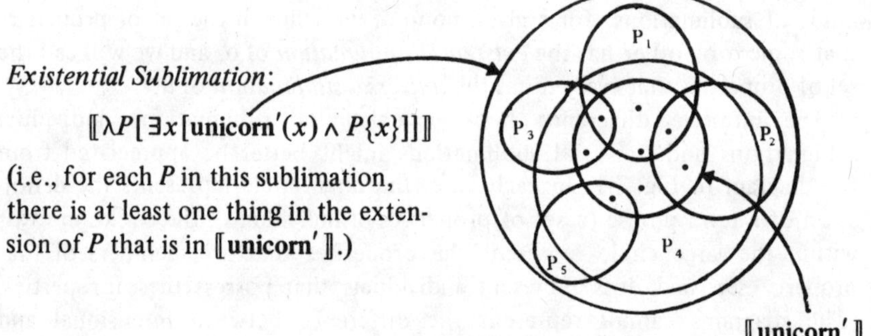
Existential Sublimation:
$[\![\lambda P[\exists x[\mathbf{unicorn}'(x) \wedge P\{x\}]]]\!]$
(i.e., for each P in this sublimation, there is at least one thing in the extension of P that is in $[\![\mathbf{unicorn}']\!]$.)
P_1
P_3
P_2
P_4
P_5
$[\![\mathbf{unicorn}']\!]$

Fig. 7-1b

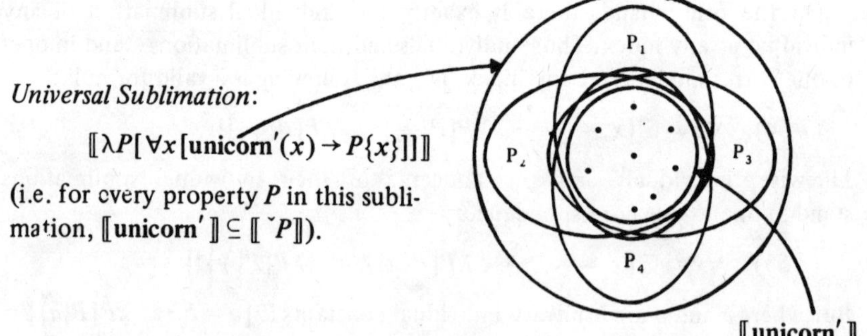
Universal Sublimation:
$[\![\lambda P[\forall x[\mathbf{unicorn}'(x) \rightarrow P\{x\}]]]\!]$
(i.e. for every property P in this sublimation, $[\![\mathbf{unicorn}']\!] \subseteq [\![\check{}P]\!]$).
P_1
P_2
P_3
P_4
$[\![\mathbf{unicorn}']\!]$

Fig. 7-1c

With these observations in mind, it is easy to see that predicating something of an individual sublimation of an individual (or concept of an individual sublimation of that individual) is tantamount to predicating something of the individual itself. For example, for every relation between individuals and sublimation-concepts of individuals, there is an exactly corresponding relation (a first-order one) that holds between individuals and those individuals of which the sublimation-concepts appear in the first relation. In *IL* there will be a precise way of describing such "corresponding" first-order relations: If R is a relation between individuals and sublimation-concepts, then $\lambda y \lambda x[\mathrm{R}(\hat{}\lambda P[P\{y\}])(x)]$ must be "that relation which holds between individuals x and y whenever R holds between x and the sublimation of y." Since such corresponding first-order relations need to be referred to frequently in translations of English, Montague introduced a special notation for them:

(7-66) $\delta_* =_{\text{def.}} \lambda y \lambda x[\delta(\hat{}\lambda P[P\{y\}])(x)]$, where $\delta \in ME_{f(TV)}$

Now we can see that the simplified translation of (7-62), repeated below, expresses something that is "tantamount", in just this way, to saying that John stands in a first-order relation to some individual x which is a unicorn:

11. $\exists x[\mathbf{unicorn}'(x) \wedge [\mathbf{seek}'(j, \hat{}\lambda P[P\{x\}])]]$

Since the higher-order relation **seek**$'$ is here asserted to hold between j and an individual-sublimation concept, this can be stated in terms of the corresponding first-order relation $\mathbf{seek}'_*$. To carry out this change, we can simply perform lambda-conversion "backwards", converting Line 12 to 13 and then 14, at which point the $\mathbf{seek}'_*$-notation becomes applicable:

(7-63)
12. $\exists x[\mathbf{unicorn}'(x) \wedge [\mathbf{seek}'(\hat{}\lambda P[P\{x\}])(j)]]$ Rel. notation
13. $\exists x[\mathbf{unicorn}'(x) \wedge [\lambda z[\mathbf{seek}'(\hat{}\lambda P[P\{x\}])(z)](j)]]$ λ-conversion
14. $\exists x[\mathbf{unicorn}'(x) \wedge [\lambda y[\lambda z[\mathbf{seek}'(\hat{}\lambda P[P\{y\}])(z)]](x)(j)]]$ λ-conversion
15. $\exists x[\mathbf{unicorn}'(x) \wedge [\mathbf{seek}'_*(x)(j)]]$ δ_* notation
16. $\exists x[\mathbf{unicorn}'(x) \wedge [\mathbf{seek}'_*(j, x)]]$ Rel. notation

Now we turn to the matter of extensional transitive verbs, such as **find**, **love** and **date**. Just as was the case with **seek**, the grammar as it stands will produce two kinds of derivations of sentences like **John finds a unicorn**, and these will have the same two patterns of reduced translations as with **seek**, e.g. (7-67) (in which **a unicorn** was introduced via S14) and (7-68) (in which S14 was not used):

(7-67) $\exists x[\mathbf{unicorn}'(x) \wedge [\mathbf{find}'_*(j,x)]]$

(7-68) $\mathbf{find}'(j, \hat{}\lambda P[\exists x[\mathbf{unicorn}'(x) \wedge P\{x\}]])$

But unlike the case of **seek**, there seems to be no ambiguity here; the only perceived reading is that of (7-67). Now there is no straightforward way to restrict the grammar so that the analysis tree which leads to (7-68) cannot be produced, but fortunately there is no real need for such a restriction. Instead, Montague restricted the semantic interpretation of **find**′ and the constants which translate the other extensional verbs in such a way that formulas like (7-68) will always be interpreted in exactly the same way as the corresponding formula like (7-67).

To capture this restriction formally, Montague turned to the device of so-called *meaning postulates*. This device, first used by Carnap 1947, is best thought of as a kind of constraint on possible models. Carnap introduced it to deal with analytically true sentences that cannot be analyzed as being logically true (true as a consequence of their syntactic form), such as *All bachelors are unmarried*. If B is the predicate "is a bachelor" and M is "is married," then Carnap's example meaning postulate is

(7-69) $\forall x[B(x) \rightarrow \neg M(x)]$.

The intent of this postulate is that in considering possible models for our language, we are to restrict ourselves to models in which this formula is true. This means, in effect, that in constructing a possible model we may still choose the extensions of non-logical constants of M and B in almost any way we wish, except that every individual in the extension of B must be excluded from the extension of M in any "admissible" model. Otherwise, no constraints are placed on the extensions of these predicates.

If we now continue to define *validity* of sentences of our language L by stipulating that "ϕ is *valid* in L iff ϕ is true in any possible (admissible) model for L,"[15] we now note that sentences like *If John is a bachelor*, *then John is not married* (formally, $[B(j) \rightarrow \neg M(j)]$) count as valid by this definition. This sentence is not valid as a result of its syntactic form and of the semantic rules of the language (as is, e.g., $[B(j) \vee \neg B(j)]$), but rather is valid just because we have declared all those models in which it could be false to be "off limits".

Certain linguists (e.g. Katz 1972 and Lakoff 1972) have strongly objected to the use of meaning postulates, because they are allegedly "ad hoc." According to Katz, there is something much more fundamental about the semantic relationship of *bachelor* and *married* than is captured by the formula above. This is a complex issue (cf. Dowty (1979) for some discussion of it), so without denying that Katz may have raised an important point here, we would merely point out that meaning postulates, in a system as precise as Montague's, offer a way of formalizing very precise and detailed relationships between word meanings of English which cannot be as accurately stated in any other known semantic theory. To invoke Chomsky's terminology, meaning postulates may not achieve the level of descriptive adequacy (much less explanatory adequacy), but they do offer a means for achieving observationally adequate statements in an area (word semantics) in which no comparably precise observationally adequate descriptions exist at present.

Let's return now to the case of extensional verbs like **find**. Unlike the case of *bachelor* and *married*, the meaning postulate we want here will not relate the meanings of two different words but will restrict the meanings of individual words in such a way that translations like (7-67) and (7-68) will be equivalent. Just what will this posutlate have to do? For simplicity, we will speak for a moment as if we were only concerned with sentences of the form **John finds** α, where α is a term phrase and thus translates into a sublimation-concept. The cases where the translation of α is an individual sublimation-concept (i.e., where α is inserted by S14, so that the translation works out to be one like (7-67)) are fine as they stand; we have already seen why this sort of case works, in effect, like a first-order statement. But suppose α is of the form **a** β and is inserted without benefit of S14; then the translation will say that John stands in the **find**′-relation to the existential sublimation of β. In this case we want to be sure that there is an individual x which is a β, such that John also stands in the **find**′-relation to the sublimation-concept of x (i.e., so that (7-68) will imply (7-67), where β replaces **unicorn**′ in both. Conversely, we want to be sure that whenever John stands in the **find**′-relation to the sublimation-concept of some individual x which is in the extension of some property β, it will also be the case that John stands in the **find**′-relation to the existential sublimation of β (so that (7-67) will imply (7-68)). Consider now the case where α is of the form **every** β. Here, the translation will say that John stands in the **find**′-relation to the universal sublimation of β, and now we want to be sure that John also stands in the **find**′-relation to the sublimation-concepts of each and every individual x that is in the extension of β. And again conversely, whenever John stands in the **find**′-relation to every individual in the extension of some property β, we want to be sure he also stands in the **find**′-relation to the universal sublimation of β. That is, we want formulas like (7-67) (where the translation of **every** α replaces that of **a unicorn**) to imply (7-68) and vice-versa. To put the matter in slightly more general terms, we want the question of to which *generic* sublimation-concepts John stands in the **find**′-relation to be determined entirely by the question of to which *individual* sublimation-concepts John stands in the **find**′-relation. How can this be stated in a general way? It turns out that we get the right results if we require that John stand in the **find**′-relation to a generic sublimation-concept if and only if that sublimation-concept contains the property of being an individual whose individual sublimation-concept John also stands in the **find**′-relation to. Generalizing this requirement to all relations δ (that translate an extensional transitive verb) and all individuals x that may be first arguments of such relations, we arrive at the meaning postulate Montague used:[16]

(7-70) MP1. $\exists S \forall x \forall \mathscr{P} \Box[\delta(x, \mathscr{P}) \leftrightarrow \mathscr{P}\{\hat{}\lambda y[S\{x, y\}]\}]$, where δ translates **find, love, lose, eat**, or **date**.

Here, S is a newly-introduced symbol for the first variable over relations-in-intension between individuals, i.e. $v_{0,\langle s,\langle e,\langle e,t\rangle\rangle\rangle}$. The variable $\mathscr{P}$ ranges over sublimation-concepts, i.e., $\mathscr{P}$ is the first variable of type $\langle s, \langle\langle s, \langle e, t\rangle\rangle, t\rangle\rangle$. Though Montague here specifies simply that there be *some* relation (in-intension) S that meets this condition, a little thought should convince the reader that $\check{} S$ can be, at each index, none other than our old friend δ_* (for each specified value of δ_*, i.e. **find**′$_*$ where δ is **find**′, **eat**′$_*$ where δ is **eat**′, etc.). That is, δ_* was defined as the relation two individuals stand in when δ holds between the first and the sublimation-concept of the second, so there is no other relation that *could* fill in for $\check{} S$ here, given that the postulate makes δ definable in terms of the individual sublimation-concepts it involves. Thus, the following holds in all models in which MP1. holds: $\forall x \forall \mathscr{P} \Box[\delta(x, \mathscr{P}) \leftrightarrow \mathscr{P}\{\hat{}\lambda y[\delta_*(x, y)]\}]$, where δ is as in MP1. This law does not hold, however, for the relation between **seek**′$_*$ and **seek**′; in other words, the generic sublimation-concepts that an individual stands in the **seek**′-relation to are NOT determined by the individual sublimation-concepts that individual stands in the **seek**′-relation to (and therefore, one can stand in the **seek**′-relation to the existential sublimation of **unicorn** without standing in the **seek**′$_*$-relation to any particular unicorn at all). Note also that Montague uses S rather than a variable over extensional relations (i.e. of type $\langle e, \langle e, t\rangle\rangle$) because this variable is bound outside the necessity operator; if an extensional variable had been used, the postulate would require that the **find**′$_*$-relation have the SAME extension at each index, which would of course be too strong.

Let us return to the translation (7-68) (that of **John finds a unicorn**, where S14 is not used).

One particular instantiation of MP1 will be the following:

(7-71) MP1′. $\forall x \forall \mathscr{P} \Box[\mathbf{find}'(x, \mathscr{P}) \leftrightarrow \mathscr{P}\{{}^\wedge\lambda y[{}^\wedge\mathbf{find}'_*\{x, y\}]\}]$

As this will be true in all admissible models, we are entitled to replace an instance of the left-hand side of the biconditional with the right-hand side (making the corresponding substitutions for $\mathscr{P}$ and x) while preserving the interpretation of the formula we started with. Thus we can continue to simplify the translation of (7-68) reducing it finally to exactly the formula (7-67):

(7-72)

1.–7.	$\mathbf{find}'(j, {}^\wedge\lambda Q \exists x[\mathbf{unicorn}'(x) \wedge Q\{x\}])$	(Cf. (7-61) above)
8.	${}^\wedge\lambda Q \exists x[\mathbf{unicorn}'(x) \wedge Q\{x\}]\{{}^\wedge\lambda y[{}^\wedge\mathbf{find}'_*\{j, y\}]\}$	From 7 by MP1
9.	$\lambda Q \exists x[\mathbf{unicorn}'(x) \wedge Q\{x\}]({}^\wedge\lambda y[{}^\wedge\mathbf{find}_*\{j, y\}])$	Brace, Down-Up
10.	$\exists x[\mathbf{unicorn}'(x) \wedge {}^\wedge\lambda y[{}^\wedge\mathbf{find}'_*\{j, y\}]\{x\}]$	Lambda conversion
11.	$\exists x[\mathbf{unicorn}'(x) \wedge \lambda y[{}^\wedge\mathbf{find}'_*\{j, y\}](x)]$	Brace, Down-Up
12.	$\exists x[\mathbf{unicorn}'(x) \wedge [{}^\wedge\mathbf{find}'_*\{j, x\}]]$	Lambda conversion
13.	$\exists x[\mathbf{unicorn}'(x) \wedge [\mathbf{find}'_*(j, x)]]$	Brace[17], Down-Up

Thus we have demonstrated that **John finds a unicorn** is indeed semantically unambiguous, thanks to MP1., in spite of the difference in its possible syntactic derivations and in the different appearances of the two respective translations.

The verb **be** is also treated as a transitive verb in PTQ and is one that turns out to be extensional just like **find**, **eat**, etc. Though Montague could have captured the extensionality of **be** by subsuming its translation under the meaning postulate MP1, he did it in a slightly different way. An example of a sentence using **be** is (7-73):

(7-73) **John is Bill**, 4
  John **be Bill**, 5
    be **Bill**

(Sentences where **be** is flanked by two proper names are not common in ordinary language, but there are examples such as *Samuel Clemens is Mark Twain, Cicero is Tully*, etc.) The verb **be** is not translated into a non-logical constant **be**′, but is one of those few "logical words" receiving a special translation:

(7-74) **be** translates into $\lambda\mathscr{P}\lambda x\mathscr{P}\{^\wedge\lambda y[x=y]\}$

This is the most complex expression assigned as a translation of any English word, and the best way to understand it is to first compute a translation using it. The translation of (7-73) is given in (7-75):

(7-75)	1. **be** ⇒ $\lambda\mathscr{P}\lambda x\mathscr{P}\{^\wedge\lambda y[x=y]\}$	Basic expression
	2. **Bill** ⇒ $\lambda P[P\{b\}]$	Basic expression
	3. **be Bill** ⇒ $\lambda\mathscr{P}\lambda x\mathscr{P}\{^\wedge\lambda y[x=y]\}(^\wedge\lambda P[P\{b\}])$	From 1, 2 by T5
	4. $\lambda x\,^\wedge\lambda P[P\{b\}]\{^\wedge\lambda y[x=y]\}$	Lambda conversion
	5. $\lambda x\lambda P[P\{b\}](^\wedge\lambda y[x=y])$	Brace Down-Up
	6. $\lambda x[^\wedge\lambda y[x=y]\{b\}]$	Lambda conversion
	7. $\lambda x[\lambda y[x=y](b)]$	Brace Down-Up
	8. $\lambda x[x=b]$	Lambda conversion
	9. **John is Bill** ⇒ $\lambda P[P\{j\}](^\wedge\lambda x[x=b])$	From 8 by T4
	10. $^\wedge\lambda x[x=b]\{j\}$	Lambda conversion
	11. $\lambda x[x=b](j)$	Brace Down-Up
	12. $j=b$	Lambda conversion

Perhaps a confusing step in this derivation will be the lambda-conversion from 3 to 4. But note that $\lambda P[P\{b\}]$ is an expression denoting a set of properties of individuals, hence $^\wedge\lambda P[P\{b\}]$ is an expression denoting a property of properties of individuals, i.e. an expression of type $\langle s, \langle\langle s, \langle e, t\rangle\rangle, t\rangle\rangle$. But this is the same type as the variable $\mathscr{P}$, so 3 is a well-formed expression of the form $\lambda\mathscr{P}[\delta](\beta)$, and it is legitimate to perform lambda-conversion on it by replacing any $\mathscr{P}$ in δ with β (which in this case is $^\wedge\lambda P[P\{b\}]$); this gives 4 exactly. Ultimately, the simple first-order identity statement $j=b$ results.

We will consider one more example with the verb **be**:

(7-76)

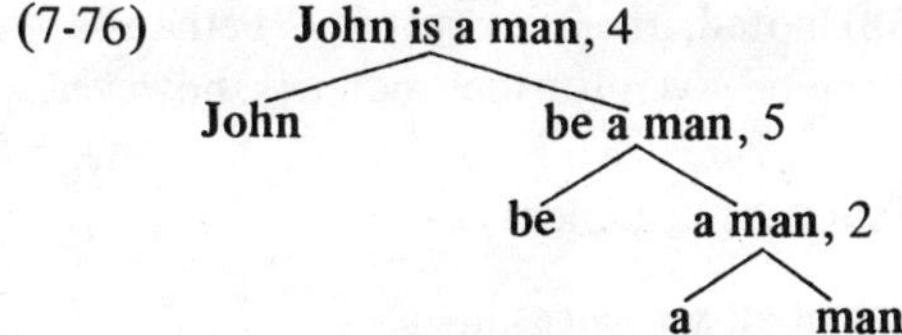

Bach (1968), like Quine (1960), suggested that this kind of sentence is not so much an identity statement as a subject-predicate sentence that ascribes the property of manhood to John. It is therefore of interest to note that in PTQ the translation of (7-76) is equivalent to **man**$'(j)$, even though the "*be* of predication" is not syntactically distinct from the "*be* of identity":

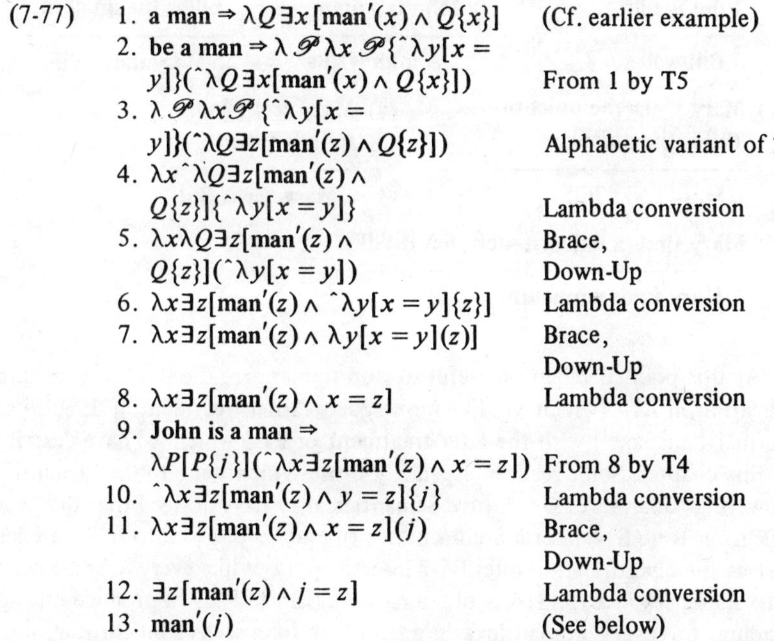

(7-77)

1.	**a man** $\Rightarrow \lambda Q \exists x[\mathbf{man}'(x) \wedge Q\{x\}]$	(Cf. earlier example)
2.	**be a man** $\Rightarrow \lambda \mathscr{P} \lambda x \mathscr{P}\{{}^\wedge\lambda y[x = y]\}({}^\wedge\lambda Q \exists x[\mathbf{man}'(x) \wedge Q\{x\}])$	From 1 by T5
3.	$\lambda \mathscr{P} \lambda x \mathscr{P}\{{}^\wedge\lambda y[x = y]\}({}^\wedge\lambda Q \exists z[\mathbf{man}'(z) \wedge Q\{z\}])$	Alphabetic variant of 2
4.	$\lambda x\, {}^\wedge\lambda Q \exists z[\mathbf{man}'(z) \wedge Q\{z\}]\{{}^\wedge\lambda y[x = y]\}$	Lambda conversion
5.	$\lambda x \lambda Q \exists z[\mathbf{man}'(z) \wedge Q\{z\}]({}^\wedge\lambda y[x = y])$	Brace, Down-Up
6.	$\lambda x \exists z[\mathbf{man}'(z) \wedge {}^\wedge\lambda y[x = y]\{z\}]$	Lambda conversion
7.	$\lambda x \exists z[\mathbf{man}'(z) \wedge \lambda y[x = y](z)]$	Brace, Down-Up
8.	$\lambda x \exists z[\mathbf{man}'(z) \wedge x = z]$	Lambda conversion
9.	**John is a man** $\Rightarrow \lambda P[P\{j\}]({}^\wedge\lambda x \exists z[\mathbf{man}'(z) \wedge x = z])$	From 8 by T4
10.	${}^\wedge\lambda x \exists z[\mathbf{man}'(z) \wedge y = z]\{j\}$	Lambda conversion
11.	$\lambda x \exists z[\mathbf{man}'(z) \wedge x = z](j)$	Brace, Down-Up
12.	$\exists z[\mathbf{man}'(z) \wedge j = z]$	Lambda conversion
13.	$\mathbf{man}'(j)$	(See below)

Line 12 is equivalent to 13 by principles of first-order logic with identity (even though it may look like 12 "says" more than 13). For the reader unfamiliar with these, the equivalence of 12 and 13 is probably best intuitively appreciated by trying to imagine how either one could be true while the other is false.

Of course, a consequence of Montague's treatment of **be** is that sentences such as **John is every man, A man is John, John is no man**, etc., will also be generated, though as Bach (1968) noted, these sound odd. Perhaps a well-motivated pragmatic explanation can be given for their oddness, however.

PROBLEM (7-11). Classify the following arguments as:

V: Valid on all derivations of all sentences involved

I: Invalid on all derivations of all sentences involved

V/I: Valid or invalid depending on the derivations of certain of the sentences

(i) **John walks.**
John is Bill.
———
∴ Bill walks.

(ii) **John walks.**
John is a man.
———
∴ A man walks.

(iii) **Mary dates the unicorn.**
Bill is the unicorn.
———
∴ Mary dates Bill.

(iv) **Mary seeks the unicorn.**
Bill is the unicorn.
———
∴ Mary seeks Bill.

(v) **Mary seeks John.**
John is Bill.
———
∴ Mary seeks Bill.

(vi) **Mary finds a unicorn such that it talks.**
———
∴ Mary finds a unicorn.

At this point it might be useful to stop to compare the treatment of quantification in L_{1E} (which was like Montague's earlier treatment in 'English as a Formal Language') with the later treatment of PTQ which we have described in this chapter. Some readers, especially those sympathetic to the "Quantifier Lowering" analysis of Generative Semantics, may have noticed that the Quantification Rule S14 inserts noun phrases (members of P_T) into full sentences, just as the quantification rules B5-7 inserted phrases like **every** α, **some** α, etc. into sentences in L_{1E}. S14 is of course necessary in PTQ to produce multiple readings for **Every woman loves a unicorn** or **John seeks a unicorn**; we could not eliminate it without losing some of these readings. But L_{1E} was able to produce some multiple readings for sentences with quantified noun phrases, even though the complicated device of letting noun phrases denote sets of properties was not employed. Does the tactic of letting noun phrases denote sets of properties really achieve anything important, in view of S14?

In fact, there are a number of advantages that the treatment of noun phrases in PTQ has over L_{1E}. First, there really is no category "noun phrase" in L_{1E}: phrases such as **every man** are introduced syncategorematically and thus belong to no category at all, while names and variables are (in terms of PTQ categories) of category *e*. Consequently, syntactic generalizations about the category "noun phrase" in some natural languages may fail to be captured (cf., e.g., languages in which names and all other noun phrases are marked systematically for various cases.)

Second, if we did not let noun phrases denote sets of properties, there would be no obvious way in Montague's framework to form disjunctions of noun phrases (and in a larger fragment, conjunctions of noun phrases) directly, by putting two noun phrases together, e.g. **John or Mary, a man or a woman**. That is, if all noun phrases were interpreted as denoting entities, it is not easy to see how we could find an appropriate entity of type *e* to assign as denotation of **John or Mary** or $\mathbf{he_0}$ **or** $\mathbf{he_1}$ in a way that permits us to get the semantics right. We would seem to be forced to adopt something like a Conjunction Reduction analysis to produce such sentences, and as we saw, such an analysis runs into problems where quantified noun phrases are involved. (Cf. also problem (7-6).)

Third, the fact that noun phrases are taken as denoting sets of properties was crucially involved in Montague's analysis of the "non-specific" *de dicto* reading of examples like *John seeks a unicorn*. If we had only names and variables of type *e* in our syntax and a quantification rule like that of L_{1E}, we could not produce this non-specific reading directly but would be forced to resort to something like a transformation that derived **John seeks a unicorn** from **John tries to find a unicorn** (where **a unicorn** could be introduced in a subordinate clause). Yet this transformational analysis encounters problems; cf. Partee (1974). Because of advantages such as these which are connected with the device of letting noun phrases uniformly denote sets of properties, we suspect that this device was largely the inspiration for the word "proper" in Montague's title 'On the Proper Treatment of Quantification in Ordinary English.'

Looking ahead to further developments of the PTQ theory by Cooper (1975), we may note that by allowing the semantic rules to assign multiple interpretations to a single analysis tree and complicating the procedure for interpreting noun phrases, Cooper is able to dispense with S14 and other quantification rules entirely, yet the treatment of noun phrases as denoting set of properties is still essential in Cooper's approach. Similarly, Cooper's proposal (1979a) for certain "pronouns of laziness" and discourse anaphora depends upon this feature.

VI. ADVERBS AND INFINITIVE COMPLEMENT VERBS

The PTQ grammar includes both sentence adverbs (members of $P_{t/t}$), such as **necessarily**, and verb-phrase adverbs (members of $P_{IV/IV}$), such as **slowly** and **voluntarily**. Both classes of adverb are introduced by functional application rules which use simple concatenation operations:

(7-78) S9. If $\delta \in P_{t/t}, \phi \in P_t$, then $F_6(\delta, \phi) \in P_t$, where $F_6(\delta, \phi) = \delta\phi$.

(7-79) T9. Functional application.

(7-80) S10. If $\delta \in P_{IV/IV}$, $\beta \in P_{IV}$, then $F_7(\delta, \beta) \in P_{IV}$, where $F_7(\delta, \beta) = \beta\delta$.

(7-81) T10. Functional application.

The adverb **necessarily** does not translate into a non-logical constant, but is given a special translation in terms of $\Box$. In this translation, p is a variable over propositions, i.e., $v_{0,\langle s,t\rangle}$:

(7-82) **necessarily** translates into $\lambda p[\Box{}^{\vee}p]$

The reader can easily confirm that, for example, **Necessarily John walks** will translate into $\Box$**walk**$'(j)$ on the simplest syntactic analysis. Actually, it is not yet clear that this will be true for *any* syntactic derivation of **Necessarily John walks**, for what happens in analyses in which **John** has wider scope than **necessarily**, e.g. in (7-83)?

(7-83)

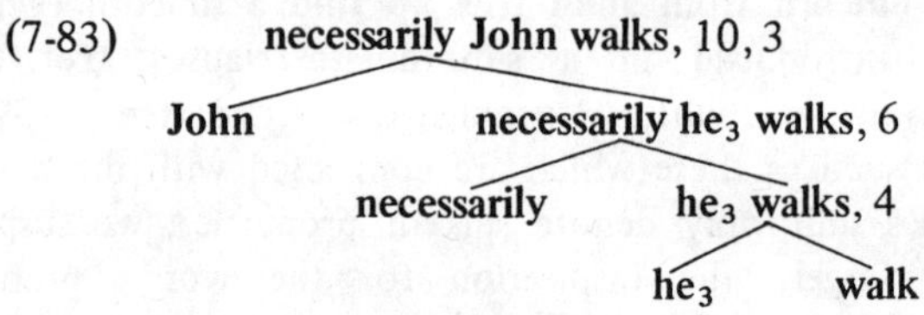

(7-84)

1.	**he**$_3$ **walks** $\Rightarrow$ **walk**$'(x_3)$	(Cf. earlier examples)
2.	**necessarily** $\Rightarrow \lambda p[\Box{}^{\vee}p]$	Basic expression
3.	**necessarily he**$_3$ **walks** $\Rightarrow$ $\lambda p[\Box{}^{\vee}p]({}^{\wedge}[\text{walk}'(x_3)])$	From 2, 1 by T2
4.	$\Box[\text{walk}'(x_3)]$	Lambda conversion, Brace Down-Up
5.	**necessarily John walks** $\Rightarrow$ $\lambda P[P\{j\}]({}^{\wedge}\lambda x_3\Box[\text{walk}'(x_3)])$	From 4 by T14

6. $\lambda x_3 \Box[\mathbf{walk}'(x_3)](j)$ Lambda conversion, Brace, Down-Up

The question now arises whether we can perform lambda-conversion on line 6 to give $\Box[\mathbf{walk}'(j)]$. The reason why there is doubt about this is that this conversion would move an expression into the scope of $\Box$, and as we saw in Chapter 6 (especially Note 4), this cannot always be allowed in *IL*. Though we moved an expression into the scope of ˆ by lambda-conversion in line 12 of (7-72), the expression so moved was the variable x, and as noted in Chapter 6, this is legitimate because the extension of a variable never varies from one index to the next. Thus the important question here is whether the extension of the non-logical constant j may vary across indices. For if it may, then line 6 asserts that the individual denoted by j at the "present" index has the property of walking at all indices, whereas $\Box[\mathbf{walk}'(j)]$ asserts that whoever is denoted by j at *each* index has the property of walking at that index. Though we noted that names like **John** are usually assumed to have invariant denotations across indices, we have said nothing that requires that this be the case in PTQ. However, Montague included the following meaning postulate in PTQ:

(7-85) MP2. $\exists x \Box[x = \alpha]$, where α is j, m, b, or n.

Since the quantifier here is outside the scope of $\Box$, this postulate requires that there be a particular individual that is identical with the denotation of j (or m, b, or n, respectively) at every index, or in other words, that these constants are "rigid designators". Hence the conversion of $\lambda x \Box[\mathbf{walk}'(x)](j)$ to $\Box[\mathbf{walk}'(j)]$ is legitimized and **Necessarily John walks** is semantically unambiguous, no matter how it is generated.

Sentences with verb-phrase adverbs such as **slowly** will be produced as in (7-86) and receive the simplified translation exemplified by (7-87):

(7-86)

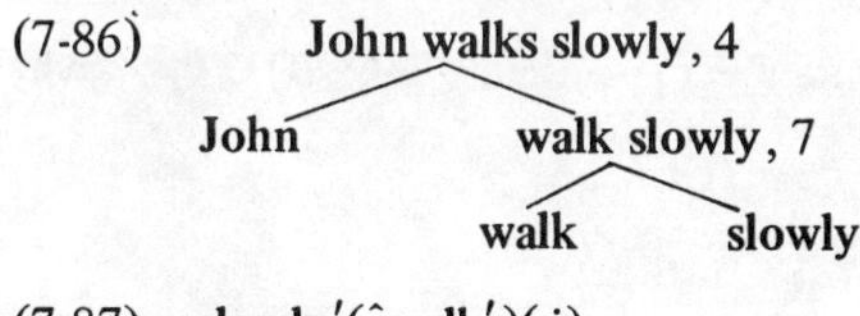

(7-87) $\mathbf{slowly}'(\hat{}\mathbf{walk}')(j)$

Here, **slowly**′ denotes a function which applies to properties of individuals (in this case the property ˆ**walk**′) and gives as value new predicates (expressions denoting sets), in this case the predicate **slowly**′(ˆ**walk**′), which is applied to j

to give a sentence. This follows the theory of predicate modifiers developed by Montague (1970), Terence Parsons (1970), and Hans Kamp (1975) and discussed in Stalnaker and Thomason (1973), so we will not dwell on this treatment at length here. As **slowly′** is treated as a non-logical constant, nothing further is prescribed by the PTQ theory about the nature of the function it denotes. However, it has often been noted that it seems to be a valid inference from "x walks slowly" to "x walks" (or, in more general terms, from "x δ's slowly" to "x δ's", where δ is any IV-phrase). Thus we may say that the extension of the predicate **slowly′**$(\hat{}\delta)$ is necessarily a subset of the extension of δ itself; for this reason Bennett (1974) adopts the term *subsective modifier* for such adverbs. This fact about the meaning of such modifiers can be guaranteed by adopting the following meaning postulate: (cf. Bennett 1974, p. 45, 74–80).

(7-88) MP10: $\forall x \forall P \Box[\gamma(P)(x) \rightarrow P(x)]$, where γ translates **rapidly** or **slowly**.

Other adverbs, however, do not have this property; from **John allegedly walks** we may not conclude **John walks**, so adverbs such as **allegedly** are to be excluded from MP10. (Cf. the discussion of adjectives such as *blue* vs. those such as *former*, *alleged* in Bennett's Chapter 2, p. 136, which is a semantically parallel case.) The postulate MP10 of course represents only one of the many facts about the meaning of **slowly** that linguists would want to capture eventually in a full analysis. See Bennett 1974 and Kamp 1975 for isolation of further semantic sub-classes of modifiers, and the latter article for further model-theoretic analysis of their meanings.

In contrast to the traditional transformational analysis of infinitive complement verbs first proposed in Rosenbaum (1967), the PTQ grammar does not derive **John tries to walk** from a structure involving the embedded sentence **John walks**. Rather, the verbs **try** and **wish** combine directly with IV-phrases (such as **walk** in this case). The rule for these is S8:

(7-89) S8. If $\delta \in P_{IV//IV}$ and $\beta \in P_{IV}$, then $F_{16}(\delta, \beta) \in P_{IV}$, where $F_{16}(\delta, \beta) = \delta$ **to** β.

(7-90) T8: Functional Application.

Note that since the syntactic category of infinitive complement verbs ($IV//IV$) is a "double slash" variant of the category of verb-phrase adverbs (IAV, which is defined as IV/IV), these verbs will be treated semantically just like the verb phrase modifiers just discussed. The translation of **John tries to walk** in (7-91) will be, in simplified form, (7-92):

(7-91)
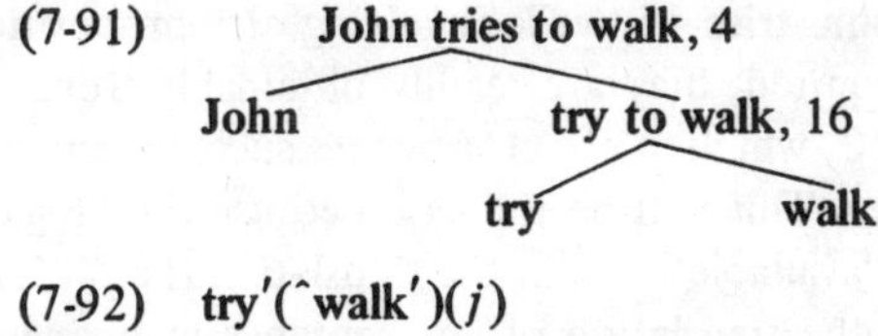

(7-92) **try**′(ˆ**walk**′)(j)

As was the case with **slowly**′, **try**′ here denotes a function which applies to the property ˆ**walk**′ and gives the new predicate **try**′(ˆ**walk**′); the meaning posulate MP10 does not of course apply to verbs such as **try** (though it may well apply to other infinitive complement verbs such as *manage*).

There are well-known syntactic arguments which are claimed to show the disadvantages of such an analysis as this over an analysis in which the complement of **try** is a full sentence, e.g., one of these involves reflexive pronouns as in *John tries to wash himself*. Quite aside from these syntactic considerations, it may also be supposed that there are purely semantic reasons why sentences such as (7-91) should be analyzed as involving embedded sentences such as *John walks*. The meaning of *John tries to walk*, after all, intuitively involves the possibility of John's walking, but not Bill's walking, or anyone else's walking. However, such a conclusion is quite unwarranted within a semantic theory such as Montague's. To follow such a line of reasoning is to make the mistake of assuming that all entailments of a sentence must be represented directly in the syntactic structure (or "logical structure") of the sentence (or at least be derivable in some very simple way from the syntactic or "logical" structure), or else not be captured by a semantic analysis at all. Though perhaps some work in Generative Semantics was based, at least implicitly, on this assumption, it is quite a doubtful one, because the entailments of a sentence can easily be shown to be infinite in number. If not all entailments can be so represented, then it is hard to justify an insistence on capturing certain entailments in this way, rather than in some other way. In the PTQ system, the entailments predicted for a given sentence by the theory arise from the interaction of (1) the translations assigned to basic expressions in the sentence and to syntactic rules (insofar as these involve logical constants), (2) the semantic rules of *IL*, insofar as these apply to logical constants and syntactic rules involved in the translation of the sentence, (3) any meaning postulates involving the non-logical constants appearing in the sentence. In short, the entailments of a sentence are defined by the semantic system of PTQ *as a whole*, and not by the translation of the sentence into *IL* considered somehow "in isolation", for this formula is not the semantic representation of the sentence *in toto*, but only one "ingredient" used in defining this interpretation.

Note that if entailments of **John tries to walk** involving the proposition expressed by **John walks** are required, they are readily obtainable from the formula $\mathbf{try}'({}^\wedge\mathbf{walk}')(j)$; cf. MP10, which in effect produces such entailments from other formulas of this form. This will be the case because the "logical subject" of **walk**$'$ is necessarily "available" within the translation (i.e., it is j), as it will always be available in the translation of any sentence involving an infinitive-complement verb.

If semantic considerations are to help decide the semantic analysis of **John tries to walk**, then these suggest, if anything, that its analysis should *not* involve an embedded sentence. This is because **John tries for Bill to walk* appears (and we stress the word *appears*) to be not merely syntactically ill-formed but meaningless. In other words, the meaning of *try*-sentences does not seem to be a compositional function of a matrix subject, a verb and an arbitrary embedded sentence, but can at best be a function of a matrix subject, a verb, and an embedded sentence *having the same subject as the matrix sentence*. Though transformational grammarians have traditionally tried to capture this fact syntactically with the infamous "like-subject constraint" on verbs such as **try** (cf. Fodor 1974 for discussion), in Montague's system this would only be a roundabout and syntactically inelegant way of stating that the meaning of the sentence is really a function of a subject, verb, and IV-phrase after all. (This fact is perhaps best appreciated by noting that if we somehow had to express the translation of **try** in terms of a constant **try**$+'$ of IL of type $\langle\langle s,t\rangle,\langle e,t\rangle\rangle$, we could still quite simply treat **try** as of category $IV/\!/IV$ and translate it as $\lambda P\lambda x[\mathbf{try}+'(x, {}^\wedge[P(x)])]$ thus still avoiding a syntactic like-subject constraint.) The syntactic arguments that **try** must have a sentential complement are, by the way, not as devastating to the PTQ theory as might be expected, when the recent proposals for possessives and reflexives in Thomason 1976 are taken into account.

At this point we are in a position to show how Montague captured the semantic equivalence of **seek** with **try to find**. As we mentioned earlier in our discussion of opaque readings with **seek**, the PTQ theory is perfectly compatible with the semantic equivalence of these two phrases (in *de dicto* and *de re* readings, respectively), though it does not require us to treat them as equivalent, much less to derive **seek** syntactically from **try to find**. The equivalence is captured by adopting the following meaning postulate:

MP9. $\forall x\forall\mathscr{P}\,\square[\mathbf{seek}'(x,\mathscr{P}) \leftrightarrow \mathbf{try}'(x, {}^\wedge[\mathbf{find}'(\mathscr{P})])]$

We can appeal to this postulate to re-express the translation of the *de dicto* reading of **John seeks a unicorn** as follows

(7-61′) (continuation of (7-61))

7. $\mathbf{seek}'(j, \hat{}\lambda P \exists x[\mathbf{unicorn}'(x) \wedge P\{x\}])$ (Cf. (7-61))
8. $\mathbf{try}'(j, \hat{}[\mathbf{find}'(\hat{}\lambda P \exists x[\mathbf{unicorn}'(x) \wedge P\{x\}])])$ From 7 by MP9

Since **find**′ is subject to MP1, we can express this last formula more perspicuously by first applying lambda-conversion "backwards" to get it into a form where MP1 is applicable, then rewriting this in terms of $\mathbf{find}'_*$:

9. $\mathbf{try}'(j, \hat{}\lambda z[\mathbf{find}'(\hat{}\lambda P \exists x[\mathbf{unicorn}'(x) \wedge P\{x\}])(z)])$ Lambda conversion
10. $\mathbf{try}'(j, \hat{}\lambda z[\hat{}\lambda P \exists x[\mathbf{unicorn}'(x) \wedge P\{x\}]\{\hat{}\lambda y[\mathbf{find}'_*(z, y)]\}])$ MP1
11. $\mathbf{try}'(j, \hat{}\lambda z[\exists x[\mathbf{unicorn}'(x) \wedge \hat{}\lambda y[\mathbf{find}'_*(z, y)]\{x\}]])$ Brace, Down-Up, Lambda conversion
12. $\mathbf{try}'(j, \hat{}\lambda z[\exists x[\mathbf{unicorn}'(x) \wedge \mathbf{find}'_*(z, x)]])$ Brace, Down-Up, Lambda conversion

This formula in (7-61′).12. asserts that John stands in the **try**-relation to a certain property – namely, that function that gives for each index the set of individuals that find some unicorn or other. The interpretation here is still "non-specific" for **a unicorn**, since different individuals may find different unicorns at a given index, and, moreover, the set of individuals that find a unicorn may itself differ from one index to another. And of course the set of individuals that find a unicorn may be empty in the actual world, though it can be non-empty in various possible worlds (and thus distinct from the set of individuals that find, say, a centaur in those worlds).

We leave it to the reader to demonstrate that the translation in (7-61′).12 is equivalent to that for **John tries to find a unicorn**, where **a unicorn** is introduced directly in the latter sentence. Likewise, the reader can easily show that the *de re* interpretations for **John seeks a unicorn** and **John tries to find a unicorn** are equivalent, i.e. are equivalent where **a unicorn** is introduced via S14 in both these sentences.

VII. *DE DICTO* PRONOUNS AND SOME PRONOUN PROBLEMS

Both linguists and philosophers have noticed sentences in which the antecedent of a pronoun has a *de dicto* reading. One such example is (7-93) (cf. Fodor 1970, Karttunen 1968, Partee 1973b):

(7-93) John tried to catch a fish and eat it.

In addition to the *de re* reading (according to which John is trying to catch and eat a particular fish), (7-93) has a reading in which **a fish** is the antecedent of **it**, yet both refer, as it were, to "the same non-specific fish." That is, there is no particular fish John is trying to catch, but his intent is to catch and eat the *same* fish, whichever fish it may be. The rules of the PTQ grammar discussed so far will not produce this second reading, however, because the only rule for "binding" subscripted pronouns (and thus giving rise to anaphoric pronouns) discussed so far is S14. This rule combines a T-phrase with a sentence, and has the semantic effect of giving the quantifier in the translation of this T-phrase wider scope than any other quantifier or operator in the sentence. But to produce a *de dicto* reading for (7-93) would require the quantifier translating **a fish** to have narrower scope than the intensional word *try*, and this is impossible. Montague saw a way out of this problem by introducing a second quantification rule like S14 except that it combines T-phrases with *IV*-phrases, rather than with whole sentences. Thus the pronoun in the *de dicto* reading of (7-93) is derived by combining **a fish** with the *IV*-phrase **catch him$_3$ and eat him$_3$** by this rule *before* the word **try** enters the derivation of the sentence. The whole analysis tree will look like (7-94) (in which we substitute the present tense for the past of example (7-93)):

(7-94)

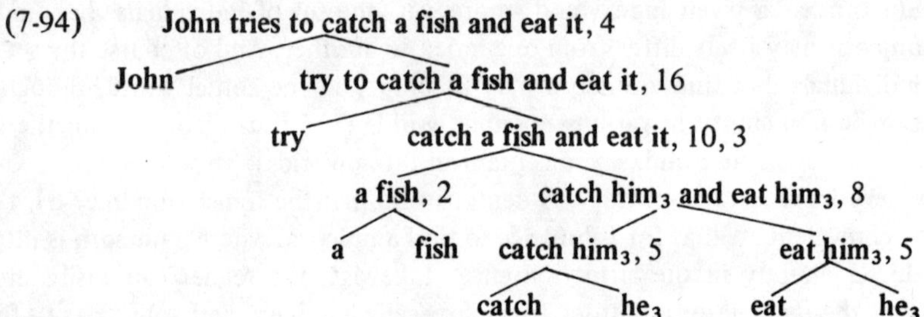

The new syntactic rule used here is S16, and it has the translation T16:

(7-95) S16. If $\alpha \in P_T$ and $\delta \in P_{IV}$, then $F_{10,n}(\alpha, \delta) \in P_{IV}$.

(7-96) T16. If $\alpha \in P_T, \delta \in P_{IV}$ and α, δ translate into α', δ' respectively, then $F_{10,n}(\alpha, \delta)$ translates into $\lambda y \alpha'(\hat{}\lambda x_n[\delta'(y)])$.

(Note that the syntactic operation schema $F_{10,n}$ that appears in this rule is the same operation schema that was used in S16 and thus does not have to be described again in this rule – this is the operation which replaces the first appropriately subscripted pronoun with the term phrase and changes all other appropriately subscripted pronouns to "anaphoric" pronouns of appropriate gender.) The translation for example (7-94) proceeds as in (7-97):

(7-97)

1.	**catch him$_3$** $\Rightarrow$ **catch**$'(\hat{}\lambda P[P\{x_3\}])$	By T5
2.	**eat him$_3$** $\Rightarrow$ **eat**$'(\hat{}\lambda P[P\{x_3\}])$	By T5
3.	**catch him$_3$ and eat him$_3$** $\Rightarrow$ $\lambda x[$**catch**$'(\hat{}\lambda P[P\{x_3\}])(x) \wedge$ **eat**$'(\hat{}\lambda P[P\{x_3\}])(x)]$	From 1, 2 by T12
4.	$\lambda x[$**catch**$'(x, \hat{}\lambda P[P\{x_3\}]) \wedge$ **eat**$'(x, \hat{}\lambda P[P\{x_3\}])]$	Relational notation
5.	$\lambda x[$**catch**$'_*(x, x_3) \wedge$ **eat**$'_*(x, x_3)]$	From 4 by MP1 (used twice)
6.	**a fish** $\Rightarrow \lambda Q \exists x[$**fish**$'(x) \wedge Q\{x\}]$	(Cf. earlier examples)
7.	**catch a fish and eat it** $\Rightarrow$ $\lambda y \lambda Q \exists x[$**fish**$'(x) \wedge Q\{x\}](\hat{}\lambda x_3[\lambda x[$**catch**$'_*(x, x_3) \wedge$ **eat**$'_*(x, x_3)](y)])$	From 5, 6 by T16
8.	$\lambda y \lambda Q \exists x[$**fish**$'(x) \wedge Q\{x\}](\hat{}\lambda x_3[$**catch**$'_*(y, x_3) \wedge$ **eat**$'_*(y, x_3)])$	Lambda conversion
9.	$\lambda y \exists x[$**fish**$'(x) \wedge \hat{}\lambda x_3[$**catch**$'_*(y, x_3) \wedge$ **eat**$'_*(y, x_3)]\{x\}]$	Lambda conversion
10.	$\lambda y \exists x[$**fish**$'(x) \wedge [$**catch**$'_*(y, x) \wedge$ **eat**$'_*(y, x)]]$	Brace, Down-Up Lambda conversion
11.	**try to catch a fish and eat it** $\Rightarrow$ **try**$'(\hat{}\lambda y \exists x[$**fish**$'(x) \wedge [$**catch**$'_*(y, x) \wedge$ **eat**$'_*(y, x)]])$	From 10 by T8
12.	**John tries to catch a fish and eat it** $\Rightarrow$ $\lambda P[P\{j\}](\hat{}$**try**$'(\hat{}\lambda y \exists x[$**fish**$'(x) \wedge [$**catch**$'_*(y, x) \wedge$ **eat**$'_*(y, x)]]))$	By T4
13.	**try**$'(j, \hat{}\lambda y \exists x[$**fish**$'(x) \wedge [$**catch**$'_*(y, x) \wedge$ **eat**$'_*(y, x)]])$	Brace, Down-Up Lambda conversion Relational notation

Note that in line 13 of (7-97), **try**$'$ still takes as its arguments an individual and a property of individuals, though here the property is specified by a lambda-abstract, not by a simple constant as in (7-92). This formula may be read as "*j* stands in the **try**-relation to the property of being a *y* such that, for some fish *x*, *y* catches *x* and *y* and eats *x*". Note that this abstractly defined property does not involve any particular fish; rather, an individual might potentially possess this property in as many "ways" as there are fish at any given index.

This new syntactic rule will give rise to additional syntactic derivations for many of the examples we discussed earlier. For example, **John finds a unicorn** can now also be produced as in (7-98):

(7-98)

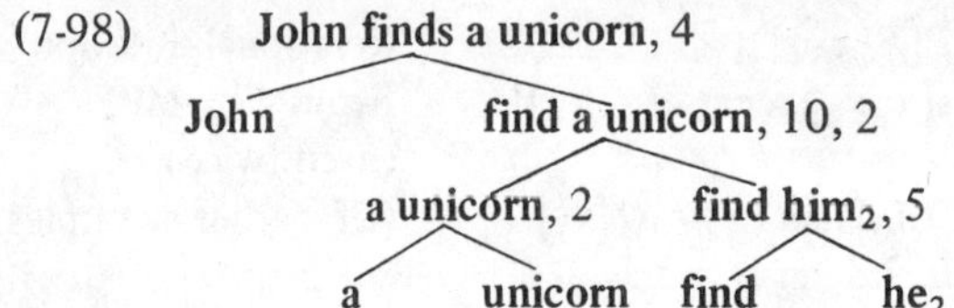

However, in all these cases the new translation produced by the derivation with S16 will be logically equivalent to that of one or more of the other derivations, so no new semantic interpretations occur, as the reader can easily confirm by working out the translations.

Unfortunately, not all pronouns whose antecedents are *de dicto* term phrases can be treated by this rule. Some simple cases where such readings ought to be produced (according to our intuitions) but cannot be produced by the PTQ grammar are (7-99) and (7-100).

(7-99) **John tries to catch a fish and he wishes to eat it.**

(7-100) **John tries to catch a fish and wishes to eat it.**

The reason why neither S14, S16, nor any similar rule involving other categories can treat the *de dicto* readings of these examples is that the pronoun and its antecedent cannot be analyzed as standing within the scope of the *same* opacity-creating operator (as was the case in (7-94)); rather, the pronoun and antecedent each stand within the scope of *different* opacity-creating words (**try** and **wish** in each case.) Thus any "quantifying" rule like S14 or S16 that applies to any syntactic "chunk" of one of these examples which is large enough to contain subscripted pronouns in the positions of both term phrases would necessarily interpret the quantifying term phrase as having wider scope than both **try** and **wish**, thus giving **a fish** a *de re* reading.

Other sentences discussed in the literature which would seem to present the same difficulty for Montague's method are (7-101) and (7-102). Here the italicized pronouns are intended to have as antecedents the italicized noun phrases.

(7-101) If John marries *a girl his parents disapprove of*, they will make life quite unpleasant for *her*.

(7-102) The agency is looking for *a model* to use in the toothpaste ad; *she* must have red hair and freckles.

Pronouns such as those in (7-99) and (7-100) have often been discussed under the rubric of *pronouns of laziness* (cf. Partee 1972, 1975), a term that originates with Geach 1962. The idea behind this name is presumably that such pronouns do not really function as bound variables, but as a sort of "lazy" way of avoiding the repetition of a longer term phrase. Thus (7-100) might be considered a "lazy" version of (7-103):

(7-103) John tries to catch a fish and wishes to eat a (the?) fish he catches.

Partee (1975) suggests that other pronouns besides those having *de dicto* antecedents might be classified as "pronouns of laziness", in particular, those cases where the PTQ grammar cannot produce for certain examples a reading that our intuitions seem to require. One such example is the (apparent) reading of (7-104) in which **every man** has wider scope than **a woman**:

(7-104) **Every man such that he loves a woman loses her.**

Though this example can be generated in such a way as to give **a woman** wide scope (i.e., a particular woman is lost by every man who loves her), it cannot be generated in such a way as to be interpreted as true in a situation where for each man there may be a different woman loved and lost by him. This is because the quantifier phrase **every man who loves a woman** syntactically contains the second quantifier phrase **a woman**, yet at the same time this second quantifier phrase appears to "bind" an additional pronoun. Thus the only way to generate the example (i.e., the tree in (7-105)) necessarily gives **a woman** wide scope;

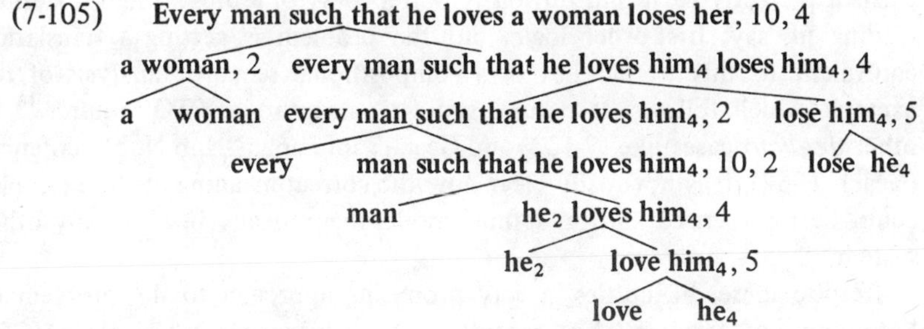

As an apparent result of the widespread use of the term *pronoun of laziness*, some writers seem to have acquired the idea that there is a *theory* of pronouns of laziness advocated by someone or other (cf. Wasow, 1975). However, this is a misconception which ought to be cleared up as soon as possible, since, to our knowledge no partially (much less completely) worked out analysis of so-called "pronouns of laziness" has ever been advanced. Note in particular that whatever such an analysis might be, it cannot simply be the old transformational "pronominalization" analysis which replaces a noun phrase with a pronoun dependent on constituent-for-constituent identity with another noun phrase, for then the transformational source for (7-105) would be (7-106), and the source for (7-100) would be (7-107):

(7-106) Every man such that he loves a woman loses a woman.

(7-107) John tries to catch a fish and wishes to eat a fish.

Yet the sentences (7-105) and (7-100) are not synonymous with their purported sources under this analysis, so the semantic analysis of them would remain totally unexplained under this treatment. A "meaning preserving" pronominalization rule for these examples would rather have to depend for its application not on simple syntactic identity, but would have to derive (7-100) from something like (7-103). That is, the "controller" for the deletion of a *NP* would not be another occurrence of that same *NP*, but a rather different syntactic unit related in a certain semantic way to the deleted *NP*. It seems doubtful that a transformation could be formulated in purely syntactic terms which accomplishes this correctly; the correctly paraphrasing "source" seems to differ syntactically from example to example (cf. Partee 1970b for discussion).

Moreover, in some cases of "pronouns of laziness" the problem seems to be a more-or-less "syntactic" one, while in other cases more fundamental semantic difficulties are present. In "extensional" cases like (7-104) there exists a perfectly clear and obviously correct way of representing the desired reading in, say, first-order logic, but the problem is getting a translation equivalent to this to fall out of a compositional semantic analysis of the example which follows its natural syntactic structure as PTQ requires.[18] In other *de dicto* cases like (7-102) and Geach's infamous "Hob-Nob" sentences (Geach 1962), it is not really clear how the correct meaning of the examples could be represented and/or defined model-theoretically in *IL* or any other system.

Despite these difficulties, a very promising approach to the problem of "pronouns of laziness" has recently been advanced by Cooper (1979).

We cannot go into Cooper's treatment here, but it seems to represent one of the first truly significant steps toward an explanation of how these pronouns are interpreted. (See also Carlson, 1977, Ch. 5, 1.0.1, for a discussion of Cooper's analysis.)

VIII. PREPOSITIONS, TENSES, AND NEGATION

Prepositional phrases are produced by the following rule of functional application; recall that IAV/T is the category of prepositions.

(7-108) S6: If $\delta \in P_{IAV/T}, \alpha \in P_T$, then $F_5(\delta, \alpha) \in P_{IAV}$.

(7-109) T6: Functional application.

(F_5 is the same syntactic operation used for combining transitive verbs with their objects: if the object is $\mathbf{he}_n$, it becomes $\mathbf{him}_n$.)

As prepositional phrases occur in the same syntactic category as verb phrase adverbs (i.e. IAV, which is IV/IV), they too will be treated semantically as functions which apply to properties to give new predicates, just as **try** and **slowly** do. Prepositions themselves, then, are treated as functions which apply to the intensions of term phrases and give such "adverb-like" functions as values. For example, the translation of (7-110) converts, by simple and familiar steps, into (7-111):

(7-110)

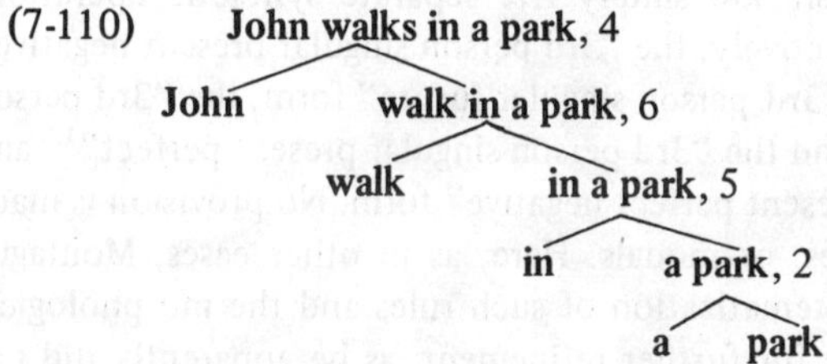

(7-111) $\mathbf{in}'(\hat{}\lambda Q \exists x[\mathbf{park}'(x) \wedge Q\{x\}])(\hat{}\mathbf{walk}')(j)$

In (7-111), as it stands, the translation of **a park** is in a non-extensional position. Thus we may not yet conclude from (7-111) that there is in fact a park in which John is walking. (Remember that the simple present in PTQ is generally best read as a present progressive.) But clearly this inference is valid, which is to say that **in** is an "extensional preposition." Montague included meaning postulate MP8 for such prepositions:

(7-112) MP8. $\exists G \forall \mathscr{P} \forall P \forall x \square[\delta(\mathscr{P})(P)(x) \leftrightarrow \mathscr{P}\{\hat{}\lambda y[[\check{}G](y)(P)(x)]\}]$, where δ translates **in**.

In this formula the new symbol G is a variable over functions from indices to functions from individuals to functions from properties to sets, namely, it is $v_{0,\langle s,\langle e,f(IAV)\rangle\rangle}$ or equivalently $v_{0,\langle s,\langle e,\langle\langle s,\langle e,t\rangle\rangle,\langle e,t\rangle\rangle\rangle\rangle}$. Note that the preposition **about**, which does occur in the PTQ fragment, has been excluded from this postulate. Thus from **John talks about a unicorn** we will *not* be able to conclude that there exists a unicorn which John is talking about.

Though this is perhaps the most complex and intuitively obscure of the meaning postulates, it is analogous to that for extensional transitive verbs and does not warrant further discussion here. Though Montague did not introduce a δ_*-notation for representing the "extensional" relation corresponding to **in**$'$ whose existence is guaranteed by this postulate (parallel to **seek**$'_*$ for **seek**$'$), we could of course introduce **in**$'_*$ as an abbreviation for $\lambda y \lambda P \lambda x[\mathbf{in}'(\hat{}\lambda Q[Q\{y\}])(P)(x)]$. The formula in (7-111) could then be rewritten, thanks to MP8, as (7-113):

(7-113) $\exists x[\mathbf{park}'(x) \wedge \mathbf{in}'_*(x)(\hat{}\mathbf{walk}')(j)]$.

Here **in**$'_*$ may be thought of as a function applying to places x and then to activities P, giving finally as value the set of individuals that do P in x.

The only remaining rules of PTQ introduce tenses and negation. While Montague's rules for these are semantically satisfactory for the sentences treated, they are syntactically somewhat superficial by current transformational standards. There are simply five separate syntactic operations described as inserting, respectively, the "3rd person singular present negative" tense form of a verb, the "3rd person singular future" form, the "3rd person singular negative future", and the "3rd person singular present perfect"[19] and the "3rd person singular present perfect negative" form. No provision is made for other tenses, auxiliaries, or modals. Here, as in other cases, Montague seems to be leaving the systematization of such rules and the morphological details of them to linguists for further refinement, as he apparently did not find such matters particularly interesting. Syntactically, the operations are treated as alternative ways (in addition to S4) of putting subject with predicate to form a sentence:

(7-114) S17. If $\alpha \in P_T$ and $\delta \in P_{IV}$, then $F_{11}(\alpha, \delta), F_{12}(\alpha, \delta), F_{13}(\alpha, \delta), F_{14}(\alpha, \delta), F_{15}(\alpha, \delta) \in P_t$, where:
$F_{11}(\alpha, \delta) = \alpha\delta'$ and δ' is the result of replacing the first verb in δ by its negative third person singular present;
$F_{12}(\alpha, \delta) = \alpha\delta''$ and δ'' is the result of replacing the first verb in δ by its third person singular future;

$F_{13}(\alpha, \delta) = \alpha\delta'''$, and δ''' is the result of replacing the first verb in δ by its negative third person singular future;
$F_{14}(\alpha, \delta) = \alpha\delta''''$ and δ'''' is the result of replacing the first verb in δ by its third person singular present perfect; and
$F_{15}(\alpha, \delta) = \alpha\delta'''''$ and δ''''' is the result of replacing the first verb in δ by its negative third person singular present perfect.

(7-115) T17. If $\alpha \in P_T, \delta \in P_{IV}$, and α, δ translate into α', δ' respectively, then:
$F_{11}(\alpha, \delta)$ translates into $\neg\alpha'(\hat{}\delta')$
$F_{12}(\alpha, \delta)$ translates into $\mathbf{F}\alpha'(\hat{}\delta')$
$F_{13}(\alpha, \delta)$ translates into $\neg\mathbf{F}\alpha'(\hat{}\delta')$
$F_{14}(\alpha, \delta)$ translates into $\mathbf{P}\alpha'(\hat{}\delta')$
$F_{15}(\alpha, \delta)$ translates into $\neg\mathbf{P}\alpha'(\hat{}\delta')$.

Note that in these translations the negation and tense operators (**P** and **F**) are given wider scope than the translation of the subject term phrase. This is no doubt deliberate as it enables us to obtain both readings of an ambiguous sentence such as **Every man doesn't run**. That is, we can also achieve the reading in which the quantifier in subject position has *wider* scope than negation by syntactically introducing the subject by S14 rather than introducing it directly. The two derivations and their respective simplified translations are given in (7-116)–(7-119):

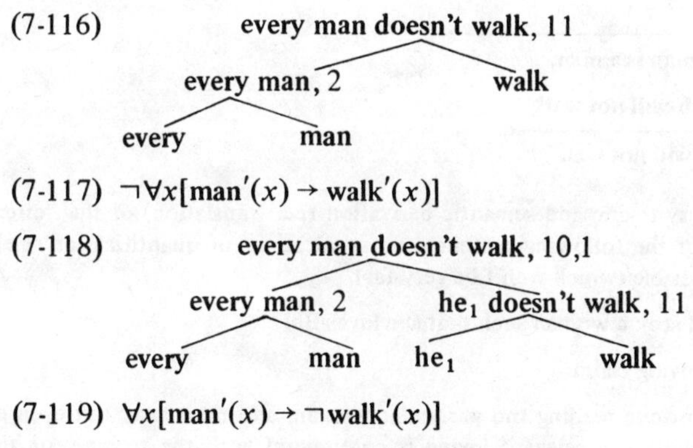

(7-117) $\neg\forall x[\mathbf{man}'(x) \to \mathbf{walk}'(x)]$

(7-119) $\forall x[\mathbf{man}'(x) \to \neg\mathbf{walk}'(x)]$

EXERCISES

1. Give an analysis tree for the sentence **John believes that a man or a woman walks** that will give a man a *de dicto* reading while a woman receives a *de re* reading. Is this a

possible reading of the English sentence, or is it a defect of PTQ to allow it? Give three more analysis trees for the same sentence, corresponding to three additional distinct interpretations PTQ provides for it. Which of these, if any, are plausible readings for the sentence?

2. Classify each of the following arguments as:

V: Valid on all derivations of all sentences involved

I: Invalid on all derivations of all sentences involved

V/I: Valid or invalid depending on derivations of certain of the sentences involved

(When a *de dicto/de re* ambiguity is possible, be sure to consider both readings for premise *and* conclusion.)

(i) **Mary talks about a unicorn such that it talks.**
∴ Mary talks about a unicorn.

(ii) **John has not walked.**
∴ John does not walk.

(iii) **John walks slowly.**
∴ John walks.

(iv) **John is Bill.**
∴ Necessarily John is Bill.

(v) ______
∴ Every man is a man.

(vi) **Every fish will not walk.**
∴ A fish will not walk.

3. Do a complete syntactic and semantic derivation (i.e. translation) of the "direct insertion" derivation of the following sentence (no applications of quantification rules) and reduce as far as possible (which won't be very far):

John will seek a woman such that she loves Bill.

Now consider the following claim:

> On the opaque reading (no particular woman, and there may not even be any women), the relevant loving is cotemporal with the seeking; on the transparent reading, the loving must be now and the seeking will be later.

(a) Is this what the PTQ analysis predicts? (b) Do you think the claim is true of English, i.e. as you understand the sentence?

4. Write an extension of the PTQ grammar which will generate the following sentences (and closely related ones) and assign correct translations for them. This may

involve new basic expressions, new translations for basic expressions, and/or new syntactic rules and translation rules.

(i) **Nothing walks.**

(ii) **No fish walks.**

(iii) **Not every fish walks.**

(iv) **John tries not to walk.**

(v) **John tries to walk and not talk.**

What readings does your fragment produce for the sentence **Every woman found nothing**? Is this in accord with your intuitions? (In connection with (iii), you might also consider the following: *Not a creature was stirring*, **Not the man walks*, **John found not every fish*, **John walks in not every garden*, *John believes that not every fish walks*. In connection with (iv) and (v) consider *John doesn't try to walk* and whether *John tries not to walk and talk* is ambiguous.)

5. Montague's rules for introducing tenses and negation in PTQ are somewhat inelegant in that they introduce each combination of tense and negation separately. Hence a total of six separate operations are needed (i.e. $F_4, F_{11}, F_{12}, F_{13}, F_{14}$ and F_{15}) to produce affirmative and negative versions of three tenses (present, present perfect, and future). Consider the possibility of employing instead a single negation rule that is independent of the rules for tense. What problems arise with this approach? Consider not only syntactic problems, but also semantic ones, i.e. the matter of assuring that tense, negation and subject term phrase are given the proper scope relation(s). You may, in addition, try to write a revision of PTQ that treats negation and tense separately but solves these problems. (Even more adventurous readers may also want to consider the assignment of types to English categories that is used in the English fragment of UG and in Thomason (1976), i.e. a system that treats the category "verb phrase" as t/T rather than IV. What syntactic options for handling negation, tenses and modal auxiliary verbs are feasible on semantic grounds in this approach that were not feasible in the PTQ type assignment? After doing this exercise, you may wish to compare your results with Bach (to appear) and Dowty (1979, Chapter 7), where this method is adopted.)

6. For (1)–(3), assume we are dealing only with models that have only *one* index: (Here and below, α' stands for the translation of the whole expression α, whether α is basic or complex.)

1. Describe the difference between $[\![$**a-unicorn'**$]\!]^{M,w,t,g}$ and $[\![$**two-unicorns'**$]\!]^{M,w,t,g}$ assuming these are translated so as to be interpreted as "at least one unicorn" and "at least two unicorns", respectively.
2. If the cardinality of the set D_e in model M is n then what is the cardinality of the set $[\![$**John'**$]\!]^{M,w,t,g}$?
3. If the cardinality of the set D_e in M is n and the cardinality of the set $[\![$**unicorn'**$]\!]^{M,w,t,g}$ is m (for some m such that $0 < m \leqslant n$), then what is the cardinality of $[\![$**a-unicorn'**$]\!]^{M,w,t,g}$ and $[\![$**every-unicorn'**$]\!]^{M,w,t,g}$?

7. For (4)–(6), assume we are dealing with models that have k indices. Then if the

cardinality of D_e in a certain model M is n and if, for a certain index ⟨ w, t⟩, the cardinality of $[\![\text{unicorn}']\!]^{M,w,t,g}$ is m (for m such that $0 < m < n$), what is the cardinality of:

4. $[\![\text{John}']\!]^{M,w,t,g}$

5. $[\![\text{a-unicorn}']\!]^{M,w,t,g}$

6. $[\![\text{every-unicorn}']\!]^{M,w,t,g}$

NOTES

[1] It is known (Bar-Hillel 1967) that categorial grammars as described by Adjukiewicz are equivalent in weak generative capacity to context-free phrase structure grammars. However, this fact is of little or no relevance to Montague's syntax, since the result applies only to what might be called "pure" categorial grammars: ones in which simple concatenation is the only way of "combining an A/B with a B to give an A", as it were. In Montague's system, the way of combining one expression with another and the syntactic deformations of the two expressions that result from this process are practically unlimited, though of course the syntactic operation associated with each syntactic rule must specify what is to be done. (The general theory of language in Montague (1970c), within which PTQ is intended to fall, does require that the syntactic operations be "unambiguous" in a very strong sense: whatever it is that results from applying a syntactic operation to its input(s), that result must be distinct from (1) any basic expression, (2) the result of applying any other operation to the same input(s) and (3) the result of applying the same or any other operation to other input(s). In other words, it must be possible to determine unambiguously from any derived syntactic expression just which basic expressions and operations were used to form it.) We know of no mathematical results about the generative capacity of Montague's syntax, but see Partee (1979a) for interesting suggestions as to how one might go about restricting the generative capacity of a Montague grammar in a linguistically interesting way.

[2] The PTQ fragment does not actually contain a category DET. Montague introduced **every**, **the**, and **a(n)** in the English syntax syncategorematically.

[3] At least this is the conclusion reached by Partee (1974), on which our presentation in this section is closely based.

[4] The phrase "its third person singular present" is deliberately informal. Montague was not especially interested in English inflectional morphology and probably assumed that anyone who cared to do so could substitute a more explicit formulation.

[5] Montague included the numbers of the syntactic operations in analysis trees not just for perspicuity, but to ensure that the "non-ambiguity" requirement of the general theory in Montague (1970c) (cf. footnote 1) is met; i.e., even if the expressions formed by two operations look alike, the number in the analysis tree makes it possible to determine just which operation was used.

[6] PTQ does not actually contain this rule, since as we pointed out in Note 2, it does not have a category of determiners. Instead, there were three distinct syntactic operations, each taking a CN as input and giving, respectively, the Term phrases **every** α, **the** α, and **a(n)** α, where α is the CN input. The resulting expressions of English produced and the interpretations assigned to them are equivalent, however. The treatment given here seems

the more linguistically natural one (especially when one considers extensions of PTQ in which more determiners than these three are included).

[7] Technically, no collision of variables would have resulted in this particular line if x had not been re-lettered, but we nevertheless advise re-lettering whenever the same variable appears with different quantifiers in the same formula, since the chance of making a clerical error by later confusing the two variables is very great.

[8] Actually, it is not completely clear that these desirable results will extend to conjunction and disjunction of all sorts of constituents without creating problems elsewhere in the fragment. A complete discussion of these problems would take us far afield, however, and these problems have only recently been noticed and have not yet received thorough investigation anywhere in the literature. Therefore we will not attempt to explicate the problem in detail here. An example of a problematic case is a sentence such as **John caught and ate a fish**. Does this sentence have only a reading in which John caught and ate the *same* fish? If so, then the transitive verb conjunction rule needed to capture this result will block the intensional reading (cf. V. below) of **John wants and needs a new car**.

[9] Montague precisely defined the notation x_n as $v_{2n,e}$ for all integers n; i.e., x_1, x_2, x_3, etc. are $v_{2,e}$, $v_{4,e}$, $v_{6,e}$, etc., respectively. The reason for using only even-numbered subscripts here is to keep these subscripted x-variables (which translate subscripted English pronouns) distinct from the variables x, y and z which are used in the translations of determiners and other logical words: x, y and z are therefore defined as $v_{1,e}$, $v_{3,e}$ and $v_{5,e}$, respectively.

[10] In cases where the binding term phrase is a proper name, such "vacuous" use of $F_{10,n}$ in the English syntax is matched by the semantically vacuous binding of the translation of the resulting expression, so that no harm is done. For example, the translation of $F_{10,5}$(Mary, he$_4$ talks) would (by the translation rule given in the text below) be a formula which reduces to λx_5[**walk**$'(x_4) \wedge$ **talk**$'(x_4)$](m), and this is an instance of the vacuous lambda-binding discussed in Chapter 6; it is equivalent to [**walk**$'(x_4) \wedge$ **talk**$'(x_4)$]. Unfortunately, such vacuous use of this quantification rule wreaks havoc with the translation if a quantified term is used. For example $F_{10,5}$ (**a unicorn, John walks**) (which yields simply **John walks**, since there is no **he**$_5$ variable at all) has a translation reducible to $\exists x$[**unicorn**$'(x) \wedge$ **walk**$'(j)$], and this is false at indices at which there are no unicorns, whether John is walking at those indices or not.

[11] Actually, there are always a denumerably infinite number of distinct analysis trees for each instance in which S14 may be used, because each of a denumerably infinite number of distinct variables might have been replaced by this rule. For example, the sentence **John walks** might be $F_{10,1}$(**John, he**$_1$ **walks**), or $F_{10,2}$(**John, he**$_2$ **walks**), or $F_{10,3}$(**John, he**$_3$ **walks**), etc.

[12] What, one might ask, is contained within this set? If there are any properties P such that the sentence **Every unicorn is** P is analytic, then P is contained within this set.

[13] There is a trap here for the unwary. One might be tempted to object at this point, "but the question whether unicorns exist should play no role in the analysis of **seek**, since when one seeks a unicorn one may not have any idea whether unicorns exist or not, or one may be mistaken about their existence." This kind of objection, however, confuses two fundamentally different matters: (1) what goes on in a person's mind when he decides to seek for something or other (and what beliefs may lead him to decide to seek something) and (2) what relation can be said to obtain among (non-linguistic and

non-mental) objects, and in particular, what the second of the two objects in this relation is, when the sentence **John seeks a unicorn** is true. Model-theoretic semantics is only concerned with the second of these two questions.

[14] In actuality, once we have made the change from sets of properties to properties of properties, there is no real reason why we should not take simply properties of *sets* of individuals as the objects of the **seek**′-relation. That is, these objects could be of type $\langle s, \langle\langle e, t\rangle, t\rangle\rangle$ rather than of type $\langle s, \langle\langle s, \langle e, t\rangle\rangle, t\rangle\rangle$. No useful semantic purpose is served by having "double" intensionality involved in the definition of these objects. The type assigned by Montague to the objects of the **seek**-relation is simply what results from the adoption of the recursive rule giving a logical type for each syntactic category, and the "double" intensionality does no harm. If we were content with simply *listing* a logical type individually for each syntactic category (and there is no reason we should not do this, since the set of categories used in the English syntax is finite), we might specify that $f(T)$ is $\langle\langle e, t\rangle, t\rangle$ (sets of sets of individuals) and that $f(TV)$ is $\langle\langle s, \langle\langle e, t\rangle, t\rangle\rangle, \langle e, t\rangle\rangle$ (relations between individuals and properties of sets of individuals), thus eliminating the "extraneous" intensionality.

[15] Or, for intensional models, "true at any index in any admissible model." Alternatively, if we define a model as Kripke did as an ordered pair consisting of a model (in our sense) and a particular index which represents the actual world now, then "truth in any admissible model" suffices, since one model (in this latter sense) may differ from another not only in the domain and interpretation of non-logical constants but also in the choice of which index is to be the actual world now; hence "true in any admissible model" in effect covers every index of every admissible model.

[16] In discussing the role of his meaning postulates in PTQ Montague speaks of "those interpretations of intensional logic in which the following formulas are true (with respect to all, or equivalently some, worlds and moments of time)." (p. 263) The reason that truth with respect to *some* worlds and times is equivalent to truth with respect to *all* worlds and times here is that all the meaning postulates involve the necessity operator, and if such a formula is true with respect to even one index in a model, it will be true with respect to all indices, given the way necessity is interpreted.

[17] The notation $\alpha\{\beta, \gamma\}$ is defined analogously to $\alpha\{\beta\}$; just as $\alpha\{\beta\}$ was defined as $[{}^{\vee}\alpha](\beta)$, so $\alpha\{\beta, \gamma\}$ is defined as $[{}^{\vee}\alpha](\beta, \gamma)$, which is in turn $[{}^{\vee}\alpha](\gamma)(\beta)$.

[18] So-called "Bach–Peters sentences" (e.g. *The man who deserved it got the prize he wanted*) also cannot be produced by PTQ (cf. Partee 1973a for explanation). Such sentences are counterexamples not just to PTQ but to any purely compositional semantic treatment of English which introduces (definite or indefinite) descriptions one at a time; that is, it is not possible to derive the meaning of the whole sentence from the meanings of the parts by the usual semantic rules for descriptions, since the meaning of *each* definite description requires, paradoxically, that the meaning of the other definite description be a part of the sentence into which the first description is introduced. Cooper's treatment of "pronouns of laziness" may be invoked here, (Cooper, 1979a), but note that this treatment gives a pragmatic account of the interpretation of "pronouns of laziness," not a purely semantic account.

[19] It is curious that Montague included the present perfect but not the simple past tense in the PTQ fragment. However, the interpretation of the present perfect is given in terms of the familiar tense-logical past tense operator (i.e., the past operator that was discussed in Chapter 5). Distinguishing the English simple past from the present perfect semantically

is, of course, a notoriously difficult problem. See Dowty (1979), Chapter 7) for a discussion of the problems involved and for an extension of the PTQ fragment which captures at least some of the differences between these two tenses.

CHAPTER 8

MONTAGUE'S GENERAL SEMIOTIC PROGRAM

Having worked our way in considerable detail through a particular grammatical and semantic proposal of Montague's about English, we will step back at this juncture to gain a larger perspective on the general framework of description within which this proposal, and the preliminary ones we developed in earlier chapters of this book, are couched. Montague termed this framework his "universal grammar", and it is his article of that title that we will now briefly explicate. (For a virtually line-by-line discussion of the article, see Halvorsen and Ladusaw [1979].) A word on terminology is in order to begin with, because Montague used the term "universal grammar" in a different sense than the one it has in linguistics. In the latter field, universal grammar is an account of those features that are common to all natural languages – in particular of the essential characteristics of natural languages, which distinguish them from other logically possible systems of communication such as artificial languages used in mathematics or computer programming, animal "languages" like that of bees, etc. In contrast to this conception, Montague used the term to refer to a mathematical framework sufficiently general to subsume a description of any system that might conceivably be termed a language, whether it is a possible natural language or not. Thus it ought to be possible in Montague's universal grammar to give a description of the Fortran programming language or of bee "language" just as readily as we were to describe a fragment of English, perhaps even more so in view of the relative simplicity of these languages.

Montague's reason for constructing such a general system was, to quote him, that "there is . . . no important theoretical difference between natural languages and the artificial languages of logicians" [UG, p. 222]. He believed that the methods of semantic analysis, in particular, which had been applied so successfully to the latter could be used with equal success on the former. This is a heterodox view among philosophers of language, most of whom hold either (a) that natural languages are too unruly to yield to these methods and must be regimented (v. Quine [1960]) before they can be applied, or (b) that natural languages are so unlike logicians' artificial, regimented languages that study of the latter is very misleading in regard to the former (v. Austin [1962]).

Montague thought of the analysis of language as a branch of mathematics rather than of psychology, as Thomason [1974a] and Partee [1979c] have pointed out. Thus he strove for generality and mathematical elegance in his general framework rather than for restrictions that would explain the limitations on possible human languages, many of which are psychological in nature and biological in origin. This does not entail that one cannot impose restrictions on his framework which could help to explain precisely those limitations. In fact, several linguists have tried their hand at this enterprise (Partee [1979a], Bach [1979]). This conception is, however, the reason why Montague himself sought mathematical elegance in his general framework sometimes even at the expense of needless complexity in his descriptions of particular languages.

In conceiving his general framework, Montague saw mathematical similarities between certain features of syntax and features of both translation and model-theoretic interpretation. Thus he sought to generalize across specific constructions of a language where that is possible. A system for syntactically generating expressions necessarily imposes a structure on the set of all expressions by virtue of the way it generates them. For instance, if **love him** is generated by using a certain operation to combine **love** and **he**, this gives rise to a structural relationship among these three expressions. Montague formalized this kind of structure as an algebra – in the sense of the mathematical theory of universal algebra (v. Cohn [1965]). And he saw similar structures in the set of translations (induced by the translation rules) and the set of semantic values (induced by the rules of model-theoretic interpretation). Thus his general framework permits one to set up two (or three) algebras – syntactic, translational if one wishes, and semantic – and define structure-preserving mappings among them (the translation function and the assignment of semantic values). Such structure-preserving mappings are called "homomorphisms" in mathematics (cf. Chapter 2, p. 43).

Our procedure now will be, first, to describe in more detail the syntactic algebra that Montague constructed; then we will describe the semantic algebra in very general and abstract terms, and discuss the homomorphic mapping between them. After that we will discuss the algebra of translations, the homomorphism from the syntactic system to it, and the interpretation of the syntactic system that is induced by the translation homomorphism if the system of translations is itself interpreted. At that point, we will go on to deal with the formalities of denotations, senses, and meanings and will show how meaning postulates fit into Montague's general framework. It is useful to think of this process as one of abstracting a general schema from the particular details of the analyses discussed so far, a schema which each of our grammars is an instantiation of.

To begin our discussion of the syntactic algebra, we note that Montague, like virtually every other logician, wished to associate meanings with a set of unambiguous syntactic expressions – that is, he imposed a 'unique readability' requirement like that which motivates the introduction of parentheses to disambiguate ordinary propositional calculus (not in Polish notation). This is not an arbitrary decision, and it does not preclude assigning meanings to ambiguous expressions. It merely necessitates doing that by, first, assigning meanings to expressions of an unambiguous "language" and, then, pairing these unambiguous expressions with the expressions of the ambiguous language we wish to describe. This procedure is nearly inescapable. It is implicit in Generative Semantics, for example, where logical forms are intended to be unambiguous expressions of meanings that natural language sentences may have and several such logical forms may be associated with a single sentence by the derivational and transderivational constraints. We will mention in passing that this method is not the only way to achieve the end of assigning several meanings to ambiguous expressions; Cooper [1975] discusses a procedure which generalizes Montague's framework by, in effect, treating a set of meanings as a single semantic value and assigning the appropriate such object to each meaningful expression of the ambiguous language being interpreted. (Katz and Fodor [1963] seem to have considered something like this to be called for.)

Given his strategy for interpreting ambiguous languages, Montague's first move is to discuss a notion of unambiguous language, or as he calls it, a disambiguated language. In order to understand what he means by "disambiguated language", which is a bit different than the usual notion of being free from structural ambiguity, we need to point out that syntactic rules can be thought of as comprising two parts: one which specifies under what conditions the rule is to be applied, and another which specifies what operation to perform under those conditions. This distinction is familiar in connection with transformational rules, which comprise a structural condition specifying, among other things, when the rule is applicable and a structural change specifying what to do to the input syntactic structure to produce the associated output structure. It can also be seen in the rules of Chapter 7, where the part about "If α is a member of P_T and δ is a member of P_{IV}, then ____ (α, δ) is a member of P_t" specifies when the rule is applicable and the "F_4" that fills in the blank is the operation. The usual notion of a structurally unambiguous language is that each expression generated by the syntactic rules as a member of a certain category has only one syntactic analysis (in effect, is generated in only one way) as a member of that category. Montague strengthens this requirement so as to ignore (a) the relativization to syntactic categories and (b) the restrictions imposed by constraining syntactic operations to apply only when permitted by the conditions stipulated in the syntactic rules. His decision would, for instance, make the unambiguous English sentence

(1) The solving of the problem required many hours of work

count as analyzable in two ways, exactly parallel to the two ways the ambiguous

(2) The shooting of the hunters was a disgrace

is analyzable, because in "generating" (1) in the second way one could ignore the fact that the verb **solve** is transitive only, never intransitive, and construct (1) as if there really were a sentence **The problem solves.**

Montague defines a *disambiguated language* ("unambiguous grammar" would be a more natural term for it) as comprising:

(i) a stock of syntactic operations (the set of all F_γ, where $\gamma \in \Gamma$, in his definition [UG, p. 225]);

(ii) a collection Δ of syntactic category names;

(iii) a set of basic expressions apportioned into syntactic categories (the X_δ's, for $\delta \in \Delta$) – he allows a basic expression to belong to more than one category but will require that it have the same meaning regardless of category membership;

(iv) a set S of syntactic rules, each rule in S having the interpretation "if ζ_0 belongs to category δ_0 and ... and ζ_{n-1} belongs to category δ_{n-1}, then $F_\gamma(\zeta_0, \ldots, \zeta_{n-1})$ belongs to category ϵ", for a particular $\gamma \in \Gamma$, where n is the number of input expressions required by the operation F_γ;

(v) a distinguished category δ_0 (not to be confused with the "δ_0" in (iv)) all expressions belonging to which will eventually be required to denote truth values;

and for technical convenience,

(vi) the set A of all expressions 'generated' by freely applying the set $\{F_\gamma | \gamma \in \Gamma\}$ of all syntactic operations to the collection $\cup_{\delta \in \Delta} X_\delta$ of all basic expressions and to the results of applying syntactic operations, whether or not these applications are in accord with the restrictions imposed by the syntactic rules.

To insure that the language is really free of syntactic ambiguity, in the sense in which Montague means this, he further requires:

(vii) that no basic expression (member of an X_δ) can also be an output of any syntactic operation;

(viii) that no expression in A can be the output of two different syntactic operations F_γ and F'_γ, and:

(ix) that no syntactic operation can produce the same output from different input expressions.

To sum up Montague's formal definition, a disambiguated language is an ordered quintuple $\langle A, F_\gamma, X_\delta, S, \delta_0\rangle_{\gamma \in \Gamma, \delta \in \Delta}$ each of whose elements is as described above.

As an instance of this definition, we will indicate how the grammar for a fragment of English discussed in the previous chapter can be seen as a disambiguated language. Note, to begin with, that the grammar would be ambiguous if we were to regard it as generating sequences of words. One of the points of that undertaking was to show how sequences such as **Every man loves a woman** are ambiguous. As disambiguated expressions we can, however, take the analysis trees of those sequences of words. Thus the first syntactic rule would technically say

(3) If the analysis tree β belongs to the category T/CN and the analysis tree ζ belongs to the category CN, then F'_2 (β, ζ) belongs to the category T, where $F'_2(\beta, \zeta)$ is the analysis tree

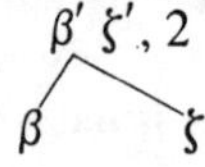

β' being the label of the root node of β less its numerical suffix (if any) and ζ' being similarly related to ζ – except that β' is **an** if β is **a** and the first word in ζ' begins with a vowel.

The second rule would be

(4) If the analysis tree ζ belongs to the category CN and the analysis tree ϕ belongs to the category t, then $F'_{3,0}(\zeta, \phi)$ belongs to the category CN, where $F'_{3,0}(\zeta, \phi)$ is the analysis tree

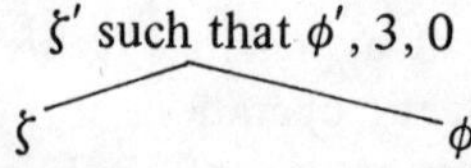

ζ' being the label of the root node of ζ less its numerical suffix (if any) and ϕ' being derived from the label of the root node of ϕ less its numerical suffix by replacing each occurrence of **he**$_0$ or

him_0 by **{he, she, it}** or **{him, her, it}** respectively, according as the first basic *CN* in ζ is of {masculine, feminine, neuter} gender.

In the less formal presentation of PTQ, reproduced in Chapter 7, the latter syntactic rule and an infinite number of others to attach relative clauses to common noun phrases were collapsed into a single cover statement. (We doubt the reader thought that presentation was lacking in formality!) Technically, however, they are not one rule but infinitely many, differing in the numeral they use in place of "0" in rule (4). The remaining "syntactic rules" of that grammar may be rewritten as real syntactic rules, in Montague's technical sense, along similar lines.

The basic expressions can be taken to be words, just as they are in the "informal" presentation. The stock of syntactic operations F_γ, for $\gamma \in \Gamma$, can be the collection of all those operations which appear in some rule of the disambiguated language. Then (a) no basic expression will be the output of any operation F_γ, (b) no expression will be the output of two different operations – because each operation suffixes a different numeral to the label of the root of the tree it produces – and (c) no operation can produce the same output from different input analysis trees – because each operation reproduces its inputs as part of its output. Thus we have a disambiguated language of analysis trees, where the set of all expressions in *A* includes trees such as

(5)

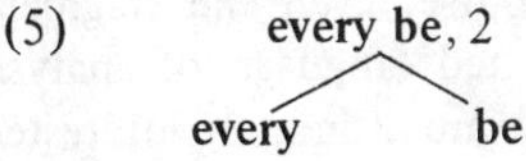

and

(6)

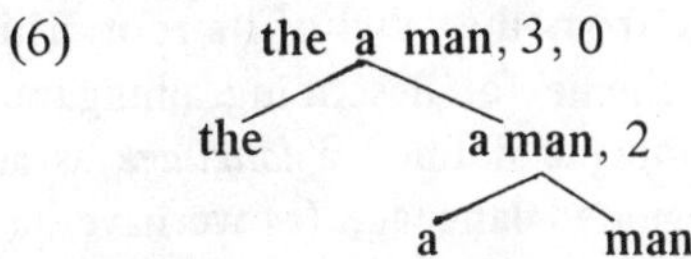

which belong to no syntactic category because they cannot be generated by application of the syntactic *rules* (but can be by application of the syntactic *operations*), along with analysis trees that do belong to syntactic categories, for example (7) and (8).

(7)

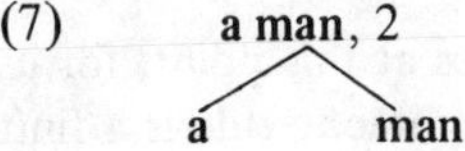

(8) 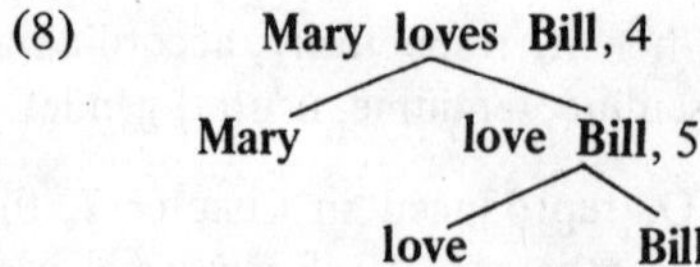

For future reference we note here that one can take the set A of all expressions of the language – the set referred to in (vi) above – as the set of elements of an algebra whose operations are the syntactic operations F_γ, for all $\gamma \in \Gamma$, of the language. This structure $\langle A, F_\gamma \rangle_{\gamma \in \Gamma}$ is a free algebra generated by the basic expressions; no element of the algebra can be expressed in two different ways as the result of applying the operations to generators. Montague uses this algebraic structure $\langle A, F_\gamma \rangle_{\gamma \in \Gamma}$ in formulating the connection between syntactic expressions and their translations or their meanings. This is a matter we will return to below.

The disambiguated language (here "unambiguous grammar" would certainly sound more natural) generates not just the set of all expressions in this free algebra, but also a set of members of each grammatical category δ in Δ. It does this in just the way one would think. The basic expressions belonging to X_δ are members of the category δ, as are all other expressions obtained by applying the syntactic operations in accordance with the restrictions imposed by the syntactic rules. This is all that Montague's definition [UG, top of p. 226] says.

Now English is an ambiguous language, of course; even the fragment Montague analyzed in PTQ. Thus the disambiguated language of analysis trees just described is not the set of expressions we are ultimately interested in. It can be related to those expressions, though, in a very simple way: just associate each (unambiguous) analysis tree with the string of words obtained by removing the numerical suffix from the label of its root. This is a very simple instance of the general scheme for describing ambiguous languages mentioned above. Formally, Montague defined a *language* as an ordered pair $\langle \mathfrak{A}, R \rangle$, where $\mathfrak{A}$ is a disambiguated language (as we have just defined that notion) and R is a binary relation whose domain is included in the set A of all expressions of $\mathfrak{A}$. R is sometimes called an ambiguating relation. In the case of PTQ, R is, as just mentioned, the set of ordered pairs $\langle \alpha, \alpha' \rangle$ such that α is an analysis tree and α' is the string of words obtained by removing the numerical suffix (if any) of the label of the root of α.

There is one other notion which Montague defines at this point, for use when he gives his theory of translation. A derived syntactic rule is a finite combination of syntactic rules of the language, by which one can produce in a single step an expression that would otherwise have to be generated in a series of steps. Derived rules arise by combining rules (or derived rules) such as (8) and (9i) through (9n) to obtain (10), where one is also given special "identity" and "constant" rules to make use of.

(8) If α_0 belongs to category δ_0 and . . . and α_{n-1} belongs to category δ_{n-1}, then $F_{\gamma_n}(\alpha_0, \ldots, \alpha_{n-1})$ belongs to category ϵ.

(9) (i) If β_0 belongs to category ζ_0 and . . . and β_{m-1} belongs to category ζ_{m-1}, then $F_{\gamma_0}(\beta_0, \ldots, \beta_{m-1})$ belongs to category δ_0.

.

.

.

(n) If β_0 belongs to category ζ_0 and . . . and β_{m-1} belongs to category ζ_{m-1}, then $F_{\gamma_{n-1}}(\beta_0, \ldots, \beta_{m-1})$ belongs to category δ_{n-1}.

(10) If β_0 belongs to category ζ_0 and . . . and β_{m-1} belongs to category ζ_{m-1}, then $F_{\gamma_n}(F_{\gamma_0}(\beta_0, \ldots, \beta_{m-1}), \ldots, F_{\gamma_{n-1}}(\beta_0, \ldots, \beta_{m-1}))$ belongs to category ϵ.

One derived syntactic rule of the PTQ fragment of English, for example, would take as inputs a T-phrase α and an IV-phrase δ and produce (the analysis tree of) the sentence $\alpha\delta$**'s or** α **doesn't walk**, a sentence that would otherwise be generable from α and δ using the rules S4, S17, and S11 and the basic expression **walk** only in a series of steps. To illustrate Montague's formal definition of derived syntactical rule, we will display this derived rule in detail. It is supposed to combine a T-phrase and an IV-phrase into a t-phrase, so it needs the sequence $\langle T, IV\rangle$ of category indices to restrict its "input" and the category index t as the place to "put" its "output". Its syntactic operation is $F_{11}(F_4, F_{17}(I_{1,2,A}, C_{\mathbf{walk},2,A}))$, where F_{11}, F_4, and F_{17} are the operations forming disjunctions, affirmative predications, and negative predications respectively; $I_{1,2,A}$ is the two-place operation on the set A of expressions which maps any pair $\langle\alpha, \delta\rangle$ of them to the first one α; and $C_{\mathbf{walk},2,A}$ is the two-place operation on A which maps any pair $\langle\alpha, \delta\rangle$ of expressions to **walk**. Thus given a pair $\langle\alpha, \delta\rangle$ of expressions F_4 yields the expression $\alpha\delta$'s; $I_{1,2,A}$ and $C_{\mathbf{walk},2,A}$ yield α and **walk** respectively; F_{17} applies to the pair $\langle\alpha$, **walk**$\rangle$, yielding α **doesn't walk**; and finally F_{11} applies to the pair $\langle\alpha\delta$**'s**, α **doesn't walk**$\rangle$ and produces $\alpha\delta$**'s or** α **doesn't walk**, which is the output we desired.

The importance of derived rules will become apparent when we discuss their role in translating expressions of one language into another. In effect, they provide a uniform means of paraphrasing things that may be said easily in the first language as a possibly more complicated expression of the second.

We turn now to the general outline of Montague's semantic framework. This outline, presented in the section of UG titled 'Semantics: Theory of Meaning', is startling in its simplicity. Essentially Montague just requires (a) that there be a set B of meanings eligible to be the semantic values of syntactic expressions – their nature is left completely open at this point – (b) that to each syntactic operation F_γ there correspond a semantic operation G_γ taking the same number of arguments and mapping (n-tuples of) meanings to meanings – this is Frege's principle of compositionality – and (c) that there be a mapping f of basic expressions to meanings. Montague could associate semantic operations with syntactic operations rather than with syntactic rules because his strong notion of disambiguation ensures that every syntactic expression is derivable in a unique way by the operations, not just the rules, of syntax.

Such an interpretation of a syntactic system uniquely determines an assignment of meanings to each expression in a natural way. Basic expressions are assigned the meaning they are mapped into by the function f mentioned in (c). Expressions derived by means of a syntactic operation F_γ – they cannot also be basic expressions – are assigned the meaning produced by the corresponding semantic operation G_γ from the meanings assigned to the inputs of the syntactic operation. Clearly each syntactic expression will be assigned exactly one meaning in this way, since each one either is a basic expression or else is derivable in a unique way from basic expressions by means of syntactic operations. Technically this meaning assignment is simply the only homomorphism that exists mapping the syntactic algebra to the semantic one and extending the mapping of basic expressions to meanings.

Even with a notion of semantic interpretation as general and skeletal as this, it is possible to say some significant things about translation from one language to another. First, we should get clear on what we mean by translation. In the case of infinite languages the most significant conception will not be simply of a function or relation mapping the sentences of one language (the source language in usual linguistic parlance) to another (the target language). The reason is that some such functions are highly idiosyncratic and ad hoc in the way they match up sentences of the two languages, not systematic or uniform. For example, many such functions are not effectively computable; that is, the translation they represent could not be carried out in an automatic way. When we consider an infinite set of expressions as translated from one language into another (not a finite set like a particular literary work), we must conceive of the translation as a systematic relation capable of being finitely described in a general and regular way if anything significant is to be true of translation in general.

Montague adopted a very strong notion of systematicity and regularity in translation, much stronger than mere effective computability of the translation function (i.e., automatability in principle). He did so in service of being able to say something very strong about the relationship between the source and target languages' meaning assignments. Roughly, his idea was that each syntactic construction of the source language L_s should be associated with a single (possibly periphrastic) construction of the target language L_t; in this way, all source language expressions having a given construction type will get translations in one and the same fashion, long-winded and roundabout though the translations might be. More precisely, he assumed (i) that translations are based on a mapping of the basic expressions of L_s to syntactically well-formed expression of L_t, (ii) all L_s expressions of a given syntactic category are translated to L_t expressions of a single corresponding syntactic category, and, (iii) this is effected by means of an association between syntactic operations of L_s and finite compositions of L_t's syntactic operations (plus "identity" and "constant" operations), i.e., what Montague calls polynomial operations over L_t's syntactic operations, where (iv) to each syntactic rule of L_s – with its operations and its category restrictions – the category correspondence mentioned in (ii) and the association of syntactic operations mentioned in (iii) determine a derived syntactic rule of L_t. (The (iv)th condition is imposed in order to assure that well-formed source language expressions translate to well-formed target language expressions, as was implied in (ii).) Referring to his definition of *translation base* [p. 232 of UG], (i) is the function j, the category correspondence of (ii) is the function g, (iii) is the association of F_γ with H_γ for all $\gamma \in \Gamma$, and (iv) is Montague's condition (5).

For example, a translation of English into Djirbal (an aboriginal language of Australia) might map English common nouns into Djirbal common nouns, English noun phrases into Djirbal noun phrases, English adjectives into Djirbal verbs (as Djirbal has no category of adjectives and what is expressed in English by adjectives is expressed by verbs in Djirbal; v. Dixon [1972]), English verbs into Djirbal verbs, etc. Then an appropriate choice of polynomial operation (finite combination of syntactic operations) of Djirbal to associate with each syntactic operation of English should insure that each syntactic *rule* of English is associated with a derived syntactic rule of Djirbal. For instance, an English rule which combines an adjective with a prepositional phrase to form an adjective phrase might be associated with a (derived) rule of Djirbal which combines a verb with a noun phrase of the appropriate case to form a verb phrase. In this way, the syntax of English will be mirrored, albeit indirectly, in Djirbal syntax.

Suppose a language L_s is translated systematically into another one L_t the way Montague assumed. His strong assumptions assure that a function mapping L_s expressions into L_t expressions is uniquely determined by the mapping of basic L_s expressions into L_t expressions and the association of L_s syntactic operations with finite combinations of L_t syntactic operations. To see this one need only consider that each L_s expression is generable in exactly one way from basic L_s expressions using L_s syntactic operations. Given any L_s expression, its translation into L_t can be obtained from its generation in L_s by (i) mapping each basic expression used into L_t and then (ii) paralleling each application of an L_s operation with the associated finite combination of L_t operations. More technically, the translation function is simply the unique homomorphism that maps L_s into L_t-as-structured-by-the-finite-combinations-of-syntactic-operations and extends the given mapping of basic L_s expressions into L_t. This function k maps each basic expression of L_s to the specified expression of L_t; and given any expressions $\zeta_0, \ldots, \zeta_{n-1}$ and (n-place) syntactic operation F of L_s, k maps $F(\zeta_0, \ldots, \zeta_{n-1})$ to $H(k(\zeta_0), \ldots, k(\zeta_{n-1}))$ where H is the finite combination of L_t operations that is associated with F. Here we see Montague making use of algebraic structure in translation, as we earlier saw him do in connection with semantic interpretation.

We note in passing that the existence of ambiguity in natural languages is no obstacle to having a translation function map each L_s expression to a single L_t expression. The reason is that Montague (and we) are assuming translation as discussed so far to be between disambiguited languages, in Montague's sense. Thus when one brings into the picture the relation between these unambiguous expressions and the actual expressions of an ambiguous language, it emerges that we are dealing here with how individual "readings" of sentences can be mapped to individual "readings" of sentences in another language.

Now translation is essentially a syntactic process, a matter of converting expressions of one language into expressions of another. And what we have said so far on the subject is indeed entirely syntactic in character. Nevertheless, the intention of translation is not simply to map source language sentences into target language sentences, but more particularly to do so in such a fashion that a sentence and its translation have the same meaning. In order to say something about this side of translation, we must assume that the source and target languages are semantically interpreted – that meanings have been assigned to their expressions. Thus let us assume that this has been done in the manner we described earlier, so that there are meaning assignments g_s and g_t which are homomorphisms from the syntactic structures of L_s and L_t respectively into algebras of meanings. What should the relation between g_s and g_t be? Letting k be the translation function from L_s into L_t, we want $g_s(\zeta)$ to be the same as $g_t(k(\zeta))$ for each expression ζ of L_s so that each expression will have the same meaning as its translation – i.e., we want $g_s = k \circ g_t$ (where $k \circ g_t$ is the composition, or relative product, of the two functions k and g_t).

We have come at last to Montague's motivation for making such strong assumptions about systematicity in translation. *If* the target language is interpreted, then there *always* exists an interpretation of the source language which is induced by its translation into the target language, regardless of whatever other interpretations (if any) the source language may have. This is a theorem that can be proved about algebraic structures of the kind that Montague takes syntactic systems, interpretations, and translation systems to have. Interestingly enough, the meaning assignment for the source language under the induced interpretation is always $k \circ g_t$. Thus we want it always to be the case that the interpretation which the source language has is identical to the induced interpretation under translation into the target language. We can assure this in various ways, of which an important one is simply to *stipulate* that the source language's interpretation is to be the induced interpretation. Such stipulation is precisely what we did in Chapter 7, where English was interpreted indirectly by translating it into the interpreted language of Intensional Logic.

Translating English into Intensional Logic was therefore not essential to interpreting the English phrases we generated; it was simply a convenient intermediate step in assigning them meanings. This step could have been eliminated had we chosen to describe the interpretation of English directly, rather than indirectly by stipulating that it be the one induced under our translation into Intensional Logic by the interpretation given to that language. This point is important, because anyone who does not appreciate it may misunderstand the role of Intensional Logic in applications of Montague's descriptive framework to natural languages.

Some writers have suggested that Intensional Logic plays a role in

'Montague grammar' like that of Logical Form in Generative Semantics or in Chomsky's current conception of grammar [1977]. This is definitely not the case. The idea is fundamentally mistaken in that translation into Intensional Logic is, as we have just seen, not in any way essential to semantic interpretation in Montague's framework – that step of PTQ is entirely eliminable without altering anything crucial about the interpretation assigned each phrase. It is further mistaken in that the particular translations assigned play no role in determining well-formedness of the syntactic structures with which they are associated, as Logical Forms may do in Chomsky [1980]. And it is also mistaken in its implication that the entailments licensed by a sentence of English are formalized by the translation of that sentence into Intensional Logic and the inference rules of that logic. The source of this error, which is less explicit in some authors than the two just commented on, is the mistaken belief that a complete and sound proof theory exists for Intensional Logic. In fact, Intensional Logic is not complete [see e.g., Gallin 1975, Chapter 1, Section 3], i.e., no effective set of inference rules exists which would allow one formally to draw all and only the logically valid inferences involving expressions of Intensional Logic. It is a mistake to think that translation into Intensional Logic plays any role in the justification of inferences involving English sentences as interpreted via Montague's framework.

It may be helpful to recall here what we said in Chapters 6 and 7 about our purpose in introducing Intensional Logic in connection with natural languages. That purpose was to have a convenient, compact notation for giving a briefer statement of semantic rules than we were able to give in earlier chapters of this book, where semantic rules were formulated rather longwindedly in English. We wished, in effect, to press Intensional Logic into service as a formalized part of our metalanguage, the part in which we would speak about the meanings of natural language phrases. Of course, Intensional Logic could not be the whole of our metalanguage since we must have ways of referring to object language (e.g., English) expressions and not just to the meanings we wish to associate with those expressions. Intensional Logic could provide us with names for meanings and we could let the rest of the metalanguage be a technical jargon, based on English, in which the names for natural language expressions were given by "syntactic variables" (such as "α" and "β") and by quotation. That would be a natural way to view the so-called translation rules we gave in Chapter 7. Montague, however, chose to view them differently – technically, as showing how the meanings of English expressions correspond to meanings of expressions of Intensional Logic. Whichever way you look at it, translation into

Intensional Logic is merely a convenience in giving the semantic interpretation of a natural language, not an essential part of the process.

To close this chapter we return to the topic of semantics in Universal Grammar, in particular the section headed 'Theory of Reference', where the central characteristics of Montague semantics are dealt with. In this section, Montague described in much greater detail the things which he and, in this book, we have taken meanings to be, exploiting the notion of truth at a possible world in a model.

We have found occasion to associate two different kinds of semantic values with expressions: senses and denotations. An expression has a particular denotation only, as we have repeatedly stressed, relative to a particular assignment of values to variables and a particular possible world (more exactly, world-time pair). Its sense does not vary with possible world or time, but the sense nevertheless is not absolutely fixed, since it may vary with assignments of values to variables. Is there, then, no semantic construct associated with an expression which is absolutely fixed by an interpretation of a language? Of course there is: to wit, a function mapping each assignment to the sense the expression has relative to that assignment. This is not an object for which we have required a name hitherto. Montague chose to call it a meaning, which is not an altogether unreasonable term for it (though "Fregean meaning" would have been a term more in the spirit of this section of UG). This function has two important properties which the meaning of any expression must have: to wit, (i) it is completely determined by an interpretation of the language, not dependent on anything nonlinguistic such as utterance context or factual circumstances, and (ii) it determines the denotation of the expression once one pins down the various parameters of context surrounding an utterance of the expression (e.g., an assignment of values to variables) and factual circumstances in the situation of utterance (i.e., a possible world and time).

What we wish our interpretation of a language to assign to each expression is its meaning. It is clear from the above discussion, however, that denotations are somehow fundamental, because every meaning we have considered is a function from assignments (and possibly other contextually variable parameters) to functions from world-time pairs to denotations. All meanings thus have the character of functions which, in effect, take several variables as arguments and yield denotations as values. Furthermore, the set of possible assignments is determined by the denotations which may be assigned as the value of a variable, and the set of world-time pairs plays a role in determining the set of possible denotations (since senses may be denoted by certain expressions). Thus the way to be more specific about meanings is to say something specific enough about denotations.

That is why Montague opened this section of his paper by specifying what are the possible denotations of various types. Two basic types of denotation which expressions may have are entities and truth values. (It is useful to think of these types of denotations as being available even if no expression of our language denotes anything of either type.) Ordered pairs consisting of a possible world an a moment of time are not a potential type of denotation (unless, of course, one chooses to let the set of entities contain these as members, which it is perfectly permissible to do.) Apart from entities, of which one specifies the domain when giving an interpretation, and truth values, which are fixed always as 0 (for falsehood) and 1 (= {0}, for truth), the only things that can be denoted are functions whose domain is either (a) the set of world-time pairs or (b) denotations of some type and whose range is a set of denotations of some type. The system of types is a kind of syntactic classification of all possible denotations into various categories.

By this point, the definition of types and of denotations of various types should hold no mystery for the reader of this book. What might be only slightly less transparent is Montague's definition of a *meaning of type* τ as a function taking a possible world (-time pair) together with a context of use to a denotation of type τ. This is simply a formal definition of the notion of (Fregean) meaning discussed in the preceding two paragraphs.

A *type assignment* is just an association of each of a language's syntactic categories with exactly one type. It is used to assure that all syntactic expressions belonging to a given category are interpreted as having meanings of the type assigned to that category. Montague calls an interpretation a *Fregean interpretation* if there is a type assignment for the language being interpreted such that (a) every basic expression is assigned a (Fregean) meaning of the type assigned to the category (or, more exactly, to each category) that the basic expression belongs to (obviously this necessitates that when some basic expression belongs to more than one category, the same type of meaning be assigned to each of those categories); (b) that for each syntactic rule of the language, every *n*-tuple of meanings having the types assigned to the syntactic categories from which the rule's inputs are to be drawn is mapped by the semantic operation which the interpretation associates with the rule's syntactic operation to a meaning of the type assigned to the syntactic category in which the rule's output is placed; and (c) all elements of the semantic algebra are (Fregean) meanings of one or another type.

It is now straightforward to define what is meant by truth of a sentence at a possible world (and time) in a context of use relative to an interpretation. Montague does this by introducing the notion of a *model*, which is just an interpretation with a distinguished possible world (-time pair) and context of use – the latter two items can be intuitively regarded as the actual world (and time) and the actual context of use. (Contexts of use here also do duty as functions assigning values to variables. Cf. p. 82; Halvorsen and Ladusaw [1979], Note 26.) Any expression of any category has a denotation in the model – the result of applying the function which is the expression's (Fregean) meaning to the distinguished world (-time pair) and context. Every sentence denotes its truth value in the model. Thus Montague's definition of Fregean interpretation is a formalization of truth-conditional, model-theoretic semantics, employing the concept of possible worlds.

One of the important uses of model-theory is, as we remarked in Chapter 1, the study of semantic properties of a language that remain invariant under certain changes of interpretation of the language. The concept of model is useful in allowing us to specify just what range of interpretations is admissible. One can distinguish a class K of admissible models, and then investigate such questions as what sentences are true in all model in K (i.e., are K-valid), what pairs $\langle S_1, S_2\rangle$ of sentences are such that S_2 is true in every member of K in which S_1 is true (i.e., are such that the sentence-type S_1 K-entails the sentence-type S_2), etc. (One can also define a concept of K-entailment holding between sentence tokens such as **I am hungry** said by one person to another and **You are hungry** said on the same occasion by the latter person to the former.)

The function of the "meaning postulates" discussed in Chapter 7 was precisely to specify the class of admissible models. Technically, one is just taking the class K to consist of exactly those pairs $\langle \mathfrak{A}, \langle\langle \mathbf{w}, \mathbf{t}\rangle, g\rangle\rangle$ such that

(a) $i \in I$ and $j \in J$, where $\mathfrak{A}$ is $\langle A, I, J, \leqslant, F\rangle$,

(b) g is a variable assignment (context), and

(c) all the "meaning postulates" are true in the model $\langle \mathfrak{A}, \langle\langle \mathbf{w}, \mathbf{t}\rangle, g\rangle\rangle$

to intermix the notation of that chapter with this chapter's notation for models.

It is often convenient to formulate restrictions on the class of admissible models by means of "meaning postulates". But it should be noted that some restrictions one might wish to impose are not expressible in the object language which one is studying interpretations of. There is no reason why one cannot nevertheless impose such restrictions, provided that they can be formulated in the meta-language within which the models that are to be admissible are described. An example of a restriction that could be stipulated this way but not by means of a "meaning postulate" is the requirement that no interpretation which appears as a part of an admissible model contain two different possible worlds which are exactly alike at all times. (The point is not that one wants to require this of all admissible models, but that if one wants to require it then this cannot be achieved through meaning postulates.)

This completes our discussion of the main points in "Universal Grammar". There is a great deal more that can be said about the definitions and remarks which Montague presented there. Much of it is very technical, however, and lies beyond the scope of this book. From this perspective, it is a great loss that Montague never had the chance to write the book he intended to write about this subject, of which UG was, in effect, only an abstract.

CHAPTER 9

AN ANNOTATED BIBLIOGRAPHY OF FURTHER WORK IN MONTAGUE SEMANTICS

In the years since 1970, when Montague wrote PTQ, at least two hundred articles inspired by this work have been published, extending and expanding it in many different ways. Some of them achieve larger or otherwise more adequate syntactic coverage of English, along with semantic interpretation of the constructions covered. Others are dedicated to analyzing languages other than English. Some present a different semantic analysis of constructions dealt with in PTQ, or introduce new ideas for semantically analyzing constructions that had not been dealt with previously. Still others attempt to elaborate the semantics to make it possible to deal with new aspects of meaning, such as presupposition.

We present here a bibliography of some of these works, to aid the reader who wishes to explore the literature of Montague "grammar" further. (It was unfortunately not possible to base this bibliography upon an exhaustive search of the literature. The omission of any papers from this bibliography should not be taken as an indication that we consider them less important than the papers listed here.) As an aid to the reader in making his way around in the substantial number of articles published so far, we will indicate for each of several largish topics which of the listed items address them in an extensive way.

Some of the work cited here consists of extensions to PTQ, while other works borrow from PTQ only the general semantic framework and certain particular analyses such as that of noun phrase meanings. We will not have the space to comment on anything approaching the full variety of work that has been done. Instead we will select certain topics and will sketch, for one of them, the outlines of what was done, so as to aid readers who wish to make a more detailed study of the work themselves.

Relative Clauses

A sensible choice of topics to begin with is relative clauses, because Montague's own treatment of them scarcely deserves the appelation "ordinary English" which he accorded it. To generate forms more colloquial than the **such that** relatives described by him requires more syntactic effort than he apparently was willing to invest. However Rodman [100], Thomason [108], and Cooper [27] give much more satisfactory treatments of this construction. They not only treat relative clauses introduced by **that**, with deletion in the subordinate clause, and **that**-less relative clauses, but also describe **wh**-moved relative clauses, including the cases with "pied piping". Moreover, the "island" constraints which limit the possibilities for forming these sorts of relative clauses are discussed in rather novel ways by Rodman and by Cooper [26]. The only major aspect of the syntax and semantics of this construction which no one has yet tried to deal with in Montague's framework is the "crossover constraints" that Postal [1971] described.

Works dealing with relative clauses include: [6, 7, 26, 27, 50, 71, 85, 92, 100, 108, 109].

Other large topics on which there is substantial published work are listed below, each with pointers to the publications catalogued in this chapter that deal in an extended way with that topic.

Passive sentences [1, 3, 4, 5, 11, 12, 23, 28, 37, 81, 91, 93, 108, 109].

Adjectives and Adverbs [22, 29, 30, 31, 59, 70, 72, 79, 88, 89, 94, 102, 103, 104, 110].

Complement Structures [2, 4, 16, 29, 33, 37, 39, 49, 70, 85, 91, 93, 96, 99, 106, 108, 109].

Questions [13, 17, 27, 29, 52, 55, 62, 64, 66, 67, 85, 98].

Deixis (Indexicals) [14, 24, 49, 55, 61].

Propositional Attitudes [16, 29, 83, 90, 95].

Presupposition [33, 47, 48, 50, 54, 64, 65, 66, 68, 79, 80, 101, 111].

Transformational Grammar and Montague Semantics [4, 23, 28, 85, 91, 93, 96].

Systematic Works [29, 46, 83].

BIBLIOGRAPHY

1. Allwood, J., 'A Montague grammar for a fragment of Swedish,' Gothenburg: Logical Grammar, Report 11 (1976).
2. Ard, J., 'Rebracketing in diachronic syntax and Montague grammar,' *Papers from*

the Parasession on Diachronic Syntax, Ed. by S.B. Steever, et al. Chicago: Chicago Linguistics Society, 1976.

3. Bach, Emmon, 'Control in Montague grammar,' *Linguistic Inquiry* **10** (1979): 515–531.
4. Bach, Emmon, 'Montague grammar and classical transformational grammar,' *Linguistics, Philosophy, and Montague Grammar*, pp. 3–50, ed. by S. Davis and M. Mithun, Austin: University of Texas Press, 1979.
5. Bach, Emmon, 'In defense of passive,' *Linguistics and Philosophy* (to appear).
6. Bach, Emmon and Cooper, Robin, 'The *NP–S* analysis of relative clauses and compositional semantics,' *Linguistics and Philosophy* 2 (1978): 145–150.
7. Bartch, R., 'Syntax and semantics of relative clauses,' *Amsterdam Papers in Formal Grammar* 1 (1976): 1–24.
8. Barwise, Jon, 'On branching quantifiers in English,' *Journal of Philosophical Logic* 8 (1979): 47–80.
9. Bennett, Michael and Partee, Barbara H., 'Toward the logic of tense and aspect in English,' MS (1972).
10. Bennett, Michael, 'Accommodating the plural in Montague's fragment of English,' *Papers in Montague Grammars*, pp. 25–64, ed. by R. Rodman, UCLA Occasional Papers in Linguistics 2 (1972).
11. Bennett, Michael, *Some Extensions of a Montague fragment of English*, UCLA Ph.D. Dissertation (1975), reproduced by the Indiana Linguistics Club.
12. Bennett, Michael, 'A variation and extension of a Montague fragment of English,' *Montague Grammar*, pp. 119–163, ed. by Barbara Partee, New York: Academic Press, 1976.
13. Bennett, M.R., 'A response to Karttunen on questions,' *Linguistics and Philosophy* 1 (1977): 279–300.
14. Bennett, Michael, 'Demonstratives and indexicals in Montague grammar,' *Synthese* 39 (1978): 1–80.
15. Bennett, Michael, 'Mass nouns and mass terms in Montague grammar,' *Linguistics, Philosophy and Montague Grammar*, pp. 263–286 ed. by S. Davis and M. Mithun, Austin: University of Texas Press, 1979.
16. Bigelow, John C., 'Believing in semantics,' *Linguistics and Philosophy* 2 (1978): 101–144.
17. Boër, Steven E., '"Who" and "whether": Towards a theory of indirect questions clauses,' *Linguistics and Philosophy* 2 (1978): 307–345.
18. Bowers, John S. and Reichenbach, Uwe K. H., 'Montague grammar and transformational grammar: a review of *Formal Philosophy: Selected Papers of Richard Montague*' *Linguistic Analysis* 5 (1979).
19. Carlson, Greg N., 'A unified analysis of the English bare plural,' *Linguistics and Philosophy* 1 (1977): 413–456.
20. Carlson, Greg N., *Reference to Kinds in English*, unpublished University of Mass. dissertation, 1978, distributed by the Indian University Linguistics Club.
21. Carlson, Greg N., 'Generics and atemporal *when*,' *Linguistics and Philosophy* 3 (1979): 49–98.
22. Cooper, R., 'Montague's semantic theory of adverbs and the VSO hypothesis,' *North East Linguistic Society* 5 (1974): 225–233.

23. Cooper, Robin, *Montague's Semantic Theory and Transformational Syntax*, Ph.D. Diss., University of Massachusetts, 1975.
24. Cooper, Robin, 'The interpretation of pronouns,' *Proceedings of the Third Groningen Round Table: Syntax and Semantics* 12, ed. by Heny and Schnelle, New York: Academic Press, 1979.
25. Cooper, Robin, 'Review of Richard Montague's *Formal Philosophy*,' *Language* 53 (1977): 895–910.
26. Cooper, Robin, 'Variable binding and relative clauses,' *Formal Semantics and Pragmatics for Natural Languages*, pp. 131–169, ed. by F. Guenthner and S.J. Schmidt, Dordrecht, Holland: D. Reidel 1979.
27. Cooper, Robin, 'A fragment of English with questions and relative clauses,' unpublished, 1978.
28. Cooper, R. and Parsons, T., 'Montague grammar, generative semantics and interpretive semantics,' *Montague Grammar*, ed. by Barbara Partee, New York: Academic Press, 1976.
29. Cresswell, M.J., *Logics and Languages*, London, England: Methuen & Co., 1973.
30. Cresswell, M.J., 'The semantics of degree,' *Montague Grammar*, ed. by Barbara Partee,' New York: Academic Press, 1976.
31. Cresswell, M.J., 'Adverbs of space and time,' *Formal Semantics and Pragmatics for Natural Languages*, pp. 171–199, ed. by F. Guenthner and S.J. Schmidt, Dordrecht, Holland: D. Reidel, 1978.
32. Davidson, D. and Harman, G. (eds.), *Semantics of Natural Language*, Dordrecht, Holland: D. Reidel, 1972.
33. Delacruz, Enrique, B., 'Factives and proposition level constructions in Montague grammar,' *Montague Grammar*, pp. 177–200, ed. by Barbara Partee, New York: Academic Press, 1976.
34. Dowty, D.R., 'Toward a semantic theory of word formation in Montague grammar,' *Texas Linguistic Forum* 2 (1975): 69–96.
35. Dowty, David, 'Montague grammars and lexical decomposition of causative verbs,' *Montague Grammar*, ed. by Barbara Partee, New York: Academic Press, 1976.
36. Dowty, D.R., 'Toward a semantic analysis of verb aspect and the English "imperfective" progressive,' *Linguistics and Philosophy* 1 (1977): 45–78.
37. Dowty, David R., 'Governed transformations as lexical rules in a Montague grammar,' *Linguistic Inquiry* 9 (1978): 393–426.
38. Dowty, David R., 'Applying Montague's views on linguistic metatheory to the structure of the lexicon,' *Papers from the Parasession on the Lexicon*, Chicago: Chicago Linguistics Society, 1978.
39. Dowty, David R., *Word Meaning and Montague Grammar*, Dordrecht, Holland: D. Reidel, 1979.
40. Dowty, David R., 'Dative "movement" and Thomason's extensions of Montague grammar,' *Linguistics, Philosophy and Montague Grammar*, pp. 153–222, ed. by S. Davis and M. Mithun, Austin: University of Texas, 1979.
41. Edmondson, J. A., 'Strict and sloppy identity in Lambda-categorial grammar,' Indiana University Linguistics Club mimeograph, 1976.
42. Edmondson, J.A. and Plank, Frans, 'Great expectations: an intensive self analysis,' *Linguistics and Philosophy* 2 (1978): 373–413.

43. Friedman, Joyce and Warren, David S., 'A parsing method for Montague grammars,' *Linguistics and Philosophy* 2 (1978): 347–372.
44. Friedman, Joyce, 'An unlabeled bracketing solution to the problem of conjoined phrases in Montague's PTQ,' *Journal of Philosophical Logic* 8 (1979): 151–169.
45. Gabbay, D.M. and Moravcsik, J.M.E., 'Branching quantifiers, English, and Montague-grammars,' *Theoretical Linguistics* 1 (1974): 139–157.
46. Gallin, Daniel, *Intensional and Higher-Order Modal Logic with Applications to Montague Semantics*, Amsterdam: North-Holland, 1975.
47. Gazdar, Gerald, *Formal Pragmatics for Natural Languages: Implication, Presupposition and Logical Form*, Indiana University Linguistics Club, 1976.
48. Gazdar, G. and Klein, E., 'Context-sensitive transderivational constraints and conventional implicature,' *Papers from the 13th Regional Meeting*, Chicago: Chicago Linguistics Society, 1977.
49. Groenendijk, Jeroen and Stokhof, Martin, 'Infinitives and context in Montague grammar,' *Linguistics, Philosophy and Montague Grammar*, pp. 287–310, ed. by S. Davis and M. Mithun, Austin: University of Texas Press, 1979.
50. Halvorsen, Per-Kristian G., *The Syntax and Semantics of Cleft Constructions*, Texas Linguistic Forum 11, University of Texas at Austin, Department of Linguistics, 1978.
51. Halvorsen, Per-Kristian and Ladusaw, William A., 'Montague's "Universal Grammar": An introduction for the linguist,' *Linguistics and Philosophy* 3 (1979): 185–223.
52. Hamblin, C. L., 'Questions in Montague English,' *Foundations of Language* 10 (1973): 41–53. Also in *Montague Grammar*, ed. by Barbara Partee.
53. Hausser, Roland, 'Scope ambiguity and scope restrictions in Montague grammars,' *Amsterdam Papers in Formal Grammar, v. 1*, ed. by J. Groenendijk and M. Stokhof, Amsterdam: Universiteit van Amsterdam, 1976.
54. Hausser, R.R., 'Presuppositions in Montague grammar,' *Theoretical Linguistics* 3 (1976): 245–280.
55. Hausser, R. and Zaefferer, D., 'Questions and answers in a context dependent Montague grammar,' *Formal Semantics and Pragmatics for Natrual Languages*, pp. 339–358, ed. by F. Guenthner and S.J. Schmidt, Dordrecht, Holland: D. Reidel, 1978.
56. Hintikka, K.J.J., 'On the proper treatment of quantifiers in Montague's semantics,' *Logical Theory and Semantic Analysis*, pp. 45–60, ed. by Sören Stenlund, Dordrecht, Holland: D. Reidel, 1974.
57. Hoepelman, J.P., 'Mass-nouns and aspects, or: Why we can't eat gingercake in an hour,' *Amsterdam Papers in Formal Grammar* 1 (1976): 132–153.
58. Janssen, T., 'A computer program for Montague grammar: theoretical aspects and proofs for the reduction rules,' *Amsterdam Papers in Formal Grammar* 1 (1976): 154–169.
59. Kamp, J.A.W., 'Two theories about adjectives,' *Formal Semantics of Natural Language*, pp. 123– 155, ed. by E.L. Keenan, Cambridge: University Press, 1975.
60. Kamp, Hans, 'Semantics versus pragmatics,' *Formal Semantics and Pragmatics for Natural Laguages*, pp. 255–287, ed. by F. Guenthner and S.J. Schmidt, Dordrecht, Holland: D. Reidel, 1978.

61. Kaplan, David, 'Demonstratives,' 1977, preliminary version.
62. Karttunen, Lauri, 'Syntax and semantics of questions,' *Linguistics and Philosophy* 1 (1977): 3–44.
63. Karttunen, F. and Karttunen, L., 'The clitic *-kin/-kaan* in Finnish,' *Papers from the Transatlantic Finnish Conference: Texas Linguistics Forum* 5, 1976, ed. by R.T. Harms, Austin: Department of Linguistics, pp. 89–118.
64. Karttunen, F. and Karttunen, L., '*Even* questions,' *North East Linguistics* Society, no. 7. 1977.
65. Karttunen, Lauri and Peters, Stanley, 'Conventional implicature,' *Syntax and Semantics 11: Presupposition*, pp. 1–56, ed. by C.-K. Oh and D. Dinneen, New York: Academic Press, 1979.
66. Karttunen, Lauri and Peters, Stanley, 'What indirect questions conventionally implicate,' *Papers from the Twelfth Regional Meeting of the Chicago Linguistics Society*, pp. 351–368, ed. by S. Mufwene, C. Walker and S. Steever, Chicago: University of Chicago Linguistics Department, 1976.
67. Karttunen, Lauri and Peters, Stanley, 'Interrogrative quantifiers,' to appear, 1979.
68. Kasher, Asa, 'Logical forms in context: Presuppositions and other preconditions,' *The Monist* 57 (1973): 371–395.
69. Kasher, A., 'A proper treatment of Montague grammars in natural logic and linguistics,' *Theoretical Linguistics* 2 (1975), 133–145.
70. Keenan, E.L. and Faltz, L., *Logical Types for Natural Languages*, to appear.
71. Klein, E.H., 'Crossing conference in a Montague Grammar,' *Pragmatics Microfiche* 2,4 (1977): A3–C8.
72. Klein, Ewan, 'A semantics for positive and compariative adjectives,' 1979, MS.
73. König, E., 'Temporal and non-temporal uses of "noch" and "schon" in German,' *Linguistics and Philosophy* 1 (1977): 173–198.
74. Kratzer, Angelika, 'What "must" and "can" must and can mean,' *Linguistics and Philosophy* 1 (1977): 337–355.
75. Kutschera, F.V., 'Partial interpretations,' *Formal Semantics of Natural Language*, pp. 156–174, ed. E.L. Keenan, Cambridge: University Press, 1975.
76. Ladusaw, William A., 'Some *any*'s mean some,' *Texas Linguistic Forum* **15** (1979): 135–142.
77. Ladusaw, William, 'Some problems with tense in PTQ,' *Texas Linguistic Forum* 6 (1977): 90–102.
78. Ladusaw, William A., *Polarity Sensitivity as Inherent Scope Relations*, Austin: University of Texas, 1979, Ph.D. Dissertation.
79. Ladusaw, William, 'The scope of some sentence adverbs and surface structure,' North East Linguistic Society, No. 8.
80. Lee, I-K., 'Syntax and semantics of Korean delimiters,' Chicago Linguistics Society **13** (1977): 302–315.
81. Lee, Kiyong, *The Treatment of Some English Constructions in Montague Grammar*, Austin: University of Texas, 1974, unpublished Ph.D. Dissertation.
82. Lee, K., 'Negation in Montague grammar,' *Chicago Linguistics Society* **10** (1974): 378–389.
83. Lewis, David, 'General Semantics,' *Semantics of Natural Language*, ed. by Donald Davidson and Gilbert Harman, Dordrecht, Holland: D. Reidel, 1972.

84. McCawley, James D., 'Helpful hints to the ordinary working Montague grammarian,' *Linguistics, Philosophy, and Montague Grammar*, ed. by S. David and M. Mithun. Austin: University of Texas Press, 1979, pp. 103–126.

85. McCloskey, James, *Transformational Syntax and Model Theoretic Semantics: A Case Study in Modern Irish*, Dordrecht, Holland: D. Reidel, 1979.

86. Montague, R., 'Comments on Moravcsik's paper,' *Approaches to Natural Language*, pp. 289–294, ed. by K.J.J. Hintikka, et al., Dordrecht, Holland: D. Reidel, 1973.

87. Montague , R. and Schnelle, H., *Universale Grammatik*, Braunschweig: Vieweg, 1972.

88. Parsons, Terence, 'Some problems concerning the logic of grammatical modifiers,' *Semantics of Natural Language*, pp. 127–141, ed. by D. Davidson and G. Harman, Dordrecht, Holland: D. Reidel, 1972.

89. Parsons, Terence, 'Type theory and ordinary language,' *Lingustics, Philosophy and Montague Grammar*, pp. 127–152, ed. by S. Davis and M. Mithun, Austin: University of Texas Press, 1979.

90. Partee, Barbara H., 'Opacity and scope,' *Semantics and Philosophy*, pp. 81–102, ed. by M.K. Munitz and Peter K. Unger, New York: New York University Press, 1974.

91. Partee, Barbara H., 'Montague grammar and transformational grammar,' *Linguistic Inquiry*,' Vol. VI. 2 (Spring, 1975) 203–300.

92. Partee, Barbara H., 'Deletion and variable binding,' *Formal Semantics of Natural Language*, pp. 16–34, ed. by E.L. Keenan, Cambridge: Cambridge University Press, 1975.

93. Partee, Barbara H., 'Some transformational extensions of Montague grammar,' *Montague Grammar*, ed. by B. Partee, New York: Academic Press, 1979.

94. Partee, Barbara, 'John is easy to please,' *Linguistic Structures Processing*, pp. 281–312, ed. by A. Zampolli, Amsterdam: North-Holland, 1977.

95. Partee, Barbara H., 'Semantics – mathematics or psychology,' *Semantics from different points of view: Proceedings of the Konstanz Colloquium on Semantics 1978*, ed. by R. Bauerle, et al., Berlin: Springer, 1979.

96. Partee, Barbara H., 'Constraining transformational Montague grammar: A framework and a fragment,' *Linguistics, Philosophy and Montague Grammar*, pp. 51–102, ed. by S. Davis and M. Mithun, Austin: University of Texas Press, 1979.

97. Partee, Barbara H., 'Montague grammar and the well-formedness constraint,' *Syntax and Semantics 10: Selections from the Third Groningen Round Table*, ed. by F. Henry and H. Schnelle, New York: Academic Press.

98. Peters, Stanley, 'What do questions mean?' *Texas Linguistic Forum* **13** (1979): 86–95.

99. Plank, F., 'Misunderstanding understood subjects: the minimal distance principle in Montague grammar,' *Amsterdam Papers in Formal Grammar*, pp. 154–215, 1976.

100. Rodman, Robert, 'Scope phenomena, "movment transformations", and relative clauses,' *Montague Grammar*, ed. B. Partee, New York: Academic Press, 1976.

101. Rohrer, C., 'Le système de Montague et les presuppositions,' *Language* **30** (1973): 111–124.

102. Siegel, Muffy, 'Capturing the Russian adjective,' *Montague Grammar*, ed. B. Partee, New York: Academic Press, 1976.

103. Siegel, Muffy, *Capturing the Adjective*, Amherst: University of Massachusetts, 1976, unpublished Ph.D. dissertation.

104. Siegel, Muffy E.A., 'Measure adjectives in Montague Grammar,' *Linguistics, Philosophy and Montague Grammar*, pp. 223–262, ed. by S. Davis and M. Mithun, Austin: University of Texas Press, 1979.

105. Thomason, R.H., 'Home is where the heart is,' Pittsburgh: University of Pittsburgh, 1974. Unpublished manuscript.

106. Thomason, Richmond H., 'Some complement constructions in Montague grammar,' *Papers for the Tenth Regional Meeting*, Chicago: Chicago Linguistics Society, 1974.

107. Thomason, R.H., 'Montague grammar and some transformations,' Pittsburgh: University of Pittsburgh, 1976, unpublished paper.

108. Thomason, Richmond H., 'Some extension of Montague Grammar,' *Montague Grammar*, ed. by B. Partee, New York: Academic Press, 1976.

109. Thomason, R., 'On the semantic interpretation of the Thomason 1972 fragment,' Pittsburgh: University of Pittsburgh, 1976, unpublished manuscript.

110. Stalnaker, R.C. and Thomason, R.H., 'A semantic theory of adverbs,' *Linguistic Inquiry* 4 (1973): 195–220.

111. Waldo, James, 'A PTQ semantics for sortal incorrectness,' *Linguistics, Philosophy and Montague Grammar*, pp. 311–331, ed. S. Davis and M. Mithun, Austin: University of Texas Press, 1979.

APPENDIX I:

INDEX OF SYMBOLS

L_0 14
$\neg, \wedge, \vee, \rightarrow, \leftrightarrow$ 15
$[\![\alpha]\!]$ 19
$\langle x, y \rangle$ 19
L_{0E} 23
$\rightarrow$ (is rewritten as) 23
1, 0 (truth values) 25
X^Y 26
$\mathscr{P}A$ 26
γ | β 29
γ $\triangle$ 29
$A \times B$ (Cartesian product) 32
$[_S\ S], [_N\ N], \ldots$ 37
$[\![\alpha]\!]^M$ 45
N, K, A, C, E ("Polish connectives) 54
| (logical connective) 54
L_1 56
$v_1, v_2, \ldots, x, y, z$ 56
$\forall, \exists$ 57
g (value assignment) 59
$[\![\alpha]\!]^{M,g}$ 60
g_u^e 62
L_{1E} 66
$L_{\mathbf{type}}$ 83
$\langle a, b \rangle$ (type) 83
e, t (as types) 83
D_x 84
$L(y)(x)$ (as notational variant of $L(x, y)$) 85
ME_a 89
$c_{n,a}$ 90
$v_{n,a}$ 91
Con_a 91
Var_a 91
$\exists!$ 94
non 94
R_o 96
R_s 96
R_r 97
L_λ 98
λ 98
$\hat{x}$ (as notational variant of λx) 100
ϕ_α^x 105
$<$ 113
i, j, k 113
$[\![\alpha]\!]^{M,\mathbf{i},g}$ 113
F, P 114
L_{1t} 115
G, H 118
$\Box, \Diamond$ 121
L_{1m} 126
W (set of possible worlds) 131
T (set of times) 131
w 131
t 131
$[\![\alpha]\!]^{M,\mathbf{w},\mathbf{t},g}$ 132
L_{1mt} 132
s 136–137
h 139
$[\![\alpha]\!]_{\mathfrak{c}}^{M,g}$ 146
$^\wedge\alpha$ 153
$^\vee\alpha$ 153

IL 154
$\langle s, a\rangle$ (type) 155
= (in IL) 159
$\gamma\{\alpha\}$ (abbreviation for $[{}^{\vee}\gamma](\alpha)$) 162
For 163
Bel 164
$\wedge, \vee$ (for $\forall$ and $\exists$) 177
W, **H** (for **F** and **P**) 177
i, j (for **w** and **t**) 177
$A/B, A//B$ 182
e, t (as categories) 182
IV, T, TV, IAV, CN, DET 183
$\mathbf{he}_0, \mathbf{he}_1, \ldots$ 184
f (function from categories to types) 187
α' (translation of α) 189
B_A 190
P_A 190
F_m (structural operation) 190–191
$\Rightarrow$ 195
$F_{n,m}$ 204
$\mathbf{him}_n$ 204
δ_* 223
$\mathscr{P}$ 226
$\alpha\{\beta, \gamma\}$ (as abbreviation for ${}^{\vee}\alpha(\beta, \gamma)$) 250
$\mathfrak{A}$ 258
$k \circ g$ (composition of functions) 263

Abbreviations from PTQ not used in this book:

$\hat{u}\phi$, where $\phi \in ME_t$	abbreviates:	$\lambda u \phi$
$\hat{u}\phi$	abbreviates:	${}^{\wedge}\lambda u \phi$
α^*, where $\alpha \in ME_{f(T)}$	abbreviates:	$\lambda P[P\{\alpha\}]$

APPENDIX II:

VARIABLE TYPE CONVENTIONS FOR CHAPTER 7

Symbol:	*Type of Variable:*	*Name of denotation:*
$x, y, z, x_1, x_2, \ldots$	e	individuals (entities)
$P, Q, P_1, P_2, \ldots$	$\langle s, \langle e, t\rangle\rangle$	Properties of individuals
p	$\langle s, t\rangle$	Propositions
$\mathscr{P}$	$\langle s, f(T)\rangle$ (or equivalently, $\langle s, \langle\langle s, \langle e, t\rangle\rangle, t\rangle\rangle$)	Properties of properties of individuals
S	$\langle s, \langle e, \langle e, t\rangle\rangle\rangle$	Relations-in-intension between pairs of individuals.
G	$\langle s, \langle e, \langle f(IAV)\rangle\rangle\rangle$	Relations-in-intension between functions from properties to sets and individuals.

APPENDIX III: *THE TEMPERATURE IS NINETY AND RISING*

We mentioned in Chapter 7 Section I.2 that Montague's original fragment in PTQ was capable of treating the puzzle created by the intensionality in examples such as Barbara Partee's *The temperature is ninety and (is) rising*, though in this text we have adopted Michael Bennett's simplification of the type assignment for English categories, a simplification that precludes Montague's solution to this particular puzzle. In this section, we will present this puzzle, explain Montague's solution to it, and then describe some of the complications that turn out to be created by this solution, complications which have led some workers in Montague Grammar to doubt whether Montague's approach to it really is preferable.

From the two premises **The mayor is John** and **The mayor walks** the conclusion **John walks** seems to follow logically, according to our intuitions. And in fact the translations of the two premises in the fragment we have presented, $\exists y[\forall x[\mathbf{mayor}'(x) \leftrightarrow x = y] \wedge y = j]$ and $\exists y[\forall x[\mathbf{mayor}'(x) \leftrightarrow x = y] \wedge \mathbf{walk}'(y)]$, do ential the translation of the conclusion, $\mathbf{walk}'(j)$, by familiar principles of first-order logic. However, the argument in (7.120)–(7.122), which is apparently parallel syntactically, obviously should not follow, as Partee pointed out to Montague:

(7-120) The temperature is ninety

(7-121) The temperature rises

(7-122) Ninety rises

To explain Montague's solution to this problem, it is necessary to return to the mapping from syntactic categories to logical types. In Chapter 7 we adopted Bennett's modification of this assignment which read as follows:

(7-3) (repeated)
1.′ $f(t) = t$
2.′ $f(CN) = f(IV) = \langle e, t\rangle$
3.′ For all categories A and B, $F(A/B) = \langle\langle s, f(B)\rangle, f(A)\rangle$.

As we mentioned there however, Montague's original assignment differed in that *CN* and *IV* were not basic categories but were defined as abbreviations for t/e and $t//e$, respectively. The type assignment was then defined by this recursive definition:

(7-2) (repeated)
1. $f(t) = t$
2. $f(e) = e$
3. For all A and B, $f(A/B) = \langle\langle s, f(B)\rangle, f(A)\rangle$.

By this definition, $f(IV) = f(CN) = f(t/e) = f(t//e) = \langle\langle s, e\rangle, t\rangle$. In other words, common nouns and intransitive verbs denoted sets of individual concepts (functions from indices to individuals) rather than sets of individuals. All of the types assigned to "higher" categories (e.g. $f(T)$, $f(TV)$, $f(IV/IV)$, etc.) bore the same relationship to each other as they bear in our fragment but differed in that each had individual concepts nested at the "bottom" of its type where it has individuals in our system (cf., if necessary, Table 7-2 on p. 187 with Table 7-3 on p. 189). A critical difference in the original PTQ system was, therefore, that a sentence such as **John walks** made the assertion that an individual concept (i.e. function from indices to individuals) "denoted" by the name **John** (via an individual sublimation) is among a set of individual concepts denoted by the verb **walk**; it did not directly make an assertion about an individual and a set of individuals. **The temperature rises** asserted that a particular individual concept (the unique concept which satisfies the predicate **temperature** at the index in question) is among the set of individual concepts denoted by **rise**. However, the meanings of the noun and verb in **John walks** were restricted by meaning postulates in an appropriate way (to be explained below) so that the truth conditions for **John walks** (and all other "extensional" examples, which constitute the great majority of English sentences) nevertheless depend entirely on whether a certain individual is in a certain set of individuals at the index in question – that is, these sentences were logically equivalent to the first-order extensional translations we have given them in our fragment. These postulates did not hold, however, for nouns such as **temperature** and **price** and verbs such as **rise** and **change**. Montague's intuitive view of the meaning of **the temperature** was that it denotes a concept which is a function from indices (world-time pairs) to numbers, in particular, a function which gives different numbers at different times and in different worlds, as the temperature rises and falls. Thus to know whether a predicate like **rise** is true of this concept at a particular index, it is necessary to know not just the current temperature (the value of the temperature concept at the present index) but also to compare it with the value of the temperature concept at earlier and/or later times.[1]

To get the meaning of **The temperature is ninety** correct under this approach, Montague analyzed the meaning of **be** as asserting not that two individual concepts are identical, but merely that the extensions of two concepts are the same at the present world and time. In the original PTQ, the variables x, y, z, x_1, x_2, ... were all variables over individual concepts, not individuals, the symbols u and v serving as variables over individuals instead. Thus the rule giving the translation of **be** was (7.123) rather than (7.124), as in our fragment:

(7.123) **be** translates into $\lambda\mathscr{P}\lambda x\mathscr{P}\{\hat{}\lambda y[x = y]\}$

(7.124) **be** translates into $\lambda\mathscr{P}\lambda x\mathscr{P}\{\hat{}\lambda y[\check{}x = \check{}y]\}$

The translations of the argument (7.120)–(7.122) then turn out to be (7.120′)–(7.122′) in PTQ:

(7.120′) $\exists y[\forall x[\textbf{temperature}'(x) \leftrightarrow x = y] \wedge \check{}y = n]$

(7.121′) $\exists y[\forall x[\textbf{temperature}'(x) \leftrightarrow x = y] \wedge \textbf{rise}'(y)]$

(7.122′) $\textbf{rise}'(\hat{}n)$

The "conclusion" (7.122′) is now of course not a valid one: since the first premise only asserts that the extension of the temperature-concept is identical with the extension of the concept of **ninety** at the current index (which concept is, as we will see below, a constant function giving the same extension at all indices), it cannot be concluded that the concept of ninety is a rising one just because the temperature-concept is a rising one.

To ensure the equivalence of other "ordinary" sentences with extensional first-order formulas, Montague introduced two meaning postulates. MP6 requires that any concept that occurs in the denotation of "ordinary" common nouns be a constant concept:

MP6. $\forall x\Box[\delta(x) \rightarrow \exists u[x = \hat{}u]]$, where δ translates any number of B_{CN} other than **price** or **temperature**.

(Recall our earlier observation that $\hat{}\alpha$ is always a constant function when α is a variable.) To forestall a possible confusion, we should point out that this postulate does not require that the denotations of common nouns like **fish** be the same at all indices, but only that the concepts within these denotations, whichever concepts they may be at a given index, all be constant functions.

To ensure that the truth conditions for sentences involving intransitive verbs depend only on the membership of individuals in a set of individuals, Montague introduces MP7; here M is used as a variable over properties of individuals, i.e. as $v_{0,\langle s,\langle e,t\rangle\rangle}$.

MP7. $\exists M\forall x\Box[\delta(x) \leftrightarrow M\{\check{}x\}]$, where δ translates any member of B_{IV} other than **rise** or **change**.

(Since M is a variable over properties, rather than a variable over sets, this postulate similarly does not require that the denotation of **walk**, etc. be the same at all indices, as a property may have different extensions at different indices.) Since the effect of this postulate is to make the set of concepts denoted by **walk**, **talk**, etc. completely definable in terms of a set of individuals that are the extensions of these concepts (and vice-versa) at each index, it is convenient to introduce a notation for this corresponding extensional set: parallel to the use of δ_* to denote the extensional relation corresponding to the translation δ of a transitive verb, Montague used δ_*, where δ translates an *intransitive* verb (or common noun, for that matter), as an abbreviation for $\lambda u \delta(\hat{}u)$, i.e. as "that set of individuals whose (constant) concepts are in the set denoted by δ." For example, the translation of **A fish walks** is, in the PTQ system, (7.125), where x is now a variable over individual concepts.

(7.125) $\exists x[\mathbf{fish}'(x) \wedge \mathbf{walk}'(x)]$

But since **fish** and **walk** are limited by MP6 and MP7, respectively, we are guaranteed that this equivalent to the extensional formula (7.117):

(7.126) $\exists u[\mathbf{fish}'_*(u) \wedge \mathbf{walk}'_*(u)]$

In the PTQ system, proper nouns such as **John**, **Mary**, **ninety**, etc. were given the translations $\lambda P[P\{\hat{}j\}]$, $\lambda P[P\{\hat{}m\}]$, $\lambda P[P\{\hat{}n\}]$, etc., respectively (rather than $\lambda P[P\{j\}]$, etc., as in our fragment). Since the names j, m, and n are required to be "rigid designators" by MP2 in (7.85) mentioned earlier (i.e. the postulate $\exists u \Box[\delta = u]$, where δ is j, m or n), the translations of sentences with proper names in subject position such as **John walks** can likewise be equivalently written as purely extensional formulas such as (7.127) in PTQ:

(7.127) $\mathbf{walk}'_*(j)$

This more complicated system of types has repercussions elsewhere in the fragment. MP7 limits only intransitive verbs, but thanks to the systematicity of the type assignment, the subjects of verbs in B_{TV}, $B_{IV/t}$ and $B_{IV//IV}$ will also be individual concepts rather than individuals. To ensure that these positions are likewise extensional, it is necessary to modify the postulate for transitive verbs, MP4, as below, and to add postulates for the other categories of verb: these cases are parallel to MP7:

MP4′. $\exists S \forall \mathscr{P} \forall x \Box[\delta(x, \mathscr{P}) \leftrightarrow \mathscr{P}\{\hat{y}[\check{}S(\check{}x, \check{}y)]\}]$, where δ translates **find**, **lose**, **love**, **eat**, etc.

MP8. $\forall \mathscr{P} \exists M \forall x \Box[\delta(x, \mathscr{P}) \leftrightarrow M\{\ x\}]$, where δ translates **seek**

MP9. $\forall p \exists M \forall x \Box[\delta(x, p) \leftrightarrow M\{\ x\}]$, where δ translates **believe, assert**

MP10. $\forall P \exists M \forall x \Box[\delta(x, P) \leftrightarrow M\{\ x\}]$, where δ translates **try, wish**

This treatment of intensionality in subject position should be compared carefully with the somewhat different treatment of the intensionality of the object position of verbs such as **seek**. The treatment of the object position of **seek** involved not merely an intension but also a higher-order relation that was not reducible to a first-order relation: because that analysis was intensional, it allowed that **John seeks a unicorn** could be true while **John seeks a centaur** was false even at an index at which the set of unicorns was the same as the set of centaurs (e.g., the empty set); yet, because it was also a higher-order relation, it could be true at an index where there were two unicorns that **John seeks a unicorn** was true even though it was true of neither of the two unicorns that he sought that particular unicorn – the treatment thus allowed for the "non-specific" character of the meaning of the object of the sentence. The treatment of the subject in **A price rises** is intensional but does not involve higher-order predication (and thus is not "non-specific"): if **A price rises** is true, then there must be at least one particular price-concept of which it is true that that concept rises.

PROBLEM A1. In PTQ Montague asserted that in view in MP6 and MP7, δ and δ_* would be interdefinable whenever δ translated a common noun or an intransitive verb mentioned in these postulates. That is, for such a δ, the formula $\forall x \Box[\delta(x) \leftrightarrow \delta_*({}^{\vee}x)]$ would be logically true. The late Michael Bennett pointed out to us that while this certainly holds for intransitive verbs, there will be cases where this formula fails for common nouns; that is, the right side of the conditional can be true for some values of x while the left is false. Explain why this is so. (HINT: consider a case where x denotes a non-rigid concept.) Why doesn't MP6 rule out this failure? Does this failure have consequences for the treatment of English?

PROBLEM A2. In sentences with a quantified NP as subject, the value of an individual concept variable in the translation will, in effect, be restricted both by MP6 (because of the common noun) and by MP7 or other verb postulate (because of the verb); consider e.g. $\exists x[\mathbf{fish}'(x) \wedge \mathbf{walk}'(x)]$. Are both postulates therefore necessary to achieve extensionality? Consider both the effect of retaining MP6 while deleting MP7 and deleting MP6 while retaining MP7. (You may wish to consider additional sentences, such as **A fish rises**.)

While Montague's use of individual concepts undeniably captures an intuitively correct aspect of the meaning of **The temperature is ninety** and **The temperature rises**, it creates problems elsewhere as it stands. Since modifiers in *IV*/*IV*, such as **slowly**, create new *IV*s from *IV*s, the postulate for **walk** will not suffice to predict the extensionality of the *IV* in (7.128), which translates (7.128′):

(7.128) **A fish walks slowly**

(7.128′) $\exists x[\mathbf{fish}'(x) \wedge \mathbf{slowly}'(\hat{}\mathbf{walk}')(x)]$

We could of course subsume **slowly**′ under the meaning postulate MP10 for **try** and **wish** (since it applies to δ of the same logical type as **slowly**). But then this would predict that **A price rises slowly** is extensional while **A price rises** is not extensional, surely an incorrect result.[2]

Another curious consequence of Montague's analysis was discovered by Anil Gupta (and passed on to us by Bennett). From the exposition of PTQ so far, the reader will no doubt expect the argument in (7.129) to be a formally valid one, as it is according to our intuitions:

(7.129) **Necessarily the temperature is the price**
The temperature rises
―――――――――――――――
The price rises

Surprisingly, this argument turns out to be invalid (on the simplest syntactic analysis, where no quantification rules are used). Its translation is (7.129′):

(7.129′) $\Box[\exists x[\forall y[\mathbf{temp}'(x) \leftrightarrow x = y] \wedge \exists z[\forall w[\mathbf{price}'(w) \leftrightarrow z = w] \wedge x = z]]]$
$\exists x[\forall y[\mathbf{temp}'(x) \leftrightarrow x = y] \wedge \mathbf{rise}'(x)]$
―――――――――――――――
$\exists x[\forall y[\mathbf{price}'(y) \leftrightarrow x = y] \wedge \mathbf{rise}'(x)]$

The first premise asserts that whatever concept is the unique temperature concept at each index has the same extension as the extension of whatever concept is the price concept at that index. However, the definite descriptions are within the scope of the necessity operator (on this analysis), so it can turn out that the concepts which satisfy the two definite descriptions may differ from index to index. Thus a counterexample to this argument can take the following form: assume a model with only three indices, calling them i_1, i_2 and i_3. The lines in the diagram below represents the values taken by four concepts c_1–c_4 at each index, where the vertical axis represents in rising values the numbers that are extensions of these concepts:

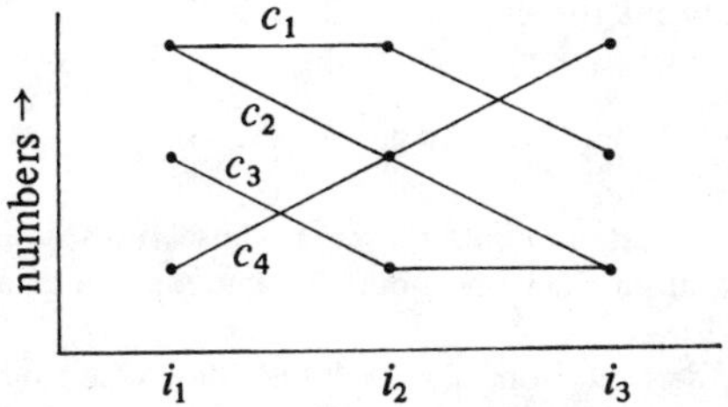

Suppose also that at i_1, c_1 is the only concept of which **temperature′** is true, and that c_2 is the only one of which **price′** is true. At i_2, **price′** is still uniquely true of c_2, but now **temperature′** is uniquely true of c_4. Finally at i_3, **price′** is uniquely true of c_2 and **temperature′** is uniquely true of c_3. Thus the first premise is true, because at each index the extensions of the appropriate pairs of concepts coincide. The second premise is also true at i_2, since c_4 is a "rising" concept at i_2 as it is diagrammed here. But the conclusion is false at i_2, since c_2 is not rising, on the natural interpretation of "rising."

PROBLEM A3. Write one or more additional meaning postulate(s) which render the argument (7.129) valid. Discuss the implications of the postulate(s) you have written.

These and other considerations suggest that a solution might be constructed similar to Montague's but with some improvements. In 'Home is Where the Heart Is,' (Thomason 1974b), Richmond Thomason proposed an analysis in which **the temperature** denotes an entity in D_e which is of a different logical "sort" than other entities – namely, a function taking numbers as values. The *IV* **be ninety** is then given a different analysis from *IV* phrases containing the "**be** of identity" (as in **The mayor is John**). In support of this approach, note that **The temperature is ninety** is paraphrasable as **The temperature stands at ninety**, etc., but other ordinary identity statements are not paraphrasable in this way. For interesting background on Montague's thought which led to this analysis and some alternatives, see Kaplan (1973a) and especially the appendices to Scott (1970).

For additional syntactic arguments that the verb **be** in **The temperature is ninety** is not the usual "**be** of identity", see Jackendoff (1979). Finally, the semantic apparatus used by Montague for the *temperature-is-ninety* puzzle is adapted by Heim (1979) in one possible analysis of the "concealed question" reading of *John knows the capital of Italy*, i.e. the reading paraphrasable as "John knows what the capital of Italy is."

NOTES

[1] For an extended analysis of various kinds of verbs whose truth conditions depend on the state of the world at more than one point in time (as Montague is suggesting here for **rise**), see Dowty (1979).

[2] Some consolation can be derived from the fact that **slowly**′ would be subject to Bennett's "subsective" meaning postulate (MP10, p. 234). By this postulate, **slowly**′(ˆ**walk**′)(ˆ*j*) entails **walk**′(ˆ*j*), and by MP7, this latter formula is logically equivalent to $\mathbf{walk}'_*(j)$. Hence the translation of **John walks slowly** entails an extensional first-order formula, but is not logically equivalent to any extensional first-order formula (while **John walks** *is* fully equivalent to an extensional first-order formula). We merely observe this fact, leaving it to the reader to decide whether this is an acceptable result or not, and similarly, whether it is acceptable that sentences with *IV*-adverbs that are *not* subject to MP10 do not even entail an extensional formula.

REFERENCES

Ajdukiewicz, Kazimierz, 'Die syntakische konnexität,' *Studia Philosophica* 1 (1935): 1–27; translated as 'Syntactic connexion,' *Polish Logic*, pp. 207–231, ed. by S. McCall, Oxford: Clarendon Press, 1967.

Akmajian, A. and Heny, F., *An Introduction to the Principles of Transformational Grammar*, Cambridge, Mass.: MIT Press, 1975.

Alston, W. P., 'Meaning,' *The Encyclopedia of Philosophy* Vol. 5, pp. 233–241, ed. by P. Edwards, New York: Macmillan, 1967.

Austin, J. L., *How to Do Things with Words*, New York: Oxford University Press, 1962.

Bach, Emmon, 'Nouns and noun phrases,' *Universals of Linguistic Theory*, pp. 91–122, ed. by E. Bach and R. T. Harms, New York: Holt, Rinehart and Winston, 1968.

Bach, Emmon, 'Montague grammar and classical transformational grammar,' *Linguistics, Philosophy, and Montague Grammar*, pp. 3–49, ed. by S. Davis and M. Mithun, Austin: University of Texas Press, 1979.

Bach, Emmon, 'Tenses and aspects as functions on verb phrases,' *Proceedings of the 1979 Stuttgart Conference on Tense and Aspect*, to appear.

Bach, Emmon and Cooper, Robin, 'The NP-S analysis of relative clauses and compositional semantics,' *Linguistics and Philosophy* 2 (1978): 145–150.

Bigelow, J. C., 'Semantics of thinking, saying and translation,' *Meaning and Translation: Philosophical and Linguistic Approaches*, ed. by M. Guenthner-Reutter and F. Guenthner, London: Duckworth, 1978a.

Bigelow, J. C., 'Believing in semantics,' *Linguistics and Philosophy* 2.1 (1978b): 101–145.

Baker, C. L., *Introduction to Generative-Transformational Syntax*, Englewood Cliffs: Prentice-Hall, 1978.

Bar-Hillel, Yehoshua, 'Indexical expressions,' *Mind* 63 (1954): 359–79.

Bar-Hillel, Y., Gaifman, C., and Shamir, E., 'On categorical and phrase-structure grammars,' *Bulletin of the Research Council of Israel* 3 (1960): 1–16; reprinted in *Language and Information*, pp. 99–115, ed. by Y. Bar-Hillel, Reading, Mass.: Addison-Wesley, 1964.

Bennett, Michael, *Some Extensions of a Montague Fragment*, UCLA Ph.D. Dissertation, 1974; reproduced by the Indiana University Linguistics Club, 1975.

Blumberg, Albert E., 'Logic, modern,' *The Encyclopedia of Philosophy* Vol. 5, pp. 12–34, ed. by P. Edwards, New York: Macmillan, 1967.

Bull, W. E., *Time, Tense, and the Verb*, Berkeley: University of California Press, 1960.

Burgess, John P., 'Logic and time,' *Journal of Symbolic Logic* 44 (1979): 566–582.

Carlson, Gregory N., *Reference to Kinds in English*, University of Massachusetts (Amherst) Ph.D. Dissertation, 1977.

Carnap, Rudoiph, *Meaning and Necessity*, Chicago: University of Chicago Press, 1947.

Chisholm, R., 'Identity through possible worlds: some questions,' *Noûs* 1 (1967): 1–18.

Chomsky, Noam, *Aspects of the Theory of Syntax*, Cambridge, Mass.: MIT Press, 1965.

Chomsky, Noam, 'Questions of the form and interpretation,' *Linguistic Analysis* 1 (1975): 75–109.

Chomsky, Noam, 'On binding,' *Linguistic Inquiry* 11 (1980): 1–46.

Church, Alonzo, 'A formulation of a simple theory of types,' *Journal of Symbolic Logic* 5 (1940): 56–68.

Church, Alonzo, 'A formulation of the logic of sense and denotation,' *Structure, Meaning and Method: Essays in Honor of Henry M. Sheffer*, pp. 3–24, ed. P. Henle, H. M. Kallen, and S. K. Langer, New York: Liberal Arts, 1951.

Church, Alonzo, *Introduction to Mathematical Logic*, Princeton: Princeton University Press, 1956.

Clifford, John E., *Tense and Tense Logic*, (*Janua Linguarum, Series Minor* 215), The Hague: Mouton, 1975.

Cocchiarella, N. B., *Tense and Modal Logic: A Study in the Typology of Temporal Reference*, UCLA Ph.D. Dissertation, 1965.

Cohn, P. M., *Universal Algebra*, New York: Harper and Row, 1965.

Cooper, Robin, *Montague's Semantic Theory and Transformational Syntax*, University of Massachusetts (Amherst) Ph.D. Dissertation, 1975.

Cooper, Robin, 'A fragment of English with questions and relative clauses,' unpublished ms, 1978.

Cooper, Robin, 'The interpretation of pronouns,' *Syntax and Semantics Vol. 10: Selections from the Third Groningen Round Table*, pp. 61–92, ed. by F. Heny and H. S. Schnelle, New York: Academic Press, 1979a.

Cooper, Robin, 'Variable binding and relative clauses,' *Formal Semantics and Pragmatics for Natural Languages*, pp. 131–169, ed. by F. Guenthner and S. J. Schmidt, Dordrecht: D. Reidel, 1979b.

Cooper, R., and Parsons, T., 'Montague grammar, generative semantics, and interpretive semantics,' *Montague Grammar*, pp. 311–362, ed. by B. H. Partee, New York: Academic Press, 1976.

Copi, I., and Gould, J., eds, *Contemporary Readings in Logical Theory*, New York: Macmillan, 1967.

Cresswell, M. J., *Logics and Languages*, London: Methuen and Co., 1973.

Cresswell, M. J., 'Hyperintensional logic,' *Studia Logica* 34 (1975): 261–292.

Cresswell, M. J., Review of *Formal Philosophy, Selected Papers of Richard Montague*, ed. with an introduction by Richmond Thomason, New Haven: Yale Univ. Press, 1976. *Philosophia* Vol. 6.1 (1976): 193–207.

Davidson, Donald, 'On saying that,' *Synthese* 19 (1968): 130–146.

Dixon, R. M. W., *The Djirbal Language of North Queensland*, Cambridge: Cambridge University Press, 1972.

Donnellan, Keith, 'Reference and definite descriptions,' *Philosophical Review* 75 (1966): 281–304.

Donnellan, Keith, 'Speaking of nothing,' *Philosophical Review* 83 (1974): 3–32.

Dowty, David R., *Word Meaning and Montague Grammar*, Dordrecht: D. Reidel, 1979.

Fillmore, Charles, *Lectures on Deixis* (Lectures delivered to the 1971 Santa Cruz Linguistics Institute); reproduced by the Indiana University Linguistics Club, 1975.

Fodor, Janet, *The Linguistic Description of Opaque Contexts*, MIT Ph.D. Dissertation, 1970; reproduced by the Indiana University Linguistics Club.

Fodor, Janet, 'Like-subject verbs and causal clauses in English,' *Journal of Linguistics* 10

(1974): 95–110.

Frege, Gottlob, 'Über Sinn und Bedeutung,' *Zeitschrift für Philosophie und philosophische Kritik* **100** (1893): 25–50; translated as 'On sense and reference,' *Translations from the Philosophical Writings of Gottlob Frege*, pp. 56–78, ed. by P. T. Geach and M. Black, Oxford: Basil Blackwell, 1952.

Gallin, Daniel, *Intentional and Higher-Order Modal Logic with Applications to Montague Semantics*, Amsterdam: North Holland, 1975.

Gazdar, Gerald, 'Unbounded dependencies and coordinate structure,' to appear in *Linguistic Inquiry*.

Geach, P. T., *Reference and Generality*, Ithaca: Cornell University Press, 1962.

Halvorsen, P.-K., and Ladusaw, W., 'Montague's "Universal Grammar": An introduction for the linguist,' *Linguistics and Philosophy* 3 (1979): 185–223.

Hankamer, Jorge, 'On the non-cyclic nature of WH-clefting,' *Chicago Linguistic Society* **10** (1974): 221–233.

Heim, Irene, 'Concealed Questions,' *Semantics from Different Points of View*, pp. 51–61, ed. by R. Bäuerle, U. Egli and A. von Stechow, Berlin: Springer-Verlag, 1979.

Henkin, Leon, 'Completeness in the theory of types,' *Journal of Symbolic Logic* **15** (1950): 81–91.

Henkin, Leon, 'Systems, formal, and models of formal systems,' *The Encyclopedia of Philosophy*, Vol. 8, pp. 61–74, ed. by P. Edwards New York: Macmillan, 1967.

Hermes, H., *Enumerability, Decidability, Computability*, Berlin: Springer Verlag, 1965.

Hintikka, Jaakko, 'Individuals, possible worlds, and epistemic logic,' *Nous* **1** (1967): 33–62.

Hughes, G. E., and Cresswell, M. J., *An Introduction to Modal Logic*, London: Methuen and Co., 1968.

Jackendoff, Ray, *Semantic Interpretation in Generative Grammar*, Cambridge, Mass.: MIT Press, 1972.

Jackendoff, Ray, 'How to keep ninety from rising,' *Linguistic Inquiry* **10.1** (1979); 172–176.

Johnson-Laird, Phillip N., *Formal Semantics and the Psychology of Meaning*, to be published in U. of Texas Sloan Foundation Conference Proceedings, to appear.

Kamp, J. A. W., 'Two theories about adjectives,' *Formal Semantics of Natural Language*, pp. 123–55, ed. by E. L. Keenan, Cambridge: Cambridge University Press, 1975.

Kaplan, David, *Foundations of Intensional Logic,* UCLA Ph.D. Dissertation, 1964.

Kaplan, David, 'What is Russell's theory of descriptions?,' *Physics, Logic and History*, pp. 277–288, ed. by W. Yourgrau and A. D. Black, New York: Plenum Press, 1970.

Kaplan, David, *The Logic of Demonstratives*, lecture presented at the University of California, Irvine, 1971.

Kaplan, David, 'Bob and Carol and Ted and Alice,' *Approaches to Natural Language: Proceedings of the 1970 Stanford Workshop on Grammar and Semantics*, pp. 490–518, ed. by J. Hintikka, J. M. E. Moravcsik, and P. Suppes, Dordrecht: D. Reidel, 1973.

Kaplan, David, 'Demonstratives: an essay on the semantics, logic, metaphysics and epistemology of demonstratives and other indexicals,' "Draft No. 2", manuscript, UCLA, 1977.

Karttunen, Lauri, *What Do Referential Indices Refer To?*, Santa Monica: The Rand Corporation (publication No. P-3554), 1968.

Karttunen, Lauri, 'Possible and must,' *Syntax and Semantics Vol. 1*, pp. 1–20, ed. by J. P. Kimball, New York: Seminar Press, 1972.

Karttunen, L., and Peters, S., 'Conventional implicature in Montague grammar,' *BLS* 1: *Proceedings of the First Annual Meeting of the Berkeley Linguistic Society*, 266–278.

Karttunen, L. and Peters, S., 'Conventional implicature', *Syntax and Semantics, Vol 11*, pp. 1–56, ed. by C.-K. Oh and D. Dinneen, New York: Academic Press, 1979.

Katz, Jerrold, *Semantic Theory*, New York: Harper and Row, 1972.

Katz, J., and Fodor, J. A., 'The structure of a semantic theory,' *Language* 39 (1963): 170–210; reprinted in *The Structure of Language* pp. 479–518, ed. by J. A. Fodor and J. Katz, Englewood Cliffs: Prentice-Hall, 1964.

Katz, J. and Postal, P., *An Integrated Theory of Linguistic Descriptions*, Cambridge, Mass.: MIT Press, 1965.

Kripke, Saul, 'A completeness theorem in modal logic,' *Journal of Symbolic Logic* 24 (1959): 1–14.

Kripke, Saul, 'Semantical considerations on modal logic,' *Acta Philosophica Fennica* 16 (1963): 83–89.

Kripke, Saul, 'Naming and necessity,' *Semantics of Natural Language*, pp. 253–355, ed. by D. Davidson and G. Harman, Dordrecht: D. Reidel, 1972.

Lakoff, George, 'Repartee,' *Foundations of Language* 6 (1970): 389–422.

Lakoff, George, 'Linguistics and natural logic,' *Semantics for Natural Language*, pp. 545–665, ed. by D. Davidson and G. Harman, Dordrecht: D. Reidel, 1972.

Lewis, David, 'Counterpart theory and quantified modal logic,' *Journal of Philosophy* 65 (1968): 113–126.

Lewis, David, 'General semantics,' *Synthese* 22 (1970): 18–67; reprinted in *Semantics for Natural Language*, pp. 169–218, ed. by D. Davidson and G. Harman, Dordrecht: D. Reidel, 1970.

Linsky, L., 'Believing and necessity,' *Proceedings and Addresses of the American Philosophical Association* 50 (1977): 526–530.

McCawley, James, 'Where do noun phrases come from?,' *Readings in English Transformational Grammar*, pp. 166–183, ed. by R. Jacobs and P. Rosenbaum, Waltham, Mass.: Ginn & Co., 1970.

McCawley, James, 'Syntactic and logical arguments for semantic structures,' *Three Dimensions in Linguistic Theory*, pp. 259–376, ed. by O. Fujimura, Tokyo: The TEC Corporation, 1973.

Mates, Benson, 'Descriptions and reference,' *Foundations of Language* 10 (1973): 409–418.

Montague, Richard, 'On the nature of certain philosophical entities,' *The Monist* 53 (1960): 159–194; reprinted in *Formal Philosophy: Selected Papers of Richard Montague*, pp. 148–187, ed. by R. H. Thomason, New Haven: Yale University Press, 1974. (ref. as 1960.)

Montague, Richard, 'Pragmatics,' *Contemporary Philosophy: A Survey*, pp. 102–122, ed. by R. Klibansky, Florence: La Nuova Italia Editrice, 1968; reprinted in *Formal Philosophy: Selected Papers of Richard Montague*, pp. 95–118, ed. by R. H. Thomason, New Haven: Yale University Press, 1974. (ref. as 1968.)

Montague, Richard, 'Pragmatics and intensional logic,' *Synthese* 22 (1970a): 68–94; reprinted in *Formal Philosophy: Selected Papers of Richard Montague*, pp. 119–147, ed. by R. H. Thomason, New Haven: Yale University Press, 1974. (ref. as 1970a.)

Montague, Richard, 'English as a formal language,' *Linguaggi nella e nella Tecnica*, pp. 189–224, ed. by B. Visentini, et al., Milan: Edizioni di Comunità, 1970b; reprinted in *Formal Philosophy: Selected Papers of Richard Montague*, pp. 108–221, ed. by R. H. Thomason, New Haven: Yale University Press, 1974. (ref. as 1970b.)

Montague, Richard, 'Universal grammar,' *Theoria* **36** (1970c): 373–98; reprinted in *Formal Philosophy: Selected Papers of Richard Montague*, pp. 222–246, ed. by R. H. Thomason, New Haven: Yale University Press, 1974. (ref. as 1970c).

Parsons, Terrence, 'A semantics for English,' ms., 1970.

Partee Barbara H., 'Negation, conjunction, and quantifiers: syntax vs. semantics,' *Foundations of Language* 6 (1970a): 153–165.

Partee, Barbara H., 'Opacity, coreference, and pronouns,' *Synthese* **21** (1970b): 359–385; reprinted in *Semantics of Natural Language*, pp. 415–441, ed. by D. Davidson and G. Harman, Dordrecht: D. Reidel, 1972. (ref. as 1970b).

Partee, Barbara H., 'Comments on Montague's paper,' *Approaches to Natural Language: Proceedings from the 1970 Stanford Workshop on Grammar and Semantics*, pp. 243–258, ed. by J. Hintikka, J. M. E. Moravcsik, and P. Suppes, Dordrecht: D. Reidel, 1973a.

Partee, Barbara H., 'The syntax and semantics of quotation,' *A Festschrift for Morris Halle*, ed. by S. R. Anderson and P. Kiparsky, New York: Holt, Rinehart and Winston, 1973b.

Partee, Barbara H., 'Opacity and scope,' *Semantics and Philosophy* pp. 81–102, ed. by M. K. Munitz and P. K. Unger, New York: New York University Press, 1974.

Partee, Barbara H., 'Montague grammar and transformational Grammar,' *Linguistic Inquiry* 6 (1975a): 203–300.

Partee, Barbara H., 'Deletion and variable binding,' *Formal Semantics of Natural Language*, pp. 16–33, ed. by E. L. Keenan, Cambridge: Cambridge University Press, 1975b.

Partee, Barbara H., 'Montague grammar and the well-formedness constraint,' *Syntax and Semantics Vol. 10: Selections from the Third Groningen Round Table*, pp. 275–313, ed. by F. Heny and H. Schnelle, New York: Academic Press, 1979a.

Partee, Barbara H., 'Constraining transformational Montague grammar: A framework and a fragment,' *Linguistics, Philosophy, and Montague Grammar*, pp. 51–102, ed. by S. Davis and M. Mithun, Austin: University of Texas Press, 1979b.

Partee, Barbara H., 'Semantics–mathematics or psychology?,' *Semantics from Different Points of View: Proceedings of the Konstanz Colloquium on Semantics*, pp. 1–14, ed. by R. Bauerle, et al., Berlin: Springer-Verlag, 1979c.

Partee, Barbara H., 'Montague Grammar, mental representation and reality,' *Proceedings of the Symposium 'Philosophy and Grammar' at Uppsala University*, ed. by S. Kanger and S. Ohman, 1979d.

Partee, Barbara H., 'Belief and the limits of semantics,' to be published in U. of Texas Sloan Foundation Conference Proceedings, forthcoming.

Pinkham, J. and Hankamer, J., 'Deep and shallow clefts,' *Chicago Linguistic Society* **11** (1975): 429–450.

Postal, Paul, 'On coreferential complement subject deletion,' *Linguistic Inquiry* **1.4** (1970), 439–500.

Postal, Paul, *Cross-Over Phenomena*, New York: Holt, Rinehart, and Winston, 1971.

Prior, A. N., *Past, Present, and Future*, Oxford: Oxford University Press, 1967.

Purtill, R. L., 'About identity through possible worlds,' *Noûs* 2 (1968), 87–89.

Putnam, Hilary, 'The meaning of "meaning",' *Language, Mind, and Knowledge*, ed. by K. Gunderson, Minnesota Studies in the Philosophy of Science VII, Minneapolis: University of Minnesota Press, 1973.

Quine, Willard V. O., 'Notes on existence and necessity,' *Journal of Philosophy* 40 (1943): 113–27.

Quine, Willard V. O., 'The problem of interpreting modal logic,' *Journal of Symbolic Logic* 12 (1947): 43–48.

Quine, Willard V. O., *Mathematical Logic*, Cambridge, Mass.: Harvard University Press, 1951.

Quine, Willard V. O., 'Reference and modality,' *From a Logical Point of View*, pp. 139–159, New York: Harper and Row, 1953.

Quine, Willard V. O., *Word and Object*, Cambridge, Mass.: MIT Press, 1960.

Rodman, Robert, 'Scope phenomena, "movement transformations", and Montague grammar,' *Montague Grammar*, pp. 165–176, ed. by B. H. Partee, New York: Academic Press, 1976.

Rosenbaum, Peter, *The Grammar of English Predicate Complement Constructions*, Cambridge, Mass.: MIT Press, 1967.

Ross, J. R., *Constraints on Variables in Syntax*, MIT Ph.D. Dissertation, 1967.

Russell, Bertrand, 'On denoting,' *Mind* 14 (1905): 479–493; reprinted in *Contemporary Readings in Logical Theory*, pp. 93–105, ed. by I. Copi and J. Gould, New York: Macmillan, 1967.

Schwartz, Stephen, *Naming, Necessity and Natural Kinds*, Ithaca: Cornell University Press, 1977.

Scott, Dana, 'Advice on modal logic,' *Philosophical Problems in Logic*, pp. 143–174, ed. by K. Lambert, Dordrecht: D. Reidel, 1970.

Strawson, Peter, 'On referring,' *Mind* 59 (1950): 320–344; reprinted in *New Readings in Philosophical Analysis*, pp. 35–50, ed. by H. Feigl, W. Sellars, and K. Lehrer, New York: Appleton-Century-Crofts, 1972.

Tarski, Alfred, 'Der Wahrheitsbegriff in den Formalisierten Sprachen,' *Studia Philosophica* 1 (1935): 261–405; translated as 'The concept of truth in formalized languages,' *Logic, Semantics, and Mathematics*, pp. 152–278, ed. by A. Tarski, Oxford: Clarendon Press.

Tarski, Alfred, 'The semantic conception of truth,' *Philosophy and Phenomenological Research* 4 (1944): 341–375; reprinted in *Semantics and the Philosophy of Language*, pp. 13–47, ed. by L. Linsky, Urbana: University of Illinois Press.

Thomason, Richmond H., 'Introduction,' *Formal Philosophy: Selected Papers by Richard Montague*, pp. 1–69, ed. by R. H. Thomason, New Haven: Yale University Press, 1974a.

Thomason, Richmond H., 'Home is where the heart is,' ms., Pittsburgh: University of Pittsburgh, 1974b.

Thomason, Richmond H., 'Some extensions of Montague grammar,' *Montague Grammar*, pp. 77–117, ed. by B. H. Partee, New York: Academic Press, 1976.

Thomason, Richmond H., 'Indirect discourse is not quotational,' *The Monist* 60 (1977): 340–354.

Thomason, R. H., and Stalnaker, R. C., 'Modality and reference,' *Noûs* 2 (1968): 359–

372.

Thomason, R. H., and Stalnaker, R. C., 'A semantic theory of adverbs,' *Linguistic Inquiry* 4 (1973): 195–220.

Van Fraassen, Bas C., *Formal Semantics and Logic*, New York: Macmillan, 1971.

Wall, Robert, *Introduction to Mathematical Linguistics*, Englewood Cliffs: Prentice-Hall, 1972.

Wasow, Thomas, 'Anaphoric pronouns and bound variables,' *Language* 51 (1975): 368–383.

ANSWERS TO SELECTED PROBLEMS AND EXERCISES

CHAPTER 2

Problems

(2-1): m^n (There are m ways of assigning an individual to the first name, m ways for the second name, etc.)

(2-3): Trees for sentence 4:

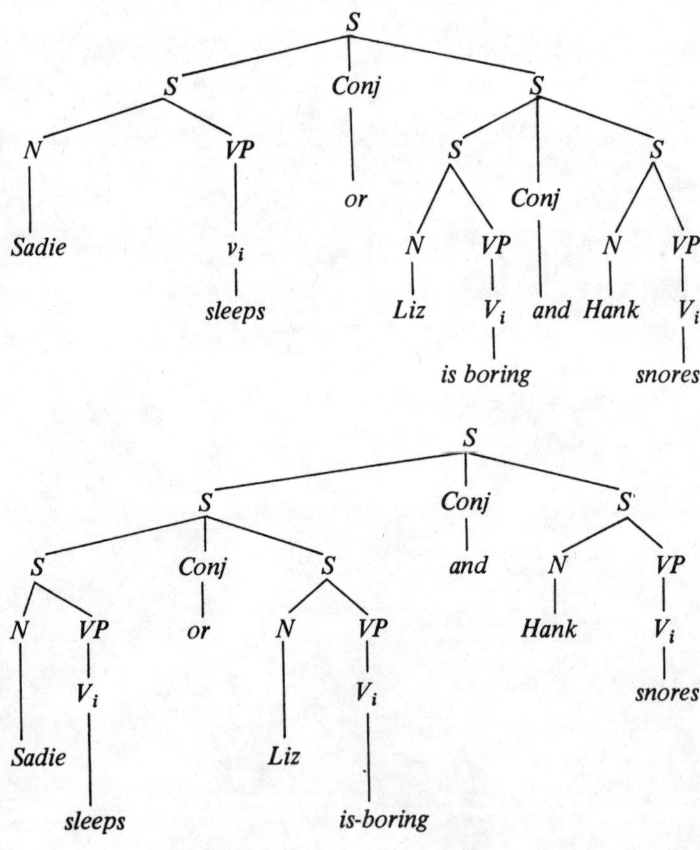

(2-4): No.

(2-5): 2^n (The number of functions in $\{0, 1\}^A$ equals the number of sets in the power set of A.)

(2-6): $[\![$*Hank sleeps*$]\!] = 0$; $[\![$*Liz is-boring*$]\!] = 1$.

(2-7): 512 ($= 2^9$). There are 2^3 distinct functions from A to $\{0, 1\}$, thus $(2^3)^3$ ways of assigning one of these functions to each of 3 individuals. For n individuals, $(2^n)^n = 2^{n^2}$

(2-9): $[\![$*if-and-only-if*$]\!]$ maps $\langle 1, 1\rangle$ and $\langle 0, 0\rangle$ into 1 and the others into 0; $[\![$*only-if*$]\!]$ maps $\langle 1, 0\rangle$ into 0 and the others into 1. Rule (2-35) suffices for these new conjunctions.

(2-10): Let *and* and *or* be basic expressions of category *Conj, Sadie, Liz,* and *Hank* basic expressions of category *N*, etc. Syntactic rules:

1. If α is a V_t and β is an N, then $\alpha\beta$ is a VP.
2. If α is a V_i, then α is a VP.
3. If α is an N and β is a VP, then $\alpha\beta$ is an S.
   etc.

(2-11): Take $[_{Conj}$ *and* $_{Conj}]$ and $[_{Conj}$ *or* $_{Conj}]$ as basic expressions of category *Conj*, $[_N$*Sadie* $_N]$, etc. as basic expressions of category *N*, and so on. The syntactic rules will be of the following form:

1. If α is a V_t and β is an N, then $[_{VP}\alpha\beta\,_{VP}]$ is a VP.

(2-13): h_R (Switzerland) $= \{\langle\text{red}, 1\rangle, \langle\text{white}, 1\rangle, \langle\text{blue}, 0\rangle\}$

(2-15): $\{0\}$. If α is Neg and ϕ is S and if ψ is S, with daughters α and ϕ (△ under Neg and under S), then $[\![\psi]\!]$ is 1 iff $[\![\phi]\!] \in [\![\alpha]\!]$, and is 0 otherwise.

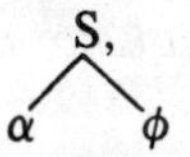

(2-17): $R = \{\langle$Anwar Sadat, Queen Elizabeth II$\rangle$, $\langle$Henry Kissinger, Queen Elizabeth II$\rangle$, $\langle$Queen Elizabeth II, Henry Kissinger$\rangle\}$

(2-18):

$$[\![and]\!] = \begin{bmatrix} 1 \rightarrow \begin{bmatrix} 1 \rightarrow 1 \\ 0 \rightarrow 0 \end{bmatrix} \\ 0 \rightarrow \begin{bmatrix} 1 \rightarrow 0 \\ 0 \rightarrow 0 \end{bmatrix} \end{bmatrix} \qquad [\![or]\!] = \begin{bmatrix} 1 \rightarrow \begin{bmatrix} 1 \rightarrow 1 \\ 0 \rightarrow 1 \end{bmatrix} \\ 0 \rightarrow \begin{bmatrix} 1 \rightarrow 1 \\ 0 \rightarrow 0 \end{bmatrix} \end{bmatrix}$$

If α is Conj, ϕ is S, ψ is S, and if ω is S, with daughters ϕ, α, ψ (△ under Conj, S, S), then $[\![\omega]\!]$ is $[[\![\alpha]\!]([\![\phi]\!])]([\![\psi]\!])$.

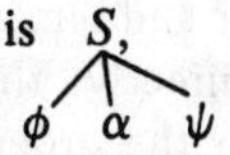

(2-20): Let "(" be a basic expression of category *LP*, ")" a basic expressions of category *RP*, etc. Let the semantic value of each be the function which maps 1 into 1 and 0 into 0. The syntactic rules and semantic rules can be reformulated along the following lines:

1. If δ is a one-place predicate, α is a name, β is an *LP*, and γ is a *RP*, then $\delta\beta\alpha\gamma$ is a sentence.
1. If δ is a one-place predicate, α is a name, β is an *LP*, and γ is a *RP*, then $[\![\delta\beta\alpha\gamma]\!] = [\![\gamma]\!]([\![\beta]\!]([\![\delta]\!]([\![\alpha]\!])))$

(2-21): Let $\wedge$, $\vee$, $\rightarrow$, and $\leftrightarrow$ be basic expressions of category *Con*(*nective*). Replace syntactic rules 4–7 by the following:

4. If ϕ is a sentence and α is a *Con*, then $\phi\alpha$ is a sentence operator.
5. If ϕ is a sentence and μ is a sentence operator, then $[\mu\phi]$ is a sentence.

(If $\neg$ were assigned as a basic expression of category sentence operator, the new rule 5 would produce $[\neg\phi]$ rather than the original $\neg\phi$ without brackets.)

Then let each *Con* be assigned a semantic value in $\left(\{0,1\}^{\{0,1\}}\right)^{\{0,1\}}$ appropriate to its truth table. The new semantic rules then become rules of functional application.

(2-23): (1) valid: *Hank snores or it-is-not-the-case-that Hank snores*; (2) true but not valid: *Liz snores*; (3) contradictory: *Hank snores and it-is-not-the-case-that Hank snores*: (4) false but not contradictory: *Hank snores*; (5) logically equivalent: *Liz sleeps and Hank snores, Hank snores and Liz sleeps*; (6) logical consequence: $\phi =$ *Liz snores* is a logical consequence of $\Gamma = \{$*Liz snores or it-is-not-the-case that Hank sleeps, Hank sleeps*$\}$.

Exercises

1. Appropriate semantic values for *Adv*'s would be functions from VP values to VP values, i.e., functions from $\{0,1\}^A$ to $\{0,1\}^A$. The corresponding semantic rule would be functional application. Sentence-adverbs would have semantic values mapping a truth value into a truth value, and there are only four such functions.

3. One need only substitute the Polish versions of formulas for their standard versions in the syntactic and semantic rules for L_0. If the connectives are assigned semantic values directly, the semantic rules become rules of functional application in which the order of function and arguments corresponds exactly to the order of the corresponding elements in the syntax.

5. Let $p, q, r, \ldots$ be basic expressions of the category sentence. Drop rules 1 and 2 from (2-2), keeping the rest as they are, and correspondingly for the semantic rules.

CHAPTER 3

Problems

(3-1): By semantic rule 8, $[\![\forall y B(x)]\!]^{M,g} = 1$ iff for every value assignment g' like g except possibly for the value assigned to y, $[\![B(x)]\!]^{M,g'} = 1$. But since $B(x)$ contains no occurrences of y, changing the value assigned to y will have no effect on the truth values of $B(x)$.

(3-4): For all M and g, $[\![[B(x) \leftrightarrow B(x)]]\!]^{M,g} = 1$ since identical expressions appear on each side of the biconditional. Thus, for all g' like g except possibly in the value assigned to x, $[\![[B(x) \leftrightarrow B(x)]]\!]^{M,g'} = 1$, and so $[\![\forall x [B(x) \leftrightarrow B(x)]]\!]^{M,g} = 1$. Since this is so for all models M, the formula is valid.

For $\exists x [M(x) \rightarrow \forall y M(y)]$, consider two cases. Case 1: $[\![\forall y M(y)]\!]^{M,g} = 1$, i.e., $F(M) = A$. Then $[\![[M(x) \rightarrow \forall y M(y)]]\!]^{M,g}$ will be true at all g since the consequent of the conditional is true. Therefore, $\exists x [M(x) \rightarrow \forall y M(y)]$ will be true with respect to model M. Case 2: $F(M) \neq$ A. Then $[\![[M(x) \rightarrow \forall y M(y)]]\!]^{M,g}$ will be true for at least one g, namely, one which assigns to x a value not in $F(M)$. Both antecedent and consequent of the conditional are false in such a case, and thus the conditional is true. Since every model is an instance of either Case 1 or Case 2, the formula is valid.

(3-5): (a) 0; (b) 1; (c) 1; (d) 0; (e) 1. In the given model none differs in truth value according to the order in which variables are quantified, but sentence (e) could do so in a different model.

Exercises

2. If the condition were dropped, we could for example apply syntactic rule B7 to the *CN fish*, the variable v_1, and the formula *Hank snores* to produce *Hank snores*. (Since there is no occurrence of v_1 in *Hank snores*, its (vacuous) replacement by *the fish* leaves the formula unchanged.) By semantic rule B7, however, assuming that the condition in question is dropped, *Hank snores* would in this case be assigned the value 0 because $[\![\textit{fish}]\!]^{M,g} = 0$. Thus, *Hank snores*, and for that matter every formula in L_{1E}, would have an infinite number of non-equivalent derivations, and the truth values of the results would be made to depend on all sorts of irrelevant matters – in the case at hand, the existence or non-existence of fish in the model.

4. Syntactic Rule: If α is a *N*, u is a variable *and* ϕ is a *For*, then ϕ' is a *For*, where ϕ' comes from ϕ by replacing the left-most occurrence of u by α and replacing all other occurrences of u by *that person*. Semantic rule: If α is

a *N*, *u* is a variable and ϕ is a *For*, then for ϕ' as in the new syntactic rule, $[\![\phi']\!]^{M,g} = 1$ iff $[\![\phi]\!]^{M,g'} = 1$, where g' is the value assignment exactly like g except that $g'(u) = [\![\alpha]\!]^{M,g}$. (Note that we do not need to add here the restricting clause "ϕ is a *For* containing at least one occurrence of u" to avoid the undesirable result that is the subject of the previous problem.) (Cf., the treatment in 'English as a Formal Language', (Montague, 1970b)).

5. Consider a model M in which *Every man loves every man* is true. Then $[\![v_1 \textit{ loves } v_2]\!]^{M,g} = 1$ for every g assigning a man to v_1 and a man to v_2. In such a model, v_1 *loves* v_1 is true for the same value assignments; therefore, *Every man loves that man* will be true. Thus, every model in which the former sentence is true is one in which the latter sentence is true, so the former logically entails the latter.

CHAPTER 4

Problems

(4-2): Syntactic rule C2 would produce $\wedge(B(j))$, for example, as a meaningful expression of type $\langle t, t\rangle$ and $\wedge(B(j))(M(d))$ as a meaningful expression of type t. The semantic rules would assign the latter formula the same denotation as $[B(j) \wedge M(d)]$, logical connectives would be treated both like their counterparts in Polish notation and in the standard way by rules 3–7.

(4-3): (i) For every predicate δ of which the predicate of predicates denoted by $c_{0,\langle\langle e,t\rangle,t\rangle}$ is true, there is some individual of whom δ is true. Alternatively, every set of individuals in the set of sets of individuals denoted by $c_{0,\langle\langle e,t\rangle,t\rangle}$ is non-empty.

(iii) There is exactly one individual who belongs to all and only those sets which are members of the set denoted by $c_{0,\langle\langle e,t\rangle,t\rangle}$.

(4-4): Four. Let the two individuals in the model be *a* and *b*. Then,

$$h = \begin{bmatrix} \begin{bmatrix} a \to 1 \\ b \to 1 \end{bmatrix} \to \begin{bmatrix} a \to 0 \\ b \to 0 \end{bmatrix} \\ \begin{bmatrix} a \to 1 \\ b \to 0 \end{bmatrix} \to \begin{bmatrix} a \to 0 \\ b \to 1 \end{bmatrix} \\ \begin{bmatrix} a \to 0 \\ b \to 1 \end{bmatrix} \to \begin{bmatrix} a \to 1 \\ b \to 0 \end{bmatrix} \\ \begin{bmatrix} a \to 0 \\ b \to 0 \end{bmatrix} \to \begin{bmatrix} a \to 1 \\ b \to 1 \end{bmatrix} \end{bmatrix}$$

(4-5): $[\![Q]\!]^{M,g}$ is that function h from $D_{\langle e,\langle e,t\rangle\rangle}$ into $D_{\langle e,\langle e,t\rangle\rangle}$ such that for any k in $D_{\langle e,\langle e,t\rangle\rangle}$ and any individuals e_1 and e_2 in A, $[h(k)](e_1)(e_2) = 1$ iff $k(e_1)(e_2) = 0$ and $[h(k)](e_1)(e_2) = 0$ iff $k(e_1)(e_2) = 1$.

(4-6): $512 (= (2^3)^3)$. $[\![R_o(K)]\!] = \{a, b\}$; $[\![R_o(L)]\!] = \{a, b, c\}$; $[\![R_s(K)]\!] = \{a, b, c\}$; $[\![R_s(L)]\!] = \{a, c\}$ (or technically, the characteristic functions of these sets). $[\![[R_o(K)](j)]\!] = 1$; $[\![[R_s(L)](m)]\!] = 1$.

(4-7): $[\![R_r]\!]^{M,g}$ is that function h from $D_{\langle e,\langle e,t\rangle\rangle}$ into $D_{\langle e,t\rangle}$ such that for all functions k in $D_{\langle e,\langle e,t\rangle\rangle}$ and for all individuals e in A, $[h(k)](e) = 1$ iff $k(e)(e) = 1$.

(4-8): $[2(5) + 3 = 13]$, true; $[2(5) + 3y = 15]$, not yet true or false, pending assignment of a value to y; $[4(7)^2 + -2(7) + 5 = 140]$, false; $\forall y[y < 7 \rightarrow 11 > (2y - 11)]$, true.

(4-10): (i) the function mapping each person into his or her height on April 2, 1980; (ii) the function mapping each day into Mickey Mantle's height on that day; (iii) same as (ii); (iv) not well formed; (v) same as (i); (vi) the function which maps each person into a function which for each day gives the height of that person on that day; (vii) the function which maps each day into a function which for each person gives the height of that person on that day.

(4-11): the function which maps each function from integers into integers into the value obtained when that function is applied at the argument 2 and then 1 is added to the result (for example, for the function which maps every integer into its cube, $\lambda f[f(2) + 1]$ assigns that function the value 9).

(4-12): Let $Q = v_{0,\langle e,\langle e,t\rangle\rangle}$. By the definition of R_o, $\forall x \forall Q[R_o(Q)(x) \leftrightarrow \exists y\, Q(y)(x)]$. Thus, $\forall Q[\lambda x R_o(Q)(x) = \lambda x \exists y\, Q(y)(x)]$, which is equivalent to $\forall Q[R_o(Q) = \lambda x \exists y\, Q(y)(x)]$, since $\lambda x R_o(Q)(x)$ is equivalent to $R_o(Q)$. Hence, $\lambda Q R_o(Q) = \lambda Q[\lambda x \exists y\, Q(y)(x)]$, that is, $R_o = \lambda Q[\lambda x \exists y\, Q(y)(x)]$. Then, for example, $R_o(L) = \lambda Q[\lambda x \exists y\, Q(y)(x)]\,(L) =$ (by lambda conversion) $\lambda x \exists y\, L(y)(x)$. This is a function which maps an individual x into 1 just in case there is some individual y such that $L(x, y)$, as desired.

(4-13): Again let $Q = v_{0,\langle e,\langle e,t\rangle\rangle}$.

$$R_s = \lambda Q[\lambda x \exists y\, Q(x)(y)]\,;\ R_r = \lambda Q[\lambda x\, Q(x)(x)].$$

Exercises

1. Note that P is here a variable of type $\langle e, t\rangle$. For concreteness, assume $g(x) = c$ and $g(P) = \{\langle a, 1\rangle, \langle b, 0\rangle, \langle c, 0\rangle\}$. Then $[\![P(x)]\!]^{M,g} = 0$ and $[\![M(x)]\!]^{M,g} = 1$, hence $[\![[M(x) \rightarrow P(x)]]\!]^{M,g} = 0$. Then $[\![\forall x[M(x) \rightarrow P(x)]]\!]^{M,g} = 0$ since $[M(x) \rightarrow P(x)]$ is false with respect to M, g. Now, $[\![\lambda P \forall x[M(x) \rightarrow P(x)]]\!]^{M,g}$

is that function h which maps members of $D_{\langle e,t\rangle}$ into $\{0, 1\}$ in such a way that for any $k \in D_{\langle e,t\rangle}$, $h(k) = 1$ iff $[\![\forall x [M(x) \rightarrow P(x)]]\!]^{M,g'} = 1$ when $g'(P) = k$. Specifically, when $k = \{\langle a, 1\rangle, \langle b, 1\rangle, \langle c, 1\rangle\}$, $h(k) = 1$, and for all other values of k, $h(k) = 0$. Thus, $[\![\lambda P \forall x [M(x) \rightarrow P(x)](B)]\!]^{M,g} = 0$, because $[\![B]\!]^{M,g}$ is $\{\langle a, 1\rangle, \langle b, 1\rangle, \langle c, 0\rangle\}$. Further, we see that $[\![\forall x [M(x) \rightarrow B(x)]]\!]^{M,g} = 0$, since $[M(x) \rightarrow B(x)]$ is false when $g'(x) = c$.

2. We must distinguish between the category of common nouns and the category of attributive adjectives while letting both be meaningful expressions of type $\langle e, t\rangle$. The syntactic rule will concatenate the two in the order adjective + noun. (If there were also multi-word attributive adjective phrases in the fragment, we would want the rule to concatenate the two in the opposite order.) Semantic rule: If α is an attributive adjective and β is a common noun, then $[\![\alpha\beta]\!]^{M,g}$ is that function h from individuals to truth values such that for any individual e in A, $h(e) = 1$ iff $[\![\alpha]\!]^{M,g}(e) = 1$ and $[\![\beta]\!]^{M,g}(e) = 1$, and $h(e) = 0$ otherwise. Alternatively, we could simply say $[\![\alpha\beta]\!]^{M,g} = [\![\lambda x [\alpha(x) \wedge \beta(x)]]\!]^{M,g}$.

5. (a)

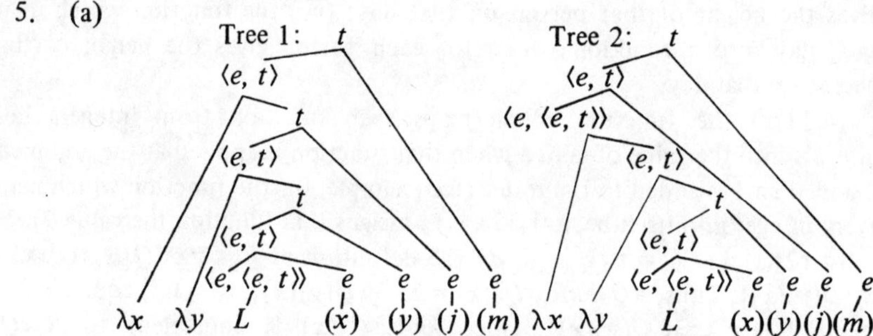

(b) The expression construed as in Tree 1 reduces to $L(m)(j)$; construed as in Tree 2 it reduces to $L(j)(m)$.

(c) The bracketed expression corresponding to Tree 1 would be $\lambda x [\lambda y [L(x)(y)](j)](m)$; that corresponding to Tree 2 would be $\lambda x [\lambda y [L(x)(y)]](j)(m)$.

CHAPTER 5

Problems

(5-1): 1 (at t_1); 1 (at t_2); 0 (at t_3).

(5-2): 0 (at t_1); 1 (at t_2); 1 (at t_3).

(5-3): Suppose $[\![\mathbf{FP}\phi]\!]^{M,i,g} = 1$ for some M, $\mathbf{i}$, and g. Then for some $\mathbf{i}'$ such that $\mathbf{i} < \mathbf{i}'$, $[\![\mathbf{P}\phi]\!]^{\mathbf{M},\mathbf{i}',g} = 1$. Hence, for some $\mathbf{i}''$ such that $\mathbf{i}'' < \mathbf{i}'$, $[\![\phi]\!]^{\mathbf{M},\mathbf{i}'',g} = 1$. But $\mathbf{i} < \mathbf{i}'' \vee \mathbf{i}'' = \mathbf{i} \vee \mathbf{i}'' < \mathbf{i}$, so $[\![\mathbf{F}\phi]\!]^{\mathbf{M},\mathbf{i},g} = 1 \vee [\![\phi]\!]^{\mathbf{M},\mathbf{i},g} = 1 \vee [\![\mathbf{P}\phi]\!]^{\mathbf{M},\mathbf{i},g} = 1$. That is, $[\![\mathbf{F}\phi \vee \phi \vee \mathbf{P}\phi]\!]^{\mathbf{M},\mathbf{i},g} = 1$. This result is independent of the choice of M, $\mathbf{i}$, and g, so the conditional is valid.

(5-4): Let M be a model containing just two times, t_1 and t_2. Suppose $t_1 < t_2$ and ϕ is true at t_2. Then $\mathbf{F}\phi$ is true at t_1, but $\mathbf{FF}\phi$ is false at t_1 since $\mathbf{F}\phi$ is false at t_2. The formula is valid in all models in which time is dense, i.e., for all t_1 and t_2 such that $t_1 < t_2$, there is a t_3 such that $t_1 < t_3 < t_2$.

(5-5): (ii) Suppose the antecedent is true for some M, $\mathbf{i}$, g, i.e., $[\![\mathbf{P}\forall u\phi]\!]^{\mathbf{M},\mathbf{i},g} = 1$. Then for some $\mathbf{i}' < \mathbf{i}$, $[\![\forall u\phi]\!]^{\mathbf{M},\mathbf{i}',g} = 1$. Hence, for that $\mathbf{i}'$, $[\![\phi]\!]^{\mathbf{M},\mathbf{i}',g^x_u} = 1$ for all $x \in A$. Suppose now the consequent is false, i.e., $[\![\forall u\mathbf{P}\phi]\!]^{\mathbf{M},\mathbf{i},g} = 0$. Then for some $a \in A$, $[\![\mathbf{P}\phi]\!]^{\mathbf{M},\mathbf{i},g^a_u} = 0$. Hence, there is no $\mathbf{i}'' < \mathbf{i}$ such that $[\![\phi]\!]^{\mathbf{M},\mathbf{i}'',g^a_u} = 1$. But this contradicts the antecedent, which guarantees the existence of just such a time, namely, $\mathbf{i}'$, such that $[\![\phi]\!]^{\mathbf{M},\mathbf{i}',g^x_u} = 1$, for all $x \in A$ (and in particular for $a \in A$.).

(5-6): (ii) Let $M = \langle A, I, <, F\rangle$, where $A = \{a, b\}$, $I = \{t_1, t_2, t_3\}$, $< = \{\langle t_1, t_2\rangle, \langle t_2, t_3\rangle, \langle t_1, t_3\rangle\}$. Let $F(t_1, B) = \{a\}$; $F(t_2, B) = \{b\}$; and $F(t_3, B) = \{a, b\}$. Then $[\![\forall u\mathbf{P}B(u)]\!]^{\mathbf{M},t_3,g} = 1$ but $[\![\mathbf{P}\,\forall uB(u)]\!]^{\mathbf{M},t_3,g} = 0$.

(5-7): $\mathbf{H}\phi = \neg\mathbf{P}\neg\phi$ by definition. The latter is true with respect to M, $\mathbf{i}$, g iff there is no time $\mathbf{i}' < \mathbf{i}$ such that ϕ is false with respect to M, $\mathbf{i}'$, g. Since ϕ is assumed to be valid in L_{1t}, such is clearly the case, and so $\mathbf{H}\phi$ is valid in L_{1t}. For any ϕ, $\mathbf{P}\phi$ is false, for example, in models containing only one moment of time; hence, $\mathbf{P}\phi$ is not valid in L_{1t}.

(5-8): (i) 1; (ii) 0; (iii) 1; (iv) 0; (v) 1.

(5-9): (i) 0; (ii) 1; (iii) 0; (iv) 1; (v) 1.

(5-10): If there is a last moment of time t_f, and $\Box\phi$ is true at this moment, then $\mathbf{F}\Box\phi$ will be false at t_f since there is no time later than t_f at which $\Box\phi$ is true.

(5-11): Let $T = \{t_i \mid i$ is a positive or negative integer or zero$\}$, ordered in the natural way. Suppose ϕ is true (in every world) at even-numbered times and false at odd-numbered times. Then at any index $\mathbf{F}\phi$ is true but $\Box\phi$ is false. Similarly, $\mathbf{P}\phi$ is true, but $\Box\phi$ is false.

(5.12): Neither $\mathbf{G}\phi \rightarrow \Diamond\phi$ nor $\mathbf{H}\phi \rightarrow \Diamond\phi$ is true in a model which contains just one moment of time t_1 such that ϕ is false at t_1.

Exercises

1. At every index, F assigns to I the value of **s** and to Y the value of **h**. Thus, the value of $L(Y)(I)$ at any index will be truth iff the speaker loves the

hearer at that index. Similarly, $L(I)(Y)$ will be true at an index just in case the hearer loves the speaker at that index.

3. (i) Suppose $[\![\Box[\phi \rightarrow \psi]]\!]^{M, w, t, g} = 1$. Then at all $w \in W$ and $t \in T$, $[\![[\phi \rightarrow \psi]]\!]^{M, w, t, g} = 1$. Thus there is no index at which ϕ is true while ψ is false; therefore it cannot be the case that $[\![\Box\phi]\!]^{M, w, t, g} = 1$ while $[\![\Box\psi]\!]^{M, w, t, g} = 0$.

(iii) Suppose $[\![\phi]\!]^{M, w, t, g} = 1$ for some $w \in W$ and $t \in T$. Then $[\![\Diamond\phi]\!]^{M, w, t, g} = 1$ since there is an index, namely $\langle w, t \rangle$, at which ϕ is true. Further, $[\![\Box\Diamond\phi]\!]^{M, w, t, g} = 1$ since at any index we still have that $\Diamond\phi$ is true at $\langle w, t \rangle$.

CHAPTER 6

Problems

(6-1): (1) t; (2) t; (3) $\langle e, t \rangle$; (4) $\langle\langle s, e \rangle, t \rangle$; (5) $\langle\langle\langle s, e \rangle, t \rangle, t \rangle$; (6) $\langle\langle s, \langle e, t \rangle\rangle, t \rangle$; (7) t; (8) $\langle\langle s, \langle e, t \rangle\rangle, t \rangle$; (9) $\langle e, e \rangle$; (10) $\langle s, \langle e, t \rangle\rangle$.

(6-2): (i) $\{a, b\}$; (ii) $\{\langle\langle w_1, t_1 \rangle, \{a, b\}\rangle, \langle\langle w_2, t_1 \rangle, \{b, c\}\rangle, \langle\langle w_1, t_2 \rangle, \{a, c\}\rangle, \langle\langle w_2, t_2 \rangle, \{a\}\rangle, \langle\langle w_1, t_3 \rangle, \{b, c\}\rangle, \langle\langle w_2, t_3 \rangle, \{a, b, c\}\rangle\}$; (iii) the function which maps each index into the function given in (ii); (iv) the function which maps $\langle w_2, t_1 \rangle$ and $\langle w_1, t_3 \rangle$ into 1 and the other indices into 0; (v) the same function as in (iv); (vi) 1; (vii) 0.

(6-3): There would be no change.

(6-4): All pairs are logically equivalent except (iii) and (vi). As a model in which the formulas in (iii) have different truth values, take $A = \{a, b\}$; $W = \{w_1, w_2\}$; $T = \{t_1\}$;

$$F(\langle w_1, t_1 \rangle, m) = \{a\} \quad F(\langle w_1, t_1 \rangle, B) = \{a\}$$

$$F(\langle w_2, t_1 \rangle, m) = \{b\} \quad F(\langle w_2, t_1 \rangle, B) = \{b\}$$

Then $[\![\Box B(m)]\!]^{M, w_2, t_1, g} = 1$ but $[\![\lambda x[\Box B(x)](m)]\!]^{M, w_2, t_1, g} = 0$.

To show that the pairs in (vi) are not logically equivalent, take the same model but let F(change′) be that function which gives at every index the following function f as value:

$$f\left(\begin{bmatrix}\langle w_1, t_1 \rangle \rightarrow a \\ \langle w_2, t_2 \rangle \rightarrow b\end{bmatrix}\right) = 1$$

$$f(\text{all other functions in } A^{W \times T}) = 0.$$

Then at any index $\exists r$ change$'(r)$ is true but $\exists x$ change$'(^{\wedge}x)$ is false since $^{\wedge}x$ can never have a value which is not a constant function from indices to individuals.

(6-5): (i) $\langle w_1, t_1\rangle \to \emptyset$

$\langle w_2, t_1\rangle \to \emptyset$

$\langle w_1, t_2\rangle \to \{a, b\}$

$\langle w_2, t_2\rangle \to \{b, c\}$

$\langle w_1, t_3\rangle \to \{a, b, c\}$

$\langle w_2, t_3\rangle \to \{a, b, c\}$

(iii) The function mapping each index into 1.

CHAPTER 7

Problems

(7-3) (i) **John walks or talks, 4**

John **walk or talk, 9**

walk **talk**

(ii) **John walks or John talks, 9**

John walks, 4 **John talks, 4**

John **walk** **John** **talk**

(i) 1.	**walk** $\Rightarrow$ **walk$'$**	Basic expression
2.	**talk** $\Rightarrow$ **talk$'$**	Basic expression
3.	**walk or talk** $\Rightarrow \lambda x\,[\text{walk}'(x) \vee \text{talk}'(x)]$	From 2, 3 by T12b
4.	**John** $\Rightarrow \lambda PP\{j\}$	Basic expression
5.	**John walks or talks** $\Rightarrow$ $\lambda PP\{j\}\,(^{\wedge}\lambda x\,[\text{walk}'(x) \vee \text{talk}'(x)])$	From 3, 4 by T4
6.	$^{\wedge}\lambda x\,[\text{walk}'(x) \vee \text{talk}'(x)]\,\{j\}$	Lambda conversion
7.	$^{\vee\wedge}\lambda x\,[\text{walk}'(x) \vee \text{talk}'(x)]\,(j)$	Brace convention
8.	$\lambda x\,[\text{walk}'(x) \vee \text{talk}'(x)]\,(j)$	Down-up cancellation
9.	$[\text{walk}'(j) \vee \text{talk}'(j)]$	Lambda conversion

(ii) 1. **walk** ⇒ **walk**′ Basic expression

2. **John** ⇒ $\lambda PP\{j\}$ Basic expression

3. **John walks** ⇒ $\lambda PP\{j\}(\hat{}\text{walk}')$ From 1, 2, by T4

4. $\hat{}\text{walk}'\{j\}$ Lambda conversion

5. $\check{}\hat{}\text{walk}'(j)$ Brace convention

6. $\text{walk}'(j)$ Down-Up cancellation

7. **John talks** ⇒ $\text{talk}'(j)$ cf. steps 1–6

8. **John walks or John talks** ⇒ $[\text{walk}'(j) \vee \text{talk}'(j)]$ From 6, 7 by T11b

(7-4): No. **A unicorn walks and talks** ⇒ $\exists x[\text{unicorn}'(x) \wedge [\text{walk}'(x) \wedge \text{talk}'(x)]]$ but **A unicorn walks and a unicorn talks** ⇒ $[\exists x[\text{unicorn}'(x) \wedge \text{walk}'(x)] \wedge \exists x[\text{unicorn}'(x) \wedge \text{talk}'(x)]]$. With **every unicorn**, however, the two translations are logically equivalent.

(7-5):

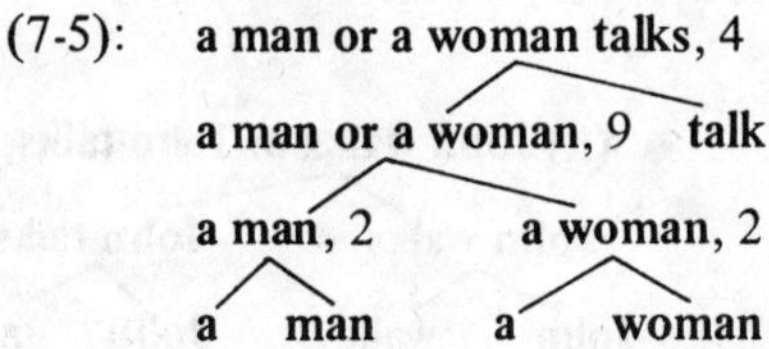

1. **man** ⇒ man′ Basic expression

2. **a** ⇒ $\lambda P[\lambda Q\exists x[P\{x\} \wedge Q\{x\}]]$ Basic expression

3. **a man** ⇒ $\lambda P[\lambda Q\exists x[P\{x\} \wedge Q\{x\}]](\hat{}\text{man}')$ From 1, 2 by T2

4. $\lambda Q\exists x[\text{man}'(x) \wedge Q\{x\}]$ Lambda conversion, brace convention, Down-Up cancellation

5. **a woman** ⇒ $\lambda Q\exists x[\text{woman}'(x) \wedge Q\{x\}]$ Cf. steps 1–4

6. **a man or a woman** ⇒ $\lambda P[\lambda Q\exists x[\text{man}'(x) \wedge Q\{x\}](P) \vee \lambda Q\exists x[\text{woman}'(x) \wedge Q\{x\}](P)]$ From 4, 5 by T13

7. **talk** ⇒ **talk**′ Basic expression

8. a man or a woman talks ⇒
$\lambda P[\lambda Q\exists x[\text{man}'(x) \wedge Q\{x\}](P) \vee$
$\lambda Q\exists x[\text{woman}'(x) \wedge Q\{x\}](P)](\hat{}\text{talk}')$ From 6, 7 by T4

9. $\lambda Q\exists x[\text{man}'(x) \wedge Q\{x\}](\hat{}\text{talk}') \vee$
$\lambda Q\exists x[\text{woman}'(x) \wedge Q\{x\}](\hat{}\text{talk}')$ Lambda conversion

10. $\exists x[\text{man}'(x) \wedge \text{talk}'(x)] \vee$
$\exists x[\text{woman}'(x) \wedge \text{talk}'(x)]$ Lambda conversion, brace convention, Down-up cancellation

This is the same translation as that for **A man talks or a woman talks.**

(7-9): **A woman such that she talks walks**, 4

a woman such that she talks, 2 **walk**

a **woman such that she talks**, 3, 4

woman **he_4 talks**, 4

he_4 **talk**

1. **he_4 talks** ⇒ $\text{talk}'(x_4)$ Cf. (7–40)

2. **woman such that she talks** ⇒ $\lambda x_4[\text{woman}'(x_4) \wedge \text{talk}'(x_4)]$
From 1 by T3

3. **a woman such that she talks** ⇒
$\lambda P[\lambda Q\exists x[P\{x\} \wedge Q\{x\}]](\hat{}\lambda x_4[\text{woman}'(x_4) \wedge \text{talk}'(x_4)])$
From 2 by T2

4. $\lambda Q\exists x[\hat{}\lambda x_4[\text{woman}'(x_4) \wedge \text{talk}'(x_4)]\{x\} \wedge Q\{x\}]$
Lambda conversion

5. $\lambda Q\exists x[[\text{woman}'(x) \wedge \text{talk}'(x)] \wedge Q\{x\}]$
Lambda conversion, Brace convention, Down-up cancellation

6. **A woman such that she talks walks** ⇒
$\lambda Q\exists x[[\text{woman}'(x) \wedge \text{talk}'(x)] \wedge Q\{x\}](\hat{}\text{walk}')$ From 6 by T4

7. $\exists x[\text{woman}'(x) \wedge \text{talk}'(x) \wedge \text{walk}'(x)]$
Lambda conversion, Brace convention, Down-up cancellation

(7-11): (i) V; (ii) V; (iii) V; (iv) V/I The first premise has two non-equivalent derivations; the conclusion has two similar derivations, but they are equivalent. The argument is valid when the first premise has **the unicorn** quantified in (the *de re* reading), invalid on the direct derivation (the *de dicto* reading); (v) V (because of the treatment of proper names as rigid designators); (vi) V.

Exercises

1.

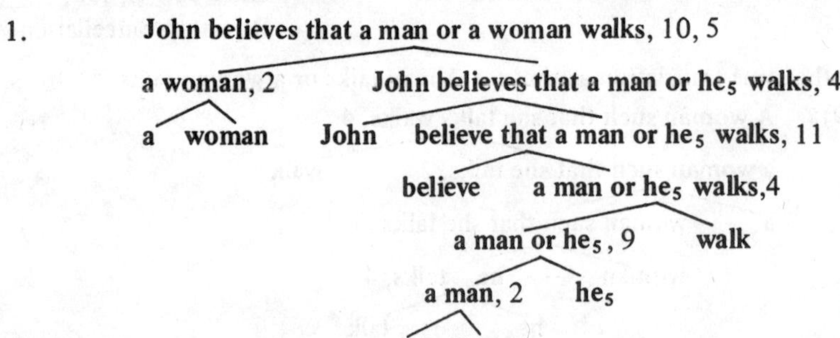

There are also analysis trees in which **a man** is *de re* and **a woman** is *de dicto*, both are *de re*, and both are *de dicto*. Of these, only the latter two are plausible readings.

2. (i) V/I There are *de dicto* and *de re* interpretations for both premise and conclusion; the only valid case is when both are *de re*. (ii) I; (iii) V (but was not valid in PTQ because MP10 (7-88) was not included there); (iv) V because of the treatment of proper names as rigid designators).

6. (1) Since there is only one index, properties may be regarded essentially as sets. $[\![$**a-unicorn**$']\!]^{M,w,t,g}$ is a collection of sets of individuals such that each set in the collection contains at least one individual which is also a unicorn, i.e., is in the set denoted by **unicorn**$'$ at M, w, t, g. The denotation of **two-unicorns**$'$ is similar except that each set in the collection contains at least two individuals which are unicorns.

(2) 2^{n-1} (Half of the 2^n distinct sets of individuals contain the individual denoted by j and half do not.)

(3) The cardinality of $[\![$**a-unicorn**$']\!]^{M,w,t,g}$ is $2^n - 2^{n-m}$. There are 2^{n-m} distinct sets which contain no unicorn, therefore $2^n - 2^{n-m}$ which do contain a unicorn. The cardinality of $[\![$**every-unicorn**$']\!]^{M,w,t,g}$ is 2^{n-m}. Take each of the 2^{n-m} sets which contain no unicorn and form the union of it with the set containing all the unicorns.

INDEX

a(n), translation of 195
abstract nouns 168
abstraction operator 98
adjectives
  intensional 144, 163
  intersective 110, 144
  further research on 270
adverbs 53
  intensional 234
  sentence 232
  verb phrase 232
  in first-order languages 53
  further research on 270
alethic logic 123
algebra
  free 258
  semantic 260
  universal 253
alphabetic variants, principle of 111, 201–202
ambiguity 78, 82
  see also ambiguous languages, scope
ambiguous languages 28, 254, 258, 262
analysis tree 70, 191, 256
analytic sentence 50
artificial languages (*vs.* natural languages) 1, 252
assignment of values to variables 59
  truth of a formula with respect to 57
autonomous syntax 82
axiomatization (of natural languages) 51–53
axioms (*or* axiom schemata) 50

Barcan Formula 129–130, 139
basic expressions 8, 14, 255–257
be
  – of identity (*vs.* be of prediction 229
  translation of 228
  original translation in PTQ 280
Bedeutung 144
belief 143, 164, 170
  paratactic theory of 174
  quotational theory of 174
  relativization to context of 175
  –sentences 165ff, 206
  see also propositional attitudes
binder 98
bound variables 57
brace notation (brace convention) 162, 193

'cap' operator
  see 'up' operator
categorematic symbols 16
categorial grammars 182, 248
categories
  'double slash' 182
  labels of 89
  lexical 24
  syntactic 42, 89, 181, 255
  (in PTQ syntax) 183
causal theory of proper names 171
character 220
characteristic function of a set 26
complement structure
  further research on 270
  sentence complements (in PTQ) 206
  verb-phrase complements (in PTQ) 234
compositionality, principle of (Frege's principle) 8ff., 42–43, 181

conjunction
  in first-order languages 15ff, 35ff
  categorematic *vs.* syncategorematic treatment of 40–41
  sentence (in PTQ) 198
  term phrase (in PTQ) 198
  verb phrase (in PTQ) 199
connectives 15ff, 35ff, 40–41
  logical 33
  see also conjunction
constant function 146
constant operations 259
contexts, role in semantic interpretation 137, 265, 267
contingent truth 122–125
contradictory sentence, definition of 48
conventional implicature 198
  see also presupposition
coordinate semantics 131
'correlative' relative clauses 215
correspondence theory of truth 4, 25
counterpart relation 130
cross-world identity problem 130
'cup' operator
  see 'down' operator

de dicto 166
  - pronouncs 237
  - readings of NPs 206, 216
de re 166, 168
  readings of NPs 207
deduction 58
  natural 50
definite descriptions 78, 197
deictic expressions 136
  see also indexical expressions
demonstratives 136
denominatum 144
denotation
  as another term for *semantic value* 84
  notation for 'possible denotation' 84
  as contrasted with *sense* 144, 265
derivation, definition of, in Phrase Structure grammar 55
  see also analysis trees
derived syntactic rule 258
detachment, rule of 50
'Determiner-Nom' analysis of relative clauses 215
Determiner-Noun Rule 194
determiners 108, 248
  see also a (n), every, the
disjunction
  see conjunction
disambiguated language 254–255, 258, 262
discourse anaphora 231
double abstracts 103
'double slash' categories 182
'Down' operator 153
down-up cancellation 154, 195

English
  fragment of 179
  syntax of 179
entailment 50–53
'eternal' models 135
events 168
every, translation of 195
Existence Predicate 129
experiences 168
extension 144
  and intension, interdefinability of 148–149
  relation-in- 160
  see also denotation
extensional (first-order) reducibility
  of higher-order verbs 224–227
  in subject position (original PTQ treatment) 278–285
extensional semantics 18

first-order language 89
first-order predicate logic 56
formation rules 14, 44
formula 57
Fragment (of English) 179
free variables 57
Fregean interpretation 266
Frege's Principle
  see Compositionality, Principle of
function 17
  characteristic (of a set) 26
  constant 146
  propositional 57

functional application 177
rules of 28, 192
future perfect tense 116

generative semantics 5, 181, 264
generative transformational grammar xi
grammar
categorial 182, 248
context free phrase structure 23, 248
generative transformational xi
Montague ix
phrase structure 54–55
PTQ 173
transformational 44, 179, 192, 214, 270
'Universal' 252

higher-order language 89
homomorphism 43, 253, 260

IL (Montague's intensional logic)
semantics of 157
syntax of 155
identity 154, 159
- operations 153
- predicate 142
impossible worlds 173
indefinite object deletion transformation 96
index 131
as argument of an intension 145
indexical expressions (deictic expressions) 136
further research on 270
indexical semantics 138
individual concepts 146, 149, 160, 279, 285
individual sublimation 220
individual terms 56
Inference, Rules of 50
infinitive complement verbs 234
intension 144
- and extension, interdefinability of 148, 149
- as distinct from *sense* 157
- of α, notation for 146
relation-in- 160

intensional constructions 143, 162ff
(in PTQ) 185, 186, 278–285
intensional isomorphism 173
intensional logic 154, 263
history of 152
interpretation induced by translation 263

K-validity 267
K-model 267
Katz-Fodor semantics 4

L_0
semantics of 16
syntax of 14
L_{0E}
semantics of 25
syntax of 23
L_1
notational variant of 83
semantics of 59
syntax of 56
L_{1E}
semantics of 72
syntax of 69
L_{type}
semantics of 92
syntax of 91
L_{1t}
syntax of 115
L_{1m}
semantics of 127
syntax of 126
L_{1mt}
semantics of 133
syntax of 132
L-truth 126
lambda conversion 99, 100, 111, 167
lambda operator 98, 177
language
ambiguous 28, 254, 258, 262
artificial (*vs.* natural) 252
- as an ordered pair $\langle \mathfrak{A}, R \rangle$ 258
disambiguated 254–255, 258, 262
first-order 89
higher-order 89
meta- 6
object- 6

language (continued)
  second-order 89
  source 260
  target 260
Law of Necessity 128
Leibnitz' Law (substitution) 142, 165, 178
lexical categories 24
lexical decomposition of seek 219, 236
lexical semantics 12
'like-subject constraint' 236
linear ordering 113
logic
  alethic 123
  first-order predicate 56
  intensional, history of 152
  modal 123
  natural 52
  second-order 52
logical connectives 33
  - consequence 49
  - equivalence 49
  - form 264
  - words 194
  see also conjunction
logical implication
  see entailment
logical words
  see logical connectives
logically true sentences 11
lower-star notation
  (for transitive verbs) 223
  (for nouns and IVs) 281

meaning
  (in UG 'General Theory of Meaning') 260
  (in UG 'Theory of Reference') 265
  David Lewis' definition 173
Meaning Postulates 224, 267
  - for extensional nouns and verbs 280
  - for prepositions 243
  for seek 236
  - for subsective modifiers 234
  - for transitive verbs 110
  - for subject position 280–282

meaningful expressions of type *a* 89
meta-language 6
meta-language variables
  see meta-variables
meta-variables 15, 29
modal logic 123
  quantification in 129
model 45
  (in UG) 267
  'eternal' 135
  K- 261
  temporal 113
model-theoretic semantics 10–11, 44–46
modally closed expressions 178
modus ponens 50
Montague Grammar ix
morphology 194, 248

names, translations of in PTQ 107, 193
  causal theory of 171
  see also rigid designators
natural kinds 171
Natural Logic 52
necessarily, translation of 232
necessary truth 122–125
necessity operator 126, 163
negation 33, 95
  - in PTQ 244, 247
  Verb Phrase 95, 104
non-logical constants 59
non-rigid designator 134
non-specific reading 143, 120, 182
non-truth-functional operator 142
notation
  brace 162
  - for intension of α 147
  - for quantifiers 177
  lower star 223
  lower star for nouns and IVs 181
  Polish 54
  predicate 98
  see also Table of Symbols
noun phrases 71, 106
'NP-S' analysis of Relative Clauses 215

object language 6
obligations 168

oblique-context
see oblique constructions
oblique constructions (oblique context) 143, 162
(in PTQ) 185, 186
opaque context
see oblique constructions
operations
constant 259
identity 259
polynomial 261
relation-reducing 96, 105
structural 190
syntactic 254–255
operator
abstraction 98
'Down' 153
lambda 98, 176–177
necessity 126, 163
non-truth-functional 142
possibility 126
tense 112
truth-functional 141
'up' 153
ordered pairs 19

paratactic theory of belief 174
passive sentences 96
further research on 270
past perfect tense 116
phrase markers 109, 190
phrase structure
- grammar 54–55
context free 23, 242
derivation in a 55
- rules 44
- tree 24
Polish notation 54
polynomial operations 261
possibility operator 126
possible denotation 84
possible worlds 3, 124–125
possible world semantics 12, 124–125
unresolved problems with 170–175
pragmatics 138
predicate
- abstracts 99
existence 129
identity 142
- logic, first-order 56
- modifiers 94
- notation 98
prepositional phrases 243
meaning postulates for 243
presuppositions 138, 198
further research on 270
principle of compositionality 8ff, 42–43 181
progressive tense 197
pronouns 68
de dicto 237
- of laziness 231, 241–242
subscripted 184, 203
proper names, causal theory of 171
property 147
(of individuals) 149, 160
propositional attitudes 170
further research on 164
see also belief
propositional function 57
propositions 144, 147, 149, 160
psychological reality 13, 80–81, 172, 253
PTQ grammar 179

quantification 68
in modal logic 129
- in PTQ 204
- rules (in PTQ) 238
substitutional theory of 58
vacuous 57, 63
quantifier lowering 230
quantifiers 56ff
notation for 177
quantifying in 168
questions, further research on 164
quotational theory of belief 174

reference 144
theory of (in UG) 265
referential theory of semantics (*vs.* theory of understanding) 172
see also truth-conditional semantics
referentially opaque constructions 143
referentially transparent constructions 143

relation 168
counterpart 120
- in extension 160
- in intension 160
- reducing operations 96, 105
relation-reducing operations 96, 105
relative clauses 211
'correlative' 215
'Determiner-Nom' syntactic analysis of 215
further research on 269
non-restrictive 214
'NP-S' analysis of 215
in transformational grammar 214
rigid designators 134, 171, 233, 281
rule(s)
derived syntactic 258
formation 14, 44
- of functional application 28, 192
- of inference 50
phrase structure 44
syntactic 190, 255
Russell's paradox 93

satisfaction of a formula by an assignment of objects to variables 57
scope
- ambiguities (in PTQ) 208–210
- of quantifiers, semantics for 63–65
- of quantifiers (in conjunction) 200
- of quantifiers and negation in PTQ 245
second-order language 89
second-order logic 52
seek 216–220
lexical decomposition of 219, 236
meaning postulate for 236
semantic representation 181
vs. translation into intensional logic 263ff
semantic value of α, notation for 19, 45
semantics
coordinate 131
extensional 18
generative 5, 181
goals of 1–3
indexical 138
Katz-Fodor 4
lexical 12
model-theoretic 10–11, 44–46
possible world 12
truth-conditional 4–10, 41–44
sense 144
(as distinct from *intension*) 157
(*vs.* meaning in 'Universal Grammar') 265
sense-data 168
sentence 57
- token 267
- type 267
set
abstractor 98
- theory 10
Sinn 144
source language (in translation) 260
speech acts 13, 138
states-of-affairs 5, 7
see also possible worlds, Index
structural description (as produced by a phrase structure grammar) 55
corresponding concept in UG 254
structural operation (syntactic operation) 190, 254–255
subject-predicate rule 191
sublimation 220
existential 221
individual 220
universal 221
subscripted pronouns 184, 203
subsective modifiers 234
meaning postulates for 234
substitutional theory of quantification 58
syncategorematic expressions 16
synonymy 49
syntactic categories 42, 89, 175, 255
(in PTQ syntax) 183
syntactic operations 254–255
syntactic rule 190, 255
derived 258

target language 260
tasks 168
tautologies 48
temporal model 113
tense operators 112

tenses 114
 future perfect 116
 in PTQ 244, 247
 past perfect 116
 progressive 197
term phrases 182
terms, individual 56
the, translation of 195
theorem 50
transformational grammar 44, 179, 192
 generative xi
 and Montague semantics, further research on 270
 relative clauses in 214
transitive verbs (two-place predicates) in L_{10} *vs.* in L_{1E} 38–39
 in PTQ 215
 meaning postulate for 226
translation 260–263
 interpretation induced by 263
 notation for 295
 - procedure in PTQ 180
truth
 correspondence theory of 4
 L- 126
 logical 11
 necessary 122–125
 - of a formula with respect to an assignment of values to variables 57
 - relative to a model 44–46
 - tables 33
 - values 25
truth-conditional semantics 4–10, 41–44
truth-functional operator 141
type assignment
 (in PTQ) 187–189
 (in UG) 266
 (in original PTQ) 278
types 155, 157, 187
 functional theory of 88

understanding (*vs.* reference) 172
'universal grammar' 252
universal sublimation 221
'up' operator 153

vacuous abstraction 101
vacuous quantification 57, 63
validity 50–53, 224
 K- 267
value assignment 57, 62
variables 68, 184
 bound 57
 free 57
 meta- 15, 29
 meta-language 15
verb-object rule 216

well-formed expressions, recursive definition of 14
word meaning 225

SYNTHESE LANGUAGE LIBRARY

Texts and Studies in Linguistics and Philosophy

1. Henry Hiż (ed.), *Questions.* 1978.
2. William S. Cooper, *Foundations of Logico-Linguistics. A Unified Theory of Information, Language, and Logic.* 1978.
3. Avishai Margalit (ed.), *Meaning and Use.* 1979.
4. F. Guenthner and S. J. Schmidt (eds.), *Formal Semantics and Pragmatics for Natural Languages.* 1978.
5. Esa Saarinen (ed.), *Game-Theoretical Semantics.* 1978.
6. F. J. Pelletier (ed.), *Mass Terms: Some Philosophical Problems.* 1979.
7. David R. Dowty, *Word Meaning and Montague Grammar. The Semantics of Verbs and Times in Generative Semantics and in Montague's PTQ.* 1979.
8. Alice F. Freed, *The Semantics of English Aspectual Complementation.* 1979.
9. James McCloskey, *Transformational Syntax and Model Theoretic Semantics: A Case Study in Modern Irish.* 1979.
10. John R. Searle, Ferenc Kiefer, and Manfred Bierwisch (eds.), *Speech Act Theory and Pragmatics.* 1980.